UNITED NATIONS CONFERENCE ON TRADE AND DEVELOPMENT

THE LEAST DEVELOPED COUNTRIES REPORT 2012

Harnessing Remittances and Diaspora Knowledge to Build Productive Capacities

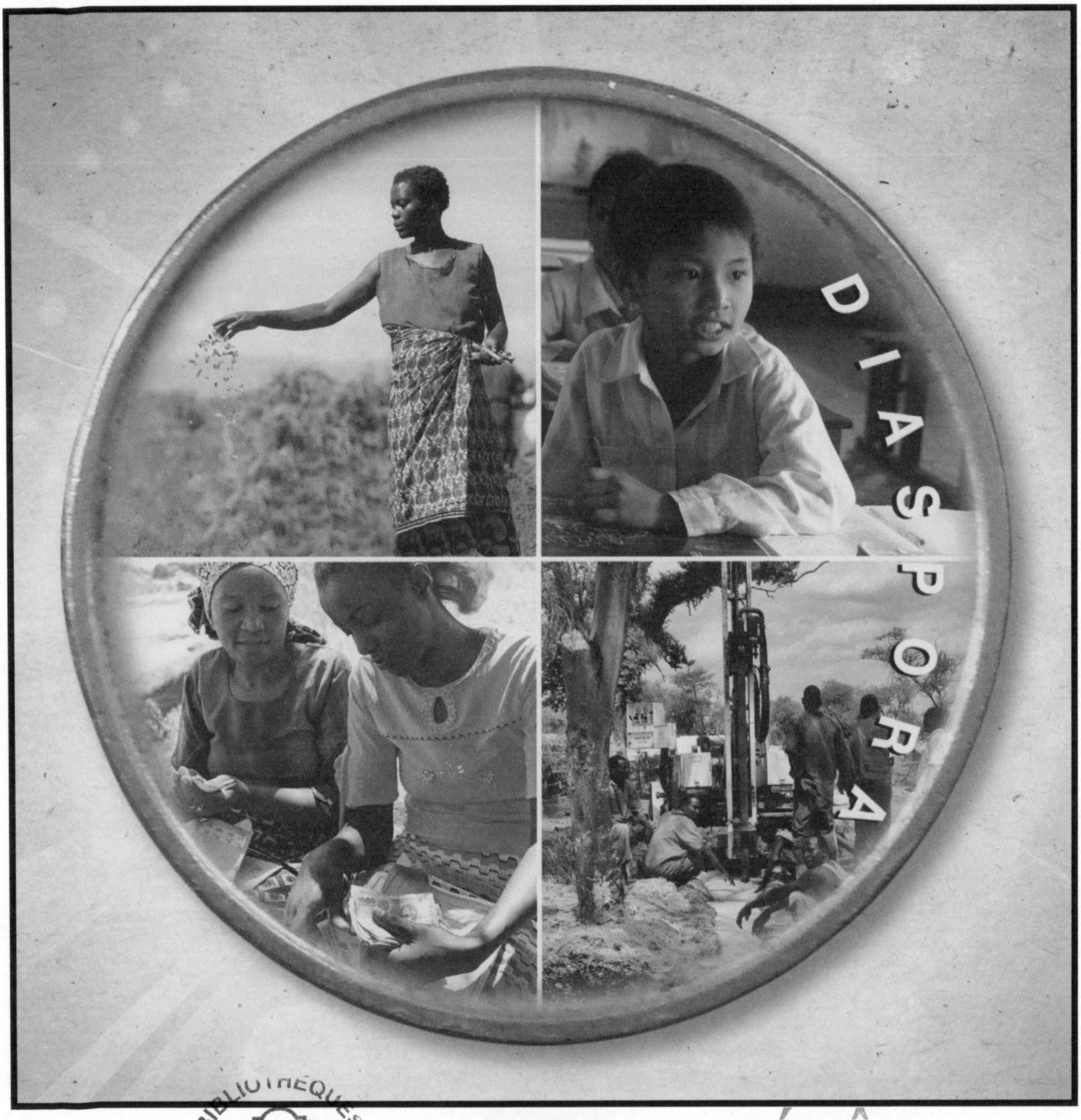

UNITED NATIONS
New York and Geneva, 2012

Note

Symbols of United Nations documents are composed of capital letters with figures. Mention of such a symbol indicates a reference to a United Nations document.

The designations employed and the presentation of the material in this publication do not imply the expression of any opinion whatsoever on the part of the Secretariat of the United Nations concerning the legal status of any country, territory, city or area, or of its authorities, or concerning the delimitation of its frontiers or boundaries.

Material in this publication may be freely quoted or reprinted, but full acknowledgement is requested. A copy of the publication containing the quotation or reprint should be sent to the UNCTAD secretariat at: Palais des Nations, CH-1211 Geneva 10, Switzerland.

The overview of this report can also be found on the Internet, in all six official languages of the United Nations, at www.unctad.org/ldcr

---

UNCTAD/LDC/2012

UNITED NATIONS PUBLICATION

Sales No. E.12.II.D.18

ISBN 978-92-1-112861-1
eISBN 978-92-1-055919-5
ISSN 0257-7550

What are the least developed countries?

Forty-eight countries are currently designated by the United Nations as "least developed countries" (LDCs). These are: Afghanistan, Angola, Bangladesh, Benin, Bhutan, Burkina Faso, Burundi, Cambodia, Central African Republic, Chad, Comoros, Democratic Republic of the Congo, Djibouti, Equatorial Guinea, Eritrea, Ethiopia, Gambia, Guinea, Guinea-Bissau, Haiti, Kiribati, Lao People's Democratic Republic, Lesotho, Liberia, Madagascar, Malawi, Mali, Mauritania, Mozambique, Myanmar, Nepal, Niger, Rwanda, Samoa, Sao Tome and Principe, Senegal, Sierra Leone, Solomon Islands, Somalia, Sudan, Timor-Leste, Togo, Tuvalu, Uganda, United Republic of Tanzania, Vanuatu, Yemen and Zambia.

The list of LDCs is reviewed every three years by the United Nations Economic and Social Council (ECOSOC), in the light of recommendations by the Committee for Development Policy (CDP). The following three criteria were used by the CDP in the latest review of the list, in March 2012:

(a) A per capita income criterion, based on a three-year average estimate of the gross national income (GNI) per capita, with a threshold of $992 for possible cases of addition to the list, and a threshold of $1,190 for graduation from LDC status;

(b) A human assets criterion, involving a composite index (the Human Assets Index) based on indicators of: (i) nutrition (percentage of the population that is undernourished); (ii) health (child mortality ratio); (iii) school enrolment (gross secondary school enrolment ratio); and (iv) literacy (adult literacy ratio); and

(c) An economic vulnerability criterion, involving a composite index (the Economic Vulnerability Index) based on indicators of: (i) natural shocks (index of instability of agricultural production; share of the population victim of natural disasters); (ii) trade-related shocks (index of instability of exports of goods and services); (iii) physical exposure to shocks (share of the population living in low-lying areas); (iv) economic exposure to shocks (share of agriculture, forestry and fisheries in GDP; index of merchandise export concentration); (v) smallness (population in logarithm); and (vi) remoteness (index of remoteness).

For all three criteria, different thresholds are used for identifying cases of addition to the list of LDCs, and cases of graduation from it. A country will qualify to be added to the list if it meets the addition thresholds on all three criteria and does not have a population greater than 75 million. Qualification for addition to the list will effectively lead to LDC status only if the government of the relevant country accepts this status. A country will normally qualify for graduation from LDC status if it has met graduation thresholds under at least two of the three criteria in at least two consecutive triennial reviews of the list. However, if the GNI per capita of an LDC has risen to a level at least double the graduation threshold, the country will be deemed eligible for graduation regardless of its performance under the other two criteria.

Only three countries have so far graduated from LDC status: Botswana in December 1994, Cape Verde in December 2007, and Maldives in January 2011. In March 2009, the CDP recommended the graduation of Equatorial Guinea. This recommendation was endorsed by ECOSOC in July 2009, but by September 2012 the General Assembly had not confirmed this endorsement. In September 2010, the General Assembly, giving due consideration to the unprecedented losses Samoa suffered as a result of the Pacific Ocean tsunami of 29 September 2009, decided to defer to 1 January 2014 the graduation of that country. In July 2012, ECOSOC endorsed the CDP's recommendation to graduate Vanuatu from LDC status.

After a CDP recommendation to graduate a country has been endorsed by ECOSOC and the General Assembly, the graduating country is granted a three-year grace period before graduation effectively takes place. This grace period, during which the country remains an LDC, is designed to enable the graduating State and its development and trading partners to agree on a "smooth transition" strategy, so that the loss of LDC status at the time of graduation does not disrupt the socioeconomic progress of the country. A "smooth transition" measure generally implies extending a concession from which the country used to benefit by virtue of LDC status for a number of years after graduation.

Acknowledgements

The Least Developed Countries Report 2012 was prepared by a team consisting of Željka Kožul-Wright (team leader), Maria Bovey, Agnès Collardeau-Angleys, Junior Davis, Pierre Encontre, Igor Paunovic, Madasamyraja Rajalingam, Rolf Traeger, Giovanni Valensisi and Stefanie West (the LDC Report team). Jayati Ghosh (consultant) also made specific inputs to the Report. Bethany Paris and Xenia Wassihun provided research assistance. The work was carried out under the overall guidance and supervision of Taffere Tesfachew, Director, Division for Africa, Least Developed Countries and Special Programmes, who also made significant inputs to the structure and content of the Report.

An ad hoc expert group meeting on "Harnessing Remittances and Diaspora Knowledge for Productive Capacities in the Least Developed Countries" was held in Geneva on 4 and 5 July 2012 to peer-review the Report and its specific inputs. It brought together specialists in the fields of remittances and diaspora knowledge networks. The participants in the meeting were: Jerónimo Cortina (University of Houston), Jérôme Elie (Graduate Institute of International and Development Studies), Olivier Ferrari (International Organization for Migration), Frank Laczko (International Organization for Migration), Tauhid Pasha (International Organization for Migration), as well as the members of the LDC Report team and the following UNCTAD colleagues: Diana Barrowclough, Ermias Biadgleng, Mussie Delelegn, Mahmoud Elkhafif and Amelia Santos-Paulino. The papers reviewed at the meeting had been prepared by Junior Davis, Željka Kožul-Wright, Igor Paunovic, Rolf Traeger and Giovanni Valensisi.

The Report draws on background papers prepared by Adamnesh Bogale, Gaye Daffé, Evans Jadotte, Nelofar Parvin, Ennio Rodríguez, Tasneem Siddiqui, Andrés Solimano and Abye Tassé. Jayati Ghosh provided the substantive editing and contributed to the overall Report. Frédéric Docquier (Université catholique de Louvain) made available the skilled migration database of Docquier et al. (2011). Useful suggestions emerged from discussions with Rudolf Anich (International Organization for Migration) and Philippe Gazagne (Graduate Institute of International and Development Studies). Comments on specific parts of the Report were received from the following colleagues from UNCTAD: Richard Kožul-Wright (Unit on Economic Cooperation and Integration among Developing Countries), Martine Julsaint Kidane, Sophia Twarog and Liping Zhang (Division on Trade in Goods and Services, and Commodities).

Maria Bovey and Stefanie West provided secretarial support. Sophie Combette designed the cover. David Neal edited the text.

Madasamyraja Rajalingam did the overall layout, graphics and desktop publishing.

The financial support of donors to the UNCTAD LDC Trust Fund is gratefully acknowledged.

Contents

BOXES

CHARTS

BOX CHARTS

TABLES

BOX TABLE

EXPLANATORY NOTES

The term "dollars" ($) refers to United States dollars unless otherwise stated. The term "billion" signifies 1,000 million.

Annual rates of growth and changes refer to compound rates. Exports are valued f.o.b. (free on board) and imports c.i.f. (cost, insurance, freight) unless otherwise specified.

Use of a dash (–) between dates representing years, e.g. 1981–1990, signifies the full period involved, including the initial and final years. An oblique stroke (/) between two years, e.g. 1991/92, signifies a fiscal or crop year.

The term "least developed country" (LDC) refers, throughout this report, to a country included in the United Nations list of least developed countries.

In the tables:

Two dots (..) indicate that the data are not available, or are not separately reported.

One dot (.) indicates that the data are not applicable.

A hyphen (-) indicates that the amount is nil or negligible.

Details and percentages do not necessarily add up to totals, because of rounding.

Abbreviations

ADB	Asian Development Bank
AfDB	African Development Bank
ATM	automated teller machine
BMANA	Bangladesh Medical Association of North America
CDP	compulsory deferred payment
CIDA	Canadian International Development Agency
CDP	Committee for Development Policy
CGAP	Consultative Group to Assist the Poor
DAC	Development Assistance Committee
DICOEX	Directorate of Chileans Abroad
DDI	diaspora direct investment
DKN	diaspora knowledge network
EAC	East African Community
EC	European Commission
ECCAS	Economic Community of Central African States
ECOSOC	United Nations Economic and Social Council
ECOWAS	Economic Community of West African States
EFTPOS	electronic funds transfer at point of sale
EU	European Union
EVI	Economic Vulnerability Index
FAISE	Fonds d'Appui aux Investissements des Sénégalais de l'Extérieur
FAO	Food and Agriculture Organization of the United Nations
FDI	foreign direct investment
GATS	General Agreement on Trade in Services
GCC	Gulf Cooperation Council
GDP	Gross domestic product
GFMD	Global Forum on Migration and Development
GMG	Global Migration Group
IDB	Inter-American Development Bank
JBFH	Japan Bangladesh Friendship Hospital
ICT	information and communication technology
IFAD	International Fund for Agricultural Development
IILS	International Institute for Labour Studies
ILO	International Labour Organization
IMF	International Monetary Fund
IOM	International Organization for Migration
IPoA	Istanbul Programme of Action (Programme of Action for the Least Developed Countries for the Decade 2011–2020)
ITC	International Trade Centre UNCTAD/WTO
KNMs	knowledge networks and markets

LDC	least developed country
LDCF	Least Developed Countries Fund
LMICs	low- and middle-income countries
MDGs	Millennium Development Goals
MFI	microfinance institution
MIDA	Migration for Development in Africa
MNO	mobile network operator
MoEWOE	Ministry of Expatriates' Welfare and Overseas Employment (Bangladesh)
M-PESA	mobile phone-based money transfer service
M-wallet	mobile wallet
MTC	mobile and telecommunications company
MTN Mobile Money	mobile phone-based money transfer service
MTO	money transfer operator
NBE	National Bank of Ethiopia
OCC	Oromo Coffee Company
ODA	official development assistance
ODCs	other developing countries
ODI	Overseas Development Institute
OECD	Organisation for Economic Co-operation and Development
PAISD	Programme d'Appui aux Initiatives de Solidarité pour le Développement
PEMEX	Petróleos Mexicanos
PIN	personal identification number
PLASEPRI	Plateforme d'Appui au Secteur Privé et à la Valorisation de la Diaspora Sénégalaise en Italie
POS	point of sale
R&D	research and development
ROCADH	Regroupement des organismes canado-haïtiens pour le développement
RQN	Return and Reintegration of Qualified Nationals
RSP	remittance service provider
SENSA	South African Network of Skills Abroad
SITC	Standard International Trade Classification
SME	small and medium-sized enterprise
STI	science, technology and innovation
TOKTEN	Transfer of Knowledge Through Expatriate Nationals
TRQN	Temporary Return of Qualified Nationals
UNCTAD	United Nations Conference on Trade and Development
UNDESA	United Nations Department of Economic and Social Affairs
UNDP	United Nations Development Programme
WB	World Bank
WEO	World Economic Outlook
WHO	World Health Organization
WFP	World Food Programme

Classifications used in this Report

Least developed countries

Geographical/structural classification

Unless otherwise specified, in this Report the least developed countries (LDCs) are classified according to a combination of geographical and structural criteria. Therefore, the small island LDCs which geographically are in Africa or Asia are grouped together with the Pacific islands, due to their structural similarities. Haiti and Madagascar, which are regarded as large island States, are grouped together with the African LDCs. The resulting groups are as follows:

African LDCs and Haiti: Angola, Benin, Burkina Faso, Burundi, Central African Republic, Chad, Democratic Republic of the Congo, Djibouti, Equatorial Guinea, Eritrea, Ethiopia, Gambia, Guinea, Guinea-Bissau, Haiti, Lesotho, Liberia, Madagascar, Malawi, Mali, Mauritania, Mozambique, Niger, Rwanda, Senegal, Sierra Leone, Somalia, Sudan, Togo, Uganda, United Republic of Tanzania, Zambia.

Asian LDCs: Afghanistan, Bangladesh, Bhutan, Cambodia, Lao People's Democratic Republic, Myanmar, Nepal, Yemen.

Island LDCs: Comoros, Kiribati, Samoa, Sao Tome and Principe, Solomon Islands, Timor-Leste, Tuvalu, Vanuatu.

Purely geographical classification

For the parts of this Report where migration flows are analysed (including on a geographical basis), LDCs have been classified according to strictly geographical criteria, as follows.

LDCs – Africa: Angola, Benin, Burkina Faso, Burundi, Central African Republic, Chad, Comoros, Democratic Republic of the Congo, Djibouti, Equatorial Guinea, Eritrea, Ethiopia, Gambia, Guinea, Guinea-Bissau, Lesotho, Liberia, Madagascar, Malawi, Mali, Mauritania, Mozambique, Niger, Rwanda, Sao Tome and Principe, Senegal, Sierra Leone, Somalia, Sudan, Togo, Uganda, United Republic of Tanzania, Zambia.

LDCs – Asia: Afghanistan, Bangladesh, Bhutan, Cambodia, Lao People's Democratic Republic, Myanmar, Nepal, Timor-Leste, Yemen.

LDC – Americas: Haiti.

LDCs – Pacific: Kiribati, Samoa, Solomon Islands, Tuvalu, Vanuatu.

Export specialization

For the purpose of analysing current trends in chapter 1, UNCTAD has classified the LDCs into six export specialization categories, according to which type of exports accounted for at least 45 per cent of total exports of goods and services in 2009–2011. The exceptions to this criterion are Bhutan, Madagascar, Mozambique, Sierra Leone and Uganda, for which a threshold of 40 per cent was used. The group composition is as follows:

Agricultural and Food exporters: Benin, Burkina Faso, Guinea-Bissau, Kiribati, Malawi, Solomon Islands, Somalia, Uganda.

Fuel exporters: Angola, Chad, Equatorial Guinea, Sudan, Yemen.

Manufactures exporters: Bangladesh, Bhutan, Cambodia, Haiti, Lesotho.

Mineral exporters: Democratic Republic of the Congo, Guinea, Mali, Mauritania, Mozambique, Sierra Leone, Zambia.

Mixed exporters: Afghanistan, Burundi, Central African Republic, Lao People's Democratic Republic, Myanmar, Niger, Senegal, Togo, United Republic of Tanzania.

Services exporters: Comoros, Djibouti, Eritrea, Ethiopia, Gambia, Liberia, Madagascar, Nepal, Rwanda, Samoa, Sao Tome and Príncipe, Timor-Leste, Tuvalu, Vanuatu.

Other groups of countries and territories

Developed economies: Andorra, Austria, Australia, Belgium, Bulgaria, Bermuda, Canada, Cyprus, Czech Republic, Denmark, Estonia, Faeroe Islands, Finland, France, Germany, Gibraltar, Greece, Greenland, Holy See, Hungary, Iceland, Ireland, Italy, Israel, Japan, Latvia, Lithuania, Luxembourg, Malta, Netherlands, New Zealand, Norway, Poland, Portugal, Romania, Saint Pierre and Miquelon, San Marino, Slovakia, Slovenia, Spain, Sweden, Switzerland, United Kingdom, United States.

Other developing countries: All developing countries (as classified by the United Nations) which are not LDCs.

Transition economies: Albania, Armenia, Azerbaijan, Belarus, Bosnia and Herzegovina, Croatia, Georgia, Kazakhstan, Kyrgyzstan, Moldova, Montenegro, Russian Federation, Serbia, Tajikistan, The former Yugoslav Republic of Macedonia, Turkmenistan, Ukraine, Uzbekistan.

Product classification

Goods: The figures provided below are the codes of the Standard International Trade Classification (SITC), revision 3.

Agriculture and Food: section 0, 1, 2 and 4 excluding divisions 27 and 28.

Minerals: section 27, 28 and 68 and groups 667 and 971.

Fuels: section 3.

Manufactures: section 5 to 8 excluding group 667.

Section 9 (Commodities and transactions not classified elsewhere in the SITC) has been included only in the total export of goods and services, but not in the goods classificaiton above, except for group 971 (Gold, non-monetary (excluding gold ores and concentrates)), which has been included in Minerals.

Services: Total services cover the following main categories: transport, travel, communications, construction, insurance, financial services, computer and information services, royalties and license fees, other business services, personal, cultural, recreational and government services.

OVERVIEW

Introduction

The uncertain global economic recovery and the worsening Eurozone crisis continue to undermine those factors that enabled the least developed countries (LDCs) as a group to attain higher growth rates between 2002 and 2008. Despite seeing real gross domestic product (GDP) grow slightly faster in 2010, the group as a whole performed less favourably in 2011, signalling challenges ahead. Indeed, with the world's attention focused on Europe, there is a danger that the international community may lose sight of the fact that in recent years, LDCs have been most affected by financial crises caused by other countries. With less diversified economies, LDCs have neither the reserves nor the resources needed to cushion their economies and adjust easily to negative shocks. Furthermore, if another global downturn hurts the growth prospects of emerging economies, LDCs, as major commodity exporters, will be directly affected. Therefore, LDCs require increased external assistance to better protect their economies against external shocks and help them manage volatility.

In May 2011, Heads of State and Government and Representatives of States gathered in Istanbul (Turkey) for the Fourth United Nations Conference on the Least Developed Countries (LDC-IV) to deliberate on the specific development challenges facing LDCs and agree on a Programme of Action for the Decade 2011–2020. The Istanbul Programme of Action (IPoA) identified eight "priority areas of action" to be implemented by both LDCs and their development partners. One of the eight priority areas is "mobilization of financial resources for development and capacity-building", and the Programme refers specifically to five sources of finance: domestic resource mobilization; official development assistance; external debt; foreign direct investment; and remittances. On the latter, the IPoA states in paragraph 123:

"Remittances are significant private financial resources for households in countries of origin of migration. There is a need for further efforts to lower the transaction costs of remittances and create opportunities for development-oriented investment, bearing in mind that remittances cannot be considered as a substitute for foreign direct investment, ODA, debt relief or other public sources of finance for development".

The Least Developed Countries Report 2012 focuses on the issue of remittances from a wider perspective. It examines the potential role of migrants or diasporas at large from LDCs as sources of development finance and also as channels of knowledge transfer and as facilitators of trade and market access opportunities in the host countries. The Report identifies policies, including policy lessons from other countries that LDCs may wish to consider in designing policy frameworks for harnessing remittances and diaspora knowledge to build productive capacities.

Remittances have attracted increasing attention in the international discourse, partly owing to their significant growth over the last decade. A growing consensus is emerging that remittances constitute a significant source of external financing, whose availability, if managed through appropriate policies, could prove particularly valuable for capital-scarce developing countries (especially those with larger diasporas).

Similarly, there is growing interest in the role that migrants, especially skilled professionals, can play as "development agents" linking home and destination countries. While concerns about the adverse impact of brain drain remain valid, as discussed in detail in this Report, the focus of the recent debate has to some extent shifted to how to engage with the diaspora and maximize its potential contribution to development, "turning brain drain into brain gain". In this respect, the emphasis has been placed not only on diaspora members' saving and investment potential, but also on their latent role as "knowledge brokers" who could facilitate the emergence of new trade patterns, technology transfer, skills and knowledge exchange. This calls for a pragmatic, context-specific policy approach to diaspora engagement.

In general, the effective mobilization of a diaspora for development depends on the existence of a critical mass of migrants in a given destination. In some cases, however, the diaspora need not be large to generate a positive development impact. Even a small number of highly skilled expatriates can create enormous benefits, in particular in poor economies with severe shortages of skilled professionals. Nevertheless, the onus of mobilizing the diaspora and transferring specialized knowledge and technology should not be placed wholly on the diaspora. Rather, the latter should be viewed as a potentially important complement to a country's development strategy; one which could be mobilized strategically within the framework of broader policy initiatives to support the financing and development of productive capacities.

Harnessing remittances for increasing productive capacities requires that these resources be considered pragmatically, with the recognition that ultimately these are private sector resources, and that due account be taken of each country's specificities, while avoiding characterizations of this phenomenon as either a "curse" or a "new development mantra". The jury is still out on whether or not they are the most stable and predictable source of development finance. While some unresolved questions remain as to their macroeconomic impact, substantial evidence suggests that remittances contribute to poverty reduction and improved health care and education. LDCs will likely be hard hit by the global economic slowdown. This will require rethinking alternative sources of development finance and the potential for tapping into LDCs' diaspora knowledge networks as sources of knowledge, entrepreneurship and trade links.

Recent economic trends in the LDCs

In 2011, LDCs grew by 4.2 per cent, 1.4 percentage points lower than the preceding year, mirroring the slowdown of growth worldwide (from 5.3 per cent in 2010 to 3.9 per cent in 2011). Given their high dependence on external economic conditions, LDCs were unable to escape this broad-based slowdown, and the rate of deceleration was similar to that of developing countries (1.3 percentage points) and advanced economies (1.6 percentage points).

In terms of country group performance, both African and Asian LDCs experienced a slowdown in 2011, and both grew by similar rates at around four per cent. For the Asian LDCs, however, the slowdown was more pronounced (over two percentage points). By contrast, GDP growth of the island LDCs (at 7.1 per cent) was much higher, compared with both the previous year and the LDC average.

The poor performance of oil-exporting LDCs in 2011 (-1.6 per cent) had a negative impact on overall LDC performance. Compared with oil exporters, LDCs specializing in exports of other products such as manufactures (6.0 per cent), services (5.7 per cent), minerals (5.8 per cent), agriculture and food (5.9 per cent) or mixed exports (5.4 per cent) fared much better. However, in terms of resource gap, indicating the extent to which countries rely on external resources to finance their domestic investment, non-oil-exporting LDCs have performed poorly. While the resource gap for LDCs as a whole fell from 6.5 per cent of GDP in 2000 to 3.9 per cent in 2010, for non-oil-exporting LDCs, it increased from 10 per cent 2000 to 13 per cent just before the global crisis and hit 14.8 per cent in 2010. One result of the increasing resource gap in non-petroleum-exporting LDCs has been a growing balance of payments vulnerability. In 2011, thirteen LDCs had current account deficits of more than 10 per cent of GDP, while five had deficits of over 20 per cent of GDP. Only five LDCs reported current account surpluses.

If this pattern continues, along with slow global recovery, it may damage employment prospects in LDCs. The significance of employment for LDCs cannot be overemphasized. The relatively young demographic structure of LDCs means that increasing cohorts of young are entering the labour market and will continue to do so. Even during the 2002–2008 boom, LDCs faced an employment challenge because of lopsided growth concentrated in resource-extractive sectors which resulted in weak job creation. This also resulted in growing informality in LDCs, even when rates of open unemployment did not increase.

The longer it takes for GDP growth to return to its pre-crisis level, the greater the likelihood of long-term unemployment and underemployment, with all of their detrimental effects on the population. Governments should thus bear in mind that additional measures are needed to minimize the adverse effects of the global crisis, and that employment creation should be at the top of their national development agendas.

Gross fixed capital formation increased slightly from 20.7 per cent of GDP in 2005–2007 to 21.6 per cent in 2008–2010. Throughout the first decade of the 21st century, it has increased slowly but surely (by three GDP percentage points). While this is positive, it compares less favourably with other developing countries (ODCs), whose gross fixed capital formation reached 30.1 per cent of GDP in 2010. If current investment trends continue, it is unlikely that LDCs will be able to catch up with ODCs in the near future. The gross domestic saving rate for the LDCs as a group was 18.9 per cent of GDP in 2005–2007, and fell to 17.7 per cent in 2008–2010.

The LDCs' trade balance improved from a deficit equivalent to 6.1 per cent of GDP in 2010 to 5.7 per cent in 2011. The value of merchandise exports from LDCs increased by 23 per cent in 2011, surpassing the pre-crisis level. The total value of merchandise exports in 2011 ($204.8 billon) was twice as high as five years ago. On the downside, merchandise exports for LDCs as a group have remained highly concentrated in a few countries. The top five exporters (Angola, Bangladesh, Equatorial Guinea, Yemen and Sudan) account for 62 per cent of all exports from LDCs. The value of merchandise imports rose sharply in 2011 (20.6 per cent) to $202.2 billion, also doubling in the last five years.

Overall trends in merchandise trade shifted the merchandise trade balance into surplus in 2011 after two years of deficits. This is important to emphasize since prior to 2006, LDCs had continuously recorded merchandise trade deficits. Yet the positive result for the group was due entirely to the African LDCs and their surplus of $21.4 billion – which in turn is driven by only a small number of countries, most notably Angola. Asian LDCs, by contrast, recorded a merchandise trade deficit of $17.5 billion in 2011, and island LDCs a deficit of $1.2 billion. Merchandise exports have continued to be dominated by petroleum, at slightly over 46 per cent of total exports.

Improved export performance by many LDCs in 2010 and 2011 was largely due to higher international commodity prices. After slumping in 2009, prices recovered rapidly, in some cases to levels higher than before the crisis. For example, food prices started to rise again in 2010 and 2011, topping pre-crisis levels. In the summer of 2012, food prices, in particular for maize and wheat, were once again on the rise due to drought in major producing countries. This will affect many poor people in LDCs, who generally spend 50 to 80 per cent of their income on food. The situation in some parts of Africa is critical, as food insecurity threatens the lives of hundreds of thousands. Governments in LDCs and their development partners must act urgently to prevent rising food prices from spiralling out of control, risking the sort of crisis experienced in 2008. In the long term, the root causes of food price increases and the issue of agricultural production in LDCs must be tackled by increasing investment in the sector and designing policies to improve productivity, in particular among small-scale farmers.

Regarding foreign investment, UNCTAD recently revised the data on inflows of foreign direct investment (FDI) to LDCs, which show that in the last decade, FDI inflows have been smaller than remittances. Unlike FDI, remittances kept increasing even during the crisis and are forecasted to grow in the medium term. In 2011, remittances to LDCs reached $26 billion. The decline in FDI inflows to LDCs for three consecutive years (from a little less than $19 billion in 2008 to $15 billion in 2011) has been largely due to disinvestment trends in Angola, tied to the oil investment cycle in that country. In the rest of the LDCs, FDI has remained relatively stable.

Official development assistance (ODA) disbursements, together with net debt relief to LDCs from all donors reporting to the Development Assistance Committee of the Organisation for Economic Co-operation and Development (OECD/DAC), reached a record level of $44.8 billion in 2010, an 11 per cent increase over 2009. In nominal terms, aid inflows to the LDCs were 3.5 times higher in 2010 than in 2000. As noted in *The Least Developed Countries Report 2011*, ODA has played an important countercyclical role in the wake of the global crisis, cushioning the impact of retreating private financial flows. While data for 2011 are still not available, there are signs of a decrease in ODA from some donor countries.

The LDCs' total debt stock reached $161 billion in 2010, only marginally higher than in 2009. Their debt service decreased slightly from $8.2 billion in 2009 to 7.6 billion in 2010. The experience of the LDCs in the last ten years shows that the key to debt sustainability is development of productive capacities. High, sustainable GDP growth and rapid expanding exports increased the debt-servicing capacity of many LDCs. While external financial resources, in particular ODA and remittances, have recently been increasingly available to LDCs, there is no guarantee that this will continue to be the case. The recent sharp decrease in FDI is instructive in this respect. Consequently, a progressive shift from reliance on external sources of finance to domestic ones to reduce their external dependence and vulnerability to external shocks and uncertainties is a major challenge for LDCs.

Sadly, given the fragile global economy, the outlook for 2013 is highly uncertain. As of mid-2012, economic activity was decelerating in a synchronized fashion in many parts of the world. The downside risks are numerous and include escalation of the Eurozone debt crisis, a rise in global energy prices due to geopolitical risks, deceleration of growth in large developing countries and fiscal retrenchment in the United States scheduled for 2013, which could have a strong negative impact on overall growth.

Against this background, the outlook for LDCs in the short- to medium-term is not encouraging. Given the growing danger that the world economy might be entering a lengthy period of stagnation and deflation, LDCs have to prepare for a relatively prolonged period of uncertainty, with possible escalation of financial tensions and real economic downturn. Trade and investment of developing countries, which are often intermediated by US and European banks, have already suffered setbacks. Prices of some commodities started to fall, in some cases abruptly, in the second quarter of 2012, partly due to slowing demand for commodities from emerging economies. If the current tendency of economic deceleration continues, commodity prices could suffer pronounced falls. Thus, LDCs may once again be exposed to external economic shocks and have to deal with a crisis that originates elsewhere. Recognizing this may allow for more effective preparation. It also lends added urgency to the need for rethinking remittances policies and the role that diasporas could play in knowledge transfer and as catalysts of industrial development and structural transformation in home countries.

Patterns of LDC emigration

Emigration from LDCs grew rapidly in 1990–2010. With 27.5 million emigrants in 2010, LDCs as a whole accounted for 13 per cent of global emigration stocks, or some 3.3 per cent of the LDC population. Over 2000–2010, the increase in emigrant stocks was fastest for African LDCs. The destination of LDC emigrants varies across regions, but most go to South Asia, the Middle East and Africa. High migration within sub-Saharan Africa probably reflects the facts that (a) much of African migration is forced (refugee flows) and by poor people, as a result of which proximity is crucial; and (b) Africans generally face great difficulty entering other countries. Among the high-income regions, only the Gulf States have a high share of South Asians, and no country has a high share of Africans. The evidence shows that some 80 per cent of LDC migrants migrate within the South, as a result of which LDCs and ODCs are important countries of destination.

In fact, refugees constitute a significant but declining share of total immigrants residing in LDCs. Their share of the total migrant stock in LDCs peaked at 44 per cent in 1995 but then declined rapidly, reflecting improved governance structures in many African countries and lessened conflict and political instability. As with conventional economic migration, when mass forced migration occurs, there is a significant loss of human and financial capital, of labour and skilled workers in the country of origin. The main countries of emigration in 2010 were Bangladesh, with 4.9 million emigrants, and Afghanistan, with two million.

Globally, developed countries tend to accept skilled immigrants but increasingly erect barriers to exclude the unskilled unless there is high demand for their labour in particular sectors (e.g. agriculture or construction). LDC migrants tend to be younger than those from other countries, with a median age of 29 years, compared with 34 in other developing countries and 43 in the developed countries.

Therefore, contrary to the general perception that LDC migration is a South–North phenomenon, the pattern of migration emerging has acquired a South–South dimension in recent decades. In 2010, high-income OECD countries (namely North America and Europe) accounted for 20 per cent of the LDC emigrant stock, while some 80 per cent were in the South. Moreover, most LDC South–South migration tends to take place between neighbouring countries, where wage differentials are in general much smaller than in South–North migration. Thus, the main LDC emigration corridors are in the South.

Concerning high-skilled migration, the majority of emigrants who have attained tertiary education tend to migrate to developed countries. In fact, Haiti (83 per cent), Samoa (73 per cent), the Gambia (68 per cent) and Tuvalu (65 per cent) have the highest emigration rates of tertiary-educated LDC population.

There are several reasons and motivations driving migration from LDCs. However, the following patterns and observations are worth noting:

- First, given the youthful demographic structure of most LDCs, young adults typically move more than older adults. This is partly due to life-cycle differences between age groups and educational levels.

- Second, men migrate more than women on average in LDCs (particularly in Asian LDCs), due to the persistence of particular gender roles in most rural societies where women have primary responsibility for child-rearing and domestic tasks. This often limits opportunities for women to migrate, the key exceptions perhaps being young, unmarried women from households where they can be absent (i.e. households where several older women already reside) or women migrating to join their partners at the destination. However, female migration has been increasing recently. When they do migrate, women migrant workers are generally employed in service activities (including the care economy), while male migrants are more likely to be found in manufacturing production and construction sectors, in addition to some services.

- Third, in LDCs migration is an important livelihood strategy and largely operates within a context of temporary (seasonal or circular) migration. The migrant remains part of the household, and is expected to send remittances home.

- Fourth, some migration occurs as a survival strategy, while some is based on a rational income-maximizing strategy to take advantage of regional or international wage differentials, irrespective of conditions at home. Educational qualifications and skills make such migration more feasible for youth.

The LDCs with the highest share of emigrants as a percentage of total LDC emigrant stocks in 2010 were Bangladesh (19 per cent), Afghanistan (8 per cent), Burkina Faso (6 per cent) and Mozambique (4 per cent). These countries were also part of the main migration corridors: Bangladesh — India, Afghanistan — Iran, Burkina Faso -

Côte d'Ivoire, Yemen — Saudi Arabia and Nepal — India. Asian LDCs like Bangladesh, Afghanistan, Yemen and Nepal tend to have India or the Middle East as a first or second country of destination. For African LDCs, the key emigration corridors are within Africa.

Inhabitants of Asian and Pacific LDCs appear to have higher propensities to migrate to non-LDCs than those of African LDCs, which recorded the highest share of emigrants residing in other LDCs in 2010. The main sources of intra-LDC migration during 2010 were in sub-Saharan Africa, particularly Eritrea, the Democratic Republic of the Congo and Sudan.

Improved international cooperation on migration and development in LDCs is needed to optimize migrant contributions at all levels. Thus, at the bilateral and regional levels, further progress is required to strengthen international cooperation.

Remittances to LDCs: Magnitude, impact and cost

Worldwide, the value of remittances began to accelerate markedly, nearly doubling between 1990 and 2000, and then tripling once again in the following decade, touching $489 billion in 2011 despite the global financial crisis. While all regions have witnessed significant expansions in remittance receipts, the rise in global remittances is chiefly driven by the surge of inflows to developing countries. Correspondingly, the developed economies' share of world remittances has been steadily declining.

As for LDCs, remittance receipts climbed from $3.5 billion in 1990 to $6.3 billion in 2000, subsequently accelerating further to nearly $27 billion in 2011. These inflows are unevenly distributed across LDCs, even more so than FDI and export revenues. Over the past decade, the top recipient, Bangladesh, expanded its share of total LDC remittance inflows from 31 to 44 per cent. During the same period, the top three LDC recipients (Bangladesh, Nepal and Sudan) also increased their overall share from 44 per cent to 66 per cent of LDC total inflows. Besides these well-known large recipients, other LDCs obtaining sizeable sums through remittances include Cambodia, Ethiopia, Haiti, Lesotho, Mali, Senegal, Togo, Uganda and Yemen.

Notwithstanding the uneven distribution, the sustained dynamism of remittance inflows to LDCs was quite general. In all but a handful of LDCs for which data are available, remittance inflows increased markedly over the last decade, growing at an annual average of 15 per cent in the median LDC. Admittedly, in the wake of the global financial crisis of 2009, remittance receipts slowed in most LDCs, even though they continued to increase with a few exceptions.

Despite some heterogeneity across countries, the value of remittances relative to GDP or export revenues has historically been much greater in LDCs than in other regions. In the median LDC, they account for as much as 2.1 per cent of GDP and 8.5 per cent of export earnings, as compared with 1.6 per cent and 4.5 per cent respectively for ODCs. This prominence is noticeable for an array of LDCs, ranging from small economies like Lesotho or Samoa, where remittances represent over 20 per cent of GDP, to traditionally large recipients such as Nepal and Haiti, where they largely exceed export earnings.

Similarly, for a number of LDCs, remittances constitute a key source of foreign financing. Over 2008–2010, recorded remittances exceeded both ODA and FDI inflows in nine LDCs, and surpassed FDI but not ODA in another eight LDC economies. Whereas by their very nature remittances are distinct from capital flows, they clearly play a significant role in providing foreign exchange for a large number of LDC countries. Consequently, it is important that LDC development strategies fully reflect the relevance of these resource flows, their intrinsic characteristics, and their underlying potential.

South–South remittance flows are particularly important for LDCs, consistent with the fact that the majority of LDC migrants actually move to other developing countries, often neighbouring ones. In 2010, it was estimated that as much as two-thirds of recorded remittances to LDCs originated in other Southern countries. Distinct regional patterns emerge, however, with respect to remittance corridors. India and the Gulf Cooperation Council (GCC) countries represent key sources of remittances for Asian LDCs; "subregional hubs" (such as Côte d'Ivoire, Kenya or South Africa) play a similar role for African LDCs, along with former colonial powers; while Pacific Islands derive the bulk of their remittances from neighbouring developed economies.

There is a compelling body of research documenting the positive impact of remittances at the household level, both in terms of poverty reduction and as a risk mitigation strategy to diversify income sources. However, evidence of their developmental impact at a macroeconomic level is far less clear-cut. The relationship between remittances and economic growth is complex and multifaceted. On the negative side, the adverse effect of remittances on labour market outcomes may reduce economic growth, especially if a culture of dependency on foreign transfers becomes gradually entrenched. Moreover, unless properly addressed, the tendency of remittances to trigger appreciations in the real exchange rate may give rise to "Dutch disease" effects, hindering much-needed structural change by undermining the competitiveness of non-traditional tradable sectors.

On the positive side, remittances may support economic growth and productive capacity development through two channels: investment and financial deepening. Indeed, remittances provide a much-needed source of foreign financing that could enhance the pace of physical and human capital accumulation (the "investment channel"). In addition, they tend to increase the availability of funds for the domestic financial system, paving the way for recipient households to demand and gain access to other financial products and services which they might not have otherwise. Besides, remittances may possibly relax financial constraints on recipient households, particularly those in rural areas, which are poorly served by existing financial intermediaries.

Even though the literature is still somewhat inconclusive on how remittances ultimately affect economic growth, there appears to be general agreement that complementary policies and sound institutions play an important role in enhancing their development impact. Governments typically have only limited room to directly affect the allocation of remittance income, since taxation or mandatory remittance requirements have historically proved rather ineffective and in most cases have simply led migrants to use informal channels to remit. Accordingly, effective mobilization of remittances for productive purposes depends on an array of policy and institutional improvements, aimed at reinforcing both the "investment channel" and remittances' impact on financial deepening.

Overall, the scope for remittances to stimulate both physical and human capital accumulation and financial development tends to be fairly positive, all the more so when a large share of remittance income is received by poor and otherwise credit-rationed households. Here, capital-scarce LDCs clearly have much to gain from remittances' potential developmental impact. Yet LDCs' structural weaknesses make it more difficult to successfully mobilize these sources of external financing for productive purposes. It is therefore essential to design appropriate strategies and policy frameworks for harnessing remittances for economic development.

Moreover, the relative stability and lower procyclicality of remittances compared with other sources of external financing is worth stressing. Due to these characteristics, an increase in the share of remittances to GDP tends to reduce the volatility of GDP growth, even after controlling for other possible determinants of growth volatility. Similarly, remittances appear to reduce the probability of sharp current account reversals, especially when they are larger than three per cent of GDP. These features may be particularly relevant in an LDC context, given that these economies have traditionally been characterized by relatively recurrent growth accelerations but nearly as frequent growth collapses, coupled with heightened balance of payments vulnerability and debt overhang.

At household level, a large body of empirical studies typically show that remittances reduce poverty. The impact of remittances on inequality is less clear-cut, especially given the selectivity underlying the migration process. As prospective migrants incur upfront costs, which are largely dependent on the destination, those belonging to the poorest households are typically unable to afford long-distance international movement or the costly bureaucratic procedures usually required to migrate to developed economies. So it is precisely the poorest who are unable to benefit from the largest differentials in terms of expected wages and consequently remit larger sums.

Migrants typically utilize a whole range of formal and informal channels for remitting, chosen on the basis of cost, reliability, accessibility and trust. Though resorting to informal remittance channels may seem a rational choice from an individual migrant's standpoint, policy-wise, formal remittance systems are preferable, even leaving aside concerns related to security, regulation or supervision. The prevalence of informal flows limits the ability of recipient countries to make optimum use of the foreign exchange sent by overseas migrants. This may limit the effects remittances have on a country's creditworthiness or in stimulating financial deepening, and encourage informal (black market) currency transactions.

Worldwide evidence shows that, as of the first quarter of 2009, the cost of remittances averaged nine per cent of the amount sent. For LDCs, the average cost of remitting was close to 12 per cent of the amount sent, 30 per cent higher than the global average. If North–South remittance costs are high, South–South remittance costs are often significantly higher. The most expensive channels for remitting transfers to LDCs are found within Africa, whereas the least expensive are from Singapore and Saudi Arabia to Asian LDCs. The implications of such high remittance costs may be significant: it is estimated that in 2010, annual remittances sent to sub-Saharan Africa could have generated an additional $6 billion for recipients if the costs of remitting money had matched the global average.

Average remittance costs naturally mask a wide range of elements that vary by corridor and remittance service provider (RSP). In general, lack of competition among RSPs appears to be a significant factor in explaining the high costs of remittances. The regulatory challenges that RSPs face vary by LDC and region, and have led to different characteristics in the respective remittance markets. For example, for the whole of sub-Saharan Africa, 65 per cent of all remittance payout locations are controlled by two money transfer operators (MTOs), namely MoneyGram and Western Union. Similarly, African governments have put into place several RSP exclusivity arrangements limiting the type of institutions able to offer remittance services to banks, thereby reducing RSP competition.

Remittance transfer payments systems in LDCs are evolving and new channels and technologies are emerging. With improving LDC infrastructure and growth in mobile bank branches and branchless banking, both urban and rural clienteles should enjoy better access to financial services. Yet despite the potential of these emerging systems, more traditional forms of RSP provision still dominate in most LDCs.

In general, as shown in this Report, remittances offer LDCs some scope for sustaining the development of productive capacities, by increasing investment in human and physical capital and stimulating financial deepening. Yet the realization of such potential is contingent upon the policy and institutional framework recipient countries put into place. In other words, owing to the intrinsic specificities of remittances as private sector financial flows, their effective mobilization for productive purposes essentially depends on the State's capacity to create a "development-centred" macroeconomic environment while also supporting the establishment of a viable and inclusive financial sector. This, in turn, warrants active engagement by diasporas and support from host countries and international development institutions.

Mobilizing the diaspora: From brain drain to brain gain

"Brain drain" generally refers to the emigration of high-skilled people with university-level education, such as physicians, engineers, scientists, managers and lawyers, as well as entrepreneurs. The main drivers of brain drain are higher income, better working conditions, career prospects in a host country, the latter's selective migration policies, adverse political and economic situations in one's home country, and lower migration costs. Worldwide, brain drain has been increasing in absolute terms. The number of high-skilled international migrants climbed from 16.4 million in 1990 to 26.2 million in 2000 (the latest year for which data are available). When the 2010 figures are finally released, they are expected to show a sharp increase in the volume of high-skilled international migration. International immigration is skewed towards highly educated people. Twenty-six per cent of all international migrants are tertiary-educated (according to data for 2000), while only 11.3 per cent of the world labour force have tertiary education. In developing countries, university-level workers account for a much lower five per cent of the labour force.

In 2000 (the year for which data are available for LDCs), high-skilled migrants accounted for one-fourth of total emigration from LDCs. This is 11 times higher than their share in the total labour force of these countries, namely, 2.3 per cent. International migration is selective (i.e. it favours high-skilled over low-skilled people), which explains this huge discrepancy. An estimated 1.3 million persons with university-level education had emigrated from LDCs by 2000, and this figure has continued to grow since then. Almost two-thirds of all LDC high-skilled emigrants live in developed countries (especially the United States), while one-third moved to other developing countries (mainly oil-exporting and neighbouring countries). The major regional source of high-skilled LDC emigrants is Asia, home to 45.9 per cent of tertiary educated migrants from LDCs, followed by African LDCs, which account for 40.4 per cent of LDC brain drain.

Brain drain can have both adverse and beneficial effects on home countries, the balance of which primarily depends on the extent of brain drain. This is measured by the brain drain rate, i.e. the number of high-skilled emigrants as a share of all nationals with the same education level. Collectively, LDCs have the highest brain drain rate among the world's major country groups, averaging 18.4 per cent, much higher than other developing countries (10 per cent). Regionally, the worst affected LDCs are Haiti, Pacific Islands and African LDCs. Six LDCs have more high-skilled professionals living abroad than at home: Haiti, Samoa, the Gambia, Tuvalu, Kiribati and Sierra Leone.

The "optimal" level of brain drain (where the net balance of positive and negative effects on the domestic home economies reaches its maximum) has been estimated at 5–10 per cent. Only five LDCs are in this range. By contrast, beyond 15–20 per cent, the likelihood increases that the negative impacts of brain drain will exceed the positive consequences. The actual brain drain rate is "high" in 30 of the 48 LDCs.

What are the main likely adverse impacts of brain drain on LDCs? First, it results in a reduction of their human capital stock and the externalities generated by highly skilled people. This can lead to lower economic and productivity growth, as well as reduced activity in science, technology and innovation (STI). Second, brain drain is especially acute in some sectors, above all health, education and scientific research. LDCs form the country group with the lowest number of doctors per population but have the world's highest medical brain drain rates. These are usually associated with higher infant and child mortality, lower vaccination rates and generally poor health-care services and national health systems. Third, through brain drain, LDC governments forego the taxes that these professional would have paid if they had stayed and worked at home. Fourth, shrinking the skilled human capital base tilts LDCs' relative endowments and comparative advantage away from skill-intensive sectors towards low-skilled activities and, possibly, natural resources. Fifth, some LDC high-skilled emigrants hold jobs with educational requirements below their training, in what is termed "brain waste", since part of their skills are not used. Sixth, the departure of the most skilled persons impairs institution-building in LDCs.

The question is: can LDCs turn brain drain into brain gain? There is evidence to show that notwithstanding the short-term adverse impacts, over the long run, countries can benefit from the additional knowledge acquired by their nationals residing and working abroad. First, it has been argued that emigration prospects may encourage people to obtain further education, which may result in brain gain, i.e. larger human capital endowments. Second, part of the remittances are used to pay for the education of family members, thereby generating brain gain. Third, high-skilled emigrants form a knowledge pool which can be organized as diaspora knowledge networks (DKNs), facilitating flows of knowledge and technology to home countries. These flows work through programmes and initiatives launched by diaspora organizations, international organizations and governments of home and host countries. They generally have positive effects, but the effectiveness of knowledge-sharing initiatives is sometimes hampered by the dispersions of projects, their failure to join actors and efforts, a dearth of resources leveraging and synergy creation, as well as little coherence with national development policies. Harnessing diaspora knowledge by creating networks has huge but still relatively unfulfilled potential for LDCs.

Fourth, the presence of diasporas can strengthen business flows between host and home countries through trade and investment links. In LDCs, diasporas have driven growth of home country goods in what has been termed "ethnic trade" or "nostalgia trade", i.e. goods exported to be consumed by the diaspora but which can potentially spread to wider markets. LDC diapora members have also propelled the growth of tourism service exports, by visiting the home country or helping to attract other tourists.

Fifth, permanent return migrants can bring with them accumulated savings, knowledge, experience and business networks, although this may depend on their motivation for return, time spent abroad, and local conditions. LDCs that are more advanced in economic diversification, structural transformation and growth have typically been more successful in attracting the voluntary return of qualified migrants who have founded new businesses and introduced economic and social innovation in the fields of science, health, education, services and industry.

Yet benefiting from a diaspora is not automatic. Tapping the potential depends on a series of institutional, economic and political conditions, still absent in most LDCs. Therefore, policy action by home and host countries and by the international community is crucial for fostering or strengthening positive diaspora effects on LDCs. Brain drain from LDCs will likely continue in the foreseeable future, due to very strong push and pull forces. These diasporas are a pool of knowledge, human and financial resources on which LDCs can draw to have them contribute to national development to a much greater extent than previously. LDC governments are at the initial stages of realizing this potential and taking action to harness it. Stronger, more systematic policy action is required in order to strengthen diasporas' contribution to LDCs. To succeed, such policy action requires mobilization and coordination of the efforts and resources of different stakeholders, especially home country institutions and firms, host country government and agents, diaspora organizations and NGOs, international organizations, and bilateral donors. Ideally, such coordination should take place upstream, i.e. at the planning stage, so as to ensure the engagement and coherence of all relevant stakeholders from the start.

Unlocking the LDCs' diaspora potential: A policy agenda for harnessing remittances and diaspora knowledge

DIASPORAS AND CAPACITY-BUILDING

Clearly, migration and its varied consequences have become increasingly significant for developing countries in general and LDCs in particular, and these trends are likely to continue into the medium-term future. The main recommendation of this Report for policymakers is to improve the current policy framework on remittances and diaspora knowledge in LDCs in order to better harness them for the development of productive capacities. Furthermore, policies on migration, remittances and diaspora engagement should not be formulated in isolation, but as an integral part of national development strategies. This will require an agency, ideally at ministerial level, to reflect the cross-cutting nature of these issues; ensure policy coherence and consistency across the board; and coordinate potential actors around a set of identified priorities. Governments in LDCs also need to be aware of the actual extent and pattern of cross-border migration, the location, spread and nature of diaspora activities, and the extent and pattern of remittances. Here, the current state of knowledge in most LDCs is relatively poor. Therefore, part of the problem is statistical in nature. There is hardly any official apparatus to report on and monitor many of the facets of migration and its results, and existing mechanisms deal mainly with remittances.

While the specific mix of policies and concrete measures for diaspora engagement will vary for each country, the overall direction should be to provide an enabling environment for development. Also, the issue of trust is crucial. While it is true that diaspora members are not motivated exclusively by commercial interests, their engagement will fail if they are only expected to contribute and receive nothing in return. This applies, for example, if LDCs wish to encourage diaspora entrepreneurs to use their savings or raise capital externally to establish productive activities in home countries. Studies on the role of the diasporas show that in some middle-income countries, entrepreneurial diasporas have been instrumental in developing the productive capacities of their home countries. For example, migrant entrepreneurs have played an important role in building knowledge-based industries in India, China, Taiwan Province of China, Israel and Ireland in the last two decades or so. A lesson from these experiences is that entrepreneurs abroad can help to develop firms at home and also serve as a two-way link for market knowledge, connections and technology transfer across countries. In LDCs, this process may be less promising in the short run because of their more limited base of human capital and venture capital to develop high-tech industries at home. Nevertheless, their entrepreneurial diasporas operating in light industry can help develop similar industries at home through contacts, know-how and other valuable inputs and capabilities developed in the host countries. They can also contribute to upgrading managerial and innovating capabilities at home.

In general, there are at least two conditions that would determine the possibilities of migrants to succeed in establishing thriving firms upon their return. The first is whether they return with more advanced knowledge and skills than before. This Report argues that this probability will increase the longer they stay as migrants in foreign countries and the more entrepreneurial experience they accumulate. The second is the existence of a favourable policy framework in their home country. They would probably need suitable financial support to start a new firm, even if they have accumulated some savings. At the very least, they should be able to obtain a loan from the financial sector under normal conditions.

Yet given the reluctance of financial institutions to extend credit to small and medium-sized enterprises (SMEs), a national development bank with special lines of credit for return migrants might be needed. In addition, return migrants might have accumulated some but not necessarily all of the requisite skills for successful entrepreneurial activity. In this case, they would need technical assistance to upgrade their managerial, technical, financial or other skills required for successfully managing an SME. Governments could provide this type of technical assistance and/or education. They could also extend support to these entrepreneurs by lowering tariffs on imports of machinery and equipment and raw materials to help them start up their businesses.

Facilitating trade-related links with host countries is another channel though which diasporas can help develop home country production and supply capacities. A positive empirical correlation has been found between the degree of international trade in source and destination countries and the size of the migrant community in both nations. The dominance of language, culture and knowledge of customer and supplier markets are all factors that help develop trade relations among nations, and the diaspora communities can be well placed for performing this role. Initially, a distinct niche for LDCs could be to seek an advantage in supplying so-called "ethnic products" or "nostalgia trade". Studies show, for example, that there is a very high participation of migrants in the United States in the market for home-country goods that are difficult to find in the host country. Each migrant spends almost $1,000 per year on nostalgia products, and the total may amount to over $20 billion annually. LDC policies could be designed to help producers become and stay competitive by upgrading their products and adapting them to changes in the final markets, and to enlist diaspora members to help with branding and marketing in the host country. Education and training of producers is crucial if they are to become competitive in foreign markets.

DIASPORAS AS SOURCES OF KNOWLEDGE AND LEARNING

Diasporas could also further structural change and economic development, by strengthening the knowledge base in home countries. A useful mechanism in this respect is the diaspora knowledge network (DKN), which consists of groups of highly skilled expatriate professionals who are interested in maintaining contacts and helping to develop their countries of origin. As knowledge is neither costless nor easily transferrable, for this to occur, proactive policies are required that incorporate this potentially key function of diasporas into governments' strategic developmental frameworks.

DKNs are understood as subsets of international knowledge networks governing the transfer of various types of knowledge, such as intellectual property, know-how, software code or databases, between dependent parties, across the economy. As such, DKNs include a platform for knowledge flows and interaction between a diaspora and local actors in a home country.

There is ample evidence from numerous case studies indicating that DKNs have played a critical role in technological upgrading, industrial development and building of productive capacities in source countries. LDCs should learn from countries that have benefited most from DKNs by designing their diaspora strategy as an integral part of industrial policy and the broader national development strategy. DKNs have effectively operated as agents of change in both developed and developing countries. There are successful cases of diaspora networks such as those formed by Indian, Chinese, Korean, Taiwanese, Vietnamese, Turkish and Bangladeshi emigrants, to name but a few.

Yet such transfer of knowledge and learning does not happen automatically: it requires an organized and coordinated diaspora network and a home-country national development strategy backed by industrial policy and active government engagement in diaspora affairs. A proactive diaspora policy is essential for ensuring that DKNs, which are in essence private voluntary networks, gain the trust and confidence needed to remain engaged and ensure that their activities exert a positive impact. As latecomers to industrial development and given their recent experience with deindustrialization, LDCs need to formulate innovative industrial policies that are compatible with both their current conditions and requirements and the rapidly evolving global context. Some LDCs have already designed industrial policies to accelerate economic diversification and structural change.

There are many reasons for promoting networks, not least of which is knowledge diffusion. DKNs can supply new technologies and inform government and other residents of the latest technological developments and those appropriate for domestic industrial needs. They can assist in matching the needs of local productive sectors with specific FDI needed for upgrading local skills and capacities. The significance of the diaspora network for industrial policy is that it makes the shift from hierarchy to search networks an essential component of industrial policy. DKNs help to link up those who want to learn with those that are already learning. Indeed, this shift from hierarchy to horizontal networks has a profound impact on global supply chains and hence on new industrial strategies, where "learning to learn" becomes an essential objective of industrial policy. However, DKNs should not be perceived as a panacea or a substitute for local efforts to build endogenous productive capabilities; rather, their role is that of additional actor in the story of growth based on domestic productive capacities.

In recent years, UNCTAD has repeatedly argued that progressive transformation in economic structure is a prerequisite for LDCs to achieve accelerated and sustained economic growth and poverty reduction. The policies and strategies needed to attain structural transformation will involve, inter alia, (a) the development of a new industrial policy based on a strategic approach that reflects the specific needs and conditions of LDCs; (b) a catalytic developmental State to compensate for the incipient and weak private sector in LDCs; (c) measures to encourage private investment in productive activities and public investment in basic infrastructure, including the development of skills and support institutions; and (d) the promotion of domestic technological learning and innovation and improvements in productivity in both agricultural and manufacturing sectors.

This Report reinforces the case for a new industrial policy in LDCs, arguing further that such a policy should reflect the role of DKNs because they carry a potentially transformative impact on knowledge accumulation, especially in accelerating technological change and direct investment. Failure to recognize this fact may mean that DKNs will remain an untapped resource and a missed opportunity.

Diasporas as sources of development finance

As noted above, one reason for the predominant use of informal channels for remitting to LDCs is the high cost of remitting through formal channels, primarily due to lack of competition. Possible policy actions to open up the remittance market to competition could include the following:

- Directly increasing the range of financial actors involved, especially in rural areas, by changing regulations to allow participation, particularly of microfinance institutions, savings and loans cooperatives, credit unions and post offices;

- Promoting partnerships among banks and microfinance institutions;

- Strengthening post office involvement by improving their Internet connectivity, increasing their technical capabilities and cash resources, and promoting a wider selection of savings products;

- Improving telecommunications infrastructure;

- Harmonizing banking and telecommunications regulations to enable banks to participate in mobile remittances;

- Actively promoting competition through specialized remittances trade fairs;

- Discouraging exclusivity agreements between all market participants, especially banks and MTOs.

These conventional measures could be accompanied by other, more innovative approaches. For example, competition could be intensified by allowing a public sector remittance service provider to operate and compete with private sector providers. This could be done by establishing a public corporation or using existing institutions like a development bank or the central bank. Such an institution would provide the same service as the private sector but would charge a lower cost for remitting. Instead of opening up its own branches, the public corporation could team up with the postal service, helping reach customers in remote areas where private financial institutions have no branches.

Use of new technologies, particularly Internet-based and mobile telephony-driven methods of transmitting funds, can be further exploited. Since the cost of remitting is highest within Africa, there is also scope for regional initiatives to bring it down, for example by coordinating measures via formal regional integration initiatives, or through the good offices of regional development banks (for example, the African Development Bank). While this could be a regional-driven process, it could also be linked to the international goal of reducing remittance costs known as the "5 x 5" initiative.

While policies to increase ease of remitting money and reduce the costs involved are clearly necessary and desirable, they need to be part of a broader macroeconomic framework to enhance the developmental role of remittances. A consistent set of trade, industrial and macroeconomic policies that sustainably foster growth and economic diversification will be crucial in ensuring that remittance flows also boost development rather than simply enhance consumption in recipient families.

At household level, governments could enhance the developmental impact of remittances by giving migrants additional incentives. For example, they could be allowed to open foreign currency accounts in the home country, and the interest rate on deposits denominated in foreign currencies could be exempted from wealth and income taxes; an option to use foreign currency deposits as collateral for obtaining preferential loans could be offered; incentives to migrants to return to the home country once they retire could be provided via double-taxation avoidance treaties with the main host countries where the majority of its migrants work; the creation of education and housing accounts at home for migrants and their families, combined with a higher rate of return on these deposits than on ordinary ones, would provide an incentive to save more out of remittances, for purposes that would encourage productive use of remittances. The appropriate mix of measures would have to be decided by competent authorities depending on the size and degree of diapora engagement.

Diaspora bonds could be attractive options for LDCs because they would increase the pool of sources for development financing. Patriotic motives for investing in diaspora bonds make these instruments at least somewhat less procyclical than other external capital flows, allowing governments to issue them in not only good but also bad times, such as natural disasters or external economic shocks.

Since remittance flows have proved fairly stable over the medium to longer term, these future-flow receivables can be used as collateral for securitization or long-term loans. For some LDCs, this could even represent the only possible access to international capital markets, increasing funds available for development, and could become a stepping stone to establish or improve international creditworthiness.

Dr. Supachai Panitchpakdi
Secretary-General of UNCTAD

CHAPTER **1**

RECENT TRENDS AND
OUTLOOK FOR THE LDCs

A. Introduction

This chapter analyses recent macroeconomic trends in LDCs and their performance in terms of economic growth, international trade and external finance. It shows that their economic performance has been substantially worse in the last three years than in the previous boom period and that some indicators have not yet reached pre-crisis levels. In addition, the current world economic situation and its implications for LDCs are analysed briefly. The main conclusion is that the growth of LDCs in the medium term will be constrained by the fragile recovery in the global economy and its negative impact on the growth of developing economies, which have been the main drivers of LDC growth in recent years. Finally, there is a small statistical annex at the end of the chapter which served as a basis for the analysis provided and which presents more detailed data at the level of national economies or different groupings of LDCs.

Given their high dependence on external economic conditions, LDCs could not escape the slowdown of growth worldwide.

B. Recent macroeconomic trends in the LDCs

1. TRENDS IN THE REAL SECTOR

The *real GDP* of the LDCs as a group grew by 4.2 per cent in 2011 (table 1), which is lower by 1.4 percentage points than the preceding year. This downward trend mirrors the slowdown of growth worldwide (5.3 per cent in 2010 and 3.9 per cent in 2011). While the coordinated fiscal and monetary easing in most developed and some developing countries provided a major stimulus for growth in 2010, the winding down of these measures in many countries, coupled with gradual intensification of fiscal austerity in most European countries, resulted in slower growth of GDP in 2011.

Given their high dependence on external economic conditions, LDCs could not escape this broad-based slowdown. Indeed, the rate of deceleration of their GDP growth in 2011 was broadly similar to that of developing countries (1.3 percentage points) and advanced economies (1.6 percentage points). It is thus evident that LDCs' recovery in terms of real GDP growth in 2010 was short lived. As shown in table 1, the GDP growth rate for LDCs in 2011 was slightly lower than the result in 2009, when, despite global recession, LDCs were the best-performing group of countries. Also, the growth rate of LDCs in 2011 was about two percentage points lower than that of other developing countries. Most importantly, it was 3.7 percentage points below the average annual growth rate attained during the 2002–2008 boom period.

The real GDP of the LDCs as a group grew by 4.2 per cent in 2011, which is lower by 1.4 percentage points than the preceding year.

In terms of country group performance, both African and Asian LDCs experienced a slowdown in 2011, and both grew by similar rates at around four per cent. However, in the case of the Asian LDCs, the slowdown of GDP growth, which was larger than two percentage points, was more pronounced. In contrast, GDP growth of the island LDCs at 7.1 per cent was much higher, compared with both the previous year and the average for the LDCs. The relatively high rate of growth of this group of LDCs was largely due to the extraordinary performance of the Democratic Republic of Timor-Leste.[1] The development of oil and gas resources in offshore waters has lifted the economic growth of the country to around 10 per cent in the last three years, and similar growth is expected in the next two years. The growth rate of GDP of the island LDCs excluding the performance of the Democratic Republic of Timor-Leste was 5.4 per cent in 2011.

Table 1. Real GDP and real GDP per capita growth rates for LDCs, developing economies and advanced economies, selected years (Annual weighted averages, percentages)											
	Real GDP						Real GDP per capita growth					
	2002–2008	2009	2010	2011	2012	2013	2002–2008	2009	2010	2011	2012	2013
Total LDCs	**7.9**	**4.9**	**5.6**	**4.2**	**5.1**	**5.5**	**5.4**	**2.5**	**3.3**	**1.9**	**2.8**	**3.2**
African LDCs and Haiti	7.8	4.2	5.0	4.1	4.9	5.3	5.1	1.5	2.4	1.5	2.3	2.6
Asian LDCs	7.5	5.9	6.4	4.2	5.4	5.9	5.5	4.1	4.6	2.5	3.6	4.1
Island LDCs	5.4	2.4	5.5	7.1	6.3	5.9	3.2	0.2	3.3	4.8	4.1	3.7
LDCs by export specialization[a]												
Oil-exporting LDCs	9.9	3.0	4.6	-1.6	1.8	3.4	7.0	0.3	1.8	-4.2	-0.9	0.7
Manufactures-exporting LDCs	6.2	5.3	5.8	6.0	6.0	6.4	4.6	3.8	4.6	4.6	4.6	5.0
Services-exporting LDCs	6.8	5.6	5.8	5.7	4.8	5.3	4.3	3.2	3.5	3.4	2.6	3.0
Mixed-exporting LDCs	9.5	6.6	6.1	5.4	6.4	6.0	6.9	4.2	3.6	3.1	4.0	3.6
Other primary commodity-exporting LDCs	6.1	4.6	5.9	5.8	6.3	6.2	3.2	1.7	3.0	2.8	3.4	3.3
Minerals-exporting LDCs	5.9	4.0	6.1	5.7	7.8	6.9	3.1	1.2	3.2	2.9	4.9	4.0
Agriculture & food-exporting LDCs	6.4	5.6	5.8	5.9	4.3	5.3	3.4	2.5	2.7	2.7	1.2	2.2
Memo Items:												
Advanced economies	2.5	-3.6	3.2	1.6	1.4	2.0	1.8	-4.2	2.7	1.0	0.9	1.5
Developing countries	7.6	2.8	7.5	6.2	5.7	6.0	6.0	1.4	6.1	5.4	4.3	4.7
World	4.6	-0.6	5.3	3.9	3.5	4.1	3.2	-1.9	4.0	3.1	2.3	2.9

Source: UNCTAD secretariat calculations based on IMF, *World Economic Outlook* database, April 2012.

Notes: LDCs' growth is calculated as the weighted average of each country's real growth (base year 2000); data for 2011 are preliminary and are forecasted for 2012–2013.

  a Classification of LDCs by export specialization is provided at the beginning of the Report (page xii).

An analysis of real GDP growth rates by country grouping according to export specialization shows that the performance of oil-exporting LDCs in 2011 (-1.6 per cent) represented an important drag on the overall performance of LDCs. This is partly a consequence of political instability which affected two of the five oil-exporting LDCs in 2011 (Sudan and the Republic of Yemen). But more generally, the performance of oil-exporting LDCs has been more erratic than the performance of other groups of LDCs in the last three years, even leaving aside political instability. This suggests that reliance on a single export sector, however dynamic it might be in some periods, has serious drawbacks.

In contrast, LDCs specialized in the export of manufactures (6.0 per cent), services (5.7 per cent), minerals (5.8 per cent), agriculture and food (5.9 per cent) and mixed exporters (5.4 per cent) all fared better in 2011 than oil-exporting LDCs. In addition, most of these groups have experienced less fluctuation in real GDP growth rates in the last three years than the oil-exporting LDCs, suggesting that more diversified economies have been less affected by the global downturn.

If the slow global recovery continues, it may lead to underutilization of resources and may also cause widespread damage to *employment* prospects in LDCs. Global unemployment started to rise again in 2011, and it has been estimated by the ILO (IILS and ILO, 2012) that some 202 million people will be unemployed in 2012. The global rate of unemployment is projected to reach 6.2 per cent in 2013, its level at the height of the 2009 financial crisis. Equally worryingly, youth unemployment rates have increased in most advanced economies and in two-thirds of the developing countries. The combination of slower economic growth and higher unemployment has resulted in an increase of the ILO's Social Unrest Index for 2011. The most heightened risk of social unrest has been estimated for sub-Saharan Africa, where the majority of LDCs are located, and the Middle East and North Africa.

The significance of the issue of employment for LDCs cannot be overemphasized. The relatively young demographic structure of LDCs means that increasing cohorts of young people are entering the labour market and will

The performance of oil-exporting LDCs has been more erratic than the performance of other groups of LDCs in the last three years, suggesting that reliance on a single export sector, however dynamic it might be in some periods, has serious drawbacks.

continue to do so for some time in the future. Even during the 2002–2008 boom period, LDCs faced an employment challenge because of the lopsided pattern of growth concentrated in resource-extractive sectors, which resulted in weak job creation. This also led to growing informality in the LDCs, even when rates of open unemployment did not increase.

The ability of LDCs to create more jobs has been hampered by the effects of the ongoing crisis because of the slowdown in export-oriented activities as well as fiscal pressures constraining public expenditure. The longer the GDP growth stays below potential, the greater the likelihood of long-term unemployment and underemployment, with long-run detrimental effects on the population. Accordingly, governments should bear in mind that additional measures are needed to minimize the adverse effects of the global crisis and that employment creation should be at the top of their national development agendas. Lack of jobs could put additional pressure on migration, an issue that is explored in more detail in chapter 2 of this Report.

Gross fixed capital formation for the LDCs as a group increased slightly from 20.7 per cent of GDP in 2005–2007 to 21.6 per cent in 2008–2010 (chart 1). Throughout the first decade of the 21st century, gross fixed capital formation in LDCs increased slowly but steadily, so that by 2010 it was three GDP percentage points higher than in 2000. While that is a positive performance, it compares less favourably with other developing countries (ODCs). In 2000, gross fixed capital formation in ODCs had already equalled 23.4 per cent of GDP. Moreover, their progress in the last ten years was much faster than in the LDCs, reaching 30.1 per cent of GDP by 2010. Thus, if the current investment trends continue, it is unlikely that LDCs will be able to catch up with other developing countries in the near future. In fact, the current level of investment is below the value of 25 per cent of GDP which is considered necessary to reach growth rates of real GDP of 7 per cent — one of the main goals of the Istanbul Programme of Action for LDCs.

Gross domestic saving rates have shown the opposite trend in the same period. The average saving rate for the LDCs as a group was 18.9 per cent of GDP in 2005–2007, declining to 17.7 per cent in 2008–2010. The biggest decline was in 2009, when it reached only 14.5 per cent of GDP. In comparison with the saving rate in 2000, however, the improvement is still significant, higher by 5.5 GDP percentage points in 2010.

As a result of these tendencies for saving and investment rates, the resource gap, indicating reliance on external resources to finance domestic investment, fell from 6.5 per cent of GDP in 2000 to only 3.9 per cent in 2010 for the LDCs as a group. For non-petroleum-exporting LDCs, however, the opposite picture emerges. Their resource gap was around 10 per cent of GDP in 2000, increasing to over 13 per cent before the crisis and averaging 14.8 per cent from 2008 to 2010. Therefore, the supply of external financial resources remains crucial for capital formation in most LDCs. Even more worrying, dependence on external resources increased in many LDCs, even during the boom period of 2002–2008. In other words, progress in domestic resource mobilization was insufficient even when average annual growth rates of GDP surpassed seven per cent.

One result of the increasing resource gap in non-petroleum-exporting LDCs has been growing vulnerability of the balance of payments, which is staggering in some cases. In 2011, thirteen LDCs had current account deficits of more than 10 per cent of GDP, while five had deficits of more than 20 per cent of GDP. At the other extreme, only five LDCs recorded current account surpluses.

The fiscal situation of LDCs was only slightly better. Ten LDCs registered fiscal surpluses in 2010, while the rest had deficits of different magnitudes. In

---

The longer the GDP growth stays below potential, the greater the likelihood of long-term unemployment and underemployment. Additional measures are needed to minimize the adverse effects of the global crisis and employment creation should be at the top of national development agendas of LDCs.

Gross fixed capital formation for the LDCs as a group increased slightly from 20.7 per cent of GDP in 2005–2007 to 21.6 per cent in 2008–2010.

If the current investment trends continue, it is unlikely that LDCs will be able to catch up with other developing countries in the near future.

In 2011, thirteen LDCs had current account deficits of more than 10 per cent of GDP, while five had deficits of more than 20 per cent of GDP.

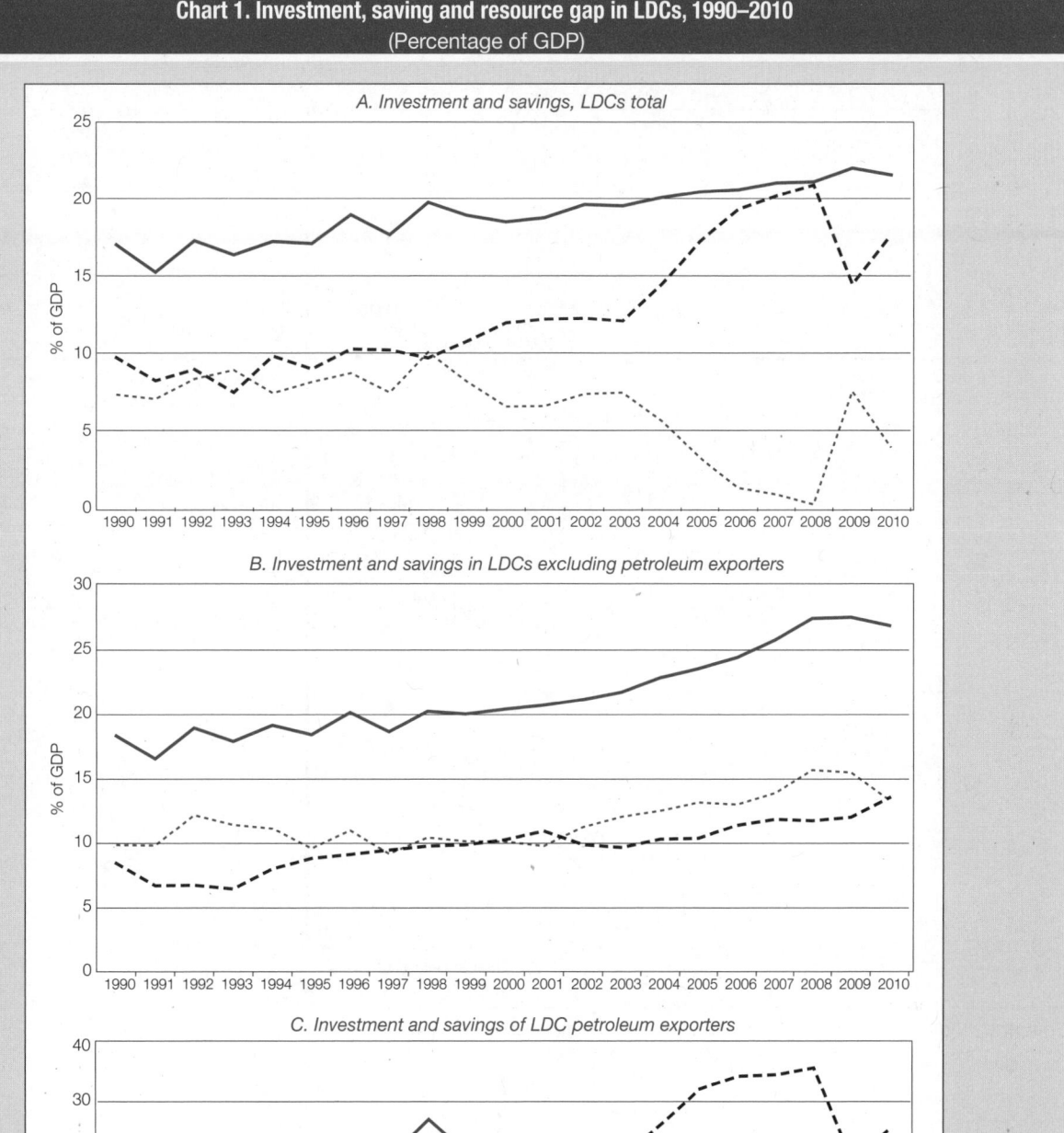

Chart 1. Investment, saving and resource gap in LDCs, 1990–2010
(Percentage of GDP)

A. Investment and savings, LDCs total

B. Investment and savings in LDCs excluding petroleum exporters

C. Investment and savings of LDC petroleum exporters

——— Gross fixed capital formation   – – – Gross domestic saving   ······· External saving (resource gap)

Source: UNCTAD secretariat calculations, based on UNCTADstat database.

six LDCs, the fiscal deficit surpassed 10 per cent of GDP. As shown in chart 2, the majority of LDCs display "twin deficits" of both fiscal balance and current account, and are located in the third quadrant,[2] which is the most vulnerable to external shocks such as sharp changes in commodity prices. Some small island LDCs (Guinea, Kiribati, Sao Tome and Principe, Tuvalu) combine very large deficits on both fiscal and current account.

Many LDCs display "twin deficits" of both fiscal balance and current account, which makes them vulnerable to external shocks such as sharp changes in commodity prices.

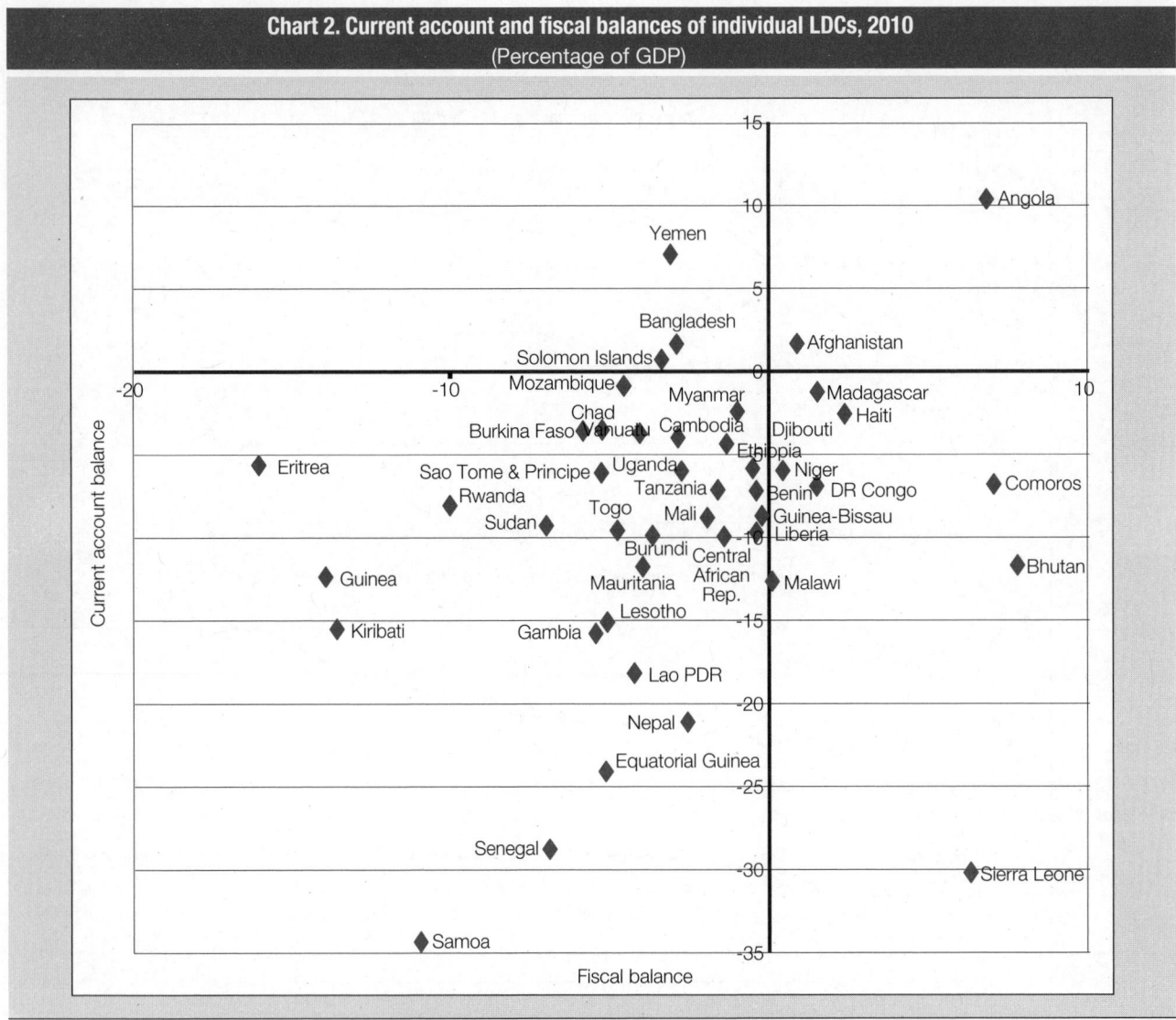

Chart 2. Current account and fiscal balances of individual LDCs, 2010
(Percentage of GDP)

Source: UNCTAD calculations based on IMF, *World Economic Outlook* database, April 2012.

2. TRENDS IN INTERNATIONAL TRADE

The *trade balance* of LDCs as a group in 2011 shows that these economies recorded a deficit of $39.8 billion, up from $37.5 billion in 2010. This was a result of a small surplus in the trade of goods ($2,639 million), which offset somewhat a much larger deficit in trade in services ($42,460 million).

In terms of share of GDP, however, the trade balance improved somewhat from a deficit equivalent to 6.1 per cent of GDP in 2010 to 5.7 per cent in 2011. While this is still slightly higher than the trade deficit recorded during the boom period, it is also a substantial improvement over the result in 2009, when it had widened to the equivalent of 10.2 per cent of GDP because of the sharp drop in exports from LDCs.

The value of merchandise exports from LDCs increased by 23 per cent in 2011, thus surpassing the pre-crisis level.

The value of *merchandise exports* from LDCs increased by 23 per cent in 2011, thus surpassing the pre-crisis level (annex table 4). The total value of merchandise exports in 2011 ($204.8 billion) was twice as high as five years previously. The change in 2011 was greatest for island LDCs, for which exports expanded by 50.8 per cent. On the downside, however, the merchandise exports of LDCs as a group have remained highly concentrated in a few countries: the top five exporters (Angola, Bangladesh, Equatorial Guinea, Yemen and Sudan) account for 62 per cent of all exports from LDCs.

The value of *merchandise imports* also increased considerably in 2011 (20.6 per cent) to reach $202.2 billion. The value of imports has also doubled in the last five years. An analysis of imports of goods by country grouping according to export specialization reveals that mixed-exporting LDCs recorded the strongest increase (36.3 per cent), followed by minerals-exporting LDCs (30.3 per cent) in 2011. In contrast, imports of goods by agriculture- and food-exporting LDCs increased by only 11.9 per cent, slightly better than the 8.6 per cent rise in 2010.

Overall trends in merchandise trade shifted the merchandise trade balance into surplus in 2011 for the LDCs as a group, after two years of deficits. This is important to emphasize since prior to 2006, LDCs had continuously recorded merchandise trade deficits. Nevertheless, the positive result for the group as a whole masks significant heterogeneity, since it was due entirely to the African LDCs and their surplus of $21.4 billion – which in turn is driven by only a handful of countries, most notably Angola. Asian LDCs, by contrast, recorded a merchandise trade deficit of $17.5 billion in 2011, while island LDCs posted a deficit of $1.2 billion.

Merchandise exports have continued to be dominated by petroleum, at slightly over 46 per cent of total exports. Since all but one of the LDC petroleum exporters are in Africa, the overall LDC trade surplus is also due to African LDCs. The list of non-petroleum export products from LDCs includes articles of apparel (5.5 per cent), clothing and textile fabrics (5 per cent), copper (4.1 per cent), natural gas (3.9 per cent) and gold (2.4 per cent).

Exports of *services* by LDCs increased by 14.4 per cent in 2011 and also surpassed the pre-crisis level. However, at $25.3 billion they are still small compared with merchandise exports and account for just one-ninth of total exports. Imports of services expanded 15.6 per cent in 2011. The services trade deficit rose from $36.5 billion in 2010 to $42.5 billion in 2011.

The gradual shift in the main markets for exports of LDCs continued in 2011, reflecting the long-term recalibration of the global economy as well as the weak economic performance of key destination markets in the North (UNCTAD, 2011a). As a group, LDCs exported more than 54 per cent of their total exports to other developing countries. China imported 26.4 per cent of total exports from LDCs, surpassing the European Union (20.4 per cent) and the US (19 per cent). Similar trends could be detected for LDC imports, with 67.8 per cent coming from other developing countries and only 29.8 per cent from developed ones. China has been growing in importance as a trade partner, and it is currently the second largest source of imports into LDCs (16.1 per cent of the total), behind the European Union (18.5 per cent).

The improving export performance of many LDCs in 2010 and 2011 was primarily due to the higher international *commodity prices*. After slumping in 2009, prices recovered rapidly, in some cases to levels higher than before the crisis. The price index for minerals, ores and metals, for example, increased by 77 per cent from 2009 to 2011, when it was 44 per cent higher than the previous peak of 2008 (table 2).

A similar trend can be observed for agricultural raw materials, whose prices were driven by very strong increases in prices of cotton, which increased nearly two and a half times from 2009 to 2011. While this clearly benefited those LDCs that are net exporters of these commodities, price volatility remains a major problem, creating vulnerability for exporters. This is evident from the last two columns of table 2 (percentage change and standard deviation), which point to high price volatility for most primary commodities of importance to LDCs.

Overall trends in merchandise trade shifted the merchandise trade balance into surplus in 2011 for the LDCs as a group, after two years of deficits...

... but it was due entirely to the African LDCs and their surplus of $21.4 billion – which in turn is driven by only a handful of countries, most notably Angola.

LDCs exported more than 54 per cent of their total exports to other developing countries in 2011.

Similar trends could be detected for LDC imports, with 67.8 per cent coming from other developing countries and only 29.8 per cent from developed ones.

Table 2. Price indices for selected primary commodities of importance to LDCs, 2008–2012 (Q1) (Price indices 2000 = 100)							
	2008	2009	2010	2011	2012 (Q1)	Standard deviation 2000–2011	% change 2000–2011
All food	**236**	**216**	**232**	**273**	**284**	**62.3**	**172.8**
Wheat	288	197	204	276	292	63.9	175.6
Rice	344	289	256	271	257	89.6	170.9
Sugar	156	222	260	318	348	76.6	217.9
Fish meal	274	298	409	372	421	102.8	272.3
Coffee, Arabica	162	167	228	321	322	70.7	209.6
Coffee, Robusta	254	179	200	275	262	69.5	160.5
Cocoa beans	291	325	353	336	377	84.1	235.7
Tea	109	127	125	140	141	22.1	39.5
Agricultural commodities	**198**	**163**	**226**	**289**	**315**	**59.3**	**189.1**
Tobacco	120	142	144	150	147	22.5	49.8
Cotton	121	106	175	258	350	50.4	158.1
Non-coniferous woods	154	154	161	158	159	23.9	58.2
Minerals, ores and metals	**337[a]**	**274[a]**	**424[a]**	**486[a]**	**435[a]**	**104.9**	**248.9**
Iron ore	494	643	1178	1348	1139	431.4	1247.7
Aluminium	166	107	140	155	161	31.9	54.8
Copper	384	283	416	487	532	149.7	386.6
Gold	312	349	440	562	496	149.3	462.2
Memo Items:							
Crude petroleum	344	219	280	368	353	99.4	268.3
Unit value index of manufactured goods exports	131	122	126	138	124a	14.4	37.7

Source: UNCTADstat, Commodity Price Bulletin; IMF, *International Financial Statistics* for Iron Ore Prices, World Bank, Development Prospect Group.
  a Estimated.

Food prices increased substantially during the boom and peaked in 2008, causing food shortages and even food riots in several LDCs. After easing somewhat in 2009, food prices started to rise again in 2010 and 2011, reaching higher levels than in the pre-crisis period. Accordingly, the food security outlook deteriorated in many LDCs since many are net food importers. The situation in some parts of Africa (mainly the Horn of Africa) was critical, as famine threatened the lives of hundreds of thousands.

After easing somewhat in 2009, food prices started to rise again in 2010 and 2011, reaching higher levels than in the pre-crisis period and the food security outlook deteriorated in many LDCs.

Whereas food prices eased somewhat after peaking in February 2012, droughts in the Sahel region and the Horn of Africa could cause the food security situation to deteriorate further. In addition, adverse weather conditions in many parts of the world (widespread drought in the United States, poor monsoon in India, and so on) and depressed output expectations are already leading to renewed increases in food prices, causing further problems for food-importing LDCs. Globally, there is a continued absence of policies that tackle the root causes of recent food price spikes (financial speculation, irresponsible land investment, inadequate policies to build buffer stocks in developing countries, neglect of small holder cultivation, disregard of food security objectives, subsidy-driven expansion of biofuel cultivation, etc.) (Wise and Murphy, 2012). In this context, there is a real possibility of renewed increases in global food prices that could once again cause widespread suffering and even famine.

3. Trends in external finance

With the exception of the petroleum-exporting LDCs, all other LDCs need external resources equivalent to almost 15 per cent of GDP to finance their current levels of investment.

One of the long-standing characteristics of LDCs is their dependence on external finance resulting from the gap between investment and domestic saving. With the exception of the petroleum-exporting LDCs, which have a negative resource gap (they invest less than they save), LDCs need external resources equivalent to almost 15 per cent of GDP to finance their current levels of investment. This leaves them vulnerable to mood swings of private capital flows.

The varying composition of external resources that finance the resource gap has very different economic effects and is thus of particular interest to LDCs. Overall trends show that private financial flows to LDCs have continued to decline for the third year in a row, mostly as a result of a further decline of FDI inflows, offset by an increase in official flows. Within private flows, however, the remittance flows have been much more stable than flows of FDI, whereas portfolio flows to LDCs are negligible. Private flows to other developing countries, in turn, have recovered to pre-crisis levels much more rapidly (portfolio inflows and remittances in 2010, and FDI in 2011). The point should also be made that ODA represents roughly half of overall external finance to LDCs, while in the case of other developing countries it is less than eight per cent of the total.

Private financial flows to LDCs have continued to decline for the third year in a row, mostly as a result of a further decline of FDI inflows, offset by an increase in official flows.

UNCTAD recently revised the data on *FDI* inflows to LDCs (UNCTAD, 2012a). According to the new data, inflows of FDI were much smaller than remittances for most of the last decade. Since remittances are one of the main topics of this Report, chapter three provides a detailed discussion of the magnitudes of these flows. It is sufficient to emphasize here that remittances have been growing even during the crisis and that they are forecasted to grow in the medium term (Mohapatra et al., 2011). In contrast, FDI inflows to LDCs have declined for three consecutive years after peaking in 2008 at a little less than $19 billion, and in 2011 amounted to only $15 billion. This is very different from the trends in other developing countries, where FDI inflows have increased steadily since 2009 (chart 3). The recent decline in FDI inflows to LDCs as a group is mainly due to disinvestment trends in Angola, tied to the oil-investment cycle in that country. In the rest of the LDCs, FDI has remained stable.

FDI inflows to LDCs have declined for three consecutive years after peaking in 2008 at a little less than $19 billion, and in 2011 amounted to only $15 billion.

Whereas FDI inflows to LDCs are still predominantly to Africa, some shifts have occurred recently. Of the total FDI flows to LDCs of $15 billion in 2011, 79 per cent went to Africa, a slight decrease from the previous year. Meanwhile, Asian LDCs received $2.8 billion in 2011, up marginally from the previous year. The concentration of FDI inflows appears to have diminished. In 2009, there were only five countries with inflows greater than $1 billion, whereas in 2011 there were nine such countries.

When analysed from the point of view of country groupings according to export specialization, FDI inflows show that all groups except the petroleum-exporting LDCs received more FDI in 2011 than in 2010. The largest increase was in the case of mineral-exporting LDCs, from $6.4 billion in 2010 to 7.2 billion in 2011. This group of LDCs received the largest share of total FDI in both 2010 and 2011. In previous years, however, petroleum-exporting LDCs were the biggest beneficiaries of FDI inflows. That changed precipitously in 2010, when they received only $2.1 billion, and FDI inflows in 2011 became negative to the tune of $1.8 billion as a result of disinvestment.

All groups except the petroleum-exporting LDCs received more FDI in 2011 than in 2010.

One key emerging trend is the recent rise of FDI outflows from LDCs. These are investments of firms based in LDCs to other countries. In 2009, FDI outflows from all LDCs amounted to $1.1 billion, nearly tripling to $3.1 billion in 2010 and continuing to increase to $3.3 billion in 2011. However, only Angola and Zambia had sums larger than $1 billion, and they accounted for three-quarters of all FDI outflows from LDCs.

Net ODA disbursements, together with net debt relief to the LDCs from all donors, reached a record level of $44.8 billion in 2010.

Data from the Development Assistance Committee (DAC) of the Organisation for Economic Co-operation and Development (OECD) show that net *Official Development Assistance* (ODA) disbursements, together with net debt relief to the LDCs from all donors reporting to the OECD/DAC, reached a record level of $44.8 billion in 2010 (chart 4). This represents an 11 per cent increase in comparison with ODA disbursements in 2009. In nominal terms, aid inflows to LDCs in 2010 were 3.5 times higher than in 2000. As noted in LDCR 2011, ODA has played an important countercyclical role in the wake of the global crisis, cushioning the impact of the retreat of private financial flows.

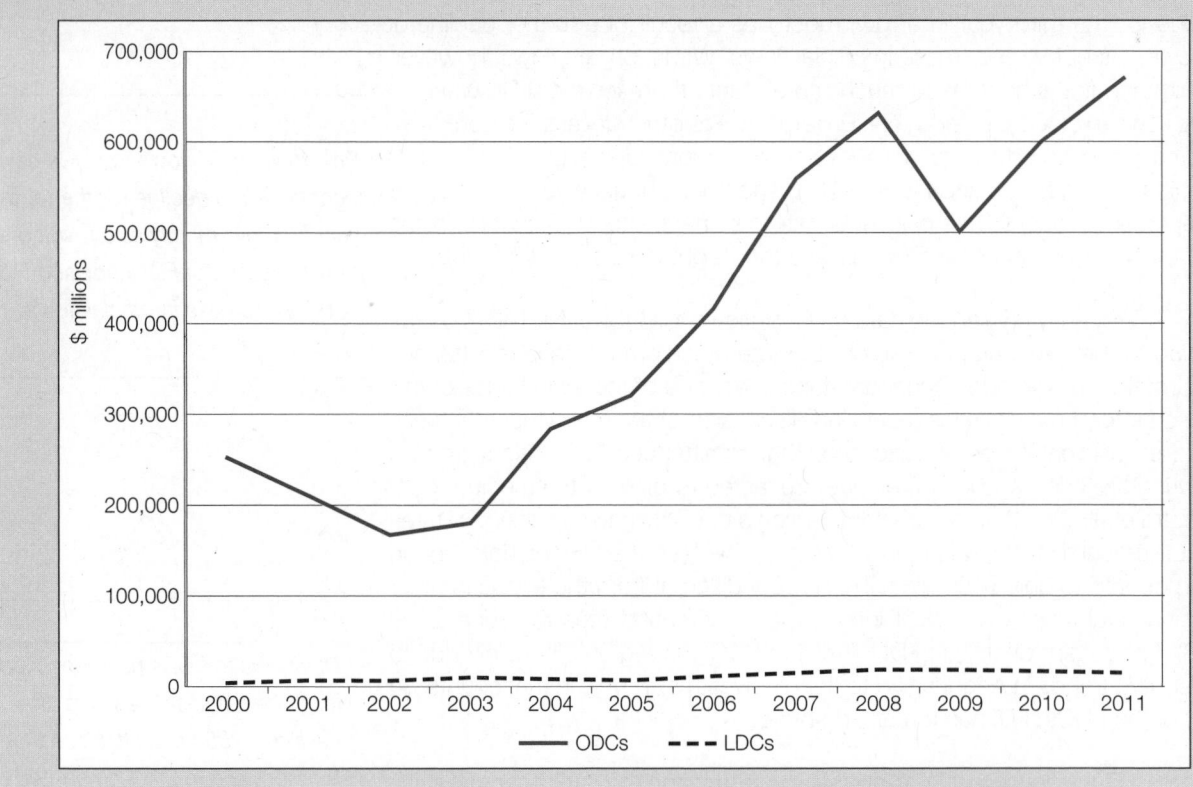

Chart 3. Inward foreign direct investment flows to LDCs and other developing countries (ODCs), 2000–2011
(Millions of current dollars)

Source: UNCTAD secretariat calculations, based on UNCTADstat database.

Preliminary data for net official development assistance from DAC and other OECD members to all developing countries show a drop of almost three per cent in 2011. It is highly likely that continuing tight budgets in OECD countries will put pressure on aid levels in coming years, thus adversely affecting development finance in LDCs.

Preliminary data for net official development assistance from DAC and other OECD members to all developing countries show a drop of almost three per cent in 2011.

Additional net debt relief to the LDCs accounted for nearly half of the increase in total ODA disbursement in 2010. This came to five per cent of total ODA disbursement in 2010, up from 1.6 per cent in 2009. Excluding net debt relief, previous trends towards a decline in the proportion of loans and increase in grants were even more pronounced in 2010. The share of grants out of net ODA flows was 98.7 per cent in 2010, whereas concessional loans accounted for a scant 1.3 per cent, down from 8.5 per cent in 2009 and 20 per cent over 2000–2005.

The LDCs' total *debt* stock reached $161 billion in 2010, only marginally higher than in 2009. Although the data for 2011 are not final, it is estimated to have increased to around $170 billion. LDCs' debt service decreased slightly from $8.2 billion in 2009 to 7.6 billion in 2010. External debt in relation to GDP fell from 29.9 per cent in 2009 to 26.7 in 2010. Compared with the situation at the beginning of the decade, when the ratio was 79.2, this is a substantial improvement. However, it is still more than eight percentage points of GDP higher than the average of developing countries. While part of this improvement was due to various debt relief initiatives, the decrease in the debt/GDP ratio was mostly due to rapid GDP growth during the boom. Similarly, debt service as a share of exports declined from 13.2 per cent in 2000 to 4.8 per cent in 2010, primarily as a result of very strong export growth.

Although the data for the LDCs' total debt stock for 2011 are not final, it is estimated to have increased to around $170 billion.

While debt sustainability indicators for the LDCs as a group have been gradually improving, in 2011 they indicated debt distress for three of them

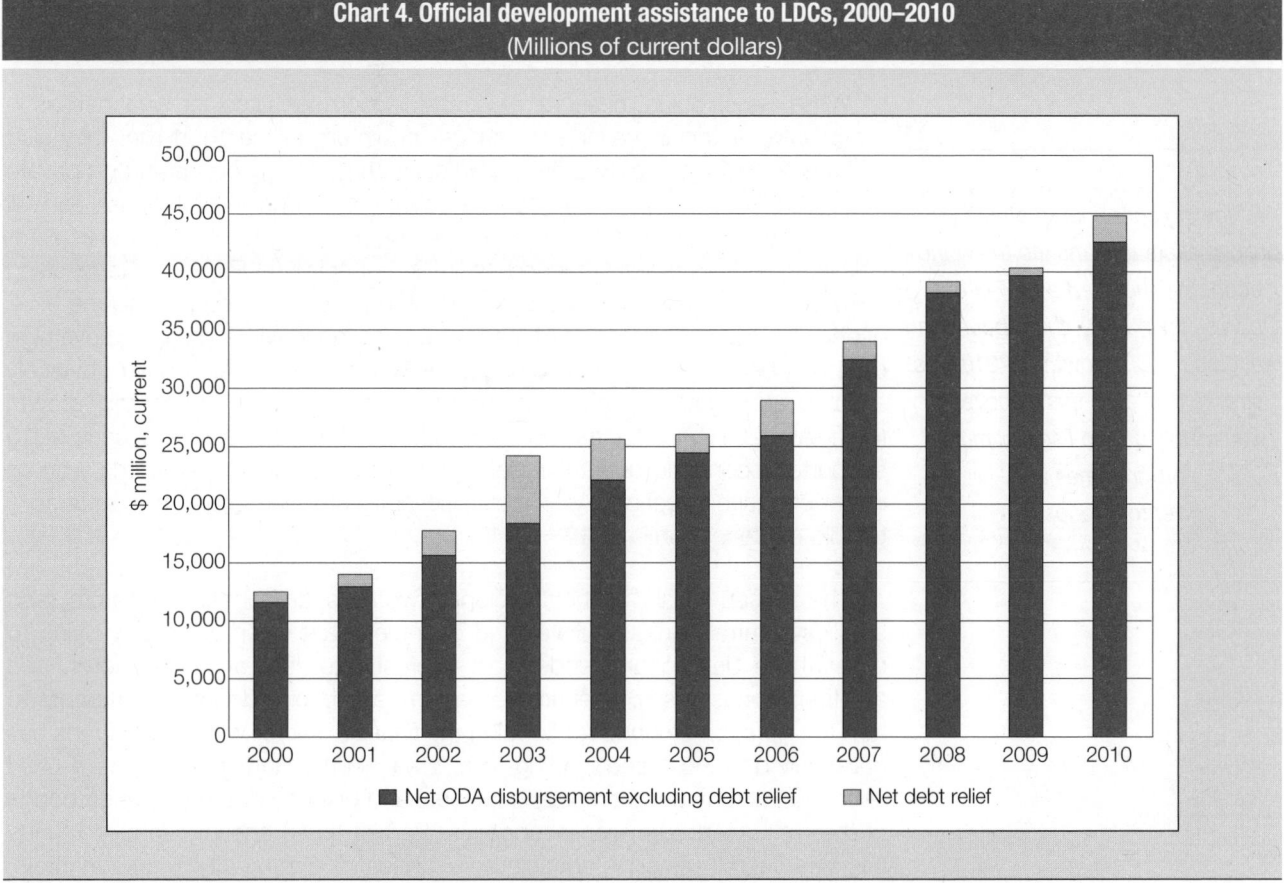

Chart 4. Official development assistance to LDCs, 2000–2010
(Millions of current dollars)

Net ODA disbursement excluding debt relief   Net debt relief

Source: UNCTAD secretariat calculations, based on OECD-DAC, *International Development Statistics*, online, July 2012.

(Comoros, Guinea and Sudan). In addition, a debt sustainability analysis shows that there were nine LDCs at high risk of debt distress in 2011. Thus, the number of LDCs in debt distress or at high risk of debt distress in 2011 remained the same overall as in 2010.

The experience of the LDCs in the last ten years shows that the key to debt sustainability is development of productive capacities. High and sustainable growth of GDP and rapid expansion of exports increased the capacity of many LDCs to service debt. While external financial resources, in particular ODA and remittances, were increasingly available to LDCs in the previous decade, there is no guarantee that this will continue to be the case in the future. The recent sharp decrease in FDI is instructive in this respect. Thus, a progressive shift from reliance on external sources of finance to domestic ones is a big challenge for LDCs. This will reduce their external dependence and vulnerability to external shocks and uncertainties.

The number of LDCs in debt distress (three) or at high risk of debt distress (nine) in 2011 remained the same overall as in 2010.

C. Current world economic situation and the short-term outlook for the LDCs

1. Current world economic situation

Following coordinated efforts by policymakers to stimulate the world economy and avert a new Great Depression in 2009, the rebound in real global GDP growth (at 5.3 per cent) in 2010 was strong. However, this "recovery" was mainly due to fiscal stimulus programmes and inventory reposition. By 2011, it was already apparent that the measures taken were not adequate to sustain the recovery, and the crisis spread to different geographic epicentres like Europe. As a result, the growth of world GDP decelerated to 3.9 per cent in 2011.

Following coordinated efforts by policymakers to stimulate the world economy and avert a new Great Depression in 2009, the rebound in real global GDP growth in 2010 was strong. However, this "recovery" was mainly due to fiscal stimulus programmes and inventory reposition.

While the stimulus measures successfully compensated for weaknesses in the private sector and averted a deeper downturn in the short run, they also created new sources of fragility. In particular, the strategy of passing on private sector losses to the public sector (by bailing out financial institutions), as well as the inevitable but necessary public sector spending to offset private sector deleveraging, has rapidly reached its limits, especially in Europe. The resulting increase in sovereign debt has brought some developed countries to the brink of default. The policy reaction of many countries faced with increasing sovereign debt has been to implement fiscal austerity measures, which have adversely affected aggregate demand and amounted to a drag on economic growth (UNCTAD, 2011b). Just as the Keynesian stimulus in 2009 and early 2010 supported economic growth, fiscal austerity from mid-2010 onwards worked in the opposite direction. As a result, several European economies entered a double-dip recession in 2012.

The present crisis in the developed world is deflationary in nature, and so most central banks in developed countries have been vigorously trying to offset these deflationary tendencies. Interest rates are at historic lows, and additional measures of quantitative easing have been adopted in attempts to turn the situation around. Yet flooding the financial sector with cheap funds has not resulted in increased lending to the real sector. Rather, banks have used cheap funds to repair their balance sheets and dispose of the sovereign bonds of the distressed European economies. Part of these cheaply acquired funds has also been invested in speculative activities on commodity futures markets, thereby inflating their prices. Thus, a combination of monetary easing and fiscal tightening has so far not resulted in a sustainable and robust recovery.

A combination of monetary easing and fiscal tightening has so far not resulted in a sustainable and robust recovery and many indicators suggest that the crisis in developed countries is nowhere near resolution.

Many indicators suggest that the crisis in developed countries is nowhere near resolution. In 2011, the unemployment rate averaged 8.6 per cent in OECD countries, well above the pre-crisis level of 5.6 per cent. The employment situation has worsened significantly in 2012. Unemployment rates in some OECD countries are now at levels of 20 per cent or more, not seen since the Great Depression. The unemployment rate in the eurozone has surpassed 11 per cent, the highest since the introduction of the euro. The unemployment rate in the US has been persistently above eight per cent for five years, suggesting that a different macroeconomic strategy is required in order to return to more normal levels of unemployment. The only bright spots in the world economy in the last three years have been some developing countries. Yet this may not last long, since growth in developing countries is intrinsically linked to growth and demand from developed countries: indeed, China, Brazil and India among others are already showing signs of growth deceleration.

2. The outlook for the LDCs

Given the fragility of the global economy, the outlook for 2012 and 2013 is subject to a high degree of uncertainty.

According to IMF forecasts, real GDP worldwide will expand by 3.5 per cent in 2012, down from 3.9 per cent in 2011. If the downside risks do not materialize, real global GDP is set to grow by 4.1 per cent in 2013. For the LDCs as a group, the IMF currently forecasts growth rates of 5.1 per cent in 2012 and 5.5 per cent in 2013. Developing countries, in turn, should attain growth rates of 5.7 per cent in 2012 and 6.0 per cent in 2013 (see again table 1).

However, given the fragility of the global economy, the outlook for 2012 and 2013 is subject to a high degree of uncertainty (UNDESA, 2012a). The downside risks are numerous and include an escalation of the eurozone debt crisis, a rise in global energy prices due to current geopolitical risks, a deceleration of growth in large developing countries, and a fiscal retrenchment in the United States, scheduled for 2013, which could have a strong negative impact on overall growth. Thus, the IMF forecasts should be considered as a best-case scenario, and policymakers should be prepared for a possible deterioration in the global economic situation.

As of mid-2012, economic activity is decelerating in a synchronized way in many parts of the world. Apart from the recession in the eurozone and the UK, economic activity is also decelerating in the US. Growth rates in India, Brazil and South Africa are also lower in 2012 than in 2011. The Chinese economy, for its part, has seen a deceleration of growth rates in the last eight quarters, as its investment-led growth falters.[3]

As of mid-2012, economic activity is decelerating in a synchronized way in many parts of the world.

The divergence in growth rates during and after the financial crisis has been interpreted in many circles as an indicator that the economies of the South are "decoupling" from the economies of the North. This interpretation, however, overlooks the reasons for the growth surge during the 2000s. International economic conditions were exceptionally conducive to growth from 2002 to 2008 (UNCTAD, 2012b). Consumption in developed economies was fuelled by cheap credit and positive wealth effects from property bubbles. This generated favourable economic conditions for developing countries, with rapidly increasing exports and remittances and surges of capital flows in the form of FDI, portfolio investment and cheap credit. Terms of trade for commodity exporters also improved.

Reduced demand for consumption goods in developed economies translates into fewer exports from China and other manufacturing hubs in developing countries, which in turn generates less demand for commodities.

However, that model was associated with increasing global imbalances, where surplus countries (including several developing countries) accumulated trillions in reserves while deficit countries accumulated trillions in debts. The financial crisis of 2009 reduced these imbalances, which are now at about half of their pre-crisis peak (UNDESA, 2012a). But one "cost" of this reduction of global imbalances has been less dynamic growth of GDP worldwide. Reduced demand for consumption goods in developed economies translates into fewer exports from China and other manufacturing hubs in developing countries, which in turn generates less demand for commodities. The vulnerability of developing countries to changes in developed economies suggests that the "decoupling" thesis is not on solid ground.

Against this background, the outlook for LDCs in the short- to medium-term is not bright.

In case the downward trajectory of the global economy intensifies, the key question is what policymakers can do to counteract it. Unfortunately, the policy space today, in both developed and developing countries, is smaller than in 2009. Larger budget deficits and increased public debt in developed countries have severely limited the perceived scope for additional fiscal stimulus. Further use of monetary policy is constrained by proximity to zero interest rates, and in any case becomes ineffective in "liquidity trap" conditions. Overcoming the risks to the global economy in this context requires globally coordinated countercyclical policies and many other bolder reforms (UNCTAD, 2011b; UNDESA, 2012a).

The pace of economic growth in China, in particular, will have a major impact on the prices of many commodities.

Against this background, the outlook for LDCs in the short- to medium-term is not bright. Given the growing danger that the world economy might be entering a lengthy period of stagnation and deflation, LDCs have to prepare for a relatively prolonged period of uncertainty, with possible escalation of financial tensions and a real economic downturn. Trade and investment of developing countries, which are often intermediated by US and European banks, have already suffered setbacks. Prices of some commodities started to decrease, in some cases abruptly, in the second quarter of 2012. If the current tendency towards economic deceleration continues, commodity prices could suffer pronounced falls. The pace of economic growth in China, in particular, will have a major impact on the prices of many commodities.

Even a partial drying up of financing options would represent a major shock to many LDCs. If, additionally, they have an export structure heavily dependent on one or a few commodities, the short-term economic outlook might be particularly challenging.

Contingency planning in LDCs should include anticipating the financing needs of governments for the current and next year, if possible.

The world economy may be entering a more turbulent and uncertain phase, in which LDCs may once again be exposed to external economic shocks and have to deal with a crisis that originates elsewhere. Recognizing this may allow for more effective preparation.

The countries most vulnerable to a deterioration of external economic conditions are LDCs with high twin deficits (Figure 2). The resource gap of many LDCs is so large that even a partial drying up of financing options would represent a major shock to these economies. If, additionally, they have an export structure heavily dependent on one or a few commodities, the short-term economic outlook might be particularly challenging. Further challenges, stemming from political unrest in Northern Africa and the Middle East, have already directly or indirectly affected some LDCs (Mali, Burkina Faso, Mauritania, Niger, Republic of Yemen).

Contingency planning in LDCs should include anticipating the financing needs of governments for the current and next year, if possible, and preparations to provide emergency support for national financial systems, as need be. Additional loans, such as those announced by China at the China-Africa meeting in July 2012, could help some LDCs cope with this difficult period.

For predominantly export-led economies, some reorientation to domestic demand may be needed. While curtailing dependence on foreign markets might be extremely difficult even in the medium term, it should certainly be a goal for most LDCs. Commodity exporters need to diversify their production and exports, and try to develop new products or upgrade existing ones. Countries running large current account deficits have to reduce them to manageable proportions.

Such diversification could be facilitated through the expansion of South–South ties and regional integration schemes that allow for productive reorientation. Reductions in external financing could be countered by innovative financial arrangements, including through regional development banks and sovereign wealth funds, along the lines of the proposal contained in LDCR 2011. Strengthening domestic resource mobilization is another important strategy, despite the constraints posed by decelerating GDP growth.

In sum, the short-term outlook for LDCs, as indeed for the world economy as a whole, is challenging. The world economy may be entering a more turbulent and uncertain phase, in which LDCs may once again be exposed to external economic shocks and have to deal with a crisis that originates elsewhere. Recognizing this may allow for more effective preparation.

Notes

1   The growth rates reported in table 1 in the text as well as annex table 1 are from the International Monetary Fund. As such, they could differ, at times even substantially, from growth rates reported by individual LDCs. The use of the IMF data instead of the data reported by countries themselves is to assure consistency across all LDCs, as well as to present forecasts for individual LDCs.

2   Data for some LDCs are missing from chart 2. One of them is Somalia, which is not reflected in the WEO database. Also, some countries with extreme values were excluded to obtain a more easily understandable picture. For example, the Democratic Republic of Timor-Leste was excluded since it had a fiscal surplus of 50.4 percent of GDP and a current account surplus of 48.1 percent of GDP in 2010.

3   The study of fast-growing economies and their subsequent slowdowns by Eichengreen et al. (2011) indicates that Chinese fast growth may come to an end in the next three to five years.

Statistical annex

Annex table 1. Real GDP growth rates for individual LDCs, selected years (Annual weighted averages, percentages)						
	2002–2008	2009	2010	2011	2012	2013
Fuel exporters	**9.9**	**3.0**	**4.6**	**-1.6**	**1.8**	**3.4**
Angola	16.6	2.4	3.4	3.4	9.7	6.8
Chad	8.9	-1.2	13.0	1.6	6.9	0.1
Equatorial Guinea	15.0	5.7	-0.8	7.1	4.0	6.8
Sudan	7.6	3.0	4.5	-3.9	-7.3	-1.5
Yemen	4.0	3.9	7.7	-10.5	-0.9	2.9
Manufactures exporters	**6.2**	**5.3**	**5.8**	**6.0**	**6.0**	**6.4**
Bangladesh	6.2	5.9	6.4	6.1	5.9	6.4
Bhutan	8.5[a]	6.7	10.6	5.9	7.0	9.9
Cambodia	10.4	0.1	6.0	6.1	6.2	6.4
Haiti	0.9	2.9	-5.4	5.6	7.8	6.9
Lesotho	3.9	3.6	5.7	4.2	5.2	2.2
Services exporters	**6.8**	**5.6**	**5.8**	**5.7**	**4.8**	**5.3**
Comoros	1.6	1.8	2.1	2.2	2.5	4.0
Djibouti	4.1	5.0	3.5	4.5	4.8	5.0
Eritrea	-0.5	3.9	2.2	8.7	7.5	3.4
Ethiopia	10.3	10.0	8.0	7.5	5.0	5.5
Gambia	3.4	6.7	5.5	3.3	-1.7	9.7
Liberia	1.3	2.8	5.0	6.4	8.8	5.1
Madagascar	5.9	-4.1	0.5	0.5	2.9	5.1
Nepal	4.0	4.4	4.6	3.5	4.2	3.8
Rwanda	7.7	4.1	7.5	8.8	7.6	7.0
Samoa	3.9	-5.4	0.2	2.1	1.4	1.9
Sao Tome and Principe	5.8	4.0	4.5	4.9	5.5	6.0
Timor-Leste	5.0	12.8	9.5	10.6	10.0	10.0
Tuvalu	0.9	-1.7	-0.5	0.4	1.5	1.3
Vanuatu	5.7	3.5	2.2	3.3	4.0	4.0
Other primary commodity exporters	**6.1**	**4.6**	**5.9**	**5.8**	**6.3**	**6.2**
Minerals	*5.9*	*4.0*	*6.1*	*5.7*	*7.8*	*6.9*
Democratic Republic of the Congo	6.4	2.8	7.0	6.9	6.5	6.7
Guinea	2.6	-0.3	1.9	3.6	4.7	4.8
Mali	4.9	4.5	5.8	2.7	6.0	5.8
Mauritania	5.6	-1.2	5.1	3.6	5.3	6.1
Mozambique	7.8	6.3	6.8	7.1	6.7	7.2
Sierra Leone	7.2	3.2	5.0	5.3	35.9	9.1
Zambia	5.7	6.4	7.6	6.6	7.7	8.3
Agriculture and food	6.4	5.6	5.8	5.9	4.3	5.3
Benin	3.8	2.7	2.6	3.1	3.5	4.7
Burkina Faso	5.8	3.2	7.9	5.6	5.0	6.4
Guinea-Bissau	2.8	3.0	3.5	5.3	4.5	4.7
Kiribati	0.6	-2.4	1.4	1.8	2.5	3.0
Malawi	5.1	9.0	6.5	5.5	4.3	4.1
Solomon Islands	7.6	-4.7	7.0	9.3	6.0	4.0
Somalia	..	..	..	..	..	..
Uganda	8.0	7.2	5.9	6.7	4.2	5.4
Mixed exporters	**9.5**	**6.6**	**6.1**	**5.4**	**6.4**	**6.0**
Afghanistan	7.7[a]	21.0	8.4	5.7	7.2	5.8
Burundi	4.4	3.5	3.8	4.2	4.8	5.0
Central African Republic	1.6	1.7	3.3	3.1	4.1	4.2
Lao People's Democratic Republic	7.5	7.6	7.9	8.3	8.4	7.1
Myanmar	12.1	5.1	5.3	5.5	6.0	5.9
Niger	5.2	-0.9	8.0	2.3	14.0	6.6
Togo	2.7	3.4	4.0	4.1	4.4	4.6
Senegal	4.8	2.1	4.1	2.6	3.8	4.5
United Republic of Tanzania	7.2	6.7	6.5	6.7	6.4	6.7

Source: UNCTAD Secretariat calculations, based on IMF, *World Economic Outlook* database, April, 2012.

Note: Data for 2011 are preliminary and are forecasted for 2012–2013.

a 2003–2008.

Annex table 2. Real GDP per capita growth rates for individual LDCs, selected years						
(Annual weighted averages, percentages)						
	2002–2008	2009	2010	2011	2012	2013
Fuel exporters	**7.0**	**0.3**	**1.8**	**-4.2**	**-0.9**	**0.7**
Angola	13.3	-0.2	0.4	0.4	6.5	3.6
Chad	5.5	-3.6	10.3	-0.8	4.3	-2.3
Equatorial Guinea	11.7	2.8	-3.6	4.1	1.1	3.8
Sudan	5.1	0.4	1.9	-6.3	-9.5	-3.9
Yemen	0.8	0.8	4.6	-13.1	-3.8	0.0
Manufactures exporters	**4.6**	**3.8**	**4.6**	**4.6**	**4.6**	**5.0**
Bangladesh	4.6	4.5	4.9	4.6	4.4	4.9
Cambodia	8.5	-1.6	4.9	5.0	5.2	5.3
Haiti	-0.7	1.2	-4.8	3.9	6.2	5.3
Lesotho	4.3	2.9	5.0	3.4	4.4	1.4
Bhutan	6.0	5.2	10.1	5.7	6.9	9.7
Services exporters	**4.3**	**3.2**	**3.5**	**3.4**	**2.6**	**3.0**
Comoros	-0.5	-0.2	-0.1	0.1	0.4	1.8
Djibouti	2.0	2.4	1.0	1.9	2.2	2.5
Eritrea	-4.1	0.7	-0.9	5.4	4.3	0.4
Ethiopia	7.4	7.2	5.5	5.0	2.6	3.0
Gambia	0.4	3.9	2.7	0.5	-4.3	6.8
Liberia	-2.0	-1.4	0.7	3.7	6.1	2.4
Madagascar	3.0	-6.6	-2.0	-2.0	0.3	2.5
Nepal	2.7	3.4	3.5	2.5	3.2	2.8
Rwanda	5.8	2.0	5.3	6.6	5.4	4.8
Samoa	3.5	-5.4	-0.3	1.5	1.4	1.3
Sao Tome and Principe	4.2	2.1	3.2	2.5	3.7	4.2
Timor-Leste	2.4	10.2	6.8	8.0	7.4	7.5
Tuvalu	..	..	..	..	..	..
Vanuatu	3.3	1.2	0.1	0.8	2.0	1.5
Other primary commodity exporters	**3.2**	**1.7**	**3.0**	**2.8**	**3.4**	**3.3**
Minerals	3.1	1.2	3.2	2.9	4.9	4.0
Democratic Republic of the Congo	3.3	-0.2	3.9	3.8	3.4	3.6
Guinea	0.5	-2.7	-0.6	1.0	2.1	2.3
Mali	1.7	1.3	2.7	-0.4	2.8	2.6
Mauritania	3.2	-3.5	2.6	1.2	2.8	3.6
Mozambique	5.7	4.2	4.7	5.0	4.7	5.1
Sierra Leone	3.6	0.7	2.3	2.7	32.4	6.3
Zambia	3.3	3.8	5.0	4.0	5.1	5.7
Agriculture and food	3.4	2.5	2.7	2.7	1.2	2.2
Benin	0.7	-0.1	-0.2	0.3	0.7	1.9
Burkina Faso	3.2	0.8	5.5	3.2	2.6	4.0
Guinea-Bissau	0.5	0.7	1.3	3.0	2.2	2.5
Kiribati	-1.3	-5.3	-0.6	-0.1	1.5	1.1
Malawi	2.6	6.0	3.5	2.5	1.4	1.2
Solomon Islands	5.4	-7.0	4.6	6.8	3.5	1.7
Somalia	..	..	..	..	..	..
Uganda	4.5	3.5	2.2	3.0	0.5	1.7
Mixed exporters	**6.9**	**4.2**	**3.6**	**3.1**	**4.0**	**3.6**
Afghanistan	4.0[a]	17.3	5.2	2.7	4.0	2.7
Burundi	2.3	1.4	1.7	2.2	2.7	3.0
Central African Republic	-0.4	-1.9	0.8	0.6	1.5	1.7
Lao People's Democratic Republic	5.6	5.6	6.0	6.3	6.4	5.1
Myanmar	9.9	3.1	3.3	3.4	3.9	3.8
Niger	2.0	-3.9	4.7	-0.8	10.6	3.4
Togo	0.1	0.9	1.5	1.6	1.8	2.0
Senegal	2.3	-0.3	1.7	0.2	1.4	2.1
United Rep. of Tanzania	5.1	4.6	4.5	4.6	4.3	4.6

Source: UNCTAD Secretariat calculations, based on IMF, *World Economic Outlook* database, April, 2012.

Note: Data for 2011 are preliminary and are forecasted for 2012–2013.

   a 2003–2008.

Annex table 3. Gross fixed capital formation in LDCs: share of GDP and annual average growth rates (Percentage)											
Country	Share of GDP (current dollars)						Annual average growth rate (constant 2005 dollars)				
	1980	1990	2000	2008	2009	2010	1980–1990	1990–2000	2000–2009	2008	2009	2010
Afghanistan	13.2	13.4	14.3	27.6	17.5	26.5	-1.6	-3.0	11.3	-5.5	-0.2	-7.3
Angola	22.8	11.7	11.7	15.8	17.1	10.3	-4.0	8.9	16.1	67.2	-15.8	-22.9
Bangladesh	21.3	20.2	23.0	24.2	24.4	24.9	3.1	9.2	7.6	1.8	6.2	5.8
Benin	21.9	13.4	18.0	20.3	21.0	20.5	-4.7	6.3	4.9	8.3	2.7	-5.9
Bhutan	32.5	31.8	50.0	38.7	41.3	42.3	6.5	9.5	-0.1	-3.9	24.0	-0.5
Burkina Faso	19.2	17.7	21.2	20.4	22.0	27.1	4.9	4.2	8.7	8.2	11.0	8.3
Burundi	17.0	21.8	13.2	14.4	14.4	13.4	4.9	-10.5	3.1	0.2	3.4	-3.1
Cambodia	9.3	8.3	18.3	17.3	20.1	16.0	5.5	15.3	12.9	15.9	18.8	-10.8
Central African Republic	6.9	11.8	11.1	11.6	11.3	11.4	7.0	-1.5	4.9	24.9	5.3	8.9
Chad	8.1	7.2	15.2	15.1	21.4	22.5	6.1	4.4	8.4	-4.7	27.6	34.0
Comoros	28.5	12.2	10.1	13.7	11.9	16.5	-6.6	-1.6	5.1	29.1	-11.6	42.0
Dem. Rep. of the Congo	20.0	12.8	3.5	21.5	19.1	26.4	0.0	-8.7	14.3	6.4	2.1	7.2
Djibouti	12.9	27.2	12.2	16.9	17.7	17.3	3.1	-9.4	23.8	16.4	-15.2	-26.3
Equatorial Guinea	13.0	58.1	61.9	30.5	70.5	61.1	11.6	54.3	16.4	28.2	38.7	-14.0
Eritrea[a]	_	_	22.0	12.7	9.1	12.3	-	14.1	-20.9	-0.5	-37.0	92.9
Ethiopia[b]	_	_	20.3	22.4	22.7	22.3	-	5.7	10.5	15.7	15.0	-0.5
Ethiopia (former)	10.0	12.5	..	..	..	..	4.2	..	..	..	..	..
Gambia	14.4	18.0	4.6	29.1	28.3	27.5	-3.4	2.3	23.2	4.5	-0.8	3.0
Guinea	20.1	34.3	35.4	21.3	16.4	18.0	8.1	2.3	14.4	34.5	19.9	11.1
Guinea-Bissau	25.1	14.7	11.3	8.6	8.4	7.2	1.7	-10.4	3.3	-13.4	7.0	-15.9
Haiti	17.9	14.3	14.3	15.1	14.3	13.1	-0.1	5.6	1.2	2.8	3.2	-6.5
Kiribati	44.0	55.9	33.2	57.8	57.6	58.6	2.6	-0.4	8.5	3.1	-2.7	1.3
Lao People's Dem. Rep.	7.4	11.3	28.3	37.1	31.1	37.1	10.7	14.8	13.3	-2.7	-11.6	33.7
Lesotho	40.3	53.0	43.2	28.5	27.8	29.9	3.8	1.5	1.4	18.0	-5.0	10.1
Liberia	21.4	10.5	7.3	20.0	20.0	20.0	-11.7	2.2	17.6	7.1	4.5	5.2
Madagascar	22.8	17.0	16.2	40.3	31.7	18.8	4.9	3.4	11.3	52.8	-26.1	-12.6
Malawi	31.6	24.4	17.5	22.6	22.6	22.3	-3.3	-4.2	18.4	23.6	9.0	26.8
Mali	17.4	20.0	18.9	18.3	20.4	21.2	4.2	2.1	7.0	-0.8	13.3	7.7
Mauritania	18.7	13.6	16.2	25.5	28.4	30.6	-3.3	2.2	17.6	-6.8	13.3	28.5
Mozambique	7.6	14.7	31.0	16.5	16.5	21.9	2.3	10.1	6.2	17.8	5.4	38.0
Myanmar	18.7	14.7	11.8	15.7	19.3	22.8	-2.7	14.5	24.0	19.6	36.7	31.7
Nepal	15.9	16.6	19.5	21.9	21.4	20.2	4.5	6.4	4.1	1.9	0.5	5.3
Niger	25.3	12.8	15.1	30.9	32.9	40.2	-10.1	3.0	11.3	19.8	5.2	32.6
Rwanda	10.8	10.9	14.2	22.7	21.6	21.0	5.0	1.1	15.3	32.1	2.6	7.3
Samoa	25.9	22.4	13.9	8.5	9.0	8.8	0.3	-4.6	-2.5	-8.5	4.3	-0.7
Sao Tome and Principe	11.4	31.3	35.8	26.7	23.4	26.1	3.1	3.6	4.3	4.1	-8.4	16.6
Senegal	16.3	16.1	22.4	27.1	23.7	27.3	4.3	6.2	6.3	7.8	-7.4	12.0
Sierra Leone	14.0	9.6	6.9	6.2	6.2	8.1	-3.7	-11.6	15.0	-3.5	4.4	25.0
Solomon Islands	22.0	17.4	18.3	18.3	18.1	19.3	1.9	0.7	21.2	14.2	-12.6	169.9
Somalia	9.8	23.0	20.4	20.1	20.0	19.9	4.7	-4.7	1.6	2.2	3.3	2.3
Sudan	19.3	16.1	9.7	18.4	18.8	18.5	-5.3	21.8	16.7	-0.3	19.8	3.2
Timor-Leste[c]	..	..	..	23.5	21.6	21.9	..	..	-0.9	26.2	3.5	7.9
Togo	29.4	14.5	15.1	14.3	16.7	17.7	-1.3	0.3	5.5	12.2	21.8	9.6
Tuvalu	74.9	68.6	11.7	77.3	76.6	77.4	6.5	-6.4	11.9	-6.7	0.6	2.7
Uganda	6.9	13.5	17.8	20.1	21.0	21.4	7.4	9.5	11.5	6.7	5.8	5.2
United Rep. of Tanzania	22.0	41.1	16.3	29.0	28.2	27.7	1.1	-1.2	12.6	7.4	10.0	8.3
Vanuatu	23.7	32.3	24.6	33.0	27.0	27.8	6.2	4.2	11.2	48.6	-15.0	8.1
Yemen[d]	31.1	11.8	16.7	19.5	20.9	17.9	-6.8	14.1	0.6	-6.2	-8.0	-7.4
Zambia	18.2	13.5	17.2	19.7	20.2	22.5	-9.0	21.0	11.7	12.1	-0.6	9.8
All developing countries	**24.9**	**22.8**	**23.3**	**28.0**	**29.7**	**29.8**	**1.8**	**6.0**	**9.0**	**6.8**	**5.8**	**10.4**
Other developing countries	**25.1**	**23.0**	**23.4**	**28.2**	**29.9**	**30.1**	**1.8**	**6.0**	**9.0**	**6.6**	**5.8**	**10.5**
LDCs	**18.6**	**17.0**	**18.5**	**21.1**	**22.0**	**21.6**	**0.6**	**6.5**	**10.2**	**12.4**	**5.1**	**3.7**
LDCs: Africa and Haiti	18.0	16.7	16.9	20.5	21.7	20.5	0.5	5.1	11.6	18.8	4.2	1.8
LDCs: Asia	20.1	17.5	20.5	22.3	22.4	23.2	0.7	8.9	8.1	2.2	6.8	6.8
LDCs: Islands	24.5	23.6	19.4	22.2	20.3	21.8	0.8	0.2	10.7	20.3	-7.6	35.3

Source: UNCTAD, UNCTADstat database, July 2012.

a For Eritrea data start in 1992.
b For Ethiopia data start in 1992.
c For Timor-Leste data start in 2003.
d Yemen prior to 1990 includes Yemen (former Arab Republic) and Yemen (former Democratic).

Annex table 4. Exports and imports of merchandise and services in LDCs, by country groups (geographic), 2006–2011
(Millions of dollars and percentage changes)

	2006	2007	2008	2009	2010	2011	change in 2010 (%)	change in 2011 (%)
Merchandise exports								
Least developed countries	102,351	128,318	169,315	130,871	166,586	204,834	27.3	23.0
LDCs: Africa and Haiti	72,901	95,045	130,618	94,654	119,445	145,490	26.2	21.8
LDCs: Asia	29,181	32,930	38,317	35,902	46,755	58,762	30.2	25.7
LDCs: Islands	269	343	379	314	386	582	22.7	50.8
Merchandise imports								
Least developed countries	101,183	123,768	161,095	153,052	167,628	202,195	9.5	20.6
LDCs: Africa and Haiti	64,454	80,179	107,030	101,857	105,099	124,089	3.2	18.1
LDCs: Asia	35,652	42,348	52,504	49,784	60,881	76,273	22.3	25.3
LDCs: Islands	1,077	1,242	1,561	1,410	1,648	1,833	16.9	11.2
Merchandise trade balance								
Least developed countries	1,168	4,550	8,219	-22,181	-1,042	2,639	95.3	353.2
LDCs: Africa and Haiti	8,448	14,866	23,588	-7,203	14,346	21,402	299.2	49.2
LDCs: Asia	-6,471	-9,418	-14,187	-13,882	-14,126	-17,512	-1.8	-24.0
LDCs: Islands	-809	-898	-1,182	-1,096	-1,262	-1,252	-15.2	0.9
Service exports								
Least developed countries	13,283	16,562	20,811	19,748	22,141	25,338	12.1	14.4
LDCs: Africa and Haiti	8,773	10,896	13,839	12,772	13,786	15,985	7.9	15.9
LDCs: Asia	4,077	5,152	6,439	6,408	7,508	8,391	17.2	11.8
LDCs: Islands	433	514	534	568	848	962	49.3	13.5
Service imports								
Least developed countries	33,281	43,095	58,824	53,373	58,638	67,798	9.9	15.6
LDCs: Africa and Haiti	26,494	35,140	49,065	44,057	47,634	55,035	8.1	15.5
LDCs: Asia	6,240	7,237	8,811	8,303	9,917	11,536	19.4	16.3
LDCs: Islands	547	718	949	1,012	1,088	1,227	7.5	12.8
Service trade balance								
Least developed countries	-19,998	-26,533	-38,013	-33,624	-36,497	-42,460	-8.5	-16.3
LDCs: Africa and Haiti	-17,721	-24,244	-35,226	-31,285	-33,848	-39,050	-8.2	-15.4
LDCs: Asia	-2,163	-2,085	-2,372	-1,895	-2,409	-3,145	-27.1	-30.6
LDCs: Islands	-114	-204	-414	-444	-240	-265	46.0	-10.2

Source: UNCTAD secretariat calculations, based on UNCTADstat database, August 2012.

Annex table 5. Exports and imports of merchandise and services in LDCs, by country groups (export specialization), 2006–2011
(Millions of dollars and percentage changes)

	2006	2007	2008	2009	2010	2011	change in 2010 (%)	change in 2011 (%)
Merchandise exports								
Oil-exporting LDCs	54,776	72,327	102,267	68,069	85,130	105,631	25.1	24.1
Manufactures-exporting LDCs	16,870	19,201	22,488	21,907	27,975	35,899	27.7	28.3
Services-exporting LDCs	3,447	4,168	5,010	4,237	5,069	6,563	19.6	29.5
Mixed-exporting LDCs	10,678	13,090	15,878	15,242	19,268	21,985	26.4	14.1
Other Primary Commodity-exporting LDCs	16,580	19,531	23,671	21,415	29,145	34,756	36.1	19.3
Minerals-exporting LDCs	12,915	14,372	17,344	14,384	21,492	26,287	49.4	22.3
Agriculture & Food-exporting LDCs	3,665	5,159	6,327	7,031	7,653	8,469	8.8	10.7
Merchandise imports								
Oil-exporting LDCs	27,073	35,452	46,646	48,742	44,237	47,267	-9.2	6.8
Manufactures-exporting LDCs	24,099	26,980	34,012	31,188	39,361	50,274	26.2	27.7
Services-exporting LDCs	12,330	14,732	20,772	19,798	20,925	23,013	5.7	10.0
Mixed-exporting LDCs	17,001	20,921	26,126	24,936	29,417	40,084	18.0	36.3
Other Primary Commodity-exporting LDCs	20,680	25,683	33,539	28,388	33,687	41,556	18.7	23.4
Minerals-exporting LDCs	13,073	15,800	20,573	16,706	21,003	27,358	25.7	30.3
Agriculture & Food-exporting LDCs	7,606	9,883	12,966	11,682	12,684	14,198	8.6	11.9
Merchandise trade balance								
Oil-exporting LDCs	27,703	36,876	55,621	19,327	40,893	58,364	111.6	42.7
Manufactures-exporting LDCs	-7,230	-7,779	-11,524	-9,281	-11,386	-14,376	-22.7	-26.3
Services-exporting LDCs	-8,883	-10,564	-15,761	-15,560	-15,856	-16,450	-1.9	-3.7
Mixed-exporting LDCs	-6,323	-7,831	-10,248	-9,693	-10,150	-18,100	-4.7	-78.3
Other Primary Commodity-exporting LDCs	-4,100	-6,152	-9,868	-6,973	-4,543	-6,800	34.9	-49.7
Minerals-exporting LDCs	-159	-1,428	-3,229	-2,322	489	-1,070	121.0	-319.1
Agriculture & Food-exporting LDCs	-3,941	-4,724	-6,639	-4,651	-5,031	-5,729	-8.2	-13.9
Service exports								
Oil-exporting LDCs	1,039	1,683	2,336	2,758	3,162	3,597	14.6	13.8
Manufactures-exporting LDCs	2,914	3,521	4,078	4,077	4,517	5,294	10.8	17.2
Services-exporting LDCs	3,525	4,340	5,917	5,125	5,521	6,690	7.7	21.2
Mixed-exporting LDCs	3,319	4,178	4,669	4,190	4,728	5,339	12.8	12.9
Other Primary Commodity-exporting LDCs	2,484	2,835	3,826	3,633	4,322	4,797	19.0	11.0
Minerals-exporting LDCs	1,505	1,626	2,314	2,037	1,972	2,257	-3.2	14.5
Agriculture & Food-exporting LDCs	980	1,210	1,511	1,596	2,350	2,540	47.3	8.1
Service imports								
Oil-exporting LDCs	15,183	20,325	30,637	27,105	27,489	32,517	1.4	18.3
Manufactures-exporting LDCs	4,151	4,921	5,922	5,647	7,365	8,481	30.4	15.1
Services-exporting LDCs	4,622	5,969	7,831	7,052	7,135	8,170	1.2	14.5
Mixed-exporting LDCs	3,687	4,437	5,259	5,134	5,710	6,505	11.2	13.9
Other Primary Commodity-exporting LDCs	5,633	7,436	9,213	8,435	10,881	12,738	29.0	17.1
Minerals-exporting LDCs	3,717	5,068	6,332	5,473	7,026	8,265	28.4	17.6
Agriculture & Food-exporting LDCs	1,915	2,368	2,881	2,961	3,854	4,473	30.2	16.0
Service trade balance								
Oil-exporting LDCs	-14,144	-18,641	-28,301	-24,347	-24,328	-28,919	0.1	-18.9
Manufactures-exporting LDCs	-1,237	-1,400	-1,843	-1,570	-2,848	-3,187	-81.4	-11.9
Services-exporting LDCs	-1,097	-1,629	-1,914	-1,927	-1,614	-1,479	16.3	8.3
Mixed-exporting LDCs	-368	-259	-590	-944	-982	-1,166	-4.0	-18.7
Other Primary Commodity-exporting LDCs	-3,148	-4,600	-5,387	-4,801	-6,559	-7,942	-36.6	-21.1
Minerals-exporting LDCs	-2,212	-3,442	-4,018	-3,436	-5,055	-6,009	-47.1	-18.9
Agriculture & Food-exporting LDCs	-936	-1,159	-1,370	-1,365	-1,504	-1,933	-10.2	-28.5

Source: UNCTAD secretariat calculations, based on UNCTADstat database, August 2012.

Annex table 6. Foreign direct investment inflows to LDCs, selected years						
(Millions of current dollars)						
Country	1985	1990	2000	2009	2010	2011
Afghanistan	..	..	0.2	75.7	211.3	83.4
Angola	278.0	-334.5	878.6	2,205.3	-3,227.2	-5,585.5
Bangladesh	-6.7	3.2	578.6	700.2	913.3	1,136.4
Benin	-0.1	62.4	59.7	134.3	176.8	118.5
Bhutan	..	1.6	0.0	18.3	16.3	13.9
Burkina Faso	-1.4	0.5	23.1	100.9	34.6	7.4
Burundi	1.6	1.3	11.7	0.3	0.8	1.7
Cambodia	0.0	0.0	148.5	539.1	782.6	891.7
Central African Republic	3.0	0.7	0.9	120.5	91.7	109.2
Chad	53.7	9.4	115.2	1,105.5	1,939.7	1,855.0
Comoros	..	0.4	0.1	13.8	3.9	6.8
Dem. Rep. of the Congo	69.2	-14.5	72.0	663.8	2,939.3	1,686.9
Djibouti	0.2	0.1	3.3	99.6	26.8	78.0
Equatorial Guinea	2.4	11.1	154.5	1,636.2	1,369.0	737.1
Eritrea	..	..	27.9	0.0	55.6	18.5
Ethiopia	0.2	12.0	134.6	221.5	288.3	206.1
Gambia	-0.5	14.1	43.5	39.6	37.2	36.0
Guinea	1.1	17.9	9.9	140.9	101.4	1,210.8
Guinea-Bissau	1.4	2.0	0.7	17.6	33.2	19.4
Haiti	4.9	8.0	13.3	38.0	150.0	181.0
Kiribati	0.2	0.3	0.7	3.2	3.7	3.9
Lao People's Dem.Rep.	-1.6	6.0	33.9	318.6	332.6	450.0
Lesotho	4.8	16.1	31.5	48.0	54.7	52.0
Liberia	-16.2	225.2	20.8	217.8	450.0	508.0
Madagascar	-0.2	22.4	83.0	1,066.1	860.4	907.4
Malawi	0.5	23.3	39.6	54.7	58.2	56.3
Mali	2.9	5.7	82.4	748.3	405.9	177.8
Mauritania	7.0	6.7	40.1	-3.1	130.5	45.2
Mozambique	0.3	9.2	139.3	892.5	989.0	2,093.5
Myanmar	0.0	225.1	208.0	963.3	450.2	850.0
Nepal	0.7	5.9	-0.5	38.6	86.7	95.5
Niger	-9.4	40.8	8.4	790.8	940.3	1,013.6
Rwanda	14.6	7.7	8.1	118.7	42.3	106.0
Samoa	0.4	6.6	-1.2	9.6	1.1	12.0
Sao Tome and Principe	..	0.0	3.8	15.5	24.6	18.0
Senegal	-18.9	56.9	62.9	320.0	266.1	286.1
Sierra Leone	-31.0	32.4	38.9	74.3	86.6	48.7
Solomon Islands	0.7	10.4	13.0	119.8	237.9	146.4
Somalia	-0.7	5.6	0.3	108.0	112.0	102.0
Sudan	-3.0	-31.1	392.2	1,816.2	2,063.7	1,936.0
Timor-Leste	0.0	0.0	0.0	49.9	26.9	20.0
Togo	16.3	22.7	41.5	48.5	85.8	53.8
Tuvalu	0.0	0.0	-0.9	2.2	1.5	1.8
Uganda	-4.0	-5.9	180.8	841.6	543.9	792.3
United Rep.of Tanzania	14.5	0.0	282.0	952.6	1,022.8	1,095.4
Vanuatu	4.6	13.1	20.3	31.7	41.1	58.2
Yemen	3.2	-130.9	6.4	129.2	-93.3	-712.8
Zambia	51.5	202.8	121.7	694.8	1,729.3	1,981.7
LDCs	**444.3**	**572.8**	**4,133.3**	**18,342.5**	**16,899.2**	**15,010.9**
LDCs: Africa and Haiti	442.8	431.0	3,122.4	15,313.8	13,858.8	11,935.7
LDCs: Asia	-4.4	111.0	975.1	2,783.0	2,699.6	2,808.1
LDCs: Islands	6.0	30.8	35.8	245.7	340.8	267.1
Other developing countries	**13,548.7**	**34,570.1**	**248,516.7**	**456,513.8**	**547,002.5**	**629,911.3**
All developing economies	**13,993.1**	**35,142.9**	**252,650.0**	**474,856.3**	**563,901.7**	**644,922.2**

Source: UNCTAD, *World Investment Report 2012*, July 2012.

Annex table 7. Foreign direct investment outflows from LDCs, selected years (Millions of current dollars)						
Country	1985	1990	2000	2009	2010	2011
Afghanistan	..	..	..	..	..	..
Angola	..	0.9	..	6.8	1,340.4	1,300.0
Bangladesh	..	0.5	2.0	29.3	15.4	9.2
Benin	..	0.3	3.6	31.2	-17.9	2.9
Bhutan	..	..	..	..	..	..
Burkina Faso	0.0	-0.6	0.2	8.5	-3.5	4.1
Burundi	-1.1	0.0	0.0	..	..	..
Cambodia	..	..	6.6	18.9	20.6	23.6
Central African Republic	0.6	3.8	..	..	..	..
Chad	0.3	0.1	..	..	..	..
Comoros	..	1.1	..	..	..	..
Democratic Republic of the Congo	..	..	-1.8	34.8	7.2	90.9
Djibouti	..	..	..	..	..	..
Equatorial Guinea	..	0.1	-3.6	..	..	..
Eritrea	-	-	..	..	..	..
Ethiopia	..	..	..	..	..	..
Gambia	..	..	..	..	..	..
Guinea	0.0	0.1	..	..	..	5.2
Guinea-Bissau	..	..	..	-2.5	5.5	1.1
Haiti	..	-8.0	..	..	..	..
Kiribati	..	..	0.1	0.2	0.3	0.5
Lao People's Democratic Republic	-0.2	0.2	9.9	1.3	5.7	7.0
Lesotho	..	..	..	..	..	..
Liberia	255.0	5.9	779.9	363.6	369.4	371.7
Madagascar	..	1.3	..	..	..	..
Malawi	..	..	-0.6	..	..	..
Mali	..	0.2	4.0	-1.0	7.4	2.4
Mauritania	..	..	..	4.3	4.1	4.2
Mozambique	..	..	0.2	-2.8	0.8	-3.4
Myanmar	..	..	..	..	..	..
Nepal	..	..	..	..	..	..
Niger	1.9	0.0	-0.6	59.3	59.7	48.4
Rwanda	..	..	..	..	..	..
Samoa	..	..	..	-1.1	..	-0.6
Sao Tome and Principe	..	..	..	0.2	0.1	0.1
Senegal	3.1	-9.5	0.6	77.1	2.2	66.4
Sierra Leone	..	0.1	..	..	5.0	..
Solomon Islands	..	..	0.1	3.0	2.3	3.6
Somalia	..	..	..	..	..	..
Sudan	..	..	..	89.2	66.1	84.5
Timor-Leste	-	-	-	..	..	..
Togo	..	..	0.4	37.4	37.2	20.4
Tuvalu	..	..	..	..	..	..
Uganda	..	..	..	..	-3.4	..
United Republic of Tanzania	..	..	..	..	..	..
Vanuatu	..	..	..	1.2	1.2	0.9
Yemen	0.5	..	-8.8	66.4	70.3	76.6
Zambia	..	..	..	269.6	1,095.4	1,150.2
LDCs	**260.1**	**-3.4**	**792.3**	**1,094.8**	**3,091.3**	**3,270.0**
LDCs: Africa and Haiti	259.8	-5.2	782.4	975.4	2,975.5	3,149.1
LDCs: Asia	0.3	0.7	9.7	115.9	112.0	116.3
LDCs: Islands	..	1.1	0.2	3.5	3.8	4.6
Other developing countries	**3,660.5**	**13,685.8**	**92,627.0**	**232,373.5**	**331,771.7**	**324,223.1**
All developing economies	**3,920.6**	**13,682.4**	**93,419.4**	**233,468.3**	**334,863.0**	**327,493.1**

Source: UNCTAD, *World Investment Report 2012*, July 2012.

Annex table 8. Total external debt and debt service payments of individual LDCs, selected years												
(Millions of dollars)												
Country	External debt[a]						Debt service[b]					
	1990	2000	2005	2008	2009	2010	1990	2000	2005	2008	2009	2010
Afghanistan	..	..	..	2,088.9	2,222.6	2,297.2	..	..	..	7.7	10.2	9.2
Angola	8,592.0	9,407.8	11,833.8	15,100.5	16,616.2	18,562.0	325.9	1,705.3	2,602.1	1,640.6	3,553.7	2,309.0
Bangladesh	12,285.3	15,534.7	18,381.5	22,879.8	23,801.6	24,962.6	735.5	766.5	799.5	888.3	954.4	1,012.7
Benin	1,119.7	1,387.8	1,537.7	916.8	1,072.4	1,221.3	37.1	74.3	47.3	58.3	36.9	42.5
Bhutan	83.5	203.8	649.2	685.5	751.9	898.2	5.2	6.7	6.8	81.5	75.5	84.2
Burkina Faso	832.0	1,422.2	1,994.2	1,669.8	1,821.6	2,053.3	34.3	46.5	45.3	45.0	42.4	50.6
Burundi	906.9	1,108.0	1,321.8	1,438.2	512.7	537.1	42.4	21.9	39.3	19.5	19.5	3.4
Cambodia	1845.0	2,627.9	3,515.3	4,215.0	4,364.0	4,676.1	30.0	31.5	31.0	42.1	49.5	62.2
Central African Republic	698.5	860.0	1,019.6	954.0	394.1	384.8	29.1	14.1	6.5	25.7	31.2	2.3
Chad	514.2	1,088.4	1,584.1	1,750.1	1,746.0	1,733.5	11.8	24.4	54.2	137.2	78.4	73.2
Comoros	187.8	226.1	278.8	279.4	277.6	485.4	1.1	3.2	4.0	12.3	11.8	4.3
Dem. Rep. of the Congo	10,258.6	11,692.4	10,600.3	12,210.5	12,276.0	5,773.7	348.1	24.8	214.2	591.9	622.9	267.6
Djibouti	155.3	258.1	406.4	698.5	755.3	751.3	11.0	13.3	15.6	29.6	35.0	33.9
Equatorial Guinea	..	..	..	..	..	..	..	..	..	..	..	..
Eritrea	-	299.9	724.5	961.4	1,018.9	1,009.8	0.0	3.0	20.2	15.6	21.6	22.4
Ethiopia[c]	8,645.2	5,494.9	6,208.1	2,879.0	5,029.5	7,147.1	236.2	137.9	93.4	111.4	103.2	191.9
Gambia	369.1	483.4	659.8	365.1	459.6	470.2	37.7	21.5	28.5	17.0	18.8	19.6
Guinea	2,478.3	3,066.4	2,898.3	3,093.7	2,915.7	2,923.0	168.3	156.7	163.5	140.6	127.1	87.4
Guinea-Bissau	694.5	947.3	1,013.0	1,085.6	1,117.6	1,094.6	8.4	5.2	6.3	9.6	10.0	17.3
Haiti	916.8	1,172.7	1,327.0	1,950.9	1,325.2	491.8	36.1	44.3	57.2	57.8	44.7	130.9
Kiribati	..	..	..	..	..	..	..	..	..	..	..	..
Lao People's Dem. Rep.	1,766.0	2,501.3	2,843.8	5,008.2	5,458.1	5,558.8	8.9	40.1	132.3	207.4	219.8	305.2
Lesotho	395.6	671.8	662.0	688.8	704.8	725.9	23.3	61.5	79.5	37.5	38.1	34.5
Liberia	2,055.6	2,792.1	3,897.6	3,128.1	1,655.6	228.0	3.2	0.7	0.9	934.4	64.0	5.5
Madagascar	3,688.9	4,691.2	3,493.5	2,075.6	2,203.2	2,295.2	222.7	116.7	78.8	32.8	50.2	55.8
Malawi	1,556.8	2,704.9	3,183.2	893.7	1,033.3	921.6	132.6	62.9	75.7	31.9	35.7	18.7
Mali	2,468.0	2,960.4	3,200.8	2,031.3	2,070.7	2,326.4	67.8	92.8	99.3	69.0	68.2	61.1
Mauritania	2,113.3	2,377.7	2,308.0	1,985.6	2,047.6	2,461.3	145.7	83.1	65.1	63.2	77.6	109.1
Mozambique	4,600.3	7,205.2	4,152.9	3,392.5	4,045.7	4,123.8	78.5	95.9	78.6	37.3	43.3	89.8
Myanmar	4,695.0	5,974.9	7,013.9	8,001.7	8,185.9	6,351.8	60.4	36.1	71.2	33.3	28.8	687.1
Nepal	1,626.9	2,867.3	3,179.6	3,685.2	3,683.0	3,702.3	67.8	101.7	117.4	161.9	176.6	186.9
Niger	1,757.6	1,708.4	2,017.4	1,002.1	1,102.7	1,126.8	98.7	26.0	40.3	29.5	45.3	27.0
Rwanda	708.0	1,270.3	1,508.9	662.8	748.9	794.6	19.8	35.6	27.6	14.3	11.3	14.5
Samoa	91.8	137.7	167.5	205.6	235.5	308.0	5.4	5.5	5.8	8.0	8.5	10.6
Sao Tome and Principe	150.0	304.0	334.7	130.8	148.8	170.2	2.8	4.3	6.6	2.3	2.1	1.6
Senegal	3,753.9	3,621.6	3,830.5	2,819.6	3,499.0	3,676.9	324.1	224.3	202.5	180.1	199.6	301.8
Sierra Leone	1,176.4	1,189.8	1,750.8	607.1	701.0	778.0	21.1	46.7	17.6	5.7	7.9	11.1
Solomon Islands	120.5	155.4	166.5	165.9	155.9	215.5	11.6	9.1	14.0	15.1	10.0	20.7
Somalia	2,370.3	2,547.9	2,730.3	2,921.6	2,943.7	2,942.4	10.7	0.0	0.1	1.7	0.0	0.0
Sudan	14,762.0	15,983.0	17,474.2	20,105.9	20,746.3	21,845.9	49.7	244.7	398.1	368.1	490.7	492.2
Timor-Leste	..	..	..	..	..	..	..	..	..	..	..	..
Togo	1,280.6	1,429.6	1,673.3	1,627.3	1,632.9	1,727.8	85.7	29.8	20.8	196.3	55.3	35.1
Tuvalu	..	..	..	..	..	..	..	..	..	..	..	..
Uganda	2,605.8	3,496.8	4,394.7	2,221.4	2,465.2	2,993.7	144.7	74.0	170.4	73.7	71.1	64.2
United Rep. of Tanzania	6,446.1	7,142.0	8,354.9	5,963.5	7,323.9	8,664.1	179.0	166.6	131.8	64.6	164.2	198.7
Vanuatu	38.2	74.5	82.1	125.8	129.8	148.3	2.4	1.9	2.6	4.5	5.6	5.9
Yemen	6,354.0	5,125.0	5,459.5	6,274.4	6,370.1	6,324.0	169.1	243.3	212.2	284.1	262.7	259.5
Zambia	6,904.8	5,722.5	5,373.2	2,974.5	3,038.9	3,688.8	200.7	185.4	281.4	166.3	169.1	147.4
LDCs[d]	**124,069.3**	**141,937.0**	**155,207.0**	**153,921.4**	**160,808.6**	**161,572.8**	**4,234.9**	**5,089.9**	**6,565.6**	**6,954.9**	**8,152.5**	**7,568.5**
LDCs: Africa and Haiti[d]	94,825.1	106,204.5	113,134.9	100,175.4	105,024.0	105,474.5	3,134.6	3,840.0	5,162.2	5,206.3	6,337.1	4,918.5
LDCs: Asia[d]	28,655.8	34,834.9	41,042.7	52,838.6	54,837.0	54,771.0	1,076.9	1,225.9	1,370.3	1,706.3	1,777.5	2,607.1
LDCs: Islands[d]	588.3	897.6	1,029.5	907.4	947.6	1,327.3	23.4	24.0	33.1	42.4	38.0	43.0

Source: UNCTAD secretariat calculations, based on World Bank, *World Development Indicators* database, online, July 2012.

    a External debt covers both long-term and short term debt as well as the use of IMF credit.

    b Debt service on total external debt.

    c Ethiopia includes Eritrea up to 1992.

    d LDC aggregates exclude missing data for Equatorial Guinea, Kiribati, Timor-Leste, Tuvalu, and for Afghanistan from 1990 to 2005.

CHAPTER **2**
HARNESSING REMITTANCES AND DIASPORA KNOWLEDGE FOR PRODUCTIVE CAPACITIES IN LDCS

A. Rationale for addressing remittances and diaspora issues

Remittances have attracted increasing attention in the international discourse, partly owing to their remarkable growth over the last decade (Ratha, 2003; Solimano, 2005; UNECA, 2007; UNDESA, 2012b; UNDP, 2009). A growing consensus is emerging that remittances constitute a significant source of external financing, whose availability, if managed through appropriate policies, could prove particularly valuable for capital-scarce developing countries (especially those with larger diasporas). The jury is still out on whether or not they are the most stable and predictable source of development finance. While some unresolved questions remain as to their macroeconomic impact, a large body of evidence suggests that remittances contribute to poverty reduction and improved health care and education.

A growing consensus is emerging that remittances constitute a significant source of external financing for capital-scarce developing countries, especially those with larger diasporas.

Similarly, there is growing interest in the role that migrants can play as "development agents" linking home and destination countries (Melde and Ionesco, 2010; World Bank, 2011a). While concerns about the adverse impact of "brain drain" remain valid, the recent debate has to some extent shifted to how to engage with the diaspora and maximize its potential contribution to development, "turning the brain drain into brain gain". In this respect, the emphasis has been placed not only on the saving and investment potential of diasporas but also on their latent role as "knowledge brokers" who could facilitate the emergence of new trade patterns, technology transfer, skills and knowledge exchange.

There is growing interest in the role that migrants can play as "development agents" linking home and destination countries

In this context, the rest of this Report addresses three main issues.

- First, it provides a baseline assessment of current patterns of migration and remittances to LDCs, analysing their importance and economic significance, the transaction costs involved, and the associated opportunities and challenges.

- Second, it assesses diaspora engagement in LDCs in relation to the process of knowledge acquisition and diffusion, shedding light on not only the risks stemming from brain drain but also on the potential scope for greater knowledge circulation.

- Finally, it provides specific policy proposals aimed at better mobilizing remittances and engaging diaspora communities for the development of LDCs' productive capacities.

The Istanbul Programme of Action for LDCs (IPoA) identified "Mobilizing financial resources for development and capacity-building" as one of the priority areas for LDCs for the decade 2011–2020.

The Istanbul Programme of Action for LDCs (IPoA) identified "Mobilizing financial resources for development and capacity-building" as one of the priority areas for LDCs for the decade 2011–2020. The programme stresses that "Remittances are significant private financial resources for households in countries of origin of migration. There is a need for further efforts to lower the transaction costs of remittances and create opportunities for development-oriented investment, bearing in mind that remittances cannot be considered as a substitute for foreign direct investment, ODA, debt relief or other public sources of finance for development" (para 126).[1]

With this in mind, it is useful to approach these issues from the perspective of the long-standing structural weaknesses that constitute the raison d'être of the LDC category. The discussion of remittances (and diaspora savings) can best be related to two key macroeconomic constraints hampering the expansion of productive capacities in LDCs, namely the low level of investment and persistent balance of payments vulnerability.[2] Indeed, LDCs' long-standing need to strengthen skill formation and knowledge creation provides the most appropriate entry point to embark on an analysis of the multiple roles that diasporas can play in catalysing knowledge circulation and technology transfer.

Capital accumulation in the LDCs has continued to proceed at a comparatively slow pace despite the growth acceleration of the last decade. With an average investment ratio of 21 per cent of GDP over the last decade compared with 26 per cent in other developing countries, LDCs' long-standing infrastructural and productivity gaps are likely to persist if not widen.[3] Similarly, since the adoption of the Millennium Declaration, most LDCs have witnessed tangible improvements in terms of literacy rates and primary school enrolment but still lag far behind other developing countries in terms of secondary and tertiary enrolment.[4] Moreover, the limited mobilization of investment in physical and human capital has traditionally been compounded by lopsided production structures largely focused on primary products and low value-added activities. This has typically resulted in heightened dependence on primary commodity exports and on imports of foreign manufactures and capital goods, leading — with a few exceptions — to chronic current account deficits and heavy reliance on foreign savings to finance capital accumulation.[5]

All sources of financing for development — whether traditional or emerging, private or public — should be mobilized in order to sustain the expansion and diversification of LDCs' productive capacities.

Moreover, even in the early and mid-2000s, when the constraints posed by a lack of investment and foreign exchange had eased somewhat, growth translated only weakly into the development of LDCs' productive capacities, which means that its benefits were short-lived. The growth experienced by many LDCs (including some of the fastest-growing ones) has been accompanied by limited economic diversification — if any — and insufficient employment creation outside traditional sectors. This, in turn, has hindered the emergence of high value-added activities, since large numbers of workers have remained confined to low-productivity jobs in the agriculture and informal sectors. As a result, the potential benefits for a very young and increasingly educated population have been largely unrealized in most LDCs (Valensisi and Davis, 2011).

LDC development strategies begin to take full cognizance of the development potential underlying migration and remittances.

Consequently, improved development finance and economic diversification towards higher value-added activities continue to pose major challenges for the world's poorest countries. In pursuit of these objectives, all sources of financing for development — whether traditional or emerging, private or public — should be mobilized in order to sustain the expansion and diversification of LDCs' productive capacities. Accordingly, it is essential that LDC development strategies begin to take full cognizance of the development potential underlying migration and remittances (as in the case of FDI, aid and other external financing flows that have traditionally received far greater attention). Harnessing remittances for increasing productive capacities requires that these resources be considered pragmatically, with the recognition that these are ultimately private sector resources, and taking into account each country's specificities, while avoiding characterizations of this phenomenon as either a "curse" or a "new development mantra" (Kapur, 2004; De Haas, 2005).[6] Remittances should be regarded as one facet of a multi-pronged effort to mobilize adequate sources of development finance; as financial inflows which could prove all the more critical in times of uncertainty and heightened volatility in the global economy.

However, the growing attention paid to remittances should in no way obscure the fact that they cannot be considered as a substitute for foreign direct investment, ODA, debt relief, internal resource mobilization or other sources of finance for development.

On the other hand, and as stated in the IPoA, the growing attention paid to remittances should in no way obscure the fact that, by their very nature, they cannot be considered as a substitute for foreign direct investment, ODA, debt relief, internal resource mobilization or other sources of finance for development. Unlike other types of private capital flows, remittances typically appear to be driven primarily by altruistic/solidarity considerations or implicit contracts with family members remaining at home (Solimano, 2005; Grabel, 2008).[7] They do not entail a corresponding accumulation of external debt and, unlike FDI or portfolio investment, are not subject to profit repatriation or sudden liquidation in times of crisis. Besides, contrary to public sources of development finance, they are comprised of a myriad of (typically small-sized) household-to-household transfers, often taking place through informal or quasi-formal channels. However, remittance flows are not without potential problems or risks (e.g. the so-called "Dutch disease"), which are discussed in chapter 3.

From a policy perspective, the distinctive features of remittances potentially provide opportunities for capital-starved economies but also present challenges in terms of their mobilization for productive purposes. Governments typically have only limited policy space to affect the allocation of remittance income, as taxation or mandatory remittance requirements have been largely ineffective (Lucas, 2008). Therefore, realizing the benefits of these additional resources for investment mainly depends on the ability of the State to create a sustainable and development-friendly institutional and macroeconomic environment, to crowd in private investment (including on behalf of remittances recipients).

When sent through formal channels, remittances can offer some scope for fostering financial deepening.

When sent through formal channels, remittances can offer some scope for fostering financial deepening, by simultaneously supplementing the availability of funds to the financial system and linking up otherwise unbanked households to the financial sector. Yet many migrants resort to informal channels precisely as a reaction to lack of trust in the financial sector and the often excessive costs of formal remittance service providers. The prevalence of informal remittance systems limits the ability of recipient countries to make best use of the additional hard currency sent by overseas migrants and may have adverse effects on monetary and exchange rate variables.

The need for a pragmatic and context-specific policy approach also applies to diaspora engagement.

The need for a pragmatic and context-specific policy approach also applies to diaspora engagement. While it is true that "brain drain" deprives the world's poorest countries of much-needed human capital and skilled professionals, the overwhelming majority of LDC migrants are not highly educated and often move to neighbouring countries with a similar level of development as their country of origin. This being so, it should be evident that the onus of transferring specialized knowledge and technology, when nurturing high-productivity high-value-added sectors, cannot (and should not) be placed wholly on the diaspora. Rather, the latter should be viewed as a potentially important complement to a country's development strategy — one which could be mobilized strategically within the framework of broader policy initiatives to support the development of productive capacities.

The diaspora should be viewed as a potentially important complement to a country's development strategy — one which could be mobilized strategically within the framework of broader policy initiatives to support the development of productive capacities.

In this respect, overseas migrants can play multiple roles in relation to their country of origin. Chart 5 provides a schematic representation of the possibilities and the multiplicity of roles that diasporas can play in contributing to productive capacities in their home countries. For instance, with reference to the expansion of productive resources, overseas migrants may provide additional physical or financial capital and/or make use of their skills and talents to strengthen knowledge accumulation in the home country. This latter aspect may be particularly relevant in countries with a sufficiently large pool of specialized professionals overseas, and may offset some of the losses stemming from brain drain. On the other hand, diaspora communities can enhance entrepreneurial capabilities in the home country by actively supporting technology transfer, knowledge circulation and diffusion, through virtual, temporary or permanent return. Finally, owing to their better knowledge of foreign markets and business practices, overseas migrants are well placed to facilitate the establishment of new international business and production linkages. Through their networks, they may effectively reduce the costs of carrying out market intelligence and cost discovery in foreign markets, integrating domestic firms into international business networks.

Chart 5. Basic elements of productive capacities in the context of diaspora investment and knowledge

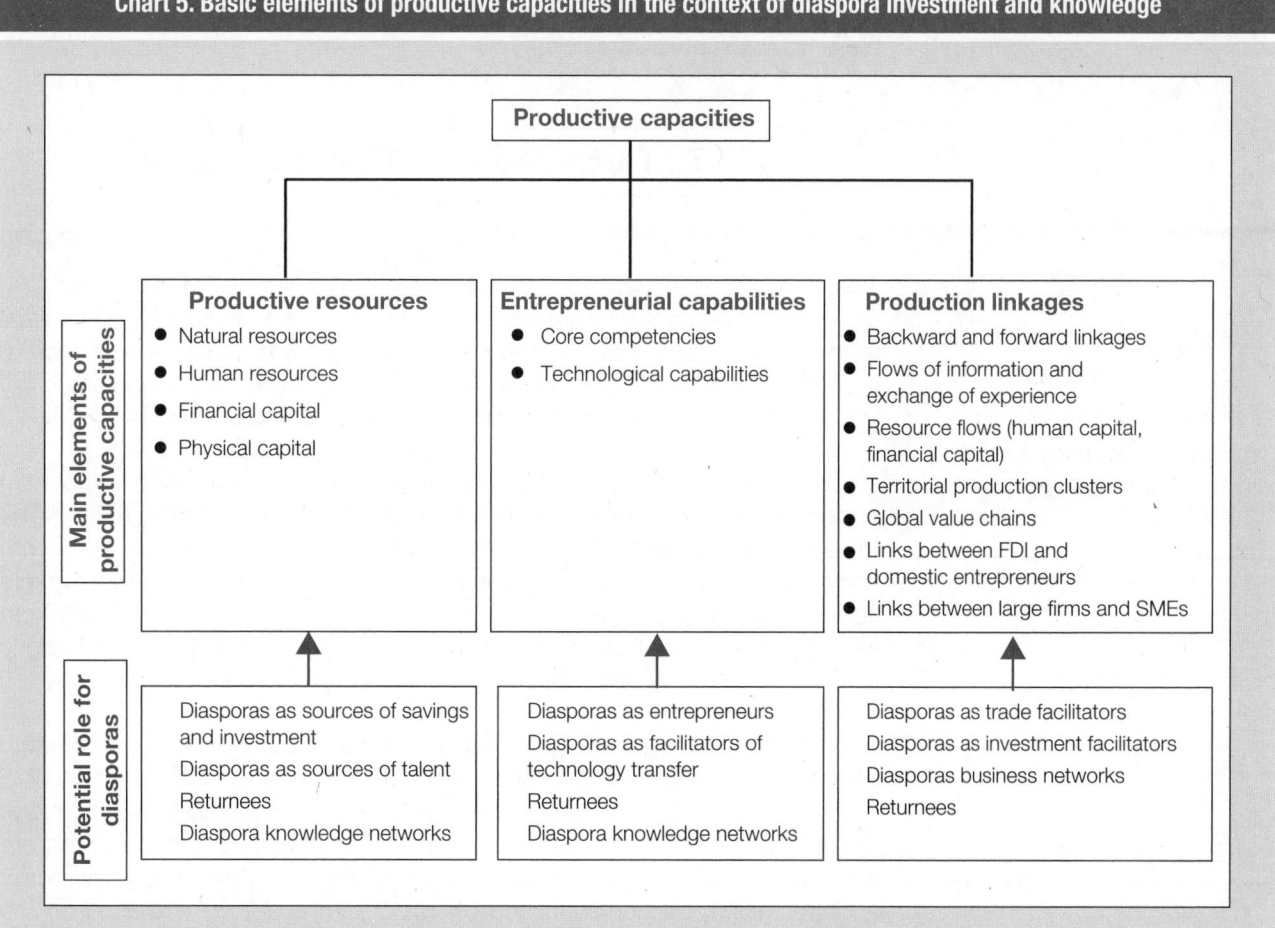

Source: Adapted from UNCTAD (2006), chart 8.

In view of the high coordination costs involved in engaging with small-scale overseas organizations, the effective mobilization of a diaspora for development usually depends on the existence of a critical mass of migrants in a given destination. Moreover, policies for diaspora engagement must also factor in the country-specific patterns of out-migration, in terms of the time horizon (seasonal, temporary, circular, or permanent migration), the skill profile of migrants, the age groups targeted (for instance overseas students with advanced degrees, professionals, or pensioners), and so on. Policies to engage with the diaspora are likely to be more promising if they adopt a strategic approach that supports the overall developmental objectives of the country.

Both the effective mobilization of remittances and the successful engagement of the diaspora for the development of productive capacities requires a coherent policy framework and the establishment of strategic partnerships to engage diaspora communities in the promotion of business linkages, technology transfer, and skills and knowledge circulation.

On the whole, both the effective mobilization of remittances and the successful engagement of the diaspora for the development of productive capacities warrant a combination of policies at multiple levels. These range from "development-friendly" macroeconomic policies aimed at stimulating greater use of remittances for productive purposes and broadening the scope for a favourable transfer of skills, knowledge and technologies to prudential financial and regulatory reforms aimed at reducing transaction costs for remittances and providing stable and secure financial contexts, and meso-level policies to promote innovation in productive sectors. All this in turn requires a coherent policy framework related to migration and remittance issues, and the establishment of strategic partnerships to engage diaspora communities in the promotion of business linkages, technology transfer, and skills and knowledge circulation.

The rest of this chapter introduces the discussion on remittances and diaspora issues by briefly reviewing LDC migration trends. It is important to emphasize that the main interest of this Report is not migration per se but rather the potential economic impact of migrants and the policies or measures that home countries can introduce to translate this potential into concrete economic benefits for society as a whole.

B. Overview of LDC migration

Although LDC migration is often assumed to be a South–North phenomenon, it has taken on a South–South dimension in recent decades.

There is no universally accepted definition of international migration. This Report adopts the definition of international migration (IOM, 2008) as "the movement of persons who leave their country of origin, or the country of habitual residence, to establish themselves either permanently or temporarily in another country".[8] This section aims to explore the nature and extent of contemporary LDC migratory patterns, especially those linked to economic factors.

On a global level, South–North migration is the fastest-growing component of permanent international migration in both absolute and relative terms.[9] The United States remains the most important migrant destination in the world, home to one-fifth of the world's migrants and the top destination for migrants from sixty sending countries. Migration to Western Europe remains largely from elsewhere in Europe. The oil-rich Gulf States have emerged as major destinations for migrants from the Middle East, North Africa and South and Southeast Asia.

Although LDC migration is often assumed to be a South–North phenomenon, it has taken on a South–South dimension in recent decades. Only 20 per cent of migrants from LDCs emigrated to high-income OECD countries (namely North America and Europe) in 2010; around 80 per cent of LDC emigrants migrate within the South (see chart 8). While migration from the African LDCs is mostly an intraregional phenomenon and often constitutes forced migration, in the case of the Asian LDCs, economic motives are more important, and migrants' preferred destinations are India and the Gulf States.

In 2010, high-income OECD countries accounted for 20 per cent of the LDC emigrant stock.

LDC migration has the potential to generate welfare gains for migrants and their countries of origin and to reduce poverty (Ratha, 2006). The benefits to countries of origin arise mainly through remittances sent home by migrants. This Report argues that there may be considerable untapped potential for leveraging remittances and other diaspora resources for the benefit of the home countries. Nevertheless, migration should not be considered a substitute for economic growth and employment generation at home. Indeed, there are potential socioeconomic costs of international migration, both for countries of origin (e.g. potential loss of skilled human capital, or so-called "brain drain") and destination countries (e.g. social cohesion). Moreover, LDC migrants may be adopting increasingly risky strategies to move, often exploring new and diverse destinations through formal and informal channels such as human traffickers (Adepoju, 2009; Hammar et al., 1997).

Around 80 per cent of LDC emigrants migrate within the South.

As of 2010, the 48 LDCs had a combined population of 832.6 million, almost 14 per cent of the world population. Some 63 per cent of the LDC population lives in Africa (526 million), 36 per cent in Asia (303 million), 0.4 per cent in island LDCs (3.4 million).

1. MAIN TYPES OF LDC MIGRATION AND DEFINITION OF TERMS

Table 3 lists some of the generic terms and definitions related to migration used in this report. Migration may be categorized according to location, type of migration and migrant. The seasonality and circularity of LDC migration has been stressed in several studies (Russell, 1990; Ratha and Shaw, 2007; Vertovec, 2007, Cali, 2010). Seasonal movements are typically those of adult males seeking off-season (i.e. post-harvest) work. Circular migration mainly involves people who migrate to augment household income with the clear intention of returning to the country of origin. An interesting distinction arises between seasonal and transhumance10 movements. In the latter, migrants have established livelihoods in two distinct areas, and have access to land and other rural productive assets in both. However, seasonal migrants mainly move to work for others, and their primary asset is their labour. In some LDCs where migrants are recruited to work abroad, contractual arrangements governing this migration require return to the country of origin at the end of the contract. Some instances of this include the Canadian Seasonal Agricultural Worker's Programme (for Mexico and the West Indies) and LDC emigration to South Africa, where there is a requirement that after two years of working in a mine, the migrant workers must return home, often repeating the process for several years if their labour remains in demand (Tati, 2008). Nonetheless, it is very difficult to estimate the extent of temporary migration or to distinguish between it and permanent migration because of limited data availability. Most accounts which exist have to be pieced together from household surveys mainly conducted at the village level. Yet this distinction is likely to be relevant in policy terms for LDCs. For example, the incentives for skill development as well as remittance flows would differ between temporary and permanent migration.

Given the youthful demographic structure of most LDCs, young adults typically move more than older adults.

Making comparisons is difficult owing to the varying definitions used in the extensive migration research literature and empirical surveys, but one thing is clear: in LDCs, cross-border migration is an important livelihood strategy for many households (Ratha, Mohapatra and Saheja, 2011). There are several examples of different types of LDC migration, but some general trends can be identified. First, given the youthful demographic structure of most LDCs, young adults typically move more than older adults (see box 2). This is in part due to life-cycle differences between age groups and levels of education (see Leliveld, 1997).

In LDCs, men migrate more on average than women (particularly in Asian LDCs) due to the persistence of particular gender roles in most rural societies where women have primary responsibility for child-rearing and domestic tasks.

Second, in LDCs, men migrate more on average than women (particularly in Asian LDCs) due to the persistence of particular gender roles in most rural societies where women have primary responsibility for child-rearing and domestic tasks. This often limits opportunities for women to migrate, perhaps with the key exceptions being young, unmarried women from households where they can be absent (i.e. households where several older women already reside) or women migrating to join their partners at the destination. Notwithstanding, female migration has been increasing recently (Ghosh, 2009). When they do migrate, women migrant workers are generally employed in service activities (including the care economy), whereas male migrants are more likely to be found in the manufacturing, production and construction sectors, in addition to some services.

Migration is an important livelihood strategy and largely operates within a context of temporary migration.

Third, in LDCs migration is an important livelihood strategy and largely operates within a context of temporary migration. The migrant remains part of the household and is expected to send remittances home. Fourth, some migration occurs as a survival strategy, while some is based on a rational income-maximizing strategy to take advantage of regional or international wage differentials, irrespective of conditions at home. Educational qualifications and skills make such migration more feasible for young people. Indeed, different types of migration coexist in the same location, with for example well-educated youth moving to urban conurbations for well-paid jobs and unskilled labourers looking for any kind of job, whether in a rural or urban locality (Thakur, 1999; Hammar et al., 1997).

Table 3. Typical migration definitions		
Term	**Definition**	**Type of migrant**
Rural	Living in, or characteristic of the countryside — areas where human settlement is not the main feature of the landscape.	Unskilled labour
Urban	An area of dense settlement, usually dominated by buildings, roads and other infrastructure. In population data, urban may be defined by the size of contiguous settlement. Periurban: an area close to and surrounding the urban.	Mainly young men Skilled vs unskilled labour White collar 'brain drain'
Circular migration	Migration that is temporary, which is not tied to seasonal factors of agricultural production (Ellis1998). Implies that the migrant returns to the area of origin. Period away may be short or long.	Guest worker Company transfer
Seasonal migration	Temporary migration which occurs in slack/off-season of farm work. Implies migration for no more than a few months at a time.	
Step migration	Migrants first move to a staging point, before moving further afield. For example, movement from village to small town to large city, to international destination.	
Chain migration	Migration where one member of the household first moves, later to be joined by others from the household.	Guest worker Company transfer
Bi- and multi-locality households	A household involving two or more geographical locations. One part of the household may live in a rural area (e.g. wife and children) while the other (e.g. husband) may live in a regional city or international destination. Stresses interaction and mobility between the two areas.	
Internal/international migration	Internal migration describes people on the move within a country; international migration involves crossing a recognized international border.	
Forced migration	This refers to refugees, internally displaced persons (IDPs) and asylum seekers. Refugee status is conferred on international migrants when a particular set of conditions linked to oppression and fear of persecution in one's home country are satisfied. Asylum seekers are those awaiting the award of refugee status.	Refugees

Source: Adapted from Toit, 1990; McDowell and de Haan, 1997; Widgren and Martin, 2002.

2. Migration to the LDCs

The global matrices of international migrant stocks spanning the period 1960–2010, disaggregated by gender and based primarily on the foreign-born concept (United Nations, 2011),[11] are the main source of globally comparable international migration data. As this reflects the stock of migrants living in a given foreign country, it is a measure of immigration (this is not the same as a measure of emigration, i.e. data for which both the source and destination of migration are known, which is based solely on World Bank (2011) estimates in a bilateral matrix of 212 countries).[12] The global stock of international migrants increased from 92 million in 1960 to about 214 million by 2010, with LDCs currently hosting some five per cent of the global stock of international migrants.

Between 1990 and 2010, the stock of international immigrants within LDCs grew very little. During this time, the migrant stock in the LDCs increased by four per cent compared with a global average of 27 per cent and increases of 20 per cent in other developing countries and 55 per cent in developed countries.

Refugees constitute a significant but declining share of the total number of immigrants residing in LDCs. Their share of the total migrant stock in LDCs peaked at 44 per cent in 1995 but then declined rapidly thereafter.

Refugees constitute a significant but declining share of the total number of immigrants residing in LDCs. In 2010, the number of refugees worldwide was 16.3 million, around eight per cent of the total number of international migrants. Refugees accounted for a higher share of the international migrant stock hosted in LDCs: their share of the total migrant stock in LDCs peaked at 44 per cent in 1995 but then declined rapidly thereafter, reflecting an improvement in governance structures in many African countries and a reduction in the level of conflict and political instability. The refugee population by country or territory of asylum in LDCs was 2.1 million in 2010 (see chart 6), accounting for 18 per cent of LDC immigrants.

Females represent about half of the global migrant stock, a share that has remained relatively stable over time. Compared with the worldwide distribution

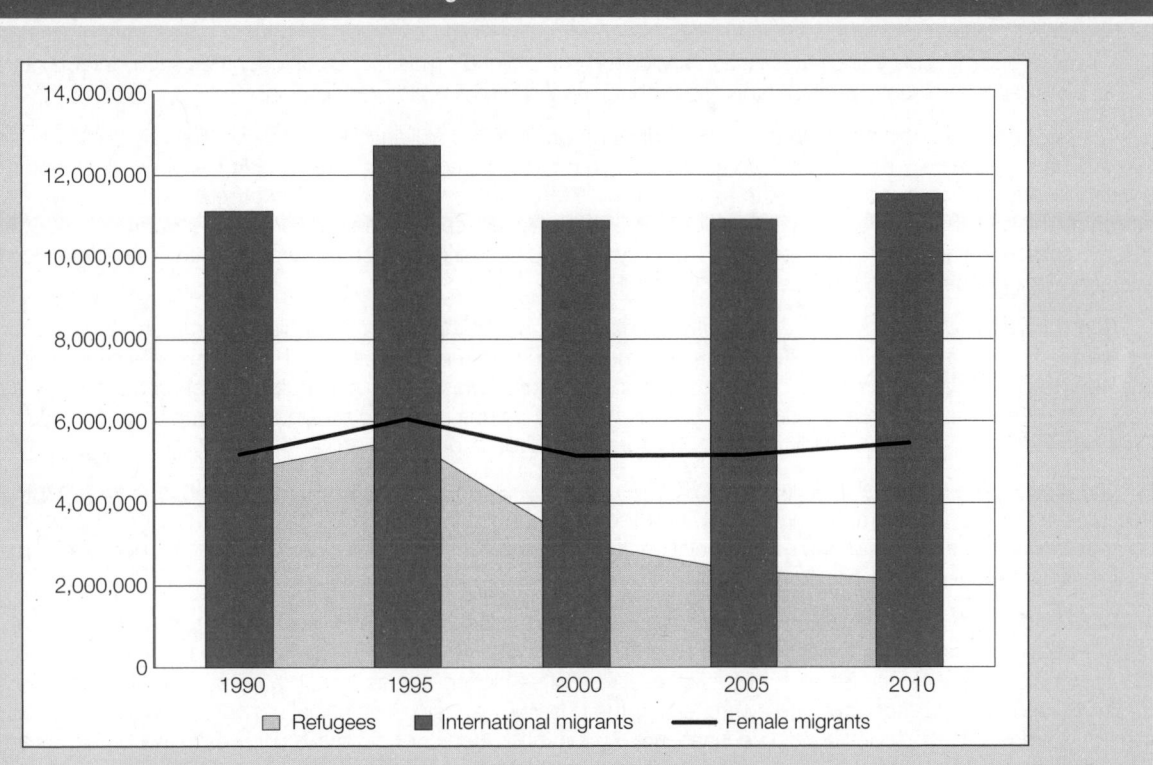

Chart 6. The international migrant stock resident within LDCs 1990–2010

Legend: Refugees — International migrants — Female migrants

Source: United Nations, Department of Economic and Social Affairs, Population Division (2011). *Trends in International Migrant Stock: Migrants by Age and Sex* (United Nations database, POP/DB/MIG/Stock/Rev.2011).

(49 per cent), the share of female migrants resident in LDCs is slightly lower, but has stayed the same at 5.4 million (47.6 per cent) over the past decade (see chart 6). The number of female migrants resident in LDCs rose by five per cent during the period 2000–2010. It also appears that the pattern of female migration is changing, as women increasingly migrate alone, rather than primarily as dependents of male migrants (United Nations, 2008). The topic of gender and LDC migration is also discussed in box 1.

The pattern of female migration is changing, as women increasingly migrate alone, rather than primarily as dependents of male migrants.

Box. 1 Gender and LDC migration

Female migration has risen mainly due to pull factors, especially growing demand for female labour in high-income countries. This can be linked to globalization, particularly the globalization of the care economy (including domestic service and health services), via the restructuring of the labour force and the generation of job opportunities specifically for women migrant workers. In Europe and North America, many migrant women find employment as domestic workers or the broader service sector. Some enter the entertainment sector, including the sex trade (Ehrenreich and Hochschild, 2003). Given that most high-income OECD households are now dual income (around 65 per cent), in 2007, an estimated six out of 10 women with dependent children (aged 0-16) were in paid employment (OECD, 2011a). This has generated an increase in the outsourcing of domestic work, creating job opportunities for LDC migrants as nannies and housekeepers. North America and Europe have ageing populations, creating more demand for elderly care and public health related services, which is increasingly being addressed through female migrant labour (Pessar and Mahler, 2003; Mahler and Pessar, 2001). A unique element of this pattern of female migration concerns what has been called "diverted mothering" — the creation of transnational families and potentially new deficits of care and nurturing in LDCs resulting from the separation of mothers and spouses from their families; often, another female member of the extended family (mother, sister, eldest daughter, etc.) takes over the care of the female migrant's children (Jones, 2008).

Migration can provide women with employment opportunities and the ability to improve their living standards in their country of origin. For example, Goldstein et al, (2000) and Essim et al., (2004) find that in Ethiopia, women migrate more than men, primarily for work-related reasons (mainly in domestic service). Migration can also provide occupational and educational opportunities for women that are often unavailable in their country of origin (Ghosh, 2009).

As previously noted, women from LDCs migrate less than men on average (particularly in Asian LDCs) due to the persistence of gender roles in most societies, whereby women have primary responsibility for child-rearing and domestic tasks. This often limits opportunities for women to migrate, with typical exceptions being young, unmarried women from households where they can be absent because of the presence of older women members, or women migrating to join their partners at the destination. Most female migrants are concentrated in low-paid care, health and light manufacturing assembly sectors.

Box. 2 Rural–urban drift and demographic factors driving LDC migration

The world's main migrations have been predominantly from rural to urban areas, and internal migration has been a major issue in development policy since the last century. Some of the world's most populous countries such as India, as well as the LDCs, are still predominantly rural, but this too is changing with more rapid urbanization.

The LDC population is projected to grow rapidly from around 850 million in 2011 to 1.2 billion by 2030 (United Nations, 2011). The economically active population (15 to 64 year old) is forecast to nearly double between 2011 and 2030. As a consequence, LDCs may need to create an estimated 170 million new jobs by 2030 in order to absorb new labour market entrants. This is a challenging task: although GDP in LDCs grew at nearly seven per cent per year during the 2000s, the rate of job creation was a mere 2.9 per cent (ILO, 2011). Most LDCs experienced jobless growth, with open unemployment at an average of six per cent during this decade (ILO, 2011).

Demographic dynamics in the LDCs appear to be sluggish and the youthful population structure is set to persist in the medium term (Valensisi and Davis, 2011). These demographic dynamics, together with high labour force participation rates, are likely to put increased pressure on domestic labour markets. Most LDCs continue to be characterized by a large rural population, with the notable exception of a few mostly small countries (Angola, Djibouti, Gambia, Liberia, Sao Tome and Principe). In 2010, less than one-third of the LDC population lived in urban areas.

The share of rural to total population in LDCs has steadily declined since 1980, and Asia has seen a particularly rapid decline since 1995. On average, annual growth of the urban population during 2000–2010 was four per cent for all LDCs, compared with 1.7 per cent for the rural population. In Africa, the figures were 4.3 per cent and 2.1 per cent respectively, as against 3.6 per cent and 1.1 per cent for Asia.

Where the incidence of migration has been recorded, the evidence is that migration is quite common, with 10 to 50 per cent of surveyed households typically having an adult migrant (World Bank, 2011b). This tends to involve young men more than other older persons and females. Migration levels are often higher from areas of low potential for farming, but much also depends on opportunity to move and awareness of the possibilities, as well as social networks and other enabling features (United Nations, 2008; McDowell and de Haan, 1997). Migration does not always imply a definitive break, as an individual often departs as part of a household livelihood strategy, in which many migrants return.

3. PATTERNS OF LDC EMIGRATION

As previously noted, the main determinants of LDC emigration may be classified as distress-push or demand-pull drivers. Distress-push emigration may be described as following from constraint-related motives (e.g. environmental degradation, poverty, displacement, conflict); whereas demand-pull emigration is driven by a desire to exploit new economic opportunities (e.g. wage differentials or employment prospects).

Emigration from LDCs grew rapidly during the period 1990–2010. In 2010, LDCs as a whole accounted for 13 per cent of global emigration stocks or approximately 3.3 per cent of the LDC population.

Chart 7 shows that emigration from LDCs grew rapidly during the period 1990–2010. With 27.5 million emigrants in 2010, LDCs as a whole accounted for 13 per cent of global emigration stocks or approximately 3.3 per cent of the LDC population (table 4). Over 2000–2010, the increase in emigrant stocks was most rapid for African LDCs.

The LDC regions where emigrants account for the highest share of population are the Pacific Island regions at 13 per cent, and Haiti in the Americas at 10 per cent. Inhabitants of island LDCs appear to have a higher propensity to emigrate than other LDCs and developing countries, mostly in the form of temporary

Table 4. LDC stock of emigrants, by regions, 1990–2010

LDC regions	Emigration stock			Regional share of LDC total emigration stock (%)			Regional emigrant stock as share of total population (%)			Percentage change in emigrant stock (%)
	1990	*2000*	*2010*	*1990*	*2000*	*2010*	*1990*	*2000*	*2010*	*2000–2010*
LDC Africa	7,676,309	9,934,059	15,183,115	47	51	55	3	3	3	53
LDC Americas	516,979	777,935	1,009,751	3	4	4	7	9	10	30
LDC Asia	7,991,115	8,521,202	11,147,518	49	44	41	4	3	4	31
LDC Pacific	87,379	121,642	136,124	1	1	0	13	14	13	12
LDC Total	16,271,782	19,354,838	27,476,508				3.2	2.9	3.3	42

Source: UNCTAD secretariat calculations based on Ratha and Shaw (2007) updated with additional data for 71 destination countries as described in World Bank (2011b).

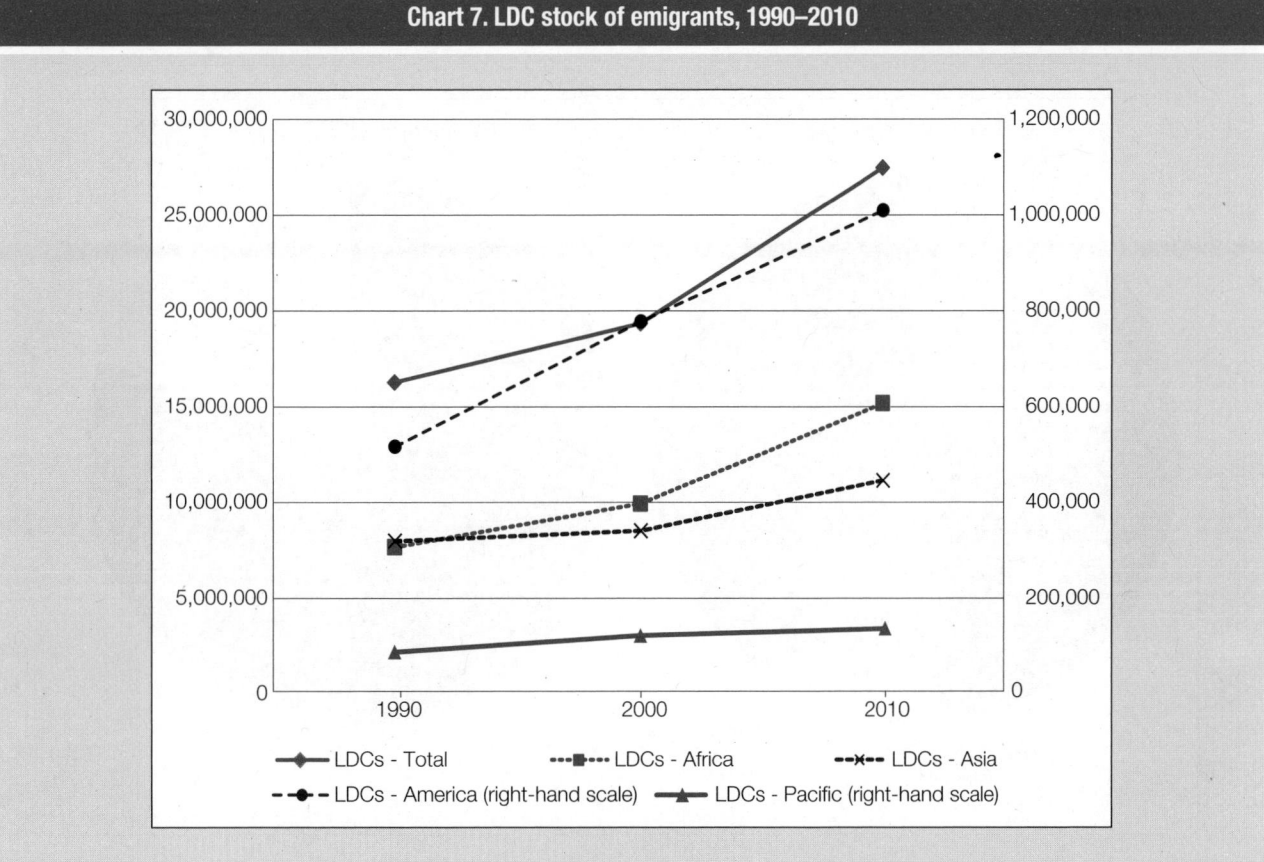

Chart 7. LDC stock of emigrants, 1990–2010

Source: UNCTAD secretariat calculations based on Ratha and Shaw (2007), updated with additional data for 71 destination countries as described in World Bank (2011b).

labour migration for work (chart 7). LDC Pacific island emigrants mainly migrate to Australia and New Zealand, both of which have initiated temporary seasonal labour schemes that attract such migrants.

The destination of emigrants from LDCs varies across regions (chart 8a). Most LDC emigrants go to South Asia, the Middle East and Africa. High migration within sub-Saharan Africa probably reflects the facts that (a) much of African migration is forced (refugee flows) and by poor people, as a result of which proximity is crucial; and (b) Africans generally face great difficulty entering other countries. Among the high-income regions, only the Gulf States have a high share of South Asians, and no country has a high share of Africans. Chart 8b shows that around 80 per cent of LDC migrants migrate within the South, as a result of which LDCs and ODCs are important countries of destination.

Globally, developed countries tend to accept skilled immigrants, but increasingly erect barriers to exclude the unskilled unless there is a high level of demand for their labour in particular sectors (e.g. agriculture or construction) (UNDP, 2009). LDC migrants tend to be younger than those from other countries, with a median age of 29 years, compared with 34 in other developing countries and 43 in the developed countries (Valensisi and Davis, 2011; Melde and Ionesco, 2010). This is closely associated with educational attainment, as the majority of emigrants who have attained at least tertiary education tend to migrate to developed countries (United Nations, 2010b). In fact, Haiti (83 per cent), Samoa (76 per cent), the Gambia (63 per cent) and Sierra Leone (53 per cent) have the highest emigration rates[13] of tertiary-educated LDC populations (World Bank, 2011a). The main LDC emigration corridors are in the South (chart 9). The main countries of emigration in 2010 were Bangladesh, with 4.9 million emigrants, and Afghanistan, with two million emigrants.

The destination of emigrants from LDCs varies across regions. Among the high-income regions, only the Gulf States have a high share of South Asians, and no country has a high share of Africans.

Chart 8. Destination of emigrants from LDCs: (a) regional breakdown, (b) high-income OECD and ODCs, 2010

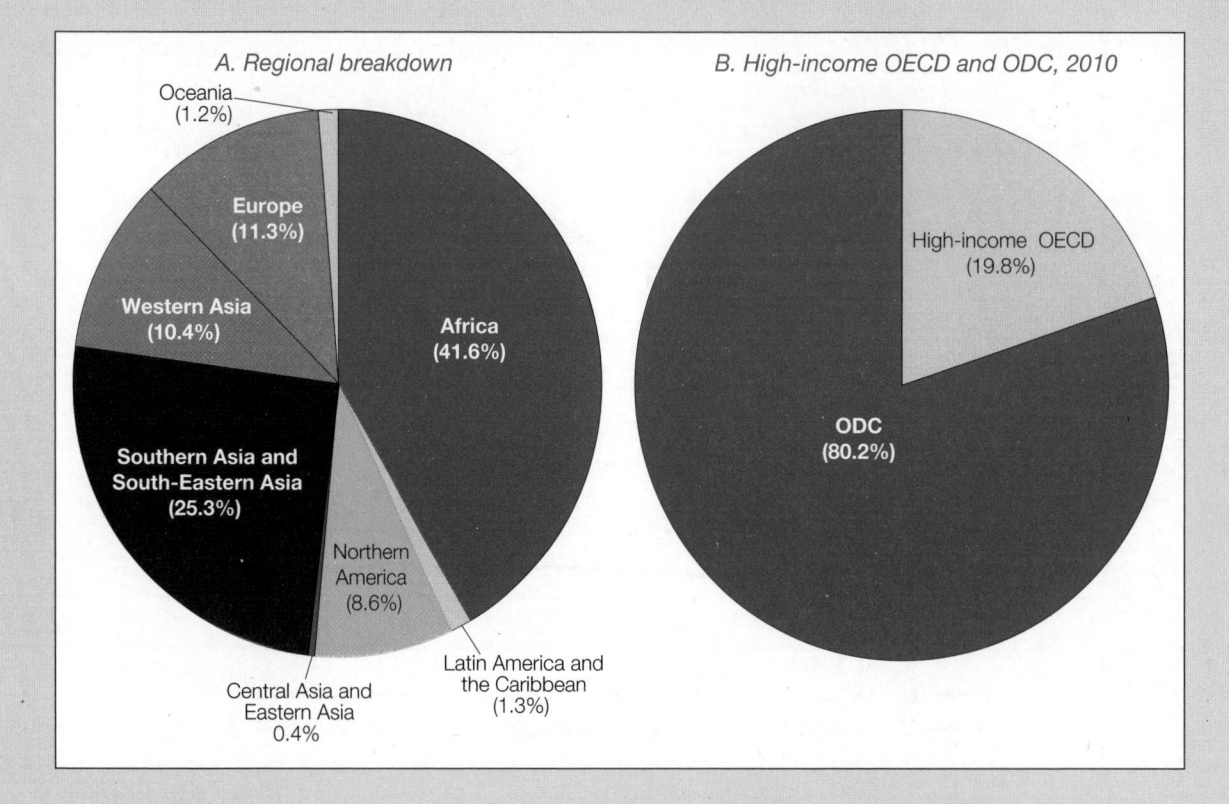

A. Regional breakdown

Oceania (1.2%)
Europe (11.3%)
Western Asia (10.4%)
Africa (41.6%)
Southern Asia and South-Eastern Asia (25.3%)
Northern America (8.6%)
Central Asia and Eastern Asia 0.4%
Latin America and the Caribbean (1.3%)

B. High-income OECD and ODC, 2010

High-income OECD (19.8%)
ODC (80.2%)

Source: UNCTAD secretariat calculations based on Ratha and Shaw (2007), updated with additional data for 71 destination countries as described in World Bank (2011b).

Note: The high-income OECD category is comprised of the United States of America, Canada and Europe.

The key determinants of LDC emigration appear to be socioeconomic circumstances, wage differentials (rural–urban as well as international), armed conflict and political unrest, along with natural disasters and climate-induced migration. Nonetheless, despite the LDCs' relative lack of productive capacities and higher average rates of poverty, they have a similar emigration rate to the global average of three per cent, which is in fact lower than the South American emigration rate.

Most LDC South–South migration tends to take place between neighbouring countries, where wage differentials are in general much smaller than in South–North migration (see chart 9). Nonetheless, despite the wage differential, the welfare and income gains from this pattern of migration are estimated to be quite significant (Ratha, 2006; Ratha and Shaw, 2007).[14]

Inhabitants of Asian and Pacific LDCs appear to have higher propensities to migrate to non-LDCs than those of African LDCs, which recorded the highest share of emigrants residing in other LDCs in 2010. Chart 10 shows that the main sources of intra-LDC migration were in sub-Saharan Africa, particularly Eritrea, the Democratic Republic of Congo and Sudan.

In 2010, the LDCs with the highest share of emigrants as a percentage of the total LDC emigrant stocks were Bangladesh (19 per cent), Afghanistan (eight per cent), Burkina Faso (six per cent) and Mozambique (four per cent). These countries were also part of the main migration corridors: Bangladesh — India, Afghanistan — Iran, Burkina Faso — Cote d'Ivoire, Yemen — Saudi Arabia and Nepal — India (table 5). Asian LDCs such as Bangladesh, Afghanistan, Yemen and Nepal tend to have India or the Middle East as the first or second country

The key determinants of LDC emigration appear to be socioeconomic circumstances, wage differentials (rural–urban as well as international), armed conflict and political unrest, along with natural disasters and climate-induced migration.

Inhabitants of Asian and Pacific LDCs appear to have higher propensities to migrate to non-LDCs than those of African LDCs.

Chart 9. Main LDC emigration corridors, 2010

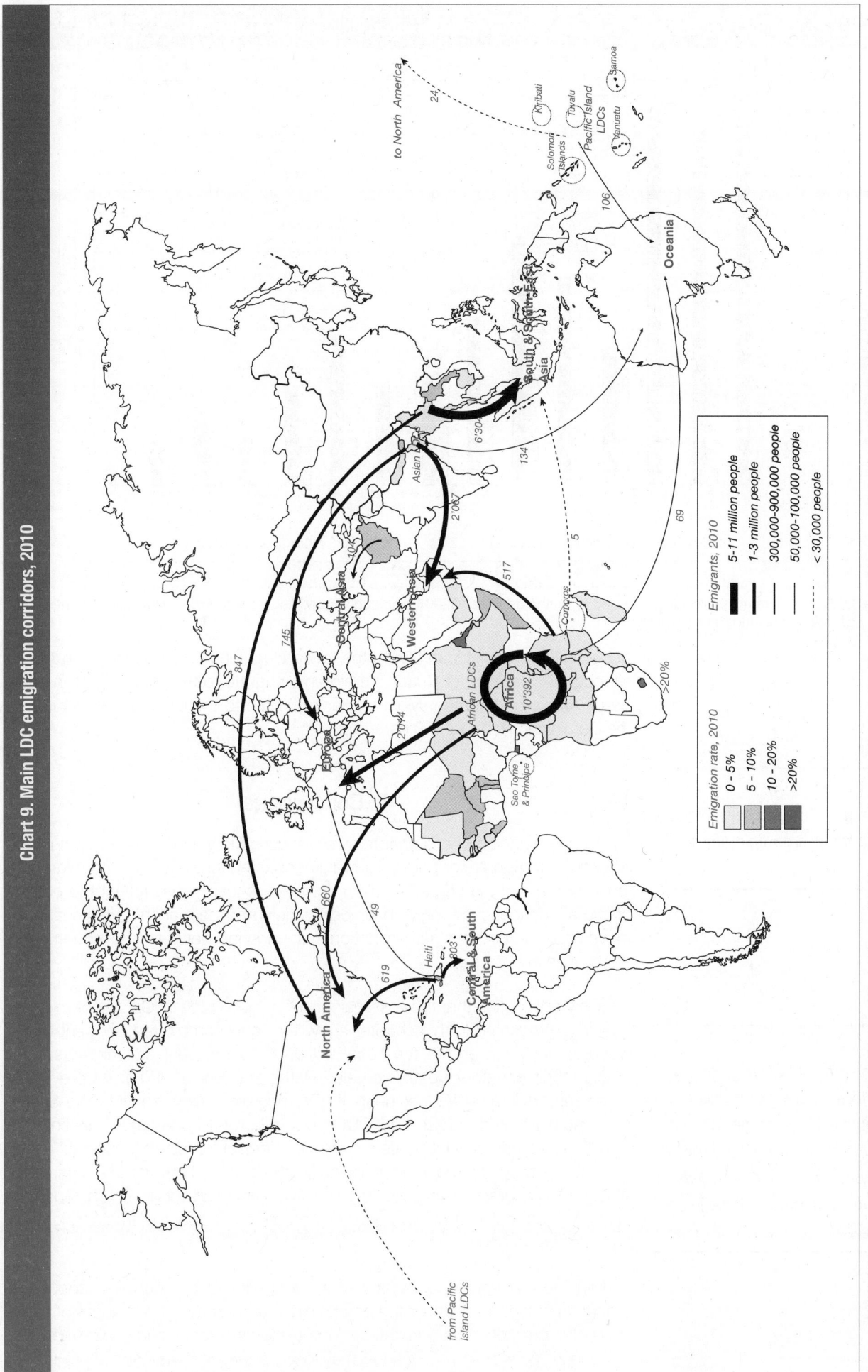

Source: UNCTAD secretariat calculations based on Ratha and Shaw (2007), updated with additional data for 71 destination countries as described in World Bank (2011b).

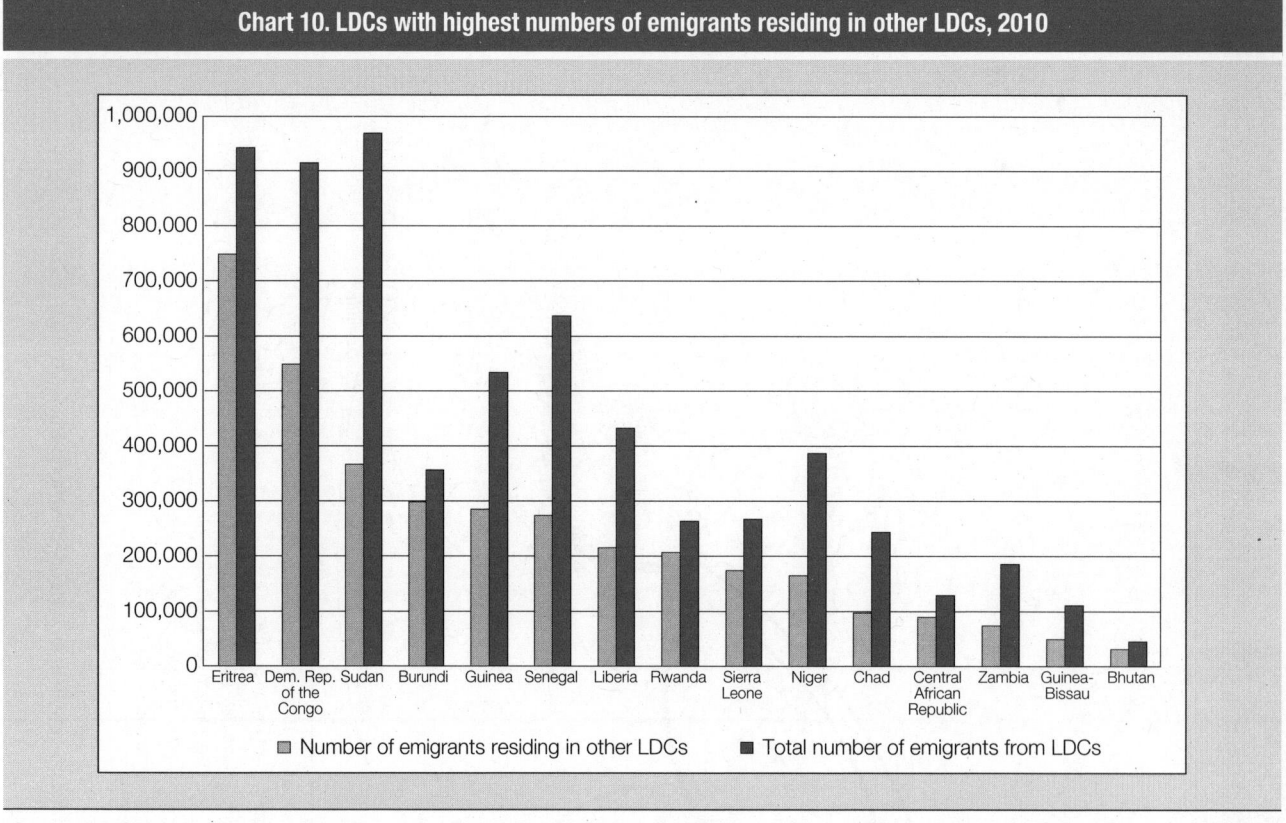

Chart 10. LDCs with highest numbers of emigrants residing in other LDCs, 2010

Legend: ▣ Number of emigrants residing in other LDCs   ■ Total number of emigrants from LDCs

Source: UNCTAD secretariat calculations, based on Ratha and Shaw (2007) updated with additional data for 71 destination countries as described in World Bank (2011b).

of destination. For African LDCs, the key emigration corridors are within Africa, although 34 per cent of Sudan's emigrants migrate to the Middle East, namely Saudi Arabia and Yemen. Most Haitians migrate to the USA (54 per cent) and the Dominican Republic (28 per cent).

4. CONCLUSIONS

At the beginning of this chapter, we discussed key migration concepts such as circular, temporary or permanent migration, step, chain and forced migration. In the context of the LDCs, circular migration concepts may reflect the pattern of migration most commonly observed, namely, non-permanent (often seasonal) movements within and across national boundaries between the countries of destination and origin.

It is worth noting that the vast majority of people in the LDCs do not migrate. The data presented in this chapter show that only some three per cent of the world's population and in the case of LDCs 3.3 per cent are migrants living outside their country of birth (see also Ratha and Shaw, 2007). As previously noted, approximately 80 per cent of LDC migrants migrate within the South, as a result of which LDCs and ODCs are important countries of destination. Moreover, as far as LDCs are concerned, cross-border migration is a key livelihood strategy for many households (Ratha et al., 2011). For example, intra-African LDC migration is significant in terms of scale and should be an important aspect of future African Union policy elaboration on labour markets, migration and refugee management.

Migration in some cases is a conscious household decision about the allocation of labour to where it earns its highest net returns, and some of these flows effectively overcome limitations in domestic insurance and capital markets. In general, economic motivations may be a strong determinant of migration;

For African LDCs, the key emigration corridors are within Africa.

Intra-African LDC migration is significant in terms of scale and should be an important aspect of future African Union policy elaboration on labour markets, migration and refugee management.

Table 5. Top 15 main emigration corridors for LDCs, 2010

Source country	Main emigration corridor			Second main emigration corridor			Third main emigration corridor			Cumulative importance of 3 main emigration corridors (%)	Total number of emigrants
	Primary emigration corridor[a]	Importance of primary corridor[b] (%)	1st country of destination	Second emigration corridor[a]	Importance of 2nd corridor[b] (%)	2nd country of destination	Third emigration corridor[a]	Importance of 3rd corridor[b] (%)	3rd country of destination		
Bangladesh	3,299,268	61	India	447,055	8	Saudi Arabia	422,325	8	Other South	77	5,384,706
Afghanistan	1,704,199	72	Iran, Islamic Republic of	215,649	9	Other South	79,444	3	Germany	85	2,350,633
Burkina Faso	1,310,892	83	Côte d'Ivoire	167,834	11	Other South	29,881	2	Niger	96	1,578,254
Mozambique	454,548	39	South Africa	159,945	14	Malawi	158,722	13	Zimbabwe	66	1,179,776
Yemen	894,109	80	Saudi Arabia	60,401	5	United Arab Emirates	58,342	5	United States	90	1,124,505
Mali	440,960	43	Côte d'Ivoire	133,464	13	Nigeria	98,799	10	Other South	66	1,013,721
Haiti	545,437	54	United States	279,216	28	Dominican Republic	73,753	7	Canada	89	1,009,432
Nepal	564,906	57	India	175,454	18	Qatar	73,154	7	Other South	83	983,156
Sudan	279,409	29	Saudi Arabia	191,103	20	Uganda	126,109	13	Yemen	62	967,980
Eritrea	458,042	49	Sudan	290,383	31	Ethiopia	90,688	10	Other South	89	942,232
Dem. Rep. of the Congo	372,964	41	Rwanda	85,476	9	Uganda	78,458	9	Congo	59	914,685
Somalia	161,179	20	Ethiopia	110,326	14	United Kingdom	109,618	13	United States	47	813,218
Uganda	531,218	70	Kenya	70,733	9	Other South	54,122	7	United Kingdom	87	758,227
Senegal	177,306	28	Gambia	91,446	14	France	81,424	13	Italy	55	636,476
Ethiopia	152,094	25	Sudan	139,693	23	United States	87,556	14	Israel	61	620,147

Source: UNCTAD secretariat calculations based on Ratha and Shaw (2007) updated with additional data for 71 destination countries, as described in the *Migration and Remittances Factbook, 2011*.

a   Denotes the number of emigrants from a source country to a particular destination country, each ranked in terms of importance as a destination for emigration.

b   Denotes the share of emigrants from a source country to a particular destination country, each ranked in terms of importance as a destination for emigration.

however, it is important to note that migration is substantially influenced by information about opportunities, networks and by social contacts that facilitate it.

As previously noted, given high rates of population and labour force growth and declining agricultural productivity, rural-to-urban migration may continue to outpace the capacity of cities to absorb large influxes of new labour. This has the potential to generate more emigration abroad, especially among youth. Indeed, it could be argued that due to the lack of employment opportunities (what the ILO terms the "decent work deficit") in LDCs, youth emigration has led to higher levels of irregular and undocumented international migration (IOM, 2008). Accordingly, for LDCs it is essential that greater emphasis be placed on creating more domestic employment and educational opportunities to upgrade skill levels in order to help check the rising tendency of irregular migration.

For LDCs it is essential that greater emphasis be placed on creating more domestic employment and educational opportunities to upgrade skill levels in order to help check the rising tendency of irregular migration.

However, migration has rapidly become a phenomenon that LDCs can no longer afford to ignore. South–South migration is also becoming more important for LDCs. For most LDCs (particularly in Africa), international migration is dominated by intraregional movements, often of refugees and seasonal (often undocumented) labour migrants. In addition, female migration is increasing and there is growing diversification of migration destinations.

A high proportion of migrants from LDCs (especially African LDCs) tend to fall into the refugee category, reflecting forced migration. As is the case with conventional economic migration, when mass forced migration occurs, there is significant loss of human and financial capital, of labour and skilled workers in the country of origin. In the case of LDCs, most of this forced migration is usually to neighbouring countries and can have damaging short-term effects, particularly in terms of strains on host resources (Lucas, 2008; Wahba and Zenou, 2011; World Bank, 2011a). Despite a declining trend, one out of five refugees worldwide still received asylum in an LDC — a disproportionate burden on national budgets and economic development that needs to be better shared with more developed countries.

Despite a declining trend, one out of five refugees worldwide still received asylum in an LDC — a disproportionate burden on national budgets and economic development that needs to be better shared with more developed countries.

Migration is increasingly an international policy priority for LDCs as well as ODCs and high-income OECD countries due to both social policy and economic concerns about managing both migrant labour flows and refugees. In the African context, for example, in July 2001 the Council of Ministers of the African Union met in Lusaka with the aim of addressing emerging migratory patterns and ensuring the integration of migration and related issues into national and regional agendas for security, stability, development and cooperation. The meeting also agreed to work towards fostering the free movement of people and strengthening intra- and inter-regional cooperation in migration matters (African Union, 2006; African Union Commission, 2004). Since 1996, both the Economic Community of West African States (ECOWAS) and the East African Community (EAC) have successfully adopted full free movement of labour conventions.

Migration is increasingly an international policy priority for LDCs as well as ODCs and high-income OECD countries due to both social policy and economic concerns about managing both migrant labour flows and refugees.

Several international initiatives and policies have also emerged around the need to develop effective migration policies on a global level. The Global Forum on Migration and Development (GFMD) has to some extent promoted international dialogue. Similarly, the Global Migration Group (GMG)[15] has played an important role in fostering better coordination and supporting the activities of Member States (for example, the collaboration between UNHCR and the International Organization for Migration in 2011 to evacuate foreign workers from Libya).

The improvement of international cooperation on migration and development in LDCs is required to optimize migrant contributions at all levels. Thus, at the bilateral and regional levels, there is a need for further progress to strengthen international cooperation.

Notes

1 In contrast, in the early 2000s, remittances and diaspora engagement were overlooked in the Brussels Programme of Action for the LDCs in 2001 and were barely mentioned in the final document of the Monterrey Consensus on Financing for Development in 2002.

2 On the analysis of economic development from the standpoint of balance of payments constrained economies refer, among others, to (Thirlwall, 2011, 1979; Chenery and Bruno, 1962; UNCTAD, 2006).

3 Over the 2000–2010 period, the investment ratio barely reached 20 per cent of GDP for both the median LDC and the weighted average of the LDC group.

4 In 2010, school enrolment rates for primary, secondary, and tertiary education were respectively 85 per cent, 32 per cent and 6 per cent in the LDCs, compared with 87 per cent, 54 per cent and 20 per cent in other developing countries.

5 Notwithstanding the recent commodity boom (2002–2008), over the past decade current account deficits in the median LDC averaged 6.5 per cent of GDP, with the LDC group as a whole posting a smaller but still negative balance (2.8 per cent).

6 The two expressions are borrowed respectively from Abdih et al. (2012) and Kapur (2004).

7 The explanation of remitting behaviour as an implicit intertemporal contract arrangement among family members goes as follows (Poirine, 1997; Brown, 1997). In a first stage, family members support the prospective migrant by covering the costs of migration (and possibly of specific human capital accumulation); expenditures which are typically paid upfront and may constitute a substantial share of his/her income. In general, the underlying "investment decision" on the part of the household may stem from the expectation of higher income streams once the migrant finds a job abroad or from the desire to diversify the sources of household income. In either case, once the migrant is settled abroad and has found a job, he/she will repay the implicit loan by transferring resources back to his/her family in the form of remittances. The enforcement of the implicit contract typically stems from family trust, solidarity and on the cost of retaliation by household and community members for breaching the agreement.

8 The importance of the concept of circular migration is clear, as it offers destination countries a steady supply of needed workers in both skilled and unskilled occupations without the requirements of long-term integration. Patterns of circular migration have the potential of providing "win-win" benefits for both countries of origin (which can benefit from the inflow of remittances while migrants are abroad and their investments and skills upon return) and countries of destination or safer legal migration).

9 It may also be the case that temporary migration is faster for South–South (IOM, 2008).

10 Transhumance migration is the seasonal movement of people with their livestock between fixed summer and winter pastures. The term is also used to denote nomadic pastoralism, the migration of people and livestock over longer distances.

11 For most countries, the definition of the stock of international migrants is the stock of foreign-born residents (close to 80 per cent of the countries), but the stock of foreign-nationals is used for some countries (close to 20 per cent of the countries). It includes refugees. The data used to estimate the international migrant stock at a particular time are obtained mainly from population censuses. The estimates are derived from the data on foreign-born population — people who have residence in one country but were born in another country. It does not account for all international migrants, as many are undocumented (illegal) and are thus not reflected in the data presented (United Nations, 2011).

12 In the World Bank data set, over one thousand census and population register records are combined to construct decennial matrices corresponding to the last five completed census rounds. It provides a comprehensive picture of bilateral global migration (i.e. the volume and rate of emigration between countries) since 1960. As previously noted, this data is available only on a decadal basis.

13 In this Report, we define the rate of emigration (or emigration rate) of a given country as the total number of emigrants expressed as a share of the total population.

14 In order to evaluate the potential gains from migration for developing countries and to illustrate key channels through which migration affects welfare, (Ratha and Shaw, 2007) undertook a model-based simulation of the economic impact of a three per cent rise in industrial countries' labour force achieved through migration from

developing countries. The assumed increase, roughly one-eighth of a percentage point a year, is close to that observed over the 1970–2000 period. The assumed rise in migration — small relative to the labour force of high-income countries but large relative to the existing stock of migrants — would generate large increases in global welfare. Migrants' real incomes roughly triple, while natives in industrial countries and those remaining in origin countries experience modest gains. By contrast, existing migrants in industrial countries experience significant losses, as they are assumed to be relatively close substitutes for the new migrants (Ratha and Shaw, 2007).

15 The Global Migration Group (GMG) is an inter-agency group bringing together heads of agencies to promote the wider application of all relevant international instruments and norms relating to migration, and to encourage the adoption of more coherent, comprehensive and better coordinated approaches to the issue of international migration.

CHAPTER

3

REMITTANCES AND THE LDCs:
MAGNITUDE, IMPACTS AND COSTS

A. Introduction

In recent years, remittances as a potential source of development finance have received greater attention from international policymakers. There is also a growing body of economic and social research highlighting the determinants, impact and significance of remittances in developing countries. In addressing these issues in an LDC context, the present chapter starts from the perspective that remittances may have multifaceted and significant impacts on recipient households, as well as at a regional and macroeconomic level. Remittances should therefore be regarded as an additional facet of LDCs' multi-pronged efforts to mobilize adequate sources of development finance.

Several empirical studies have shown that many of the effects remittances have — whether positive or negative — are contingent upon the financial, institutional and macroeconomic setting in recipient countries. Policy can therefore play a fundamental role in enhancing the developmental impact of remittances and harnessing resources for structural transformation.

Against this background, the primary objective of this chapter is to provide an evidence-based assessment of (a) current patterns of remittances to LDCs; (b) their importance for recipient LDC economies and the associated development opportunities and challenges; and (c) the transaction costs involved in remitting to LDCs. Finally, the chapter outlines some key policy issues related to remittances, which will be elaborated upon in chapter 4.

Remittances may have multifaceted and significant impacts on recipient households, as well as at a regional and macroeconomic level; they should therefore be regarded as an additional facet of LDCs' multi-pronged efforts to mobilize adequate sources of development finance.

B. The magnitude of remittances for LDCs

1. LDCs FROM A GLOBAL PERSPECTIVE

Before entering into a detailed discussion of remittance flows, a few considerations are needed about the data used in this report. The lack of systematic and reliable data invariably constrains the analysis of international migration and remittances, as openly acknowledged in the literature (World Bank 2006a, Grabel 2008, UNDP 2009, Melde and Ionesco 2010, among others). These data limitations, which are particularly pronounced in the LDC context, are discussed in detail in box 3.

Even with the caveats of data problems, the international debate increasingly recognizes that remittances constitute a sizable and relatively stable source of external financing, whose availability could prove particularly valuable for developing countries. After FDI, recorded remittances constitute the second largest external financial flow to developing countries, and their value far outstrips total ODA, although, unlike the latter, they are not necessarily directed from rich to poor countries.

The expansion of the global value of remittances accelerated markedly during the early and mid-2000s. They nearly doubled between 1990 and 2000 (chart 11) and then tripled once again in the following decade, touching $489 billion in 2011 notwithstanding the global financial crisis. Such a fast pace of growth is remarkable even when compared with corresponding trends of other financial flows.[1] Moreover, with the rate of emigration hovering around three per cent worldwide for the last 25 years, a similar boom of recorded remittances reflects not only the increase in migrant stock proceeding in tandem with demographic dynamics but also a sharp rise in the average amount remitted per migrant.[2]

The international debate increasingly recognizes that remittances constitute a sizable and relatively stable source of external financing, whose availability could prove particularly valuable for developing countries.

The global value of remittances doubled between 1990 and 2000 and then tripled once again in the following decade, touching $489 billion in 2011.

Box 3. Remittances, definitional issues and data limitations

According to the IMF's Balance of Payments and International Investment Position Manual, remittances represent a source of household income from abroad arising from the temporary or permanent movement of people to foreign economies (IMF, 2010). In line with common practice, in this chapter remittances are intended, unless otherwise specified, as the sum of three distinct items recorded in the balance of payment:

(a) *Workers' remittances*, which are recorded under the heading "current transfers" in the current account, and consist of "all current transfers in cash or in kind made or received by resident households to or from nonresident households" (IMF 2011, A5.7 page 273);[1]

(b) *Compensation of employees*, recorded under the "primary income" subcategory of the current account, and referring to "the income of border, seasonal, and other short-term workers who are employed in an economy where they are not resident and of residents employed by nonresident entities" (IMF 2011, A5.6 page 272); and

(c) *Capital transfers between households* which are reported in the capital account.

Though some empirical works focus only on the item "workers' remittances", the broader definition used here, which corresponds to IMF's notion of "personal remittances" (IMF 2011), is believed to capture more adequately the size of workers' remittances.

Leaving aside definitional issues, three main sets of problems limit the overall quality of existing remittances statistics, as openly acknowledged in the literature (World Bank, 2006a; Grabel, 2008; UNDP, 2009; Melde and Ionesco, 2010, among others). First, several countries do not report remittances data, thereby reducing the coverage of available statistics regardless of the definition of remittances used. This is the case, for instance, of the Central African Republic, the Democratic Republic of Congo, and Somalia, all of which are believed to receive significant remittance flows. As noted in Kapur 2004, these gaps in data availability refer in many instances to those countries, such as Afghanistan or Somalia, where persistent economic difficulties may render remittances even more critical to a household's livelihood and economic activity.

Second, countries reporting data sometimes fail to implement in a standardized manner the IMF guidelines concerning the classification of remittances' flows. The latter problem arises above all with the distinction between "workers' remittances" and "compensation of the employees". Although data coverage and comparability have significantly improved over the last decade, as a consequence of these persistent limitations they are still incomplete, particularly in the context of the LDCs. Another clear example of the poor data quality is the fact that the worldwide sum of remittance inflows does not match the sum of outflows: in 2009, they were respectively $416 billion and $282 billion (World Bank, 2011).[2]

Third, official statistics only record those sums which transit through formal intermediaries (banks, bureaux de change, money transfer operators, etc.); and not in-kind transfers or other informal channels such as "hawala" systems.[3] In this regard, World Bank estimates suggest that informal flows could add at least 50 per cent to the reported remittances flows, with significant variation across regions (Maimbo et al., 2003 and World Bank 2006a). This measurement problem is likely to be particularly acute in the case of LDCs, given that informal channels tend to be used disproportionately where the financial sector is either absent — as in conflict and post-conflict countries — or in any case weak (World Bank 2006a). According to Freund and Spatafora (2005), for instance, informal remittances accounted for 54 per cent of the total in Bangladesh and an astounding 80 per cent of the total in Uganda. In the same vein, Maimbo et al. (2003) place the share of unreported remittances in Sudan and Tanzania at 55 and 58 per cent, respectively.

[1] According to IMF's 2011 Balance of Payments and International Investment Position Manual (6th edition), the traditional denomination "workers remittances" is now to be replaced by "personal transfers" (A5.7 page 273).

[2] In the text below, unless otherwise specified the term "remittances" will be used to refer to "remittance inflows".

[3] While historically associated with the Middle East and South Asia, informal fund transfer systems are now widely used in the whole developing world. They go under different names in various regions: Hawala in Arab countries, Fei-Ch'ien in China, Padala in the Philippines, Hundi in India, Hui Kuan in Hong Kong, and Phei Kwan in Thailand.

In fact, all regions of the world have witnessed significant expansions in remittance receipts (chart 12), with generalized acceleration in the last decade.[3] The increase in global remittances is chiefly driven by the surge of inflows to developing countries, which include many of the world's largest remittances recipients. Indeed, since remittance inflows to transition economies and developing countries alike — whether LDCs or non-LDCs — have grown at a much faster rate in the past two decades than those directed to developed economies, the developed economies' share of world remittances has been steadily declining (chart 13). At present, developed countries receive approximately 25 per cent of the world's total remittances, down from 50 per cent of the total in the early 1990s. Conversely, developing countries excluding LDCs account for upwards of 60 per cent of the total, while LDCs and transition economies receive roughly six per cent each.

The increase in global remittances is chiefly driven by the surge of inflows to developing countries. The fallout of the global financial crisis appears to have reinforced this prominence.

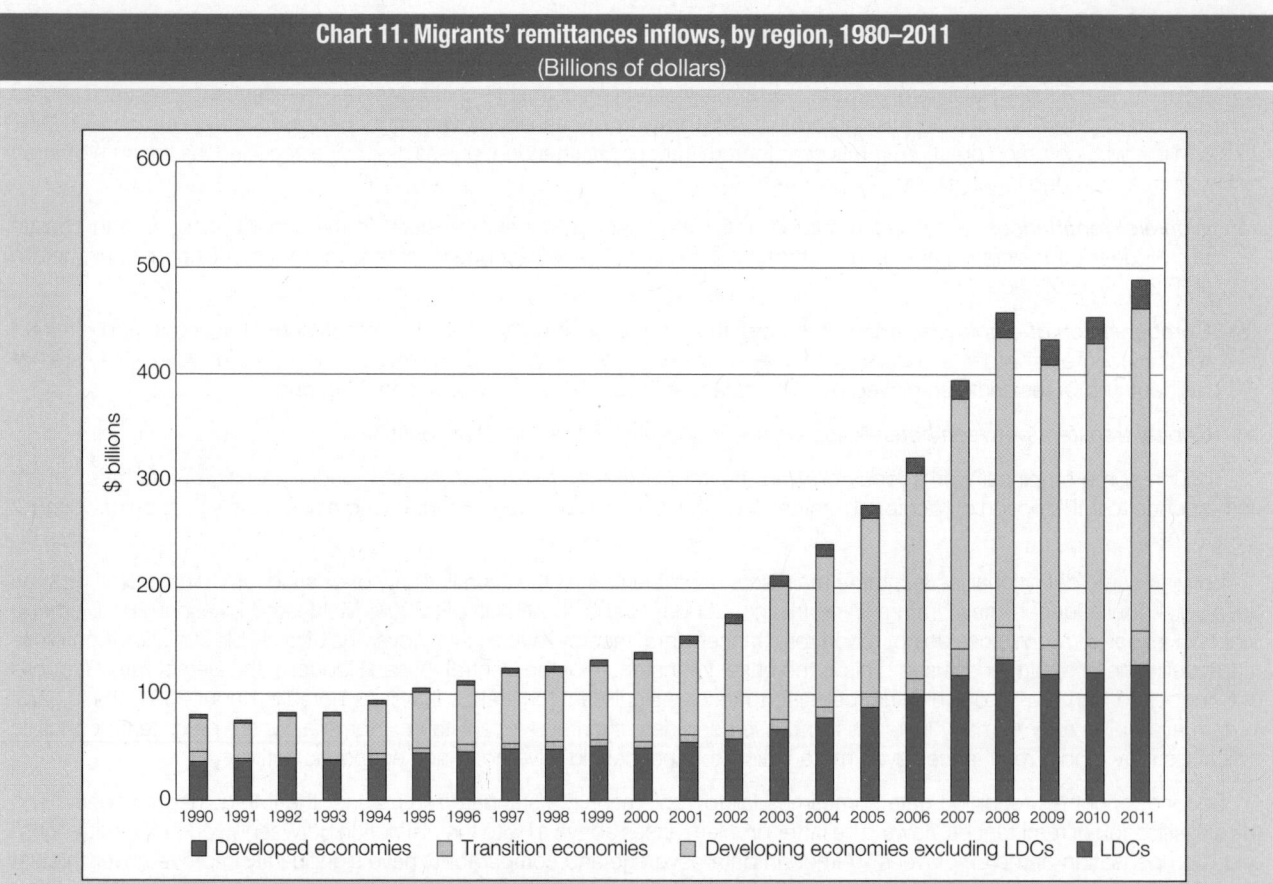

Chart 11. Migrants' remittances inflows, by region, 1980–2011
(Billions of dollars)

600
500
400
300
200
100
0
$ billions
1990 1991 1992 1993 1994 1995 1996 1997 1998 1999 2000 2001 2002 2003 2004 2005 2006 2007 2008 2009 2010 2011
Developed economies
Transition economies
Developing economies excluding LDCs
LDCs

Source: UNCTAD secretariat calculations, based on UNCTADstat database.

Chart 12. Growth rate of remittances receipts, by decade and region
(Percentage)

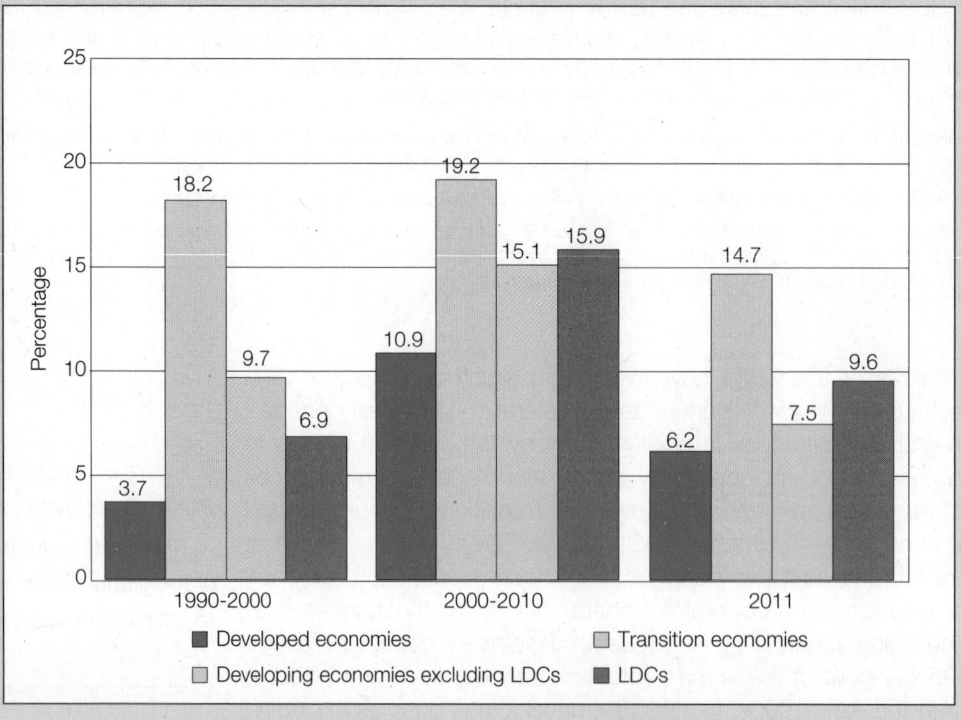

25
20
15
10
5
0
Percentage
3.7
18.2
9.7
6.9
10.9
19.2
15.1
15.9
6.2
14.7
7.5
9.6
1990-2000
2000-2010
2011
Developed economies
Transition economies
Developing economies excluding LDCs
LDCs

Source: UNCTAD secretariat calculations, based on UNCTADstat database.

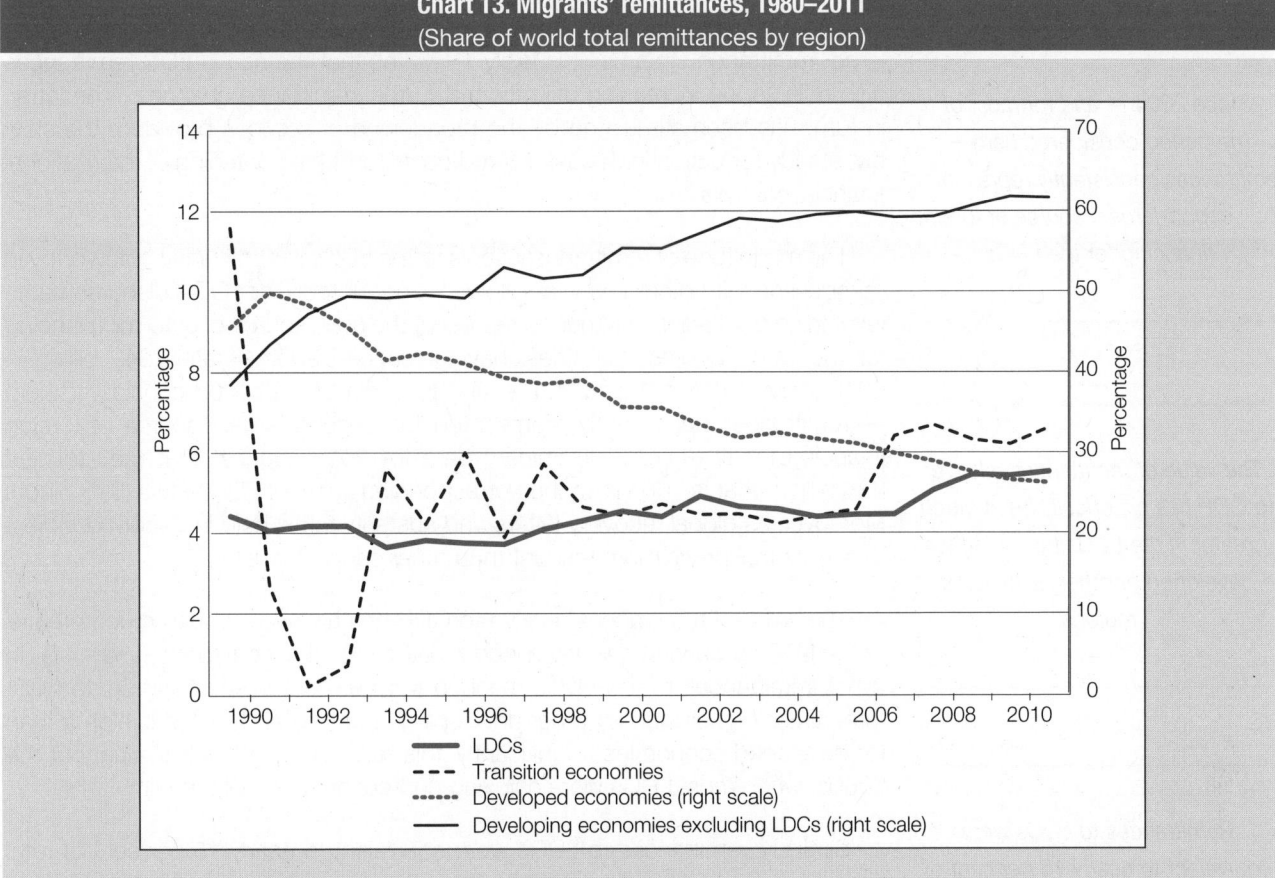

Chart 13. Migrants' remittances, 1980–2011
(Share of world total remittances by region)

Legend:
— LDCs
- - - Transition economies
····· Developed economies (right scale)
— Developing economies excluding LDCs (right scale)

Source: UNCTAD secretariat calculations, based on UNCTADstat database.

The fallout of the global financial crisis appears to have reinforced this prominence of developing countries. Remittances to LDCs continued their upward trend notwithstanding the global recession, albeit at a much slower pace, while inflows to other developing countries, as well as transition economies, suffered a slump in 2009 but quickly rebounded. Conversely, three years after the onset of the crisis, remittances inflows to developed economies remain significantly below their pre-crisis peak.

In addition, it is likely that the burgeoning importance of developing countries with respect to global remittances is even more pronounced than official figures indicate. World Bank estimates suggest that informal flows could add at least 50 per cent to reported remittances flows, and developing countries are likely to account for the bulk of these unreported transfers (World Bank 2006a).

With regard to the LDCs, remittance receipts climbed from $3.5 billion in 1990 to $6.3 billion in 2000, subsequently accelerating further to touch nearly $27 billion in 2011. A number of concurring factors explain such a rapid surge, especially when the notorious limitations of remittance data are taken into consideration (see box 2). The boom in LDC remittances partly reflects the steady increase in the stock of emigrants originating from LDCs, from 16 million people in 1990 to 19 million in 2000, and as many as 27 million in 2010 (i.e. a 42 per cent increase in the stock of LDC emigrants during the last decade). In part, it may also follow from a gradual rise in the importance of "economic migration" (especially to fast-growing developing countries) and since 1995 a corresponding decline in the number of refugees and forced migrants, who tend to remit much lower sums. In addition to these factors, as the number of LDCs reporting remittance data has grown from 22 in the year 1980 to 39 since 2006, the increase in total remittances also depends, at least to some extent, on the improved quality of the data.[4] Nonetheless, the average amount remitted by each

Remittance receipts to the LDCs climbed from $3.5 billion in 1990 to $6.3 billion in 2000, subsequently accelerating further to touch nearly $27 billion in 2011.

LDC emigrant also appears to have increased over the period considered. This may be partly due to gradual improvements in migrants' earnings translating into larger remittance streams; it is likely, however, that the rise in LDC remittances also reflects the increasing utilization of formal remittance channels. The latter, in turn, has been stimulated by the broadening of services provided, the slow but steady reduction in the associated costs, and the tightening of international financial controls.[5]

The magnitude of remittance inflows to the LDCs is particularly noteworthy in comparison with other financial inflows.[6] Undoubtedly, net ODA disbursements (excluding debt relief) continue to represent the main source of external financing for the world poorest countries, having reached approximately $42 billion in 2010 (chart 14). Yet since 2004 — and for most of the period considered here — remittances consistently represented the second-largest source of foreign financing for the LDCs. Preliminary data for 2011 suggest that they totalled $26 billion, that is, 1.8 times the corresponding value of FDI inflows ($15 billion) Moreover, as global recovery falters and austerity takes hold in donor countries, they may well prove more resilient than other capital flows.

The value of remittances relative to GDP has historically been much greater in the LDCs than in either developed or other developing regions (chart 15). In 2010, remittances to the LDCs reached 4.4 per cent of their aggregate GDP, three times higher than for other developing countries and 14 times higher than for developed economies. Significantly, this ratio remained high throughout the 2000s, when most LDCs were enjoying unprecedented GDP growth.[7]

Similarly, remittances to LDCs were equivalent to nearly 15 per cent of total export revenues in 2011, more than three times as much as in other developing countries (chart 16). Most of the decline in the trend for LDCs took place in the 1990s, while the ratio between remittances and total export revenues remained broadly constant in the 2000s. Thus, the recent dynamics of recorded remittances have roughly paralleled those of exports of goods and services, notwithstanding the well-known "commodity boom" and the eruption of the global crisis.

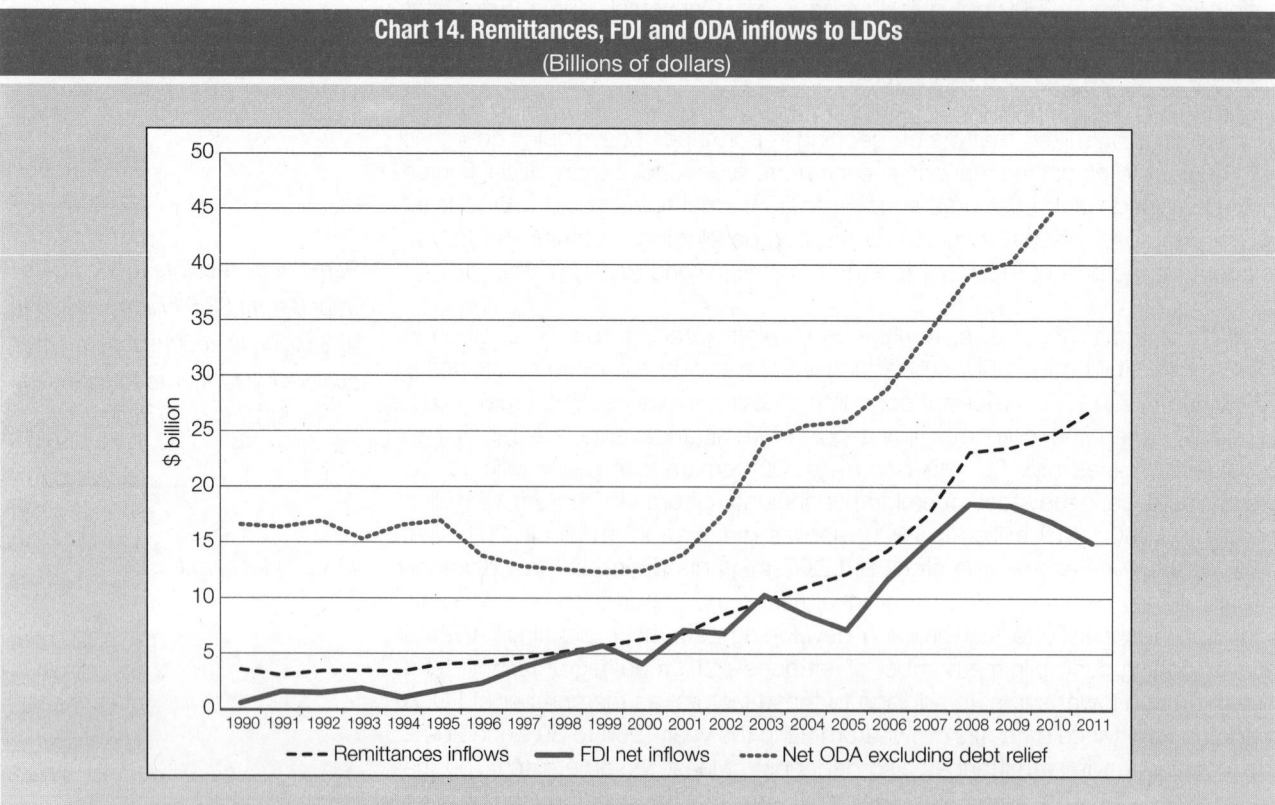

Chart 14. Remittances, FDI and ODA inflows to LDCs
(Billions of dollars)

Source: UNCTAD secretariat calculations, based on UNCTADstat, *World Development Indicators,* and OECD-DAC online databases.

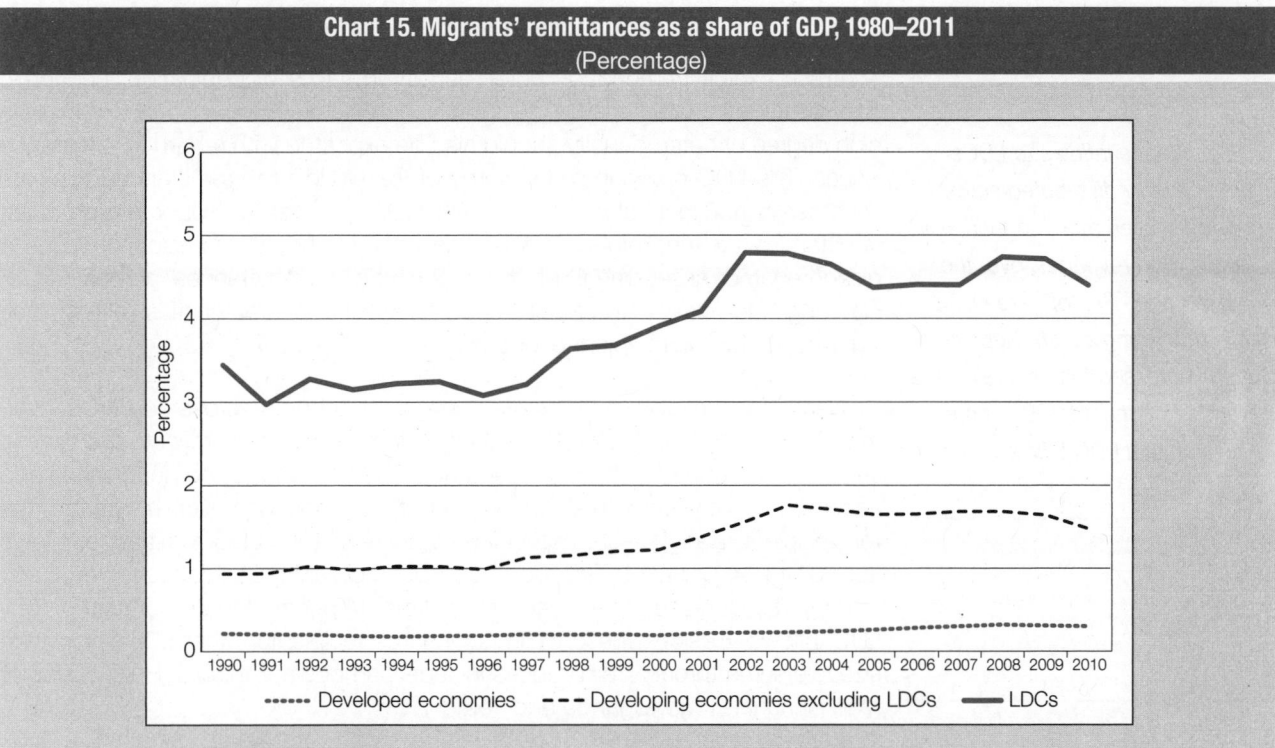

Chart 15. Migrants' remittances as a share of GDP, 1980–2011
(Percentage)

Source: UNCTAD secretariat calculations, based on UNCTADstat database.

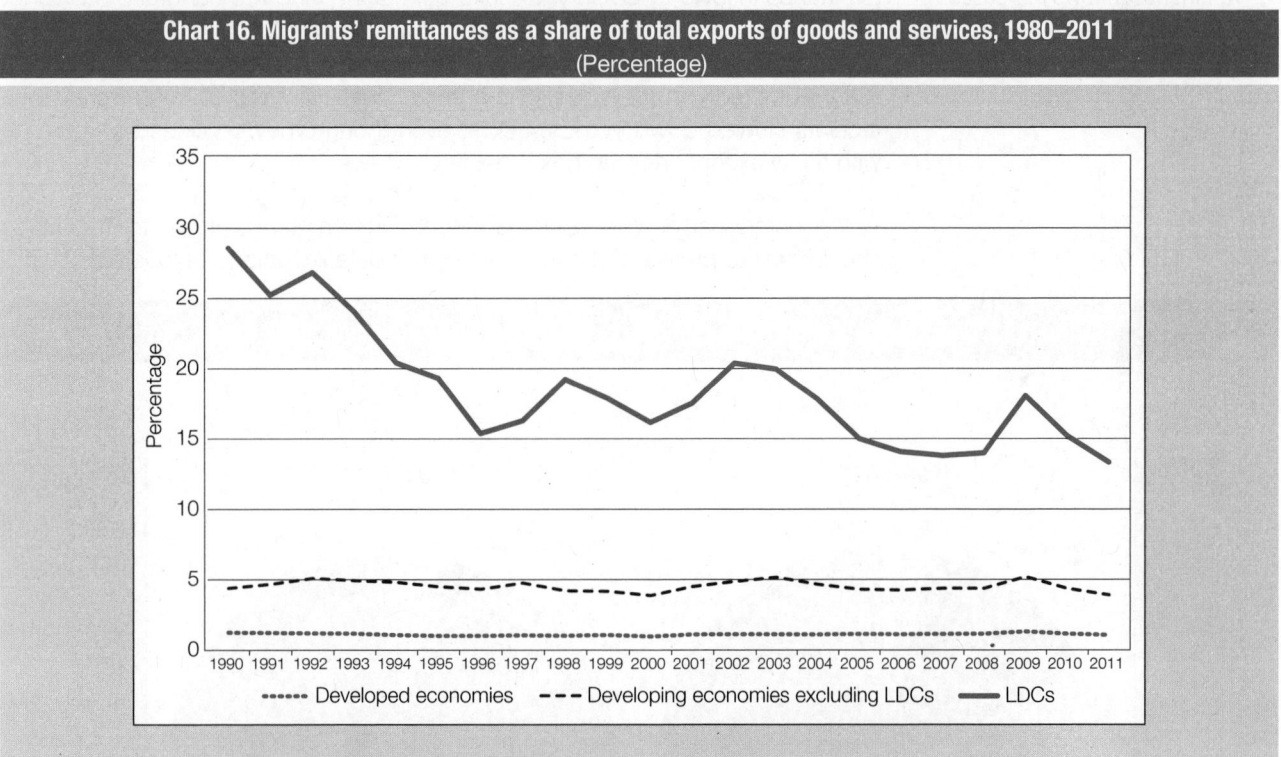

Chart 16. Migrants' remittances as a share of total exports of goods and services, 1980–2011
(Percentage)

Source: UNCTAD secretariat calculations, based on UNCTADstat database.

Although LDC remittances form a relatively small share of the global total, they play a disproportionately important role in LDCs compared with other economies (Ratha 2003, IMF 2005). Remittances had become an important means of LDC integration into the world economy even during the period when they were relatively marginalized in terms of world trade and investment flows. Currently, while LDCs represent 12 per cent of global population, their contribution to world GDP and exports is only one per cent and their share of global FDI is just under three per cent, yet they account for six per cent of global cross-border remittances.

2. Remittances across LDC economies

LDCs exhibit tremendous heterogeneity in terms of population, economic size, structural characteristics, geography and historical legacies; accordingly, a high degree of heterogeneity should also be expected with regard to remittance issues. The LDC group includes some of the world's top remittance recipients (whether in nominal value or relative to GDP), as well as countries for which remittances are negligible. Against this background, this section provides a disaggregated assessment of the magnitude of remittances across LDCs, clarifying the extent to which country-specific characteristics affect their significance for the recipient economy.

Remittance inflows to LDCs are unevenly distributed across countries, even more so than FDI and export revenues, over the last decade. The top three LDC recipients (Bangladesh, Nepal and Sudan) increased their overall share from 44 per cent to 66 per cent of total LDC inflows.

Remittance inflows to LDCs are unevenly distributed across countries, even more so than FDI and export revenues, a fact which partly reflects the varying size of each country's stock of emigrants. Chart 17 shows the persistence and accentuation of skewed distribution over the last decade. Over this period, the top recipient, Bangladesh, expanded its share of total LDC remittance inflows from 31 to 44 per cent. The top three LDC recipients (Bangladesh, Nepal and Sudan) also increased their overall share from 44 per cent to 66 per cent of total LDC inflows. Besides these well-known large recipients, other LDCs obtaining sizeable sums through remittances include Cambodia, Ethiopia, Haiti, Lesotho, Mali, Senegal, Togo, Uganda and Yemen.

In all but a handful of LDCs remittance inflows increased markedly over the last decade.

Notwithstanding the uneven distribution, the sustained dynamism of remittance inflows to LDCs was quite general. In all but a handful of LDCs for which data are available, remittance inflows increased markedly over the last decade (chart 18), growing at an annual average of 15 per cent in the median LDC. Admittedly, in the wake of the global financial crisis of 2009, remittance receipts slowed down in most LDCs, even though they continued to increase with a few exceptions (see box 4 below).

As noted earlier, the sustained boom in remittance flows to the LDCs should be interpreted with caution in light of data limitations.[8] Nonetheless, it is

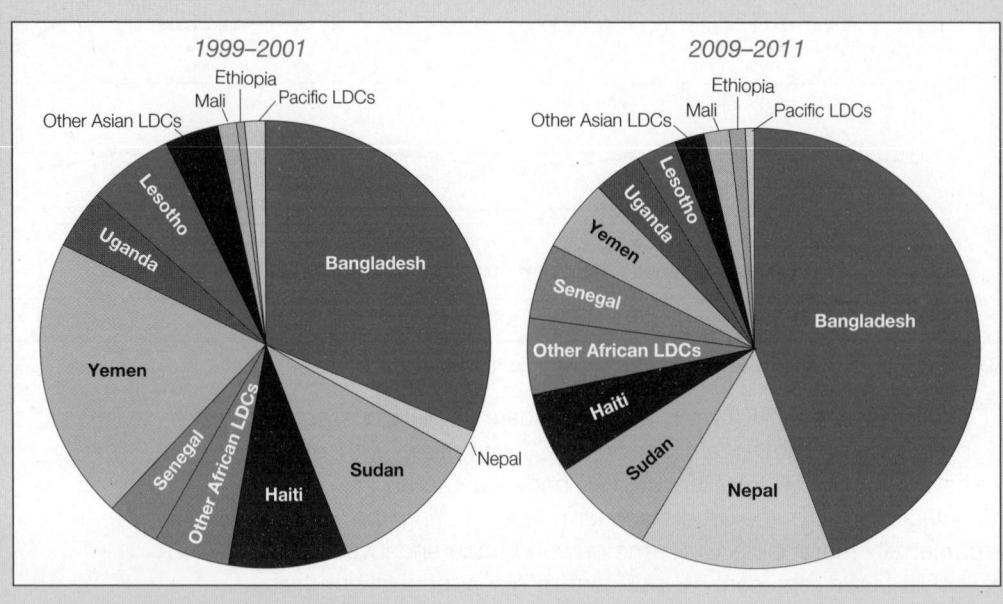

Chart 17. Distribution of remittances inflows across LDCs, 1999-2001 and 2009–2011

Source: UNCTAD secretariat calculations, based on UNCTADstat database.

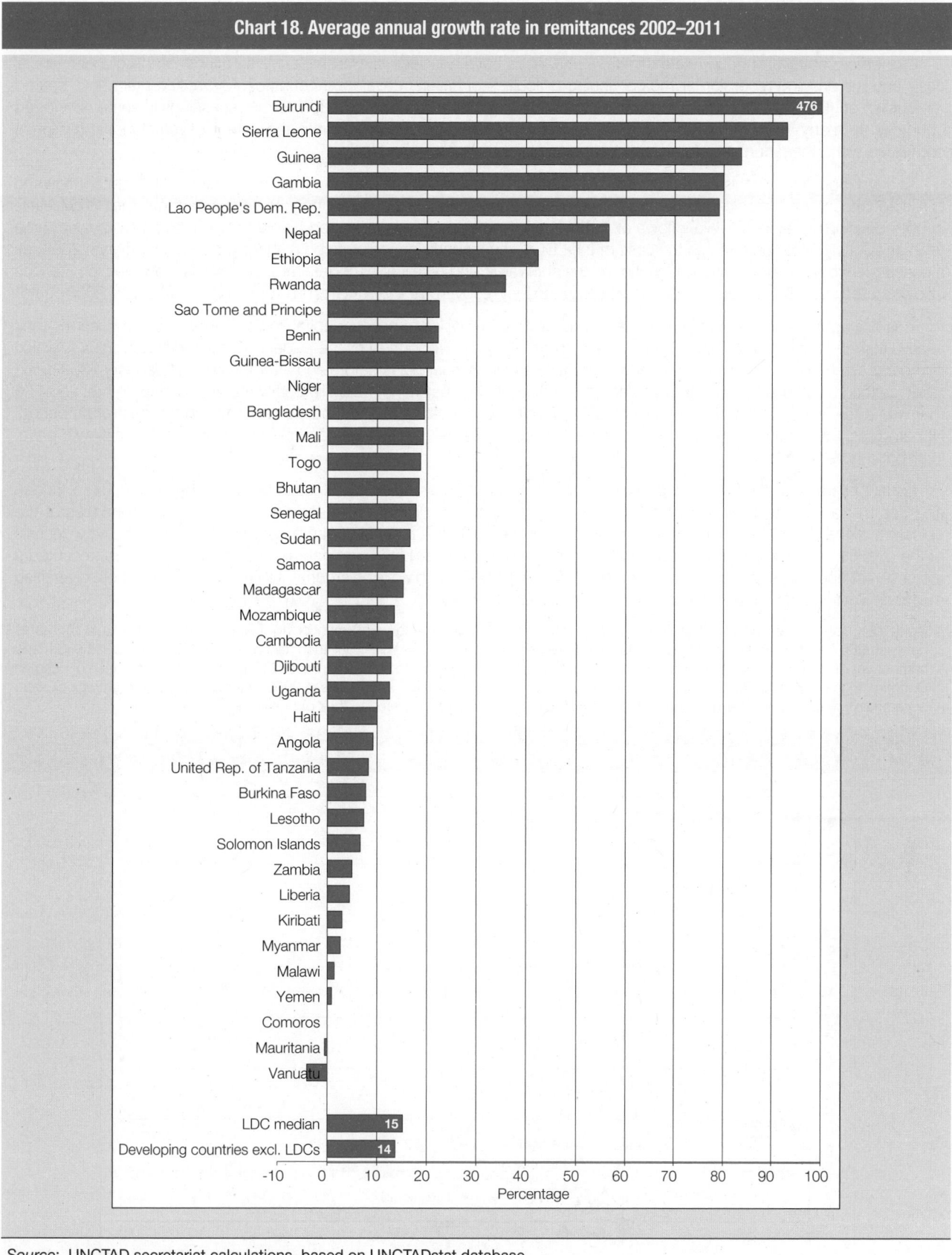

Chart 18. Average annual growth rate in remittances 2002–2011

Source: UNCTAD secretariat calculations, based on UNCTADstat database.

noteworthy that remittances to LDCs have also increased in per capita terms, despite rapid demographic dynamics in the recipient countries. On a per capita basis, recorded remittance flows to the LDCs rose from an average of $7 in 1990 to nearly $30 in 2010, with a doubling of this quantity since 2005. Table 6 shows that a rising trend in per capita remittance receipts since 1990 holds for the overwhelming majority of the LDCs. It also reveals that remittances represent a sizeable inflow of resources relative to GDP per capita, not only in

Box 4. Remittances and the global financial crisis

Like other capital and trade-related flows, remittances have not been spared the adverse effects of the global financial crisis and the ensuing recession or the continuing difficulties of several developed countries. Migrant workers have shared the burden of gloomy labour market conditions, with faltering global recovery and double-dip recessions in some developed countries. In many ways, however, the fallout of the crisis has provided insight into the extent of remittances' resilience compared with other sources of foreign exchange, and the reasons behind it.

To shed more light on this aspect, box table 1 compares recent trends, pre- and post-crisis, for private capital inflows to LDCs and to low- and middle-income countries (LMICs). Interestingly, in 2010, remittances were well above their 2007 levels in both developing regions, while inflows of FDI and portfolio investments remained below their corresponding value three years previously. More precisely, in the case of the LDCs, remittances indeed suffered a sharp growth slowdown in 2009, as a consequence of the downturn, but continued their upward trend, albeit at a modest rate. For LMICs, however, remittances inflows stalled in 2009 but picked up one year later, when they recovered the ground lost and actually surpassed the 2008 peak.[1]

This distinct behaviour of remittances, as opposed to other types of private capital flows, stands out and confirms their relative resilience to shocks. With regard to LDCs, this finding is corroborated by the evidence depicted in box chart 1, which compares three-year growth rates in remittances inflows to individual LDCs before and after the crisis (1 January 2009 being taken as the cut-off point). As a matter of fact, the overwhelming majority of LDCs lie below the red 45-degree line, showing that with a few exceptions the expansion of LDCs' remittances receipts has indeed slowed down in the post-crisis period. Nonetheless, even in the post-crisis triennium, the value of migrants' remittances continued to climb, albeit at a slower pace, in all but a dozen LDCs.

Equally interesting, countries whose remittances were worst hit by the crisis (Ethiopia, Guinea, Liberia, Sao Tome, Sudan and Zambia) appear to be those whose diaspora communities are largely concentrated in developed economies at the epicentre of the crisis (United States, France, United Kingdom). In this respect, it can be argued that, given the very genesis of the global financial crisis, the predominantly South–South nature of LDC migration and remitting channels represented a factor of resilience. This finding is consistent with (UNCTAD, 2010a) and with the argument that countries with more diversified migration destinations are likely to have more resilient remittances.

[1] Incidentally, the different behaviour of FDI and portfolio investment flows is also worth mentioning. FDI inflows rose at double-digit rates between 2007 and 2008, notwithstanding financial distress in developed economies, but then fell sharply both in LDCs and LMICs, and had not yet recovered their peak level by 2010. Conversely, the notorious flight to safety manifested itself right after the collapse of Lehman Brothers, triggering immediate outflows of portfolio investments from both LDCs and LMICs in 2008. Although by 2010 both regions were once again witnessing positive inflows of portfolio investments, neither had recovered to their pre-crisis level.

Box chart 1. Remittances to LDCs before and after the global recession

Source: UNCTAD secretariat calculations, based on UNCTADstat database.
Note: Data for Bhutan start in 2007.

Box 2 (contd.)

Box table 1. Private capital inflows in times of crisis (Value in 2007=100)					
	Type of private capital flow	2007	2008	2009	2010
To LDCs	Remittances	100	132.5	135.1	141.7
	FDI net inflows	100	116.5	112.6	92.6
	Portfolio equity, net inflows	100	-101.8	-8.2	82.9
To LMICs	Remittances	100	116.4	110.3	116.9
	FDI net inflows	100	116.6	74.6	94.9
	Portfolio equity, net inflows	100	-40.1	82.1	97.5

Source: UNCTAD secretariat calculations based on *World Development Indicators* online database.
LMIC = Low- and middle-income countries.

Table 6. Remittances inflows to LDCs, 1990–2010 (Decreasing rank in 2010)					
	Current $ per capita				Share of GDP per capita 2010 (%)
	1990	*2000*	*2005*	*2010*	
Samoa	265.73	254.89	609.90	783.51	23.44
Lesotho	261.03	243.44	292.16	343.53	35.03
Haiti	8.56	66.86	105.50	147.48	24.07
Nepal	..	4.57	44.42	115.79	21.65
Senegal	19.62	24.56	72.55	108.26	10.48
Kiribati	71.60	83.32	76.10	88.71	6.04
Bangladesh	7.40	15.18	30.69	72.97	10.88
Gambia	10.35	10.79	39.44	66.94	11.56
Yemen	125.39	72.67	62.12	62.44	4.34
Togo	7.33	7.14	35.60	55.26	10.53
Djibouti	..	16.79	31.98	36.73	2.86
Sudan	2.34	18.74	26.45	32.60	1.79
Guinea-Bissau	0.98	6.47	14.55	31.76	5.89
Mali	12.33	6.48	13.45	28.38	4.74
Benin	21.17	13.36	22.63	28.03	3.78
Uganda	..	9.83	11.32	27.36	5.37
Vanuatu	56.00	187.30	24.14	26.82	0.91
Cambodia	..	9.68	14.95	22.71	2.85
Comoros	22.69	21.33	18.66	16.33	2.22
Sao Tome and Principe	2.67	3.29	9.83	12.09	0.94
Sierra Leone	0.01	1.72	0.47	9.80	2.79
Rwanda	0.37	0.82	2.27	9.71	1.82
Liberia	..	..	10.01	7.87	3.60
Bhutan	..	..	..	7.80	0.38
Lao People's Democratic Republic	2.60	0.12	0.14	6.59	0.63
Guinea	3.12	0.14	4.60	6.05	1.42
Burkina Faso	14.98	5.48	3.99	5.77	1.11
Niger	1.78	1.32	5.11	5.67	1.59
Mozambique	5.20	2.02	2.84	5.64	1.38
Ethiopia	0.10	0.81	2.34	4.16	1.28
Zambia	..	..	4.62	3.34	0.27
Solomon Islands	..	10.58	15.25	3.10	0.26
Myanmar	0.15	2.30	2.82	2.77	0.32
United Republic of Tanzania	..	0.24	0.50	0.55	0.11
Mauritania	6.87	0.76	0.66	0.55	0.05
Madagascar	0.70	0.73	0.61	0.48	0.11
Angola	..	0.29	0.42	0.47	0.01
Burundi	..	..	0.01	0.43	0.25
Malawi	..	0.07	0.07	0.06	0.02
LDCs	**7.01**	**9.54**	**16.36**	**29.57**	**4.01**

Source: UNCTAD secretariat calculations, based on UNCTADstat database.

small economies such as Samoa, Lesotho, Kiribati, Gambia or Djibouti but also in large recipient countries.

As evident from chart 19, whether in relation to GDP (panel A) or to export earnings (panel B), remittances play a prominent role in the median LDC, accounting for as much as 2.1 per cent of GDP and 8.5 per cent of export earnings, as compared with 1.6 per cent and 4.5 per cent, respectively, for other developing countries. This prominence is noticeable for an array of LDCs,

Chart 19. Remittances as a share of GDP and exports of goods and services, 1998–2011
(Percentage)

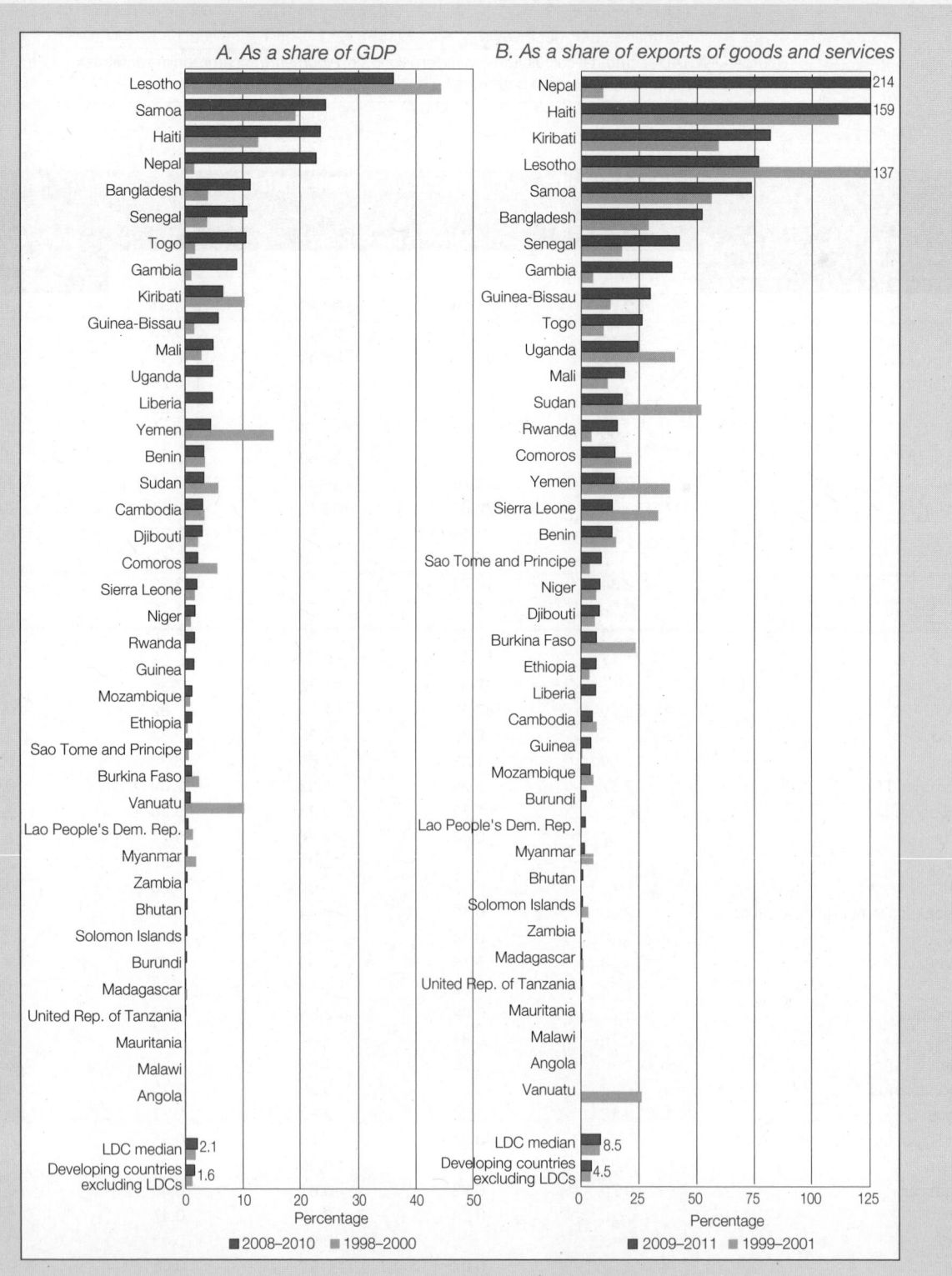

Source: UNCTAD secretariat calculations, based on UNCTADstat database.

ranging from small economies like Lesotho or Samoa — where remittances represent over 20 per cent of GDP — to traditionally large recipients such as Nepal and Haiti, where they largely exceed export earnings.

For a number of LDCs, remittances constitute a key source of foreign financing (chart 20). Over 2008–2010, recorded remittances exceeded both ODA and FDI inflows in nine LDCs (Bangladesh, Haiti, Lesotho, Nepal, Samoa, Senegal, Sudan, Togo and Yemen). In addition, remittances surpassed FDI but not ODA in another eight LDC economies (Benin, Burundi, Comoros, Ethiopia, Gambia, Guinea-Bissau, Kiribati and Uganda).

Whereas by their very nature remittances are distinct from other international financial flows, they clearly play a significant role in providing foreign exchange for a large number of LDC countries. It is therefore important that LDC development strategies take full account of the relevance of these flows of resources, of their intrinsic characteristics, and of their underlying potential.

Whether in relation to GDP or to export earnings, remittances play a prominent role for an array of LDCs, and constitute a key source of foreign financing; over 2008–2010, they exceeded both ODA and FDI inflows in nine LDCs and they surpassed FDI but not ODA in another eight LDC economies.

Chart 20. Remittances inflows to LDCs compared with other capital flows
(2008–2010 period average)

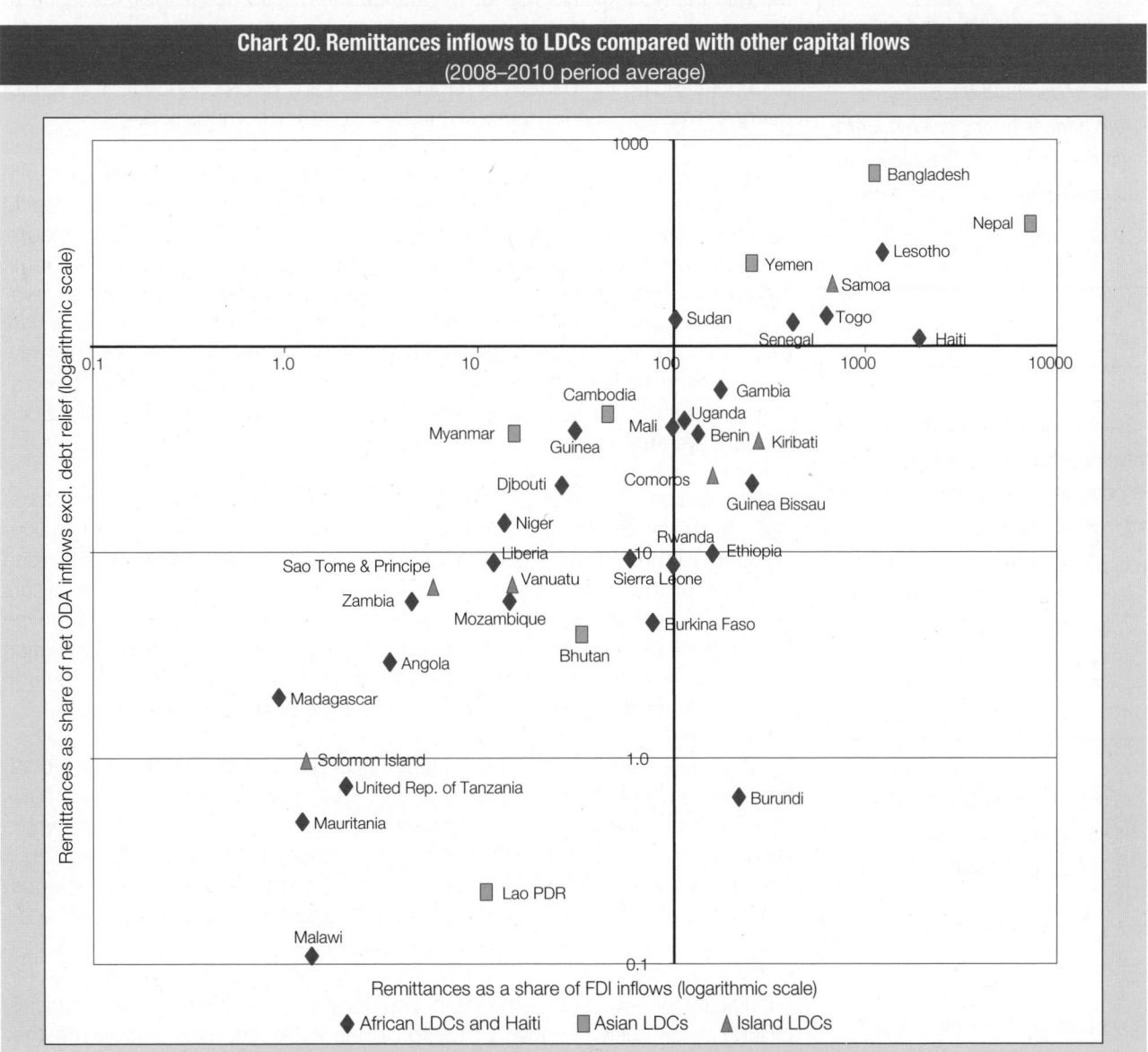

Source: UNCTAD secretariat calculations, based on UNCTADstat, *World Development Indicators,* and OECD-DAC online databases.

3. REGIONAL PATTERNS AND REMITTANCE CORRIDORS

The historical context (for example colonialism) and the "geography" of remittances represent additional elements from both the analytical and the policymaking point of view. A number of reasons explain this relevance. First, geographical and cultural proximity is one of the key determinants of migration costs, which in turn affect the size of migrant stocks from any given country to another. As a consequence, proximity factors, coupled with differences in economic development and labour market conditions in the origin and destination countries, concur to determine the size of bilateral remittance flows. Second, in the LDC context, proximity factors appear to influence the cost of remitting and possibly also the choice of channel for sending money back home, thereby affecting the amount of foreign exchange ultimately available to the receiving economy. Third, bilateral exchange rate movements, which are contingent upon the precise pattern of remittances either from or to any given country, may also determine variations in remittance receipts. Similarly, the geographical distribution of remittances may also affect their resilience to idiosyncratic shocks, to the extent that business cycles in the country of origin and in the destinations are not closely correlated.[9] This highlights the importance of understanding the pattern of remittances to any given country (in the light of geographical and cultural factors) and their currency composition.

LDC development strategies should take full account of the relevance of these flows of resources, of their intrinsic characteristics, and of their underlying potential.

South–South flows are particularly important for LDCs, consistent with the fact that the majority of LDC migrants actually move to other developing countries, often to neighbouring ones (Ratha and Shaw, 2007). Even though workers migrating to developed economies are typically in a position to remit greater amounts of money, in 2010, it was estimated that as much as two-thirds of recorded remittances to LDCs originated in other Southern countries (UNCTAD, 2011a). Arguably, the prominence of South–South remittances may well be even higher than the above estimates suggest, given that "hawala" channels may be expected to be prevalent among countries with less developed financial systems.

From the analytical and policy-making point of view, it is important to understand the pattern of remittances to any given country (in the light of geographical and cultural factors) and their currency composition.

South–South remittance flows are particularly sizeable in the case of large LDC recipients. Seven of the top ten – or twelve of the top twenty – remittance corridors to the LDCs are South–South. These include several corridors linking countries of the Gulf Cooperation Council (GCC) and India to large recipients such as Bangladesh, Nepal, Sudan and Yemen, in addition to a few intra-African corridors to Lesotho and Uganda. Besides, corridors connecting destination countries in the developed world (notably the UK, the USA or France) to large LDC recipients also feature prominently in the list of top remitting corridors.

Even though workers migrating to developed economies are typically in a position to remit greater amounts of money, in 2010, it was estimated that two-thirds of recorded remittances to LDCs originated in other Southern countries

There are distinct regional and subregional patterns of remittance corridors, as documented in chart 21 and table 7.[10] The significance of remittance flows from neighbouring countries is apparent in the case of African LDCs, where relatively large sums of money are sent from subregional "poles" such as Kenya and Uganda in East Africa, Nigeria and Côte d'Ivoire in West Africa, and South Africa. The weight of the corridors linking Saudi Arabia with Sudan, and Israel with Ethiopia, represent notable exceptions to the above sub-Saharan African pattern, but again they are largely driven by considerations of historical and cultural proximity. Other prominent corridors in sub-Saharan Africa typically include those linking African LDCs to developed economies with which they retain historical and cultural ties. This is particularly the case of corridors linking France, the UK, and other European countries with their former colonies, but also of those connecting the United States with countries such as Liberia and Sierra Leone.

There are distinct regional and subregional patterns of remittance corridors.

In the case of African LDCs, relatively large sums of money are sent from subregional "poles" such as Kenya and Uganda in East Africa, Nigeria and Côte d'Ivoire in West Africa, and South Africa.

In the case of the Asian LDCs, conversely, India and GCC countries are by far the primary sources of remittances, whereas funds sent from developed

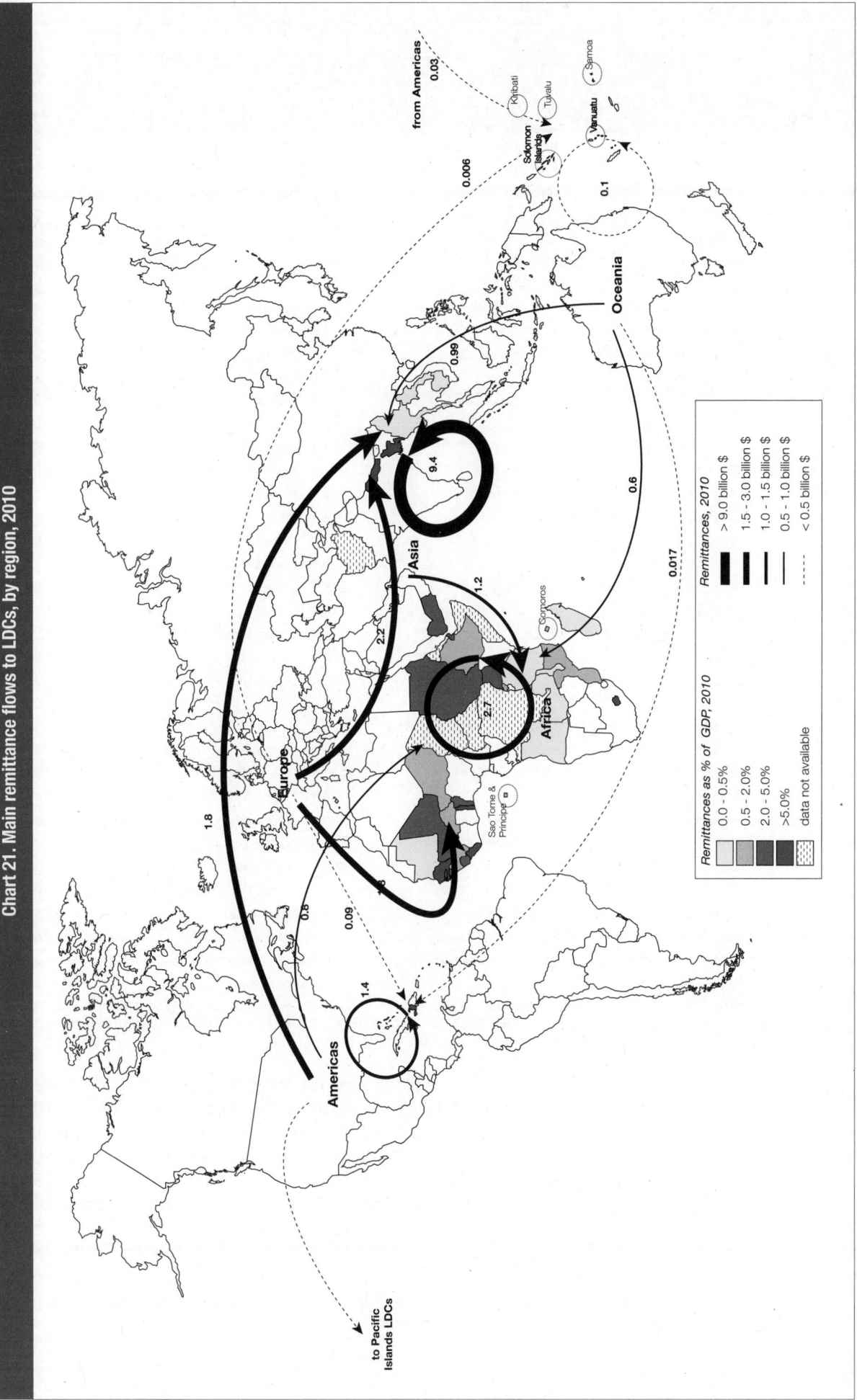

Chart 21. Main remittance flows to LDCs, by region, 2010

Source: UNCTAD secretariat calculations, based on World Bank dataset. Bilateral remittance 2010 estimates using migrant stocks, destination and source country incomes; http://econ.worldbank.org/ WBSITE/EXTERNAL/EXTDEC/EXTDECPROSPECTS/0,,contentMDK:22803131~pagePK:64165401~piPK:64165026~theSitePK:476883,00.html

Table 7. Top remittance corridors by recipient LDC							
	Main corridor		Second main corridor		Third main corridor		Cumulative importance of the 3 main corridors for the recipient country (%)
Recipient country	Sending country	Remit-tances inflows in 2010 ($ million)	Sending country	Remit-tances inflows in 2010 ($ million)	Sending country	Remit-tances inflows in 2010 ($ million)	
Benin	Nigeria	87.4	France	28.4	Togo	24.0	59
Burkina Faso	Côte d'Ivoire	32.9	Italy	1.4	France	0.7	90
Burundi	United Rep. of Tanzania	0.8	Uganda	0.5	Belgium	0.3	49
Comoros	France	9.9	Madagascar	0.5	Egypt	0.2	96
Djibouti	France	18.1	Ethiopia	3.3	Canada	1.7	82
Ethiopia	United States	148.3	Israel	64.8	Sudan	26.0	62
Gambia	Spain	20.3	United States	10.7	United Kingdom	6.2	61
Guinea	France	11.6	Côte d'Ivoire	11.3	Senegal	6.7	45
Guinea-Bissau	Portugal	11.1	France	4.9	Spain	3.5	72
Lesotho	South Africa	457.0	Mozambique	19.2	United States	1.6	95
Liberia	United States	32.3	Guinea	7.8	Côte d'Ivoire	4.2	77
Madagascar	France	8.0	Canada	0.3	Belgium	0.2	85
Malawi	United Kingdom	0.3	Zimbabwe	0.2	South Africa	0.1	69
Mali	Côte d'Ivoire	121.0	France	91.1	Nigeria	37.3	65
Mauritania	France	0.5	Spain	0.3	Senegal	0.3	60
Mozambique	South Africa	51.9	Portugal	24.7	Malawi	7.8	72
Niger	Nigeria	14.6	Côte d'Ivoire	13.8	Benin	11.8	58
Rwanda	Uganda	25.1	Belgium	15.3	United Rep. of Tanzania	10.2	56
Sao Tome & Principe	Portugal	1.2	Angola	0.4	Cape Verde	0.1	92
Senegal	France	309.8	Italy	248.1	Gambia	152.4	61
Sierra Leone	United Kingdom	11.1	United States	10.2	Guinea	9.1	63
Sudan	Saudi Arabia	1025.5	Uganda	407.1	United States	270.6	54
Togo	France	61.2	Nigeria	54.3	Germany	49.6	55
Uganda	Kenya	326.2	United Kingdom	176.4	United States	87.4	76
United Rep. of Tanzania	United Kingdom	4.5	Canada	3.2	Kenya	2.5	58
Zambia	United Kingdom	23.4	United Rep. of Tanzania	9.0	United States	6.5	55
Haiti	United States	1055.0	Dominican Republic	178.9	Canada	129.7	91
Bangladesh	India	3768.9	Saudi Arabia	1249.2	United Kingdom	1113.9	55
Cambodia	United States	179.5	France	80.2	Australia	36.0	81
Lao People's Dem. Rep.	United States	0.6	France	0.2	Thailand	0.1	87
Myanmar	Thailand	55.6	United States	48.6	Australia	11.9	75
Nepal	Qatar	1125.2	India	960.9	United States	428.4	72
Yemen	Saudi Arabia	1039.4	United States	134.8	United Arab Emirates	122.0	88
Kiribati	United States	2.4	Germany	2.0	New Zealand	1.3	65
Samoa	New Zealand	65.8	United States	31.4	Australia	26.6	87
Solomon Islands	Australia	1.5	New Caledonia	0.4	New Zealand	0.3	80
Vanuatu	Australia	2.9	France	1.4	New Caledonia	0.7	72

Source: UNCTAD secretariat calculations based on World Bank dataset Bilateral remittance 2010 estimates using migrant stocks, destination and source country incomes; http://econ.worldbank.org/WBSITE/EXTERNAL/EXTDEC/EXTDECPROSPECTS/0,,contentMDK:22803131~pagePK:64165401~piPK:64165026~theSitePK:476883,00.html

In the case of the Asian LDCs, India and GCC countries are by far the primary sources of remittances, whereas funds sent from developed economies account for only some 30 per cent of the total.

economies in Europe or North America account for only some 30 per cent of the total. This is especially true for Bangladesh, Nepal and Yemen, even though the corridors linking the UK to its former colonies are also important (table 7). For small LDC recipients in South-East Asia, on the other hand, a large share of remittances originate from the United States — and to a lesser extent France — though the amounts sent are negligible compared to the receipts of other Asian LDCs. Finally, unlike the other LDC regions, developed countries account for the majority of remittance inflows to Pacific Islands and Haiti. In this respect, the United States is, broadly speaking, the main source of inflows, followed by Australia and New Zealand in the case of the Pacific Islands; and the Dominican Republic and Canada for Haiti.

C. The development impact of remittances

In sections A and B, we have presented clear evidence of the growing value of remittances to the LDCs, and of their importance as a source of external financing. Given the magnitudes involved, it is likely that they affect not only the recipient households but also a number of macroeconomic variables, ranging from investments, labour supply and real exchange rates to the potential creditworthiness of a country, etc. These overlapping effects, in turn, set in motion complex adjustment processes whose ultimate outcomes typically depend on country-specific conditions.

This section reviews the current evidence on the development impact of remittances, distinguishing between the macroeconomic and microeconomic spheres. As noted by Chami et al. (2008), empirical studies in this field have widened the scope of research, refining the methodologies applied and moving from country case-studies to cross-sectional and panel data analyses. This section focuses only on those issues which are deemed critical in the context of the LDCs. With regard to macroeconomic impacts, four main questions will be addressed:

1. Do remittances have an impact on economic growth?
2. To what extent do they smooth GDP fluctuation and current account volatility?
3. Do remittances have an impact on the creditworthiness of the recipient country?
4. Is there a risk that remittances may fuel real exchange rate appreciation or real estate bubbles in recipient countries?

With regard to microeconomic effects, the discussion will focus on the impact of remittances on poverty reduction and diversification of households' income sources, as well as the different uses of remittance income.

There is a compelling body of research documenting the positive impact of remittances at the household level, both in terms of poverty reduction and as a risk mitigation strategy to diversify sources of income. However, the evidence on their developmental impact at a macroeconomic level is far less clear-cut. Migrants' remittances may indeed contribute to the development of productive capacities by sustaining investment in human and physical capital and stimulating financial deepening. However, the realization of such potential is largely contingent upon the policy and institutional frameworks which recipient countries put in place. In this respect, while capital-scarce LDCs have much to gain from the potential developmental impact of remittances, their structural weaknesses also make it more difficult to successfully mobilize these sources of external financing for productive purposes.

1. MACROECONOMIC ISSUES

a) Do remittances have an impact on economic growth?

The relationship between remittances and economic growth is complex and multifaceted, as remittances affect a recipient country's economy through a number of overlapping channels. Since remittances represent a household-to-household transfer, their receipts directly increase the real disposable income of the recipient families, allowing them to improve their standard of living. By doing so, they correspondingly boost aggregate demand through either consumption

Developed countries account for the majority of remittance inflows to Pacific Islands and Haiti.

There is a compelling body of research documenting the positive impact of remittances at the household level, both in terms of poverty reduction and as a risk mitigation strategy to diversify sources of income.

The evidence on their developmental impact at a macroeconomic level is far less clear-cut.

Migrants' remittances may contribute to the development of productive capacities. However, the realization of such potential is largely contingent upon the policy and institutional frameworks which recipient countries put in place.

or investment spending, with the multiplier being dependent on the specific use of remittance income.

Migration and remittances also affect labour supply directly or indirectly. On the one hand, outward migration reduces labour supply, which may put upward pressure on domestic wages in the short term. On the other hand, the receipt of remittances may be expected to raise the "reservation wage", thereby reducing the incentive to work for household members in the country of origin. For example, Kim (2007) finds evidence that remittances have a negative effect on labour market outcomes in Jamaica. Jadotte (2009) finds the same in the case of Haiti, for both hours worked and for labour market participation. However, other empirical studies have yielded contrasting evidence. Ducanes and Abella (2008) show that among Filipino households, those with migrants abroad tend to display a higher participation in the labour market, once the working age population attending schools is factored in. Cox-Edwards and Rodríguez-Oreggia (2009) also find limited evidence of labour force participation effects of long-term remittances in Mexico.[11]

The relationship between remittances and economic growth is complex and multifaceted, as remittances affect a recipient country's economy through a number of overlapping channels.

Generally speaking, it could be argued that the reduced incentive to work is likely to be more pronounced in remittance-dependent small economies, especially in the presence of large differentials between the domestic wage and the wage prevailing in destination countries. This is notably the case for several SIDS located at a small distance from much more developed economies.[12] Yet this concern is plausibly less serious in the LDC context, where underemployment and low-value-added informal activities prevail and capital – not labour – is the scarce factor. Indeed, both Jadotte (2009) and Kim (2007) note that the negative impact on labour supply is quantitatively small, as a result of which adverse effects on output are unlikely to be significant.

In the short run (i.e. with fixed capital stock and productivity), aggregate supply is unlikely to keep pace with the expansion in aggregate demand financed by remittance inflows. Consequently, large inflows of remittances may be expected to worsen the trade balance of the recipient country. Relative prices of non-tradables may then tend to increase vis-à-vis tradables, leading to appreciation of the real exchange rate, even as the inflows of financial resources sent by overseas migrants help to finance the trade deficit.

On the negative side, the adverse effect of remittances on labour market outcomes may reduce economic growth if a culture of dependency becomes gradually entrenched or if remittances trigger appreciations in the real exchange rate.

Whether these short-run dynamics can be expected to improve or dampen the recipient country's growth performance depends essentially on the impact of remittances on the expansion of productive capacities. On the negative side, the adverse effect of remittances on labour market outcomes may reduce economic growth if a culture of dependency on foreign transfers becomes gradually entrenched. Moreover, unless properly addressed, the tendency of remittances to trigger appreciations in the real exchange rate may give rise to "Dutch disease" effects, impairing much-needed structural change by undermining the competitiveness of non-traditional tradable sectors.

On the positive side, remittances may support economic growth and productive capacity development through two non-mutually exclusive channels: investment and financial deepening.

On the positive side, remittances may support economic growth and productive capacity development through two non-mutually exclusive channels: investment and financial deepening. Indeed, remittances provide a much-needed source of foreign financing that could accelerate the pace of physical and human capital accumulation (the "investment channel"). In addition, they tend to increase the availability of funds for the domestic financial system, paving the way for recipient households to demand and gain access to other financial products and services which they might not have otherwise. Besides, remittances may possibly relax financial constraints on recipient households, particularly those in rural areas which are poorly served by existing financial intermediaries.

Given that the overall impact of remittances on growth is ambiguous at a theoretical level, whether or not the positive effects outweigh the negative impacts is a purely empirical question, the answer to which depends on a host of country-specific factors, ranging from the pattern of migration and its underlying distributive consequences to institutional quality and financial development. Most econometric analyses investigating the relationship between remittances and GDP per capita growth have relied on the standard growth regression framework, including additional control variables accounting for remittance receipts and other plausible growth determinants. This empirical literature has so far yielded mixed results, as well as highlighting a number of methodological problems ranging from measurement and specification issues to reverse causality and unobservable heterogeneity.[13]

Econometric analyses investigating the relationship between remittances and GDP per capita growth have yielded mixed results.

On one hand, some cross-sectional studies document an adverse effect of workers' remittances on economic growth, traceable to reduced working efforts (Chami et al., 2005, 2008) or deteriorating institutional quality (Abdih et al., 2012). In the same vein, Acosta et al. (2009) build a two-sector dynamic stochastic general equilibrium model based on the El Salvadorian economy, confirming that remittances hamper growth through a decline in labour supply and an increase in consumption demand biased toward non-tradables, as with the "Dutch disease".

Yet the above claims are at odds with other empirical research, which actually fails to detect any robust statistically significant relationship between remittances and growth (IMF, 2005; Pradhan et al., 2008; Giuliano and Ruiz-Arranz, 2009).[14] Moreover, a number of others studies — particularly those with a strong emphasis on the time dimension, such as dynamic panel data — document instead a positive and statistically significant influence of remittances on per capita GDP growth (Glytsos, 2005; Acosta et al., 2008; Catrinescu et al., 2009; Mundaca, 2009; Ziesemer, 2009, 2012).

Remittances appears to sustain growth by easing credit and liquidity constraints in countries with poorly developed financial sectors.

Along similar lines, but by means of a completely different framework, namely a traditional Keynesian macroeconomic model focusing on five Mediterranean countries (Egypt, Jordan, Greece, Morocco and Portugal) — Glytsos (2005) obtains a positive effect of remittances on economic growth, with average investment and income multipliers of 2.3 and 0.6 respectively.[15]

As for the "financial deepening channel", the influence of remittances appears to be twofold. First, they appear to sustain growth by easing credit and liquidity constraints in countries with poorly developed financial sectors, thereby "substituting" for financial development. Consistent with this view, those studies adding to a standard growth regression both a remittance variable and an interaction of that variable with a proxy for financial development find a significant positive coefficient for the former and a significant negative coefficient for the latter (World Bank, 2008; Giuliano and Ruiz-Arranz, 2009).[16] Second, remittances directly foster financial deepening, especially when transferred through formal financial institutions, by stimulating demand for new products and services. Aggarwal et al. (2006) document this robust positive impact of remittances on a panel of 99 countries, even after controlling for other factors that affect financial development, and regardless of whether financial development is measured in terms of the ratio of deposits or credit to GDP. Various econometric studies focused on Latin American and Caribbean countries reach the same conclusion, namely, that remittances are strongly associated with greater banking breadth and depth, increasing the number of branches and accounts per capita, and the ratio of deposits to gross domestic product (World Bank, 2008; Anzoategui et al., 2011; Demirgüç-Kunt et al., 2011).[17] In the African context, these findings are corroborated by the analysis of several household surveys, which demonstrate how, for a given income quintile, the probability of having a bank account is considerably higher for households receiving remittances (World Bank, 2011a).

Remittances directly foster financial deepening, especially when transferred through formal financial institutions, by stimulating demand for new products and services.

Even though the literature is still somewhat inconclusive on how remittances ultimately affect economic growth, there appears to be general agreement on the fact that complementary policies and sound institutions play an important role in enhancing their development impact (World Bank, 2008; Pradhan et al., 2008; Catrinescu et al., 2009). Governments typically have only limited room to directly affect the allocation of remittance income, since taxation or mandatory remittance requirements have historically proved rather ineffective and in most cases have simply led migrants to use informal channels to remit (Lucas, 2008). In the light of the inherently private nature of remittance flows, the effective mobilization of remittances for productive purposes depends on a whole array of policy and institutional improvements, aimed at reinforcing both the "investment channel" and the impact of remittances on financial deepening. This may entail a range of policy interventions, from "development-centred" macroeconomic and regional development policies aimed at crowding in private investments to appropriate financial and regulatory reforms designed to reduce transaction costs and promote greater financial inclusion and credit provision for SMEs.

There appears to be general agreement that complementary policies and sound institutions play an important role in enhancing the development impact of remittances.

Overall, there is some scope for remittances to stimulate physical and human capital accumulation as well as financial development; all the more so when a large share of remittance income is received by poor and otherwise credit-rationed households. In this respect, capital-scarce LDCs clearly have much to gain from the potential developmental impact of remittances. However, LDCs' structural weaknesses make it more difficult to successfully mobilize these sources of external financing for productive purposes. It is therefore essential to design appropriate strategies and policy frameworks for harnessing remittances for economic development.

Capital-scarce LDCs clearly have much to gain from the potential developmental impact of remittances. However, their structural weaknesses make it more difficult to successfully mobilize these sources of external financing for productive purposes.

b) To what extent do remittances smooth GDP fluctuation and current account volatility?

It is true that remittance flows tend to be correlated with the macroeconomic performance of source countries and could thus partially transmit macroeconomic fluctuations from source to recipient countries.[18] Yet unless business cycles are closely synchronized across both sets of countries, remittances can be expected to play a somewhat more stabilizing role. In addition, remittances tend to be more resilient to downturns than other sources of foreign exchange for several reasons, as confirmed in the aftermath of the 2009 global recession (see box 3). First, as remittances are sent by the accumulated flows of migrants and not only by the new migrants of recent years, they tend to be more persistent over time. Second, as remittances typically account for a minor share of a migrant's income, the latter often cushions a temporary fall in earnings by reducing other costs while continuing to send money back home. Third, the tightening of border controls and fear of unemployment back home may encourage the migrant to stay abroad longer (i.e. increase the duration of migration) and continue to send money overseas. Finally, returning migrants are likely to take back accumulated savings, which are counted as remittances.[19]

Remittances tend to be more resilient to downturns than other sources of foreign exchange.

Equally important, unlike purely investment-driven sources of capital flows, remittances also encompass an altruistic/insurance component, and can thus have a stabilizing effect on the recipient economies. For example, remittance receipts rose during the so-called "tequila crisis" in Mexico in 1994–1995, and during the Asian crisis of 1997 in Korea and the Philippines. Besides, it has been noted that they tend to increase in response to natural disasters and political conflicts, in countries that have a larger emigrant stock as a share of the home country population (Mohapatra et al., 2009). In Haiti, for example, remittance receipts increased by over $100 million a year in the biennium following the devastating earthquake of January 2010, which corresponds to an average annual growth rate of eight per cent.[20] Similarly, in West African countries, remittances appear to play a significant role in smoothing GDP fluctuations induced by climatic variability (Couharde, Davis and Generoso, 2011).

Several studies covering large samples of countries and using different estimation strategies (ranging from instrumental variables to generalized method of moments) have shown that an increase in the share of remittances to GDP tends to reduce the volatility of GDP growth, even after controlling for other possible determinants of growth volatility (IMF, 2005; Bugamelli and Paternò, 2008; Chami et al., 2010). This finding highlights another potential channel through which remittances may sustain economic progress in recipient countries, namely by reducing growth volatility, which in itself is detrimental to economic growth. This may be particularly relevant in an LDC context, given that these economies have indeed been traditionally characterized by relatively recurrent growth accelerations but nearly as frequent growth collapses (UNCTAD, 2010a).

Several studies have shown that an increase in the share of remittances to GDP tends to reduce the volatility of GDP growth, even after controlling for other possible determinants of growth volatility.

From a macroeconomic point of view, the relative stability of remittances as compared with other sources of external financing is worth stressing. As shown in chart 22, over the period 1980–2010, remittance inflows to the LDCs displayed the lowest volatility, as measured by the standard deviation of the ratio between the relevant inflow and GDP.[21] Among the sources of foreign exchange available to the world's poorest countries, the volatility of ODA net disbursements was nearly twice as high, while FDI and export revenues displayed even higher instability over time. In addition, over the same period, remittances appear to be characterized by considerably lower procyclicality than other types of flows, including both aid and FDI.[22]

The relative stability and lower cyclicality of remittances as compared with other inflows may have beneficial implications for the recipient country's external accounts.

This relative stability and lower cyclicality of remittances as compared with other inflows may have beneficial implications for the recipient country's external accounts. A comparison of the stabilizing impact of aid and remittances in 82 developing countries (including 26 LDCs) spanning the period 1980–1995 reveals that remittances, like aid, behave in a rather acyclical way with respect to exports (Guillaumont and Le Goff 2011). However, as remittances are on average less volatile than aid, and aid is less volatile than exports, both flows tend to dampen the instability of export revenues in the majority of countries (ibid.).[23]

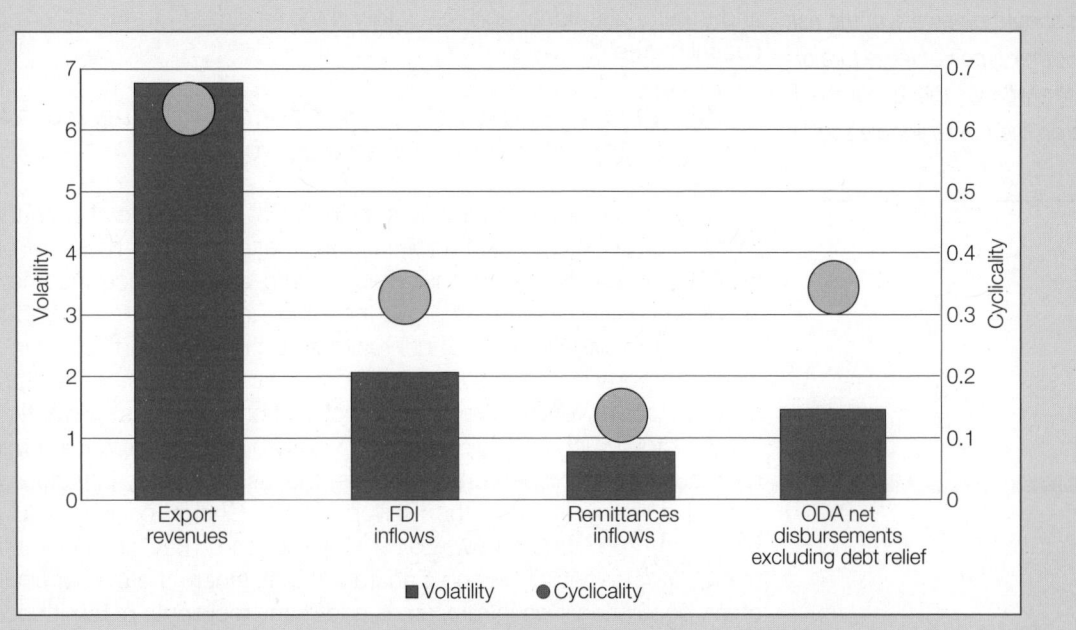

Chart 22. Volatility and cyclicality of foreign exchange flows to LDCs, 1980–2010

■ Volatility ● Cyclicality

Source: UNCTAD secretariat calculations, based on UNCTADstat, *World Development Indicators,* and OECD-DAC online databases.
Note: For the definition of volatility and cyclicality refer to the main text.

In the context of the LDCs, whose export structures are concentrated within a narrow range of products, the stabilizing effect of ODA and remittances can play an important role in reducing the impact of adverse terms of trade shocks. Remittances, especially when they are larger than three per cent of GDP, also appear to reduce the probability of sharp current account reversals by reducing the sensitivity to a decline in international reserves (Bugamelli and Paternò, 2009).

c) Do remittances have an impact on the creditworthiness of the recipient country?

By increasing the level and the stability of foreign exchange receipts, remittances may improve the creditworthiness of the recipient country, boosting its ability to repay external debt.

By increasing the level and often the stability of foreign exchange receipts as well, remittances may improve the creditworthiness of the recipient country, boosting its ability to repay external debt — at least insofar as they transit through formal financial channels. This is illustrated in chart 23, which compares the ratio of debt service to export earnings (a standard indicator of debt sustainability), both including and excluding remittances from the computation. Across LDCs, the inclusion of remittances lowers the indicator of debt burden by roughly one percentage point on average. The benefit is significantly larger for some Pacific Island LDCs and other traditional recipients.

Acknowledging the growing importance of remittances for low-income countries, the World Bank and the International Monetary Fund have gradually moved towards a revision of the Debt Sustainability Framework, so as to account for the impact of remittances on debt repayment capacity as well as on the probability of default (IMF and World Bank, 2009 and 2012). The full operationalization of this revision is hampered by the poor quality of remittance data, as a result of which only eight countries had their risk of debt distress assessed using remittances in the 2010–2011 biennium (IMF and World Bank, 2012).

Given the relative stability of remittances and the underlying implications for a country's creditworthiness, one potential mechanism for enhancing their developmental impact could be to use them as collateral for securitization or for long-term syndicated loans. This could reduce the (often prohibitive) costs LDCs face on international capital markets, potentially broadening their access to long-term development finance. This policy option is discussed in detail in chapter 5, which also highlights the possible synergies between this measure and other institutional and regulatory reforms aimed at strengthening domestic capital markets.

Large remittance recipients, however, should be aware of the risk that, like other types of large foreign exchange inflows, these may put pressure on the non-tradable sector.

d) Is there a serious risk that remittances may fuel real exchange rate appreciation or real estate bubbles?

Large remittance recipients should be aware of the risk that, like other types of large foreign exchange inflows, these may put pressure on the non-tradable sector. Since a considerable share of remittance income is typically spent on housing, be it to improve the living standards or as a deliberate saving strategy, this situation could fuel real estate bubbles, particularly in large cities where property is one of the most favoured asset classes. Several practitioners, for instance, have observed that transfers from overseas migrants, along with other factors such as rapid economic growth and an expanding middle class, have pushed up property markets over the last few years in various developing countries, ranging from the Philippines to Ghana or Nepal (Buckley and Mathema, 2007 and Chow, 2011). This concern may be partly attenuated in most LDCs (especially in sub-Saharan Africa), where the overwhelming majority of the population lives in rural areas and many recipients of remittances are rural dwellers.

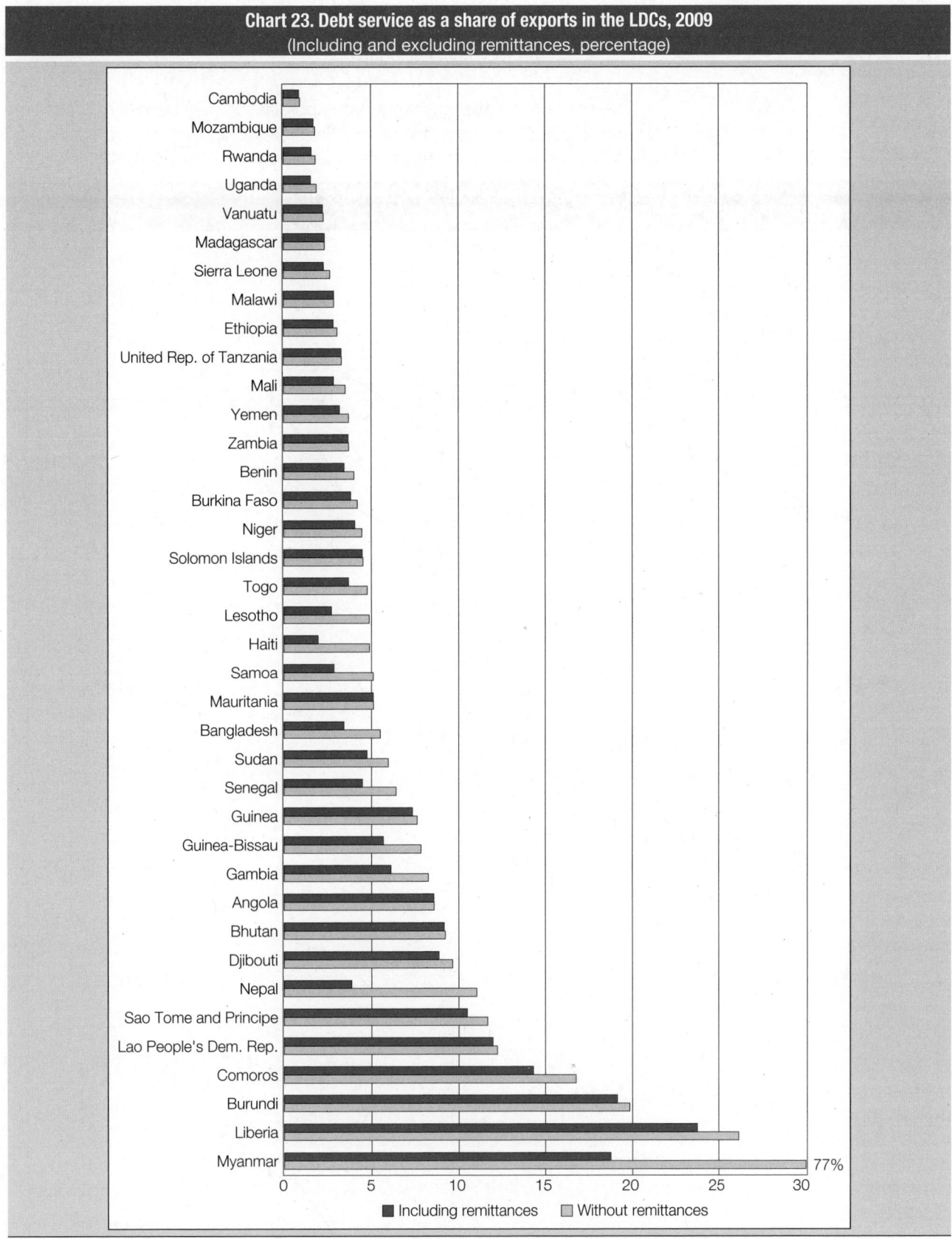

Chart 23. Debt service as a share of exports in the LDCs, 2009
(Including and excluding remittances, percentage)

Source: UNCTAD secretariat calculations, based on UNCTADstat, *World Development Indicators,* and OECD-DAC online databases.

Large inflows of remittances may also be associated with appreciation of the real exchange rate, weighing down domestic competitiveness and hindering economic growth (i.e. the so-called "Dutch disease"). This risk appears to be more pronounced in Latin American and Caribbean economies, where — according to (Amuedo-Dorantes and Pozo, 2004) — a doubling of workers' remittances could result in real exchange rate appreciation of some 22 per cent.[24] However, there is little evidence of such an effect in broader samples of developing countries or in the context of sub-Saharan Africa (Rajan and Subramanian, 2005; World Bank, 2011a).

The possibility of real exchange rate appreciation may be less of a concern for most LDCs. Focusing on the six most remittance-dependent LDC economies (i.e. those where remittances represent the highest share of GDP), chart 24

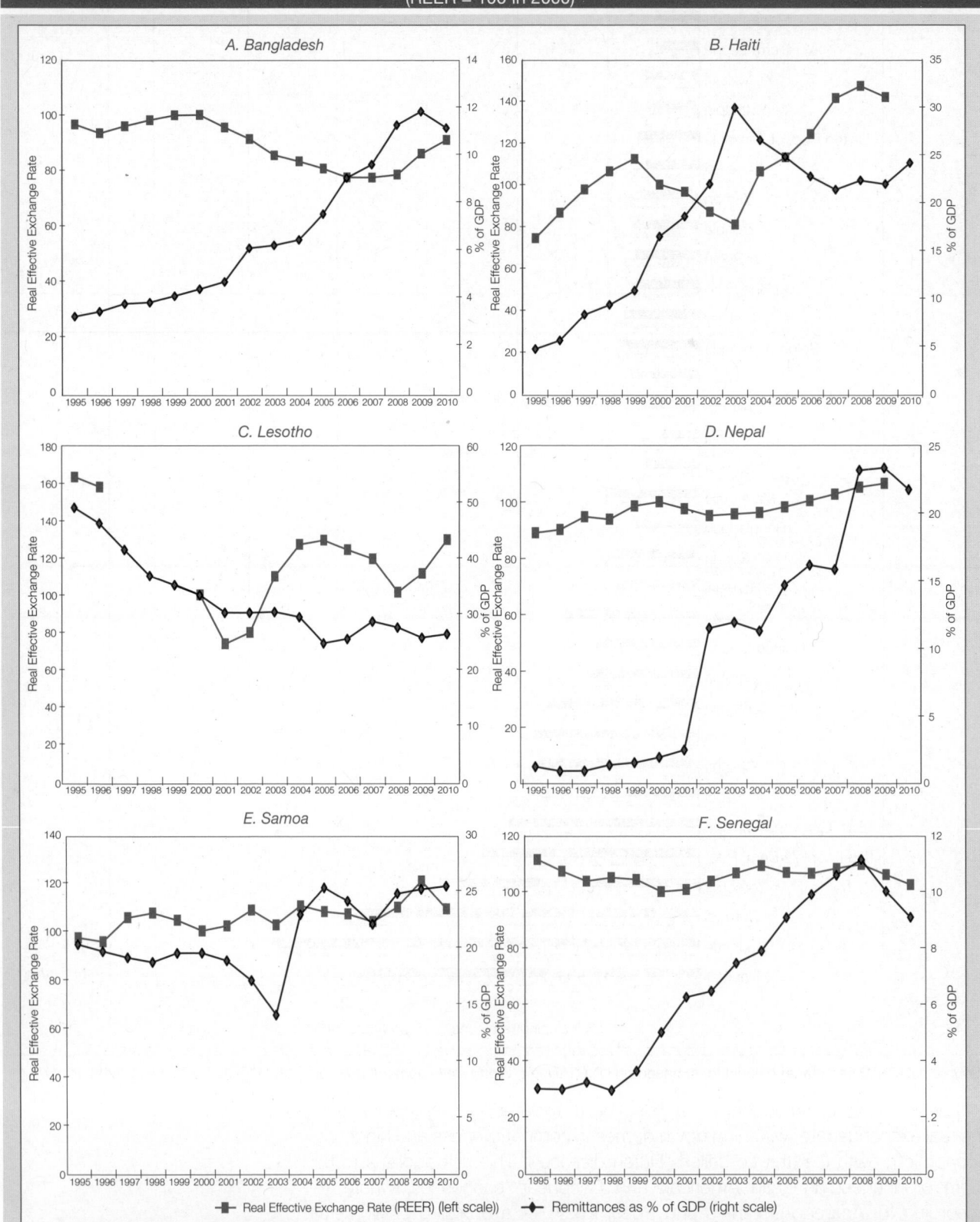

Chart 24. Real effective exchange rate, selected LDCs, 1995–2010
(REER = 100 in 2000)

A. Bangladesh   B. Haiti   C. Lesotho   D. Nepal   E. Samoa   F. Senegal

Real Effective Exchange Rate (REER) (left scale))   Remittances as % of GDP (right scale)

Source: UNCTAD secretariat calculations, based on UNCTADstat database.

shows that only in the case of Haiti — and to a much lesser extent Samoa — was the surge in remittances associated with a discernible appreciation in the real exchange rate. In the case of Senegal and Bangladesh, on the other hand, the boom in remittance inflows did not seem to have a similar effect, while even in Nepal — where remittances climbed from five per cent of GDP to 20 per cent in the span of a decade — the real exchange rate appreciated only marginally.

Of course, this does not mean that LDCs should be complacent and overlook the potentially adverse implications of remittances, and other foreign exchange inflows, on domestic competitiveness. Particularly when the overall macroeconomic environment discourages the channelling of remittance incomes towards investment, the boost provided to disposable income and aggregate demand may conflict with persistent supply-side bottlenecks. This may ultimately undermine domestic competitiveness, and require some degree of proactive monetary and exchange policy interventions to restore macroeconomic conditions that are conducive to growth and economic diversification. In any case, insofar as LDCs put in place sustainable exchange rate and fiscal policies while crowding in private investment and fostering financial deepening, the positive effects of growing remittance inflows are likely to outweigh the modest appreciations typically witnessed in the LDC context.

On average, a 10 per cent increase in per capita international remittances leads to a 3.5 per cent reduction in the proportion of people living below the poverty line.

2. MICROECONOMIC ISSUES

In the typical developing country, remittances account for approximately 30 to 40 per cent of a recipient household's income. As a result, they can contribute towards poverty reduction while raising the household's savings and investments, including through better access to health and education. Empirical studies, whether at the country level or across a broad range of economies, typically show that remittances reduce standard poverty measures (Adams, 2011; World Bank, 2011a). An often-cited cross-sectional study based on household surveys for 71 developing countries shows that both international migration and remittances have a statistically significant effect on poverty reduction, whether measured through the headcount ratio or the poverty gap (Adams and Page, 2005). Using instrumental variables to control for reverse causality, the authors find that, on average, a 10 per cent increase in per capita international remittances leads to a 3.5 per cent reduction in the proportion of people living below the poverty line and a 3.9 per cent reduction in the poverty gap. These findings are basically confirmed by another study of 10 Latin American countries, employing a two-stage Heckman model to control for selection bias, which find that international remittances have a positive and statistically significant poverty-reducing effect. Similarly, according to the study by (Anyanwu and Erhijakpor, 2010) covering a sample of 33 African countries for the period 1990–2005, a 10 per cent increase in reported international remittances as a share of GDP leads to a 2.9 per cent decline in the share of people living in poverty, with similar declines also occurring for the depth and severity of poverty. Besides, remittances (whether national or international) appear to contribute to household income smoothing and to a diversification of sources of income, broadly in line with the tenets of the New Economics of Labour Migration.

Remittances appear to contribute to household income smoothing and to a diversification of sources of income.

The impact of remittances on inequality is less clear-cut, especially in view of the selectivity underlying the migration process.

The impact of remittances on inequality is less clear-cut, especially in view of the serious econometric concerns related to reverse causality and above all to the selectivity underlying the migration process. As prospective migrants incur upfront costs which are largely dependent on the destination, those belonging to the poorest households are typically unable to afford long-distance international movement or the costly bureaucratic procedures usually required to migrate to developed economies. So it is precisely the poorest who are unable to benefit from the largest differentials in terms of expected wages and who consequently remit larger sums. As a result, international migration in many cases appears to have a regressive impact on inequality (Adams, 2011). Consistent with this finding, recent household surveys show that more than half of households in Burkina Faso, Ghana and Nigeria and 30 per cent of households in Senegal receiving remittances from outside Africa are in the top two consumption quintiles (World Bank, 2011a). Conversely, households receiving remittances from other African countries or domestic sources tend to be more evenly distributed across consumption expenditure quintiles, although these flows of remittances tend to be significantly lower than remittances from outside the region. Once again, however, country-specific conditions matter. For example, in Fiji and Tonga — where migration to neighbouring developed economies (i.e. Australia or New Zealand) is relatively more affordable — remittances are found to have a positive effect not only on poverty but also on income distribution (Brown and Jimenez, 2007).[25]

In terms of uses of remittance income, while it is true that a substantial portion is spent on food and housing, this should not be taken to mean that "remittances are predominantly spent on excessive consumption" (De Haas, 2005). On the contrary, a significant proportion of remittances is typically used for human capital accumulation, namely health and education expenditures. Household surveys conducted by the World Bank in Burkina Faso, Kenya, Nigeria, Senegal, and Uganda show, for instance, that the share of international remittance income spent on health and education ranged between 10 to 32 per cent, albeit with some variability across destination and source regions (chart 25). Accordingly, remittances are typically found to improve health and education outcomes, even though the absence of a migrant family member may to some extent erode part of these benefits (Amuedo-Dorantes et al., 2010; Amuedo-Dorantes and Pozo, 2010; Adams, 2011).

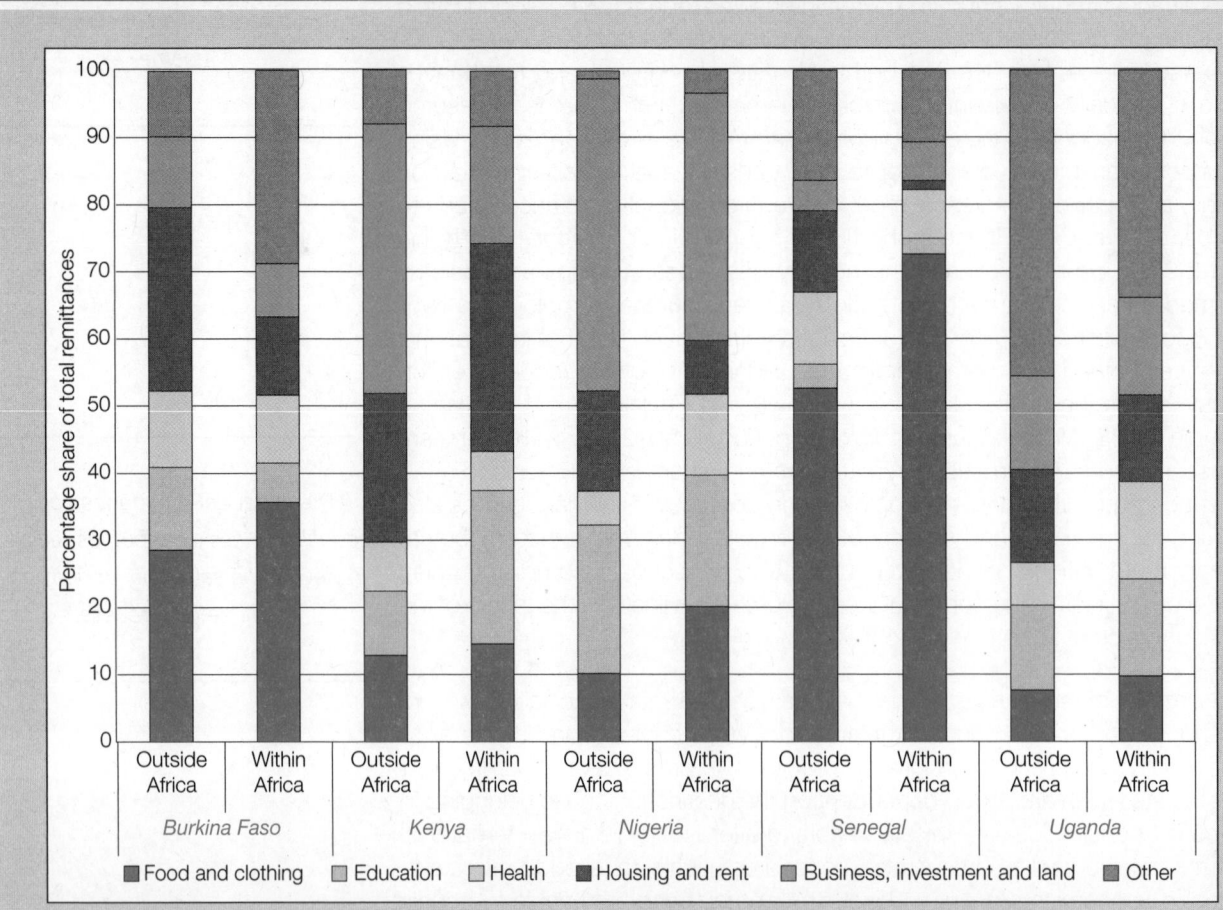

Chart 25. Use of remittances by recipient household in selected African countries, by source of remittance

Source: UNCTAD secretariat calculations, based on World Bank (2011a).

Equally important, a significant share of remittances is also spent on physical investment. For example, it is estimated that some 20 per cent of the capital invested in 6,000 microenterprises in urban Mexico was financed by remittances (Woodruff and Zenteno, 2007). Similarly, household surveys from the six sub-Saharan African countries mentioned above show that on average, 20 per cent of international remittance income is spent on physical capital investments such as buying land or equipment, starting a business, or improving a farm (chart 25).

Interestingly, the selectivity of migration may also be linked to households' use of remittance income. Given their state of deprivation, the poorest households are likely to use a relatively higher share of remittance income on subsistence items such as food and clothing. Conversely, in relatively wealthier settings, remittances respond more to strategies of risk diversification and investment, so there is a larger share of income financing productive assets. The evidence reported in chart 25, which compares the use of remittance income by source, is consistent with this reasoning.

Given the relatively shallow levels of financial development in most LDCs, the potential linkages between remittances and household access to financial services are worth noting. Especially in rural areas, the receipt of remittances often constitutes the only relationship poor people have with the formal financial system. So they potentially provide an opportunity for financial intermediaries to "get to know" otherwise unbanked recipients, paving the way for the latter to obtain new financial products, for saving as well as credit purposes (Orozco and Fedewa, 2006). Consistent with this, data from recent household surveys conducted in Africa and in Latin American and Caribbean economies demonstrate how households that receive remittances typically have better access to financial services, such as bank accounts (World Bank, 2008, 2011a).

Especially in rural areas, remittances often constitute the only relationship poor people have with the formal financial system. So they potentially pave the way for households to obtain new financial products, for saving and credit purposes.

D. Remittance payment systems and LDCs

In most LDC remittance corridors, the cost of sending remittances is still high relative to the often low incomes of migrant workers. At the 2009 G8 Summit in L'Aquila, countries pledged to reduce the cost of sending remittances by half (from 10 to 5 per cent) in five years. As a result of this commitment, the Global Remittance Working Group and the World Bank initiated the 5x5 objective, which is based on the BIS-World Bank General Principles for International Remittance services.[26] However, in an LDC context, it is unclear as to whether the target has been achieved and whether the problem of persistently high costs is due to sending country or recipient country factors. In this section, we consider the costs of remittances in terms of socioeconomic factors, industry market structure, government policies and regulations that affect the costs borne by remitters.

Migrants typically utilize a whole range of formal and informal channels for remitting, chosen on the basis of cost, reliability, accessibility and trust.

1. THE COSTS ASSOCIATED WITH REMITTING

Migrants typically utilize a whole range of formal and informal channels for remitting, chosen on the basis of cost, reliability, accessibility and trust. Formal channels include money transfer services by banks and non-bank financial institutions, such as bureaux de change, and dedicated money transfer operators (MTOs) like Western Union and MoneyGram. The former enables financial transfers from a bank account in the host country to a foreign account through an international funds transfer. These require considerable administration, and the process may take several days. Formal financial institutions tend to have higher overhead costs than MTOs due to their network of branches and automated teller machines (ATMs) and regulatory compliance requirements, which feed into higher remittance fees. In the LDCs, the majority of MTO transactions involve the receipt of funds, and because MTOs tend to have smaller networks than commercial banks, they tend to focus on serving specific populations and geographic niches. These channels are changing in LDCs with the growth of Internet-based firms and new forms of service provision, such as the option to have goods delivered or to purchase vouchers for redemption in shops in the home country.

In some African LDCs — although it is difficult to determine the extent of this practice — diaspora organizations facilitate remittance transfers, both formally or informally (Melde and Ionesco, 2010). In addition, bus, coach and courier companies that transport money or goods as part of their regular and official services also offer domestic and intraregional remittance transfer (formal but non-financial) services. Informal systems of remittance transfers in LDCs tend to have many similarities, whether in Africa, Asia or the Middle East, as nationals of most LDCs tend to send money with friends, relatives or carry it themselves. Other informal systems include hawala or hundi services or are single-destination services provided by individual business people (see section B.2). For example, Somali refugee communities in Nairobi, Kenya often use informal agents with radio or satellite phones to Somalia to manage money transfers home (Omer, 2003; Kabbucho et al., 2003).

Though resorting to informal remittance channels may be a rational choice from the point of view of the individual migrant, from a policy perspective, formal remittance systems are preferable.

Informal and formal remittance channels are utilized for different reasons. In some cases, formal transfers can be slow, expensive and bureaucratic and incur additional charges, while in other instances they may be more cost-effective than informal channels. On the other hand, the latter tend to be inherently more risky, as usually there are no official means for loss recovery if the money is not successfully delivered. In addition to the formal and informal remittance channels discussed below, there are also new and emerging innovations in the remittance transfer and payment systems, such as mobile money, which are discussed further on in section 2.[27]

For LDCs, the average cost of remitting was close to 12 per cent of the amount sent, 30 per cent higher than the global average.

Though resorting to informal remittance channels may be a rational choice from the point of view of the individual migrant, from a policy perspective, formal remittance systems are preferable, even leaving aside concerns related to security, regulation or supervision. The prevalence of informal flows limits the ability of recipient countries to make the best use of the foreign exchange sent by overseas migrants. This may reduce the effects remittances have on a country's creditworthiness or in stimulating financial deepening, and encourage informal (black market) currency transactions.

The Remittance Prices Worldwide database collected by the World Bank Payment Systems Group shows that, as of the first quarter of 2009, the cost of remittances averaged nine per cent of the amount sent (see chart 26). For LDCs, the average cost of remitting $200 was close to 12 per cent of the amount sent, 30 per cent higher than the global average.

For most LDCs, the cost of formal money transfer is in the range of 4–25 per cent of the value sent, and the price depends on informal networks, aggregate volume and competition as well as on the availability of banking institutions and technology.

Chart 27 shows the spread between the minimum and maximum amounts charged on average by remittance service providers (RSPs) in countries sending remittances to LDCs, reflecting both destinations and providers. It also reflects disparities in the cost structures between the major sending countries and within each sending country. For example, Saudi Arabia and the UAE have the lowest total average cost. Among the G8 countries, the UK and the USA are below the world average, at 6.9 per cent and 7.7 per cent respectively. South Africa is the costliest G20 remittance-sending country in the G20 group, with an average of 19 per cent to LDCs as compared to an average of 16 per cent to other developing countries (ODCs). For most LDCs, the cost of formal money transfer is in the range of 4–25 per cent of the value sent, and the price depends

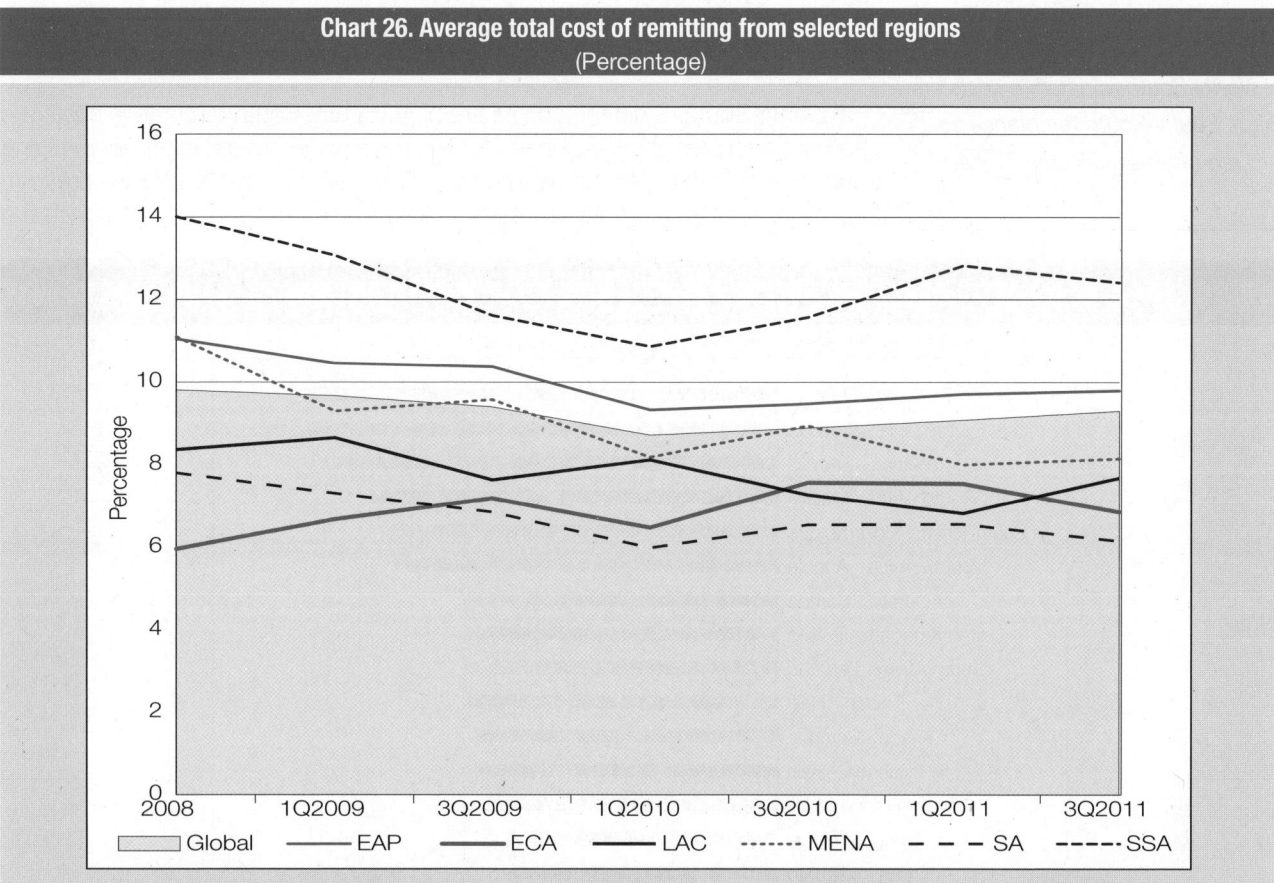

Chart 26. Average total cost of remitting from selected regions
(Percentage)

Source: The World Bank Group, *Remittance Prices Worldwide: Making Markets More Transparent*, online at remittanceprices.worldbank.
org (accessed May, 2012; first quarter 2012 data).

Notes: EAP = East Asia and Pacific; ECA = Europe and Central Asia; LAC = Latin American countries;
MENA = Middle East and North Africa; SA = South Asia; SSA = Sub-Saharan Africa.

Chart 27. Country remittance average service provision costs across providers and LDC destinations
(Percentage)

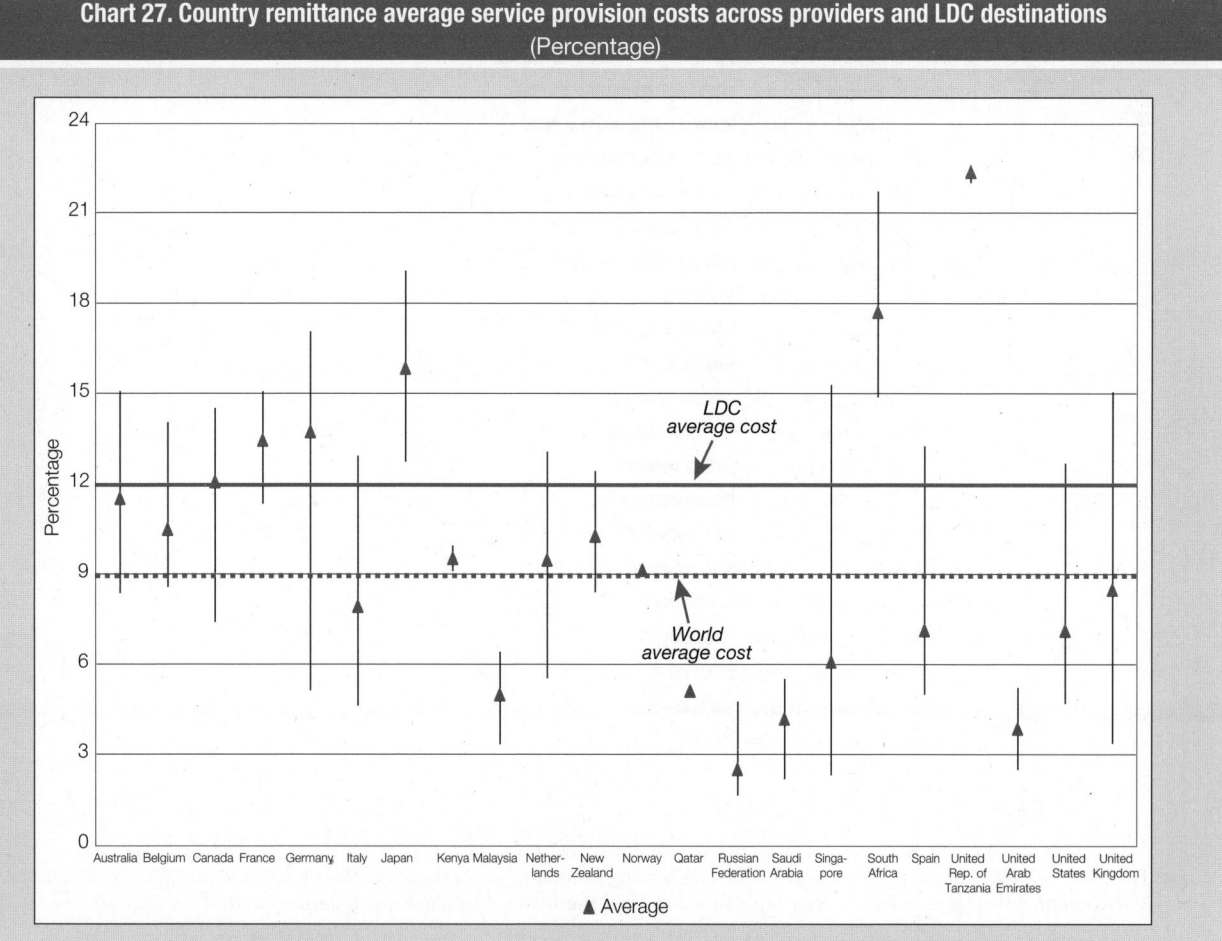

Source: UNCTAD secretariat calculations, based on The World Bank Group, *Remittance Prices Worldwide: Making Markets More Transparent,* online at remittanceprices.worldbank.org (accessed May, 2012; first quarter 2012 data).

If North–South remittance costs are high, South–South remittance costs are often significantly higher.

on informal networks, aggregate volume and competition as well as on the availability of banking institutions and technology.

If North–South remittance costs are high, South–South remittance costs are often significantly higher (see chart 28). The most expensive channels for remitting transfers to LDCs are found within Africa, whereas the least expensive are from Singapore and Saudi Arabia to Asian LDCs. Remitters to Asian LDCs face the

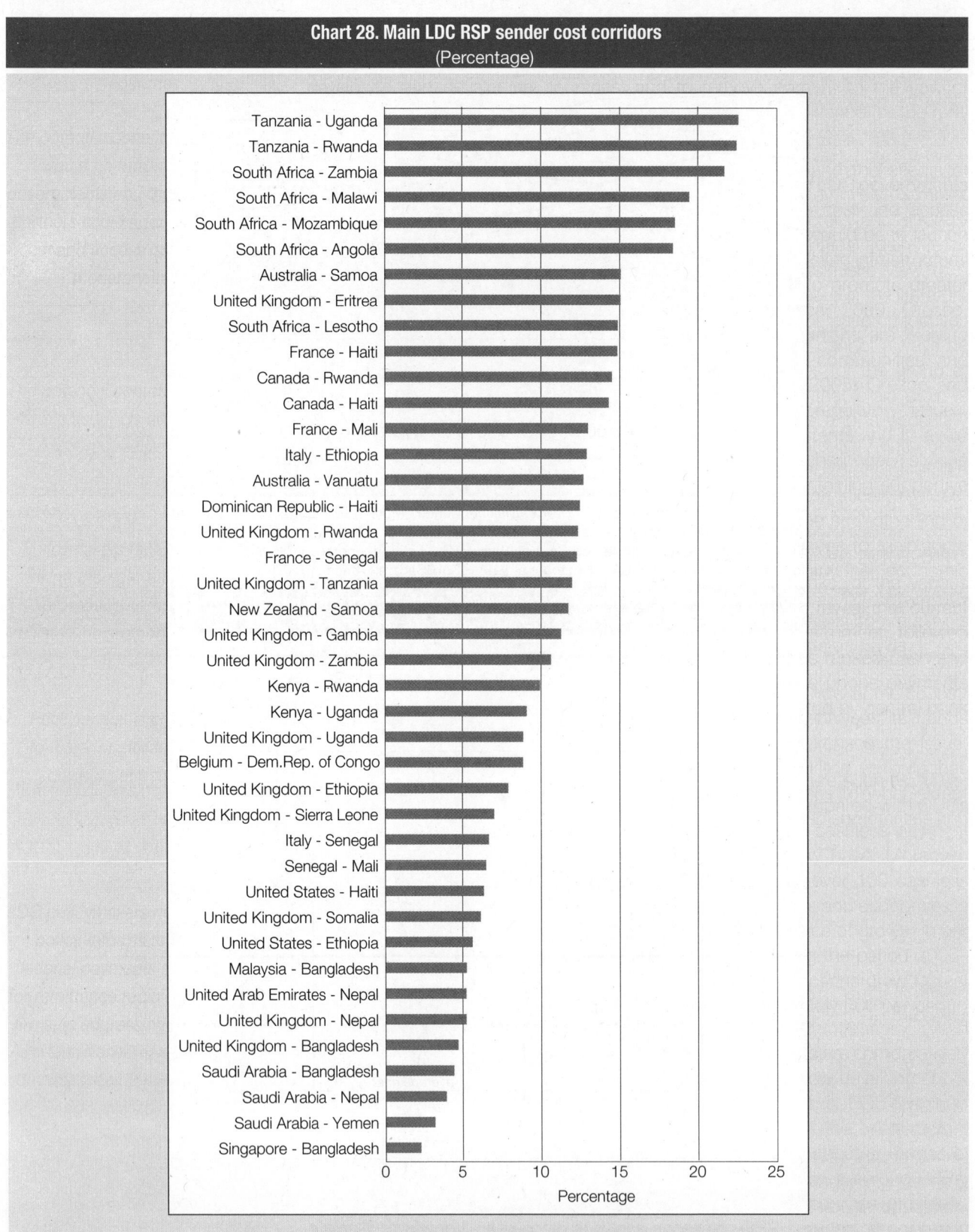

Chart 28. Main LDC RSP sender cost corridors
(Percentage)

Source: UNCTAD secretariat calculations, based on The World Bank Group, *Remittance Prices Worldwide: Making Markets More Transparent,* online at remittanceprices.worldbank.org (accessed May, 2012; first quarter 2012 data).

lowest average costs for sending remittances; they also tend to encounter lower spreads between the minimum and maximum average cost (six per cent), compared with 12 per cent for Pacific LDCs and 20 per cent for African LDCs. One possible reason is that Asian LDCs have a higher than average estimated number of RSPs per sending country, compared with African LDCs and Haiti. Asian LDCs also face lower average exchange rate margin costs than African and Pacific LDCs.[28] For example, exchange rate margins in Bangladesh, Nepal and Yemen are on average 1.3 per cent.[29] For 16 African LDCs, the margin is on average 2.9 per cent, whereas for five Pacific LDCs, the average is 4.6 per cent. Although the major MTOs are present in the Asian market, they face greater competition due to the absence of exclusivity agreements[30] and the proliferation of new technologies, such as mobile phone transfers and transfer cards, which have helped to reduce costs.

There is significant variation across Africa (chart 29a): while most African corridors have average remittance costs of 22 per cent, the cost is only 10 per cent for remittances sent from Kenya. For remitters sending from the UK to Rwanda and Uganda, the average cost is lower than from Tanzania, at 12 per cent and 8 per cent respectively (chart 28). Sending remittances within Africa is thus prohibitively expensive, and costs nearly twice as much as sending the same amount of money between Singapore and Bangladesh (chart 28). In Kenya, banks sending remittances to African LDCs are on average around 19 per cent more expensive than MTOs, and almost three times more expensive than MTOs in South Africa and Tanzania. For sending remittances from the UK to Rwanda and Zambia, banks are on average 35 per cent more expensive than MTOs.

The implications of such high remittance costs may be significant. The World Bank has estimated that in 2010, annual remittances sent to sub-Saharan Africa could have generated an additional $6 billion for recipients, if the costs of remitting money had matched the global average (Ratha et al., 2011). In many LDCs, the remittance market exhibits a low level of competition with very little financial institutional presence, in particular in rural areas. For example, for the whole of sub-Saharan Africa, 65 per cent of all remittance payout locations are controlled by two MTOs (MoneyGram and Western Union). Similarly, African governments have put in place several RSP exclusivity arrangements limiting the type of institutions able to offer remittance services only to banks, thus reducing RSP competition (Ratha et al., 2011).

Pacific LDCs also face an average cost of remitting to the region which is significantly higher than the global average, though somewhat lower than within Africa. Chart 29(c) shows that across most corridors (such as Australia-Samoa), the average remittance cost is 15 per cent of the amount remitted when sent from Australia and 11 per cent when sent from New Zealand. These relatively high costs may in part reflect the relatively small and remote nature of many Pacific economies, which could be limiting the extent to which RSPs can leverage "economies of scale" (that is, falling average costs as the number of transactions increases) to reduce costs. However, as in the case of sub-Saharan Africa, other factors such as regulatory, competition and infrastructure issues may also play a role.[31]

Average remittance costs naturally mask a wide range of elements that vary by corridor and RSP. By corridor, Solomon Islands and Vanuatu have the highest average fees from both Australia and New Zealand. Average costs vary from 10 per cent (New Zealand to Kiribati) to 17.5 per cent (Australia to Solomon Islands). In competitive markets, fees imposed on remittance services should reflect their cost of provision by RSPs, allowing for a profit margin. More competitive markets are usually associated with low profit margins and prices to consumers that closely reflect the cost of providing this service, as firms are

The most expensive channels for remitting to LDCs are found within Africa, whereas the least expensive are from Singapore and Saudi Arabia to Asian LDCs.

In 2010, annual remittances sent to sub-Saharan Africa could have generated an additional $6 billion for recipients, if the costs of remitting money had matched the global average.

For sub-Saharan Africa, 65 per cent of all remittance payout locations are controlled by two MTOs (MoneyGram and Western Union).

African governments have put in place several RSP exclusivity arrangements limiting the type of institutions able to offer remittance services only to banks, thus reducing RSP competition.

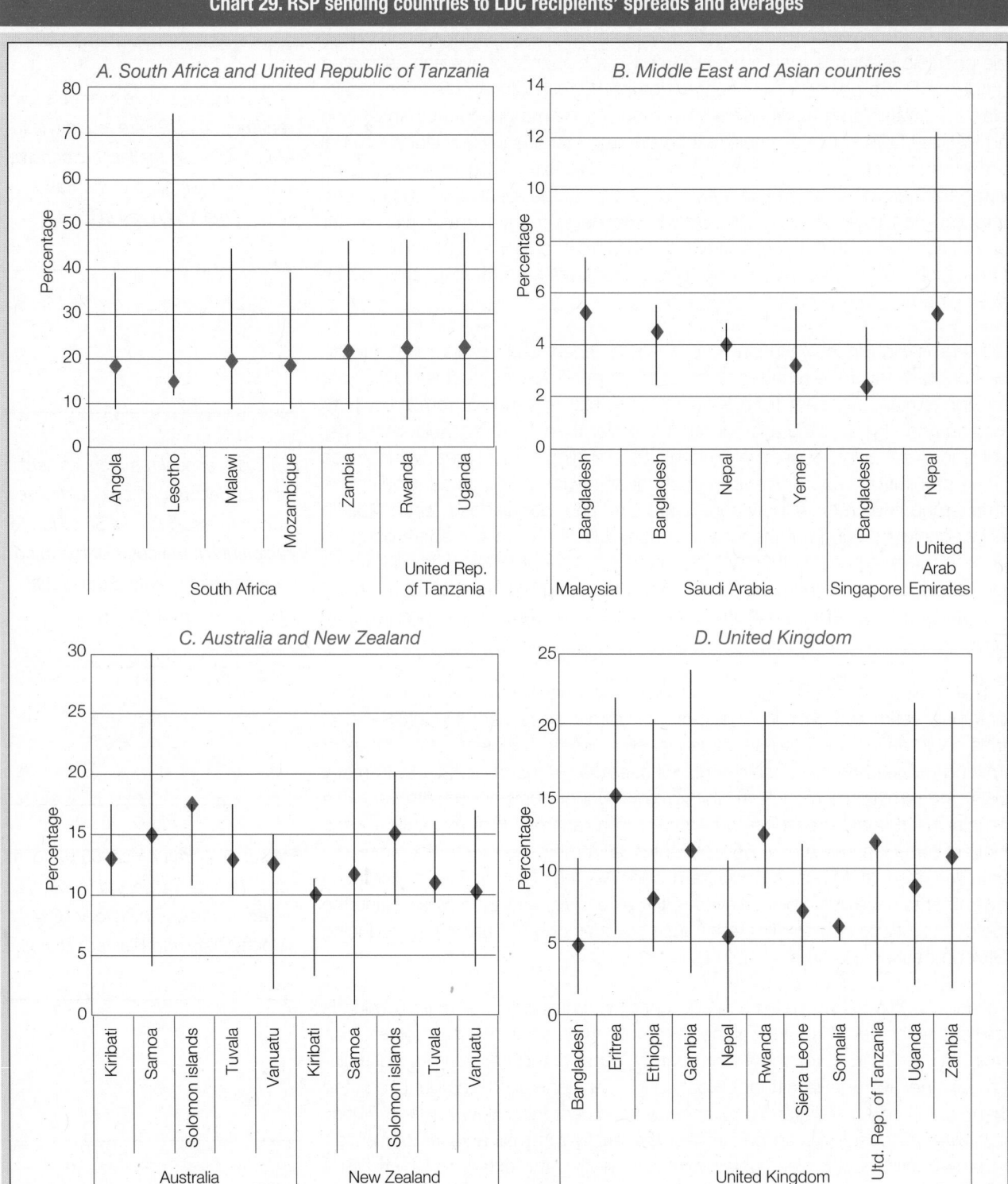

Chart 29. RSP sending countries to LDC recipients' spreads and averages

◆ Average

Source: UNCTAD secretariat calculations, based on The World Bank Group, *Remittance Prices Worldwide: Making Markets More Transparent,* online at remittanceprices.worldbank.org (accessed May, 2012; first quarter 2012 data).

unable to charge fees greatly in excess of their costs without losing market share to competitors. Among RSPs, financial institutions are on average around 22 per cent more expensive than MTOs in Australia and 10 per cent more expensive in New Zealand, although at an individual RSP level, the lowest cost providers in some New Zealand remittance corridors are banks. However, several studies suggest that remittance charges tend to decline with volume sent, and this is particularly true as regards charges for amounts ranging from $150 to $300 (Ratha et al., 2011; CGAP, 2010).

Competitive markets for transfer services tend to develop in areas where there are large immigrant populations, generating economies of scale that reduce transaction and transfer costs. The cost of formal international transfers to rural areas tends to be high (Orozco, 2010) and access to remittance outlets can present a problem for rural residents. Formal banking procedures (such as documentation requirements) and physical access difficulties constitute major barriers for the rural population (World Bank, 2005). The weak institutional capacity of rural finance providers is also related to the limited availability of educated and well-trained people in smaller rural communities — this is particularly an issue for community-based microfinance institutions (MFIs).

Accessible and low-cost money transfer mechanisms are not only needed for international remittances but also for domestic ones, i.e. for money sent from urban to rural areas or from one agricultural region to another (Wimaladharma et al., 2004; Pradhan et al., 2008). In Viet Nam, it was found that seven out of every eight transfers are domestic, although they make up only half the value of international remittances (Sander, 2003). Since international travel can be expensive, domestic remittances are particularly relevant to the rural poor (Faini, 2006).

In general, the lack of competition among RSPs appears to be a significant factor in explaining the high costs of remittances. The regulatory challenges that RSPs face vary by LDC and region, and have led to different characteristics in the respective remittance markets (UNCTAD, 2010b). Some of these are summarized in table 8 below and discussed in the next section of this chapter.

2. Emerging remittance transfer payment systems

Remittance transfer payments systems in LDCs are evolving, and new channels and technologies are emerging. In most LDCs, there is little interoperability between bank ATM and point-of-sale (POS)[32] networks, a factor which limits customer numbers and therefore the financial viability of these networks. Most bank branch and ATM networks are located in major population centres, limiting rural access. With improving LDC infrastructure and the growth in mobile bank branches and branchless banking, both urban and rural clientele

Accessible and low-cost money transfer mechanisms are not only needed for international remittances but also for domestic ones, i.e. for money sent from urban to rural areas.

The lack of competition among RSPs appears to be a significant factor in explaining the high costs of remittances.

Remittance transfer payments systems in LDCs are evolving, and new channels and technologies are emerging.

Table 8. Regulatory challenges facing international RSPs in LDCs	
Issues generic to international RSPs	• Acquiring the necessary authorization of non-bank entities to provide cross-border transfer services in LDCs often incurs high transaction costs. • Hard currency out-of-country transfer regulations, remittance service providers (RSPs) compliance with exchange control and reporting requirements are arduous and costly in some LDCs. • Exchange control regulations that require customers to provide reporting documentation in person may prevent mobile international remittance models from growing sustainably. Also, exchange controls and foreign currency rationing in LDCs may pose a significant barrier to South-South regional mobile international remittance development.
RSP exclusivity agreements	• In LDCs, often the largest MTOs enter into exclusive payment agreements with those banks that have the widest retail network, and that sometimes no other (non-bank) institutions are allowed to pay remittances. • Moreover to enter these markets, RSPs face a situation where the few banks allowed to pay remittances cannot sign an agreement with a new (possibly more efficient) RSP due to the exclusivity agreement; often other potential payment partners, such as MFIs or post offices, are prohibited from offering remittance services.
Issues specific to international remittances through mobile money	• Since 9/11, the existing international framework and national measures for anti-money laundering (AML) and combating the financing of terrorism (CFT) may have had far-reaching effects for LDCs. The introduction of stricter AML/CFT regulations (such as record-keeping and customer ID compliance regulations) may have unintentionally reduced the access of LDC populations to formal financial services. • AML/CFT requirements vary by country for both mobile RSPs and mobile money more generally. However, in many LDCs cross-border transactions now involve stricter compliance and increased requirements.
Mobile money specific issues	• Authorization of cash-in and cash-out services outside of bank branches in some LDCs is still greatly restricted. • In many LDCs, Central Bank authorities restrict the development of mobile international remittance deployments by not currently allowing the use of non-bank agents in fund transfer transactions.

Source: UNCTAD secretariat summary based on World Bank (2011a) and CGAP (2010).

access to financial services should improve. In LDCs, there are now more mobile subscriptions than bank accounts (chart 30). The UNCTAD Information Economy Report (2010b) shows that there is rapidly growing interactive connectivity in LDCs, which could facilitate access to financial services and low-cost mobile micro-insurance products. However, as noted in table 8, regulatory issues have arisen as a result of concerns at the international level about money laundering and the financing of terrorist activities (IMF, 2012).

> *There is rapidly growing interactive connectivity in LDCs, which could facilitate access to financial services and low-cost mobile micro-insurance products.*

Chart 31 shows a schematic of potential branchless banking options for remittance transfer in LDCs. There are four emerging delivery models of relevance to LDCs:

1. M-wallets (mobile money) to facilitate cash-in;
2. Customer m-wallets to enable cash-out;
3. Agent m-wallets (mobile money) to enable cash-out.
4. Prepaid cards that can be topped up directly from one sending country to enable cash-out (CGAP, 2012).

UNCTAD (2012c) has categorized mobile money services into three groups: (i) M-transfers: where money is transferred from one user to another, often referred to as person-to-person (P2P) transfers, which may be domestic or international; (ii) M-payments: where money is exchanged between two users with an accompanying exchange of goods or services; and (iii) M-financial

---

Chart 30. Bank accounts and mobile subscriptions per 1000 inhabitants, selected LDCs, 2010

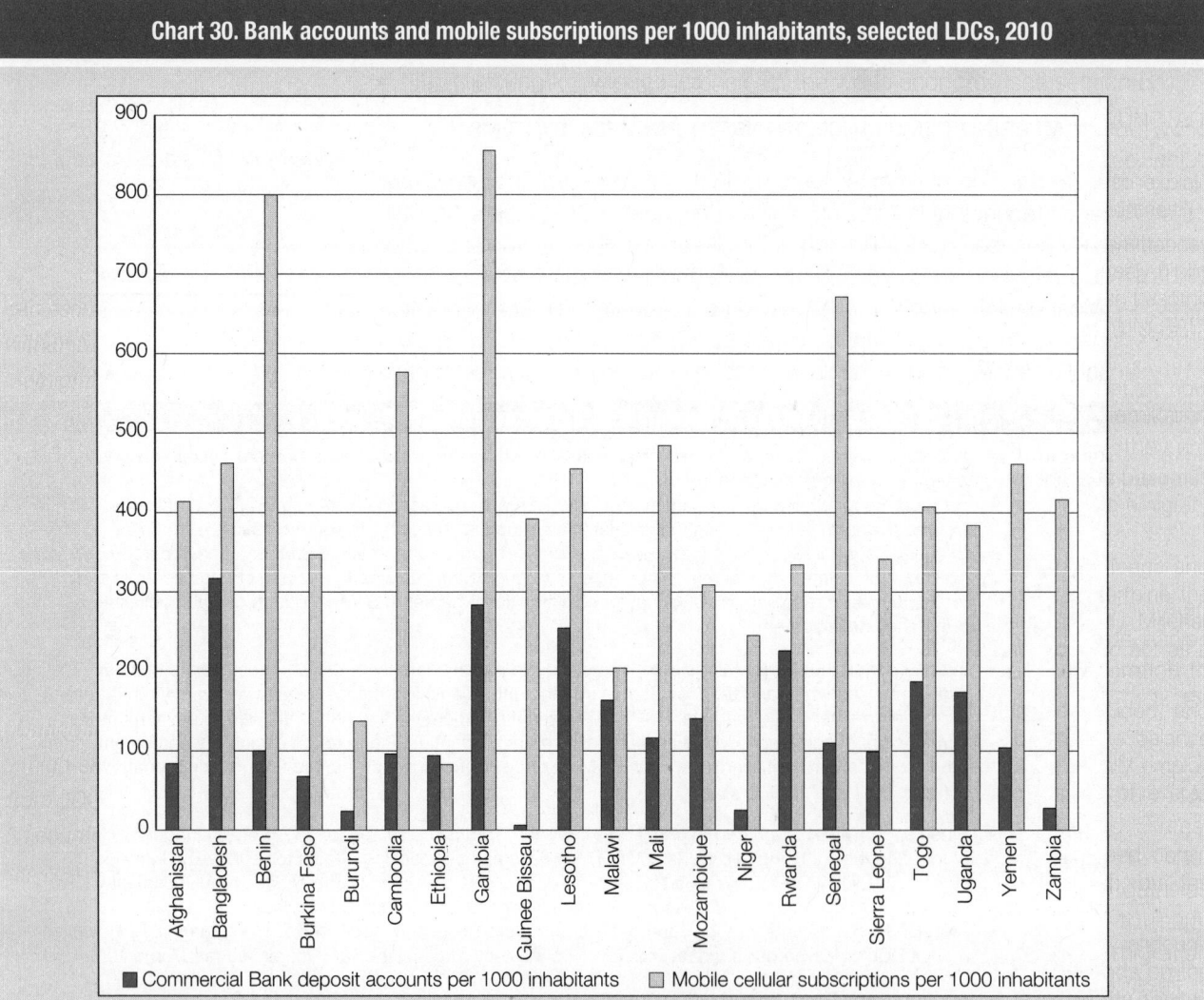

■ Commercial Bank deposit accounts per 1000 inhabitants   ▨ Mobile cellular subscriptions per 1000 inhabitants

Source: UNCTAD secretariat calculations, based on International Telecommunications Union ICT statistics at http://www.itu.int/ITU-D/ict/statistics, accessed in May, 2012. CGAP (2010).

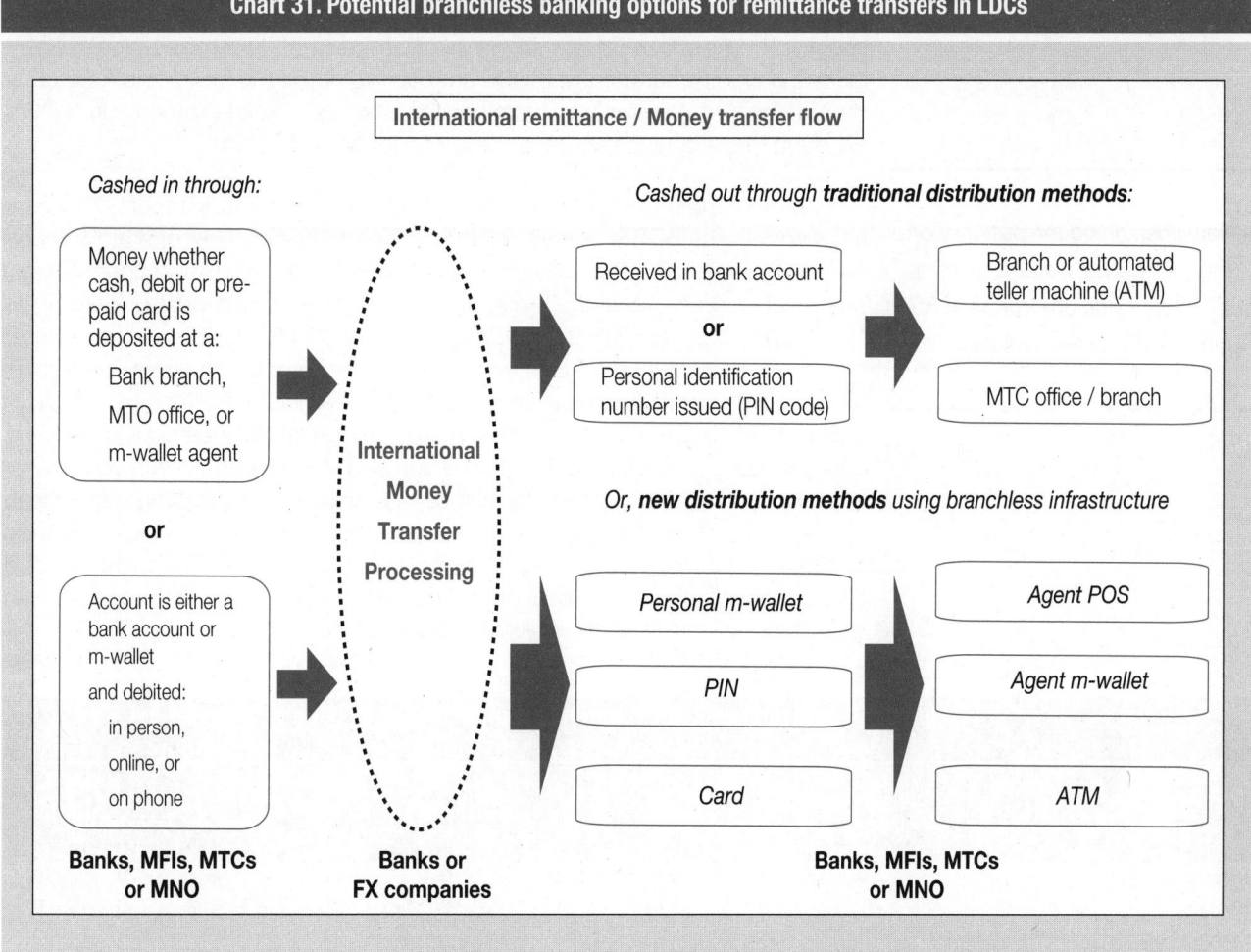

Chart 31. Potential branchless banking options for remittance transfers in LDCs

Source: Adapted from CGAP (2012).
Note: Mobile Telecommunications Company (MTC), Mobile Network Operator (MNO) (technology providers enhancing ATM interoperability with banks). Regarding mobile cash-in or cash-out methods, irrespective of how a sender transmits funds, these funds are stored in an m-wallet which can be used for mobile transactions or cashed through an MNO agent network.

services: where mobile money may be linked to a bank account to provide the user with a whole range of transactions (savings, credits) that they would ordinarily access at a bank branch (see chart 31).

Within Africa, the East African Community (EAC) is at the frontier of both mobile money transfer technology and payment systems. Nonetheless, most mobile money services across EAC are essentially domestic between urban and rural areas, with m-transfers accounting for the bulk of transactions (CGAP, 2012; UNCTAD, 2012c). Mobile money services may be gradually replacing traditional, often insecure informal methods of sending money.

The UNCTAD (2012c) study focusing on the EAC notes that some M-PESA agents perform informal cross-border mobile money transfers between Uganda and Kenya. Also, Western Union has already integrated its system with a number of mobile money platforms in the EAC in order to allow international remittances to be converted and credited directly to a user's mobile money account. At present, this movement is only one way and the service is currently operational on M-PESA in Kenya and MTN Mobile Money in Uganda. Clearly, this reflects potential nascent demand for mobile money remittance services, and could help facilitate growth in cross-border mobile money transfers and regional trade within the EAC. In addition, similar cash-in and cash-out mobile money transfer services are being established in other LDCs such as Bangladesh (Banglalink), Burkina Faso, Madagascar, Samoa and Tanzania.

Mobile money services may be gradually replacing traditional, often insecure informal methods of sending money.

Moreover, Western Union has established strategic alliances with MTN Uganda and Roshan in Afghanistan which will allow senders to remit funds directly to a recipient's mobile wallet from any of Western Union's agent locations worldwide. Clearly, MNOs are positive about the prospects for greater deployment of international remittances through mobile money in LDCs, although these benefits are most likely of a long-term nature.

Notwithstanding the potential of these emerging systems, in most LDCs more traditional forms of RSP provision still dominate.

Notwithstanding the potential of these emerging systems, in most LDCs more traditional forms of RSP provision still dominate. LDC MTOs operate through their own chain stores or a range of existing outlets, for example supermarkets, pharmacies, other transfer agents, bureaux de change and post offices. Since MTOs often partner with other outlets, they usually face lower operating costs than banking institutions. RSPs generate revenue through transfer fees, foreign exchange margins and delayed transfers (to earn interest income). Table 9 shows that MTO participation in the remittance market in African LDCs is heavily concentrated in the hands of Western Union and MoneyGram, which account for approximately 70 per cent of the market — five per cent above the pan-African average. Most financial market regulations in Africa only allow banks to provide remittance services (see table 8). Approximately 51 per cent of payments and 65 per cent of all pay-out locations are serviced by banks in partnerships with either MoneyGram or Western Union (IFAD, 2009).

Table 9. MTO participation in the remittance market in African LDCs
(Percentage)

	Western Union	Money-Gram	Coinstar	Money Express	Express funds international	Express Money Transfer	Trans-horn Money Trans	Money Transfer	Other
Angola	30	65	0	0	0	0	0	0	5
Benin	64	5	2	18	0	0	11	0	0
Burkina Faso	65	11	2	12	0	0	11	0	0
Burundi	85	3	3	0	0	0	10	0	0
Central African Republic	96	4	0	0	0	0	0	0	0
Chad	59	23	3	15	0	0	0	0	0
Comoros	67	5	2	0	0	0	0	0	26
Democratic Republic of the Congo	45	3	29	0	0	0	23	0	0
Djibouti	67	6	17	0	0	0	0	0	11
Equatorial Guinea	80	0	20	0	0	0	0	0	0
Eritrea	7	10	0	0	0	0	0	7	76
Ethiopia	33	14	2	0	0	24	0	0	28
Gambia	63	23	3	4	0	0	0	1	7
Guinea	66	18	1	5	0	0	1	0	9
Guinea-Bissau	64	13	8	0	0	0	0	0	15
Lesotho	0	12	0	0	0	0	0	0	88
Liberia	0	98	0	0	0	0	0	0	2
Madagascar	86	14	0	0	0	0	0	0	0
Malawi	43	38	5	0	0	0	0	0	14
Mali	77	14	1	3	0	0	5	0	0
Mozambique	37	17	0	0	0	0	0	0	47
Niger	63	12	0	13	0	0	1	0	11
Rwanda	79	3	0	0	0	0	18	0	0
Sao Tome and Principe	50	50	0	0	0	0	0	0	0
Senegal	38	9	21	15	0	0	17	0	0
Sierra Leone	32	36	1	0	0	0	4	6	21
Somalia	0	0	0	0	0	0	0	0	100
Sudan	41	0	54	0	0	0	0	2	2
Togo	50	7	1	26	0	0	16	0	0
Uganda	50	32	3	0	0	0	0	0	15
United Republic of Tanzania	44	9	0	0	0	0	0	0	47
Zambia	39	61	0	0	0	0	0	0	0
LDC average	**51**	**19**	**6**	**3**	**0**	**1**	**4**	**1**	**16**

Source: Adapted from IFAD (2009).

However, table 10 shows that although there is scope for greater participation of MFIs and post offices in providing remittance pay-out and transfer services in African LDCs, the market for these services is still dominated by banks, which account for 53 per cent of inbound payment of remittances in African LDCs. Although post offices have a strong geographical presence in African LDCs, they lack the necessary human capital, communications infrastructure and cashflow to participate effectively in the remittance pay-out market. Similarly, MFIs only account for five per cent of African LDC inbound payment of remittances by institution yet tend to have a greater institutional presence in rural areas, where most Africans still reside. Much of this is concentrated in six African LDCs: Rwanda, Burundi, the Central African Republic, Mali, Uganda and Togo (see table 10).

In LDCs, MFIs actually have a greater network and reach in rural areas than either commercial banks or cooperatives, especially as compared with ODCs (see table 11). However, efforts to promote competitive and reliable fund transfer services and to adopt technology that lowers the cost and improves the efficiency of financial services delivery to the rural population have been constrained by a lack of infrastructure and supportive legal frameworks. The rural poor would benefit directly from policies and regulatory systems that raise

There is scope for greater participation of MFIs and post offices in providing remittance pay-out and transfer services in African LDCs.

Efforts to promote competitive and reliable fund transfer services have been constrained by a lack of infrastructure and supportive legal frameworks.

Table 10. African LDC inbound payment of remittances by institution, 2010 (Percentage)						
	Bank	Forex	MFI	Other	Post	Retail
Angola	100	0	0	0	0	0
Benin	26	0	0	8	54	11
Burkina Faso	31	2	2	14	38	13
Burundi	68	0	21	11	0	0
Central African Republic	70	0	20	0	0	10
Chad	53	0	0	47	0	0
Comoros	12	0	9	0	76	3
Democratic Republic of the Congo	25	0	0	67	0	9
Djibouti	23	0	0	23	46	8
Equatorial Guinea	75	0	0	13	13	0
Eritrea	42	58	0	0	0	0
Ethiopia	89	0	0	10	1	0
Gambia	34	42	0	15	1	9
Guinea	47	6	0	28	0	19
Guinea-Bissau	26	26	0	48	0	0
Lesotho	100	0	0	0	0	0
Liberia	69	0	0	28	0	3
Madagascar	52	6	0	24	18	0
Malawi	70	10	0	15	0	6
Mali	59	0	17	15	9	0
Mozambique	100	0	0	0	0	0
Niger	33	0	6	18	28	14
Rwanda	63	0	24	9	4	0
Sao Tome and Principe	100	0	0	0	0	0
Senegal	13	0	9	26	53	0
Sierra Leone	62	20	0	16	0	3
Somalia	0	0	0	0	0	100
Sudan	18	46	7	29	0	0
Togo	23	0	14	25	38	0
Uganda	63	0	17	19	1	0
United Republic of Tanzania	65	0	0	10	25	0
Zambia	84	0	0	5	11	0
Average	53	7	5	16	13	7

Source: Adapted from IFAD (2009).

Table 11. LDC bank branches per hundred thousand adults, 2010			
	Commercial banks	Cooperatives	SSFIs	MFIs
LDC average	2.9	2.9	0.6	3.7
ODC average	16.0	2.5	1.5	1.6

Source: UNCTAD secretariat calculations based on CGAP (2010).
SSFIs = Specialized State Financial Institutions; MFIs = Microfinance Institutions.

confidence in the role of MFIs and other non-bank financial institutions and rural savings mobilization. They would also benefit if MFIs, post offices and banks acted as channels for rural payments and for the transfer of remittances. Efforts to promote partnerships between the private sector and governments (in both developed and developing countries) and to remove barriers to the flow of remittances also have the potential for improving access to finance for the rural poor and local SMEs.

The potential benefits of remittances would be maximized if LDC governments and their development partners could address transaction cost and access issues related to monetary transfers.

The potential benefits of remittances would be maximized if LDC governments and their development partners could address transaction cost and access issues related to monetary transfers. One way of doing this would be to launch initiatives with bilateral and multilateral partners to address existing infrastructural and regulatory barriers. In addition, there may be a need to promote greater competition among remittance service providers (Mundaca, 2009; Orozco, 2007; Sander, 2003). Microfinance institutions and credit unions are likely to be a key link in channelling remittances, particularly to rural communities, and in facilitating financial intermediation (Maimbo and Ratha, 2005; Orozco and Fedewa, 2006). However, promoting competition raises regulatory issues, primarily to ensure the reliability and integrity of transfer systems and to avoid their abuse (e.g. for money laundering). Policymakers face a challenge in striking the right balance between promoting competition and maintaining supportive regulations.

Policymakers face a challenge in striking the right balance between promoting competition and maintaining supportive regulations.

Data from the World Bank's Global Payments Systems survey, 2010 (2011c) about the relative importance, as rated by LDC central banks, of the various payment instruments for sending and receiving remittances, reveal that current account transfers are perceived as the most important instrument, followed by cash. For receiving remittances, most LDC central banks ranked cash and current account transfers as the most important and mobile phone payments as the least important. The ratings are similar to those reported by central bank respondents in ODCs.

Chart 32 shows the lack of cashless payment infrastructure such as ATMs, point-of-sale terminals, debit and credit cards in LDCs as compared with ODCs and developed economies. Although the expansion of the cashless payment infrastructure is increasing in LDCs, this is from a very low base. Moreover, in developed countries, an individual performs on average over 100 cashless transactions per year, while this same indicator is 19 for ODCs and economies in transition and less than 1 for LDCs. However, there is evidence of growth in per capita cashless transactions in both LDCs and ODCs during the period 2006–2009 (see chart 32). Within the LDC group, cashless transactions grew fastest in African LDCs during the period 2006–2009 (by approximately 500 per cent).

LDC policymakers need to introduce policy reforms to improve the national payments system, not just for remittance recipients but also for firms, in addressing the prevalence of more expensive cash-based transactions in LDCs.

In sum, it is clear that remittance payment systems in LDCs are comparatively limited and mainly located in urban centres. Moreover, the slow development of access channels to initiate and deliver cashless payments (e.g. POS terminals in many LDCs, together with inadequate interoperability of the infrastructure that already exists) has constrained access to modern and cheaper modes of accessing remittance services. It is likely that limited competition among RSPs, especially banking institutions, MTOs and other payment services providers, typically results in higher costs and less access to RSP services, especially in rural areas. Accordingly, LDC policymakers need to introduce policy reforms to improve the national payments system, not just for remittance recipients

Chart 32. Recent trends in LDC cashless payment systems 2004–2010

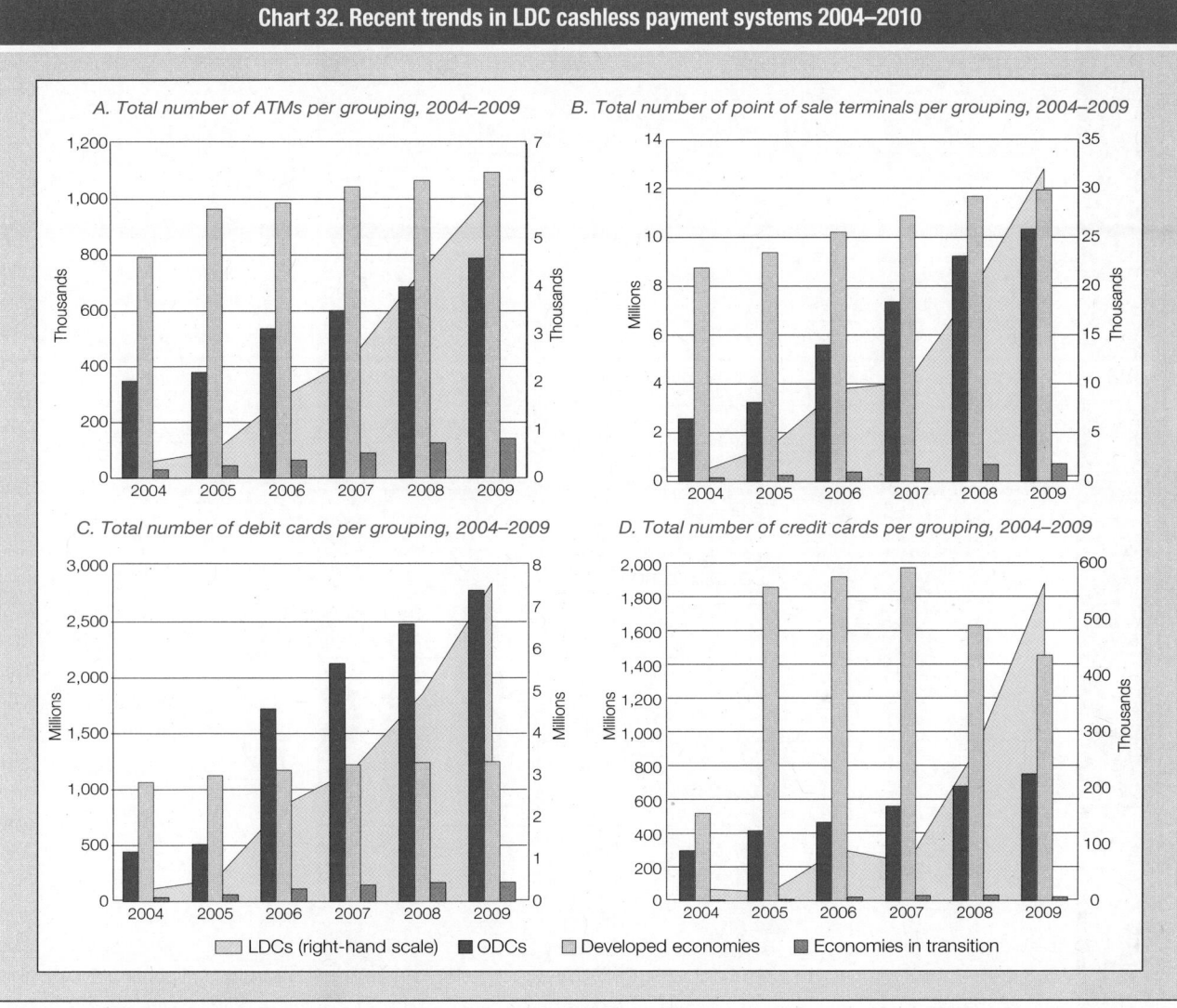

A. Total number of ATMs per grouping, 2004–2009

B. Total number of point of sale terminals per grouping, 2004–2009

C. Total number of debit cards per grouping, 2004–2009

D. Total number of credit cards per grouping, 2004–2009

☐ LDCs (right-hand scale) ■ ODCs ☐ Developed economies ■ Economies in transition

Source: UNCTAD secretariat calculations, based on World Bank Global Payment Systems Survey, 2010 at http://www.worldbank.org/paymentsystems.

but also for firms, in addressing the prevalence of more expensive cash-based transactions in LDCs.

Policies are also required to improve competition and regulation of the RSPs through greater transparency by providing more information about the service (price, speed, foreign exchange charges, etc.) (table 12). In an LDC context, this raises concerns about RSP services and appropriate consumer protection (see World Bank (2011b). Also, LDC-based RSPs face some financial risk (e.g. if liquidity is supplied to disbursing agents), legal and operational risks, and the threat of fraud.

Good governance and risk management practices by RSPs are required to help make remittance services safer and help protect LDC consumers.

There are of course cost implications for effective transparency and accountability mechanisms, which may well be passed on to customers. Therefore, good governance and risk management practices by RSPs are required to help make remittance services safer and help protect LDC consumers. Table 12 summarizes an initial assessment of the transparency of remittance services based on a selected sample of LDCs, and suggests that LDC RSPs in general, as compared with ODC RSPs, have a similar and reasonable regulatory framework in place (see table 12). Nonetheless, in an LDC context, we have highlighted the importance of RSP competition and the need to remove entry barriers for other potential remittance service providers, such as post offices and MFIs. This approach, particularly in an African LDC context, would be enhanced by the removal of exclusivity conditions (as opposed to an agent choosing to offer only one remittance service).

Table 12. Transparency of remittance services in selected LDCs, 2010

Country	Burundi	Dem. Rep. of the Congo	Eritrea	Ethiopia	Malawi	Mauritania	Nepal	Rwanda	Samoa	Sierra Leone	United Rep. of Tanzania	Timor-Leste	Uganda	Yemen	Zambia	LDC (%)	ODC (%)
a. RSPs are legally required to disclose fees applied.		x	x	x	x	x		x	x		x	x	x		x	73	44
b. RSPs are subject to different legal requirements as to fees disclosed, depending on the destination country.											x					7	23
c. RSPs are legally required to disclose foreign exchange rate applied.		x	x	x	x	x			x		x		x		x	60	65
d. RSPs are legally required to disclose taxes applied.			x	x	x	x					x				x	40	19
e. RSPs are legally required to disclose speed of the transfer.				x		x					x				x	27	21
f. RSPs are legally required to disclose available complaint mechanisms.											x				x	13	44
g. RSPs must inform customers on the details of the transaction before they perform it.	x		x	x		x	x	x	x	x	x				x	67	53
h. RSPs must provide customers with receipt containing the details of the transaction.	x		x	x	x	x	x	x	x	x	x		x	x	x	87	79

Source: World Bank (2011c) at http://www.worldbank.org/paymentsystems.
RSP = remittance service providers.

E. Conclusions

The evidence presented in this chapter highlights the importance of remittances to LDCs, not only in terms of the increasing value of these resources but also relative to the size of the recipient economies or to other sources of external financing. Notwithstanding some heterogeneity across individual countries, remittances appear to play a more prominent role in LDC economies than in other developing countries. There are distinct regional and subregional patterns of remittances, underscoring the significance of South–South flows not only in Asia but also within sub-Saharan Africa.

If the rise in remittances has increased the availability of external financing for LDCs, the developmental impact of this evolving reality is subject to a number of caveats. Migrants' remittances undoubtedly exert a positive effect at household level, in terms of poverty reduction as well as mitigation of adverse income shocks. It is less clear as to whether they contribute to the structural transformation of recipient countries or merely supplement disposable income with negligible (or possibly even adverse) consequences for long-term development.

Overall, the chapter shows that remittances do offer some scope to sustain the development of productive capacities, by increasing investment in human and physical capital and by stimulating financial deepening. However, the realization of such potential is contingent upon the policy and institutional framework which recipient countries put in place. In other words, owing to the intrinsic specificities of remittances as private sector financial flows, their effective mobilization for productive purposes essentially depends on the capacity of the State to create a "development-centred" macroeconomic environment while also supporting the establishment of a viable and inclusive financial sector. This, in turn, warrants a combination of policies at multiple levels, ranging from traditional macroeconomic policies capable of crowding in private investment and/or avoiding exchange rate appreciation to appropriate financial and regulatory reforms aimed at fostering financial deepening, thereby stimulating greater use of remittances for productive purposes.

Particularly in an LDC context, leveraging remittances to extend access to financial services will also require engaging with a broad range of financial actors, along with commercial banks and RSPs. State banks, post offices, microfinance institutions and agricultural development banks may have extensive branch networks that can be used to extend access to rural financial services quickly and relatively cheaply and reach out to a broad array of potential customers, from SMEs to micro-entrepreneurs. However, it is clear that greater competition in the RSP market involving a wider range of financial institutions with greater rural market penetration would be desirable in most LDCs.

Since LDCs typically face disproportionately high costs for remittance services, the chapter has also highlighted the role of RSPs and retail payment systems, payment platforms and instruments. In this respect, harnessing the development potential of remittances will require stronger competition in the remittance market and greater attention to regulation (clearing and settlement, capital adequacy, exchange controls, disclosure and cross-border arbitration). Wider LDC adoption of the 5x5, BIS-World Bank General principles for International Remittance services might facilitate this process. This and other policy proposals introduced in the present chapter will be elaborated upon in chapter 4 of this report.

Notwithstanding some heterogeneity across individual countries, remittances appear to play a more prominent role in LDC economies than in other developing countries.

Remittances do offer some scope to sustain the development of productive capacities.

Their effective mobilization for productive purposes essentially depends on the capacity of the State to create a "development-centred" macroeconomic environment while also supporting the establishment of a viable and inclusive financial sector.

Notes

1 In nominal terms, for instance, net ODA disbursements (excluding debt relief) declined from $57 billion in 1990 to $48 billion in 2000 then rose steadily over the 2000s, peaking at $125 billion in 2010, that, is, 2.6 times their value at the beginning of the decade. Conversely, global FDI flows rose from $207 billion in 1990 to $1,401 billion in 2000, peaking at $1,975 billion in 2007, but have not yet recovered since then: in 2011, they still totalled $1,524 billion.

2 Since recorded migrant stock does not capture short-term migration, it is also possible that such migration, including GATS-related movement, increased in this period.

3 It is worth noting that the rapid growth rate of remittance inflows to transition economies during the 1990s largely reflects the disruption of the Soviet Union and the consequent abrupt surge in both migrant stocks and international remittances.

4 Note, however, that improvements in the country coverage of the series only explain a minor part of the rise of LDC remittance inflows. When the analysis is limited to the 22 LDC countries with consistent data series over the 1980–2011 period, remittances grew at a rate very similar to the total figure (nearly 12 per cent per year), climbing from $2 billion in 1990 to nearly $20 billion in 2011.

5 In the wake of 9/11, the strengthening of financial controls led to the disruption of some informal "hawala" networks, leading migrants to switch to formal remittance channels (Maimbo and Ratha, 2005; Grabel, 2008).

6 The comparison between remittances and other types of foreign exchange inflows (such as export revenues, ODA, or FDI) makes sense from a national accounting point of view, but one should bear in mind that the former are radically distinct from other capital flows insofar as they are intrinsically linked to international migration. For a discussion of some delicate consequences of migration for home countries, notably the "brain drain", see chapter 4.

7 On the patterns of growth followed by the LDCs in this period, refer to (UNCTAD, 2010a, 2011a; Valensisi and Davis, 2011).

8 Data problems, including the presence of frequent zero entries, may also explain unrealistically high growth rates for remittance inflows to some recipient countries.

9 For instance, countries like Ethiopia and Haiti, which receive the bulk of remittances from the USA and other developed economies, were typically more adversely hit by the fallout of the global financial crisis than other LDCs, such as Bangladesh Lesotho or Nepal, whose diasporas mainly reside in other developing countries (UNCTAD, 2010a).

10 Unfortunately, the lack of adequate time series impedes an assessment of how remittance patterns to LDCs have evolved over time: estimates of bilateral remittance flows are only available for 2010.

11 The authors explain this finding, arguing that a persistent flow of remittances becomes an integral part of a household's income generation strategy and that the emigrant worker remits to simply replace his/her lost contribution to the household.

12 For instance, MacMaster (1993: 279) notes that "In the Cook Islands, Tonga and Western Samoa these [remittances] are a mixed blessing as they undermine the incentive to work and are rarely spent on productive investment." Similarly, Mitchell (2006: 21) voices the concern that "Remittances create dependency and act as a disincentive to the mobilization of domestic resources."

13 While differing in terms of country/time coverage, control variables included, and definition of remittances used (either "personal remittances" or only the balance of payment item "workers' remittances"; see box 3), these studies usually employ instrumental variable techniques or panel data methods to address issues of reverse causality and unobservable heterogeneity.

14 In the last two of the three papers referenced above, the authors indeed obtain a positive effect for the remittance variable on GDP per capita growth, but the corresponding coefficient is not significant.

15 All the authors referenced above have left aside distributional issues, although admittedly the propensity to save out of remittances income also depends on the affluence of the recipient households. Here, distributional aspects will be treated below.

16 Note that the idea that remittances "substitute" for a viable financial sector is contradicted by (Mundaca, 2009), who, however, does not include any interaction

between remittances and financial development. Incidentally, also observe that (Giuliano and Ruiz-Arranz, 2009) fail to obtain a statistically significant coefficient for the remittance variable in the growth regression, unless when they also include a variable for financial development, and the interaction between the two.

17 Interestingly, the positive effect of remittances on financial deepening appears to be stronger in terms of saving instruments than of access to credit, in line with the idea that remittances might ease credit constraints, thereby reducing the need for external financing from financial institutions (Anzoategui et al., 2011; Demirgüç-Kunt et al., 2011).

18 For example, the financial and housing crisis in the USA quickly triggered steep reductions of remittance receipts in many Central American economies and in Mexico.

19 It is worth noting that the gender dimension could also affect the sensitivity of remittances to business cycles. As women migrants are largely employed in the services sectors (especially as caregivers and housemaids), they tend to be less affected by business cycles than male migrants typically working in manufacturing and construction. Hence, countries with a higher proportion of female migrants tend to have less cyclicality in remittance transfers (Ghosh, 2009; UNDP, 2009).

20 Interestingly, the USA, where nearly half of the Haitian diaspora resides, favoured this process by granting temporary protected status for 18 months to Haitians already in the country. The temporary protected status allowed over 200,000 Haitians residing in the USA without proper documents to live and work legally, without fear of deportation. It also allowed them to send money home quickly and efficiently through formal remittance channels (Migration and Development Brief 12).

21 This definition of volatility is consistent with the one employed in (IMF, 2005).

22 Cyclicality in this case is measured as the correlation between detrended relevant inflows and detrended GDP growth. For all series, the Hodrick-Prescott filter has been used to separate the trend from the cyclical component, setting the smoothing parameter equal to 7, in line with standard practice.

23 Using a slightly different approach, (Neagu and Schiff, 2009) find that for a panel of 116 countries, remittances tend to be more stable and less procyclical than FDI but more erratic than ODA, which in turn tends to be countercyclical.

24 This point appears to be confirmed by other studies as well (World Bank, 2008; Acosta et al., 2009).

25 The positive impact of remittances on inequality (and not just on poverty measures) in the Pacific region is likely to be explained not only by geographic proximity, but also by the existence of specific policy frameworks favouring circular migration between Australia or New Zealand and several Pacific Islands.

26 The World Bank – 5x5 General Principles for International Remittances Services are as follows:

GP1: The market for remittances should be transparent and have adequate consumer protection;

GP2: Improvements to payment system infrastructure that have the potential to increase the efficiency of remittance services should be encouraged;

GP3: Remittance services should be supported by a sound, predictable, non-discriminatory and proportionate legal and regulatory framework;

GP4: Competitive market conditions, including appropriate access to domestic payments infrastructures, should be fostered in the remittance service industry; and

GP5: Remittance services should be supported by appropriate governance and risk management practices.

27 UNCTAD (2012c) defines mobile money as funds stored using the SIM (subscriber identity module) in a mobile phone as an identifier as opposed to an account number in conventional banking. Mobile money banking works as follows: (i) notational equivalent is in value issued by an entity (i.e. an MTO) and is kept in a value account on the SIM within the mobile phone that is also used to transmit transfer or payment instructions, while the corresponding cash value is normally held in a bank; (ii) the balance on the value account may be accessed via the mobile phone, which is also used to transmit instant transfer or payment instructions (UNCTAD, 2012c).

28 The exchange rate spread is the difference between the exchange rate applied by the RSP to convert, for example, dollars into local currency and the interbank (market) exchange rate. RSPs usually offer the sender a less favourable exchange rate than the market rate.

29 A survey of the charges borne by LDC remitters suggests that they vary according to whether money is transferred in local or foreign currency. RSPs (including MTOs) tend to charge more when the amount is sent in dollars (this is an additional source of profit for the RSP and an additional cost component). Conversely, if the money is sent in local currency at lower fees, the recipient loses a percentage of the remittance in the foreign exchange rates. In LDCs, a growing number of companies offer money transfers in dollars. However, it should be noted that this activity does not necessarily guarantee that received remittances will not include detrimental exchange rate charges, as banks can sell dollars at adverse exchange rates (in an LDC context, this is a subject requiring further research but is currently beyond the scope of this report). Nevertheless, it should be noted that the lower costs of delivering funds in dollars are not a complete saving for the recipient with a different national currency, as he or she will still need to convert the dollars into local currency, an operation which entails a transaction cost.

30 According to the World Bank Global Payments Systems Survey of 2010 (2011), a number of RSPs reported that in some countries, the largest MTOs enter into exclusive payment agreements with those banks that have the widest retail networks and that sometimes no other (non-bank) institutions are allowed to pay remittances. In response, regulators in some countries, including Nigeria and Ethiopia, have banned exclusive remittance agreements. They report that a number of new providers have entered the market as a result and that prices have fallen.

31 Pacific LDCs might reasonably expect a more than proportionate increase in remittances from a reduction in the related transaction costs, as remittances appear to have a negative cost-elasticity with respect to the fixed fee component of money transfer costs (Ratha and Shaw, 2007; Ratha, Mohapatra and Saheja, 2011; Gibson et al., 2006).

32 Point of sale (POS), such as electronic funds transfer at a point of sale (EFTPOS), is a payment system involving electronic funds transfers based on the use of debit and credit at terminals located at points of sale.

CHAPTER **4**
MOBILIZING THE DIASPORA:
FROM BRAIN DRAIN TO BRAIN GAIN

A. Introduction

The present chapter analyses two aspects of international migration in the LDCs not yet discussed in this Report. First, it studies the flows of knowledge and technology stemming from the international movement of labour — particularly from the migration of so-called high-skilled persons — , their impact on the human capital endowment and technological accumulation of LDCs, and the emergence of diaspora knowledge networks. Second, the chapter examines the impact of international migration on the business activities of these countries through two mechanisms: international trade and investment flows between home and host countries; and returnee entrepreneurship.

Brain drain is more prevalent in LDCs than in other developing countries.

The issues of brain drain, brain gain, brain circulation and the effects of diaspora networks on home countries are very contentious. They involve complex processes produced by economic, political and social factors and strongly influenced by policies in both sending and receiving countries. Mainstream academic and policy discussions have swung from a pessimistic view to a rather optimistic position on these processes. A significant share of the literature is theoretical, but lacks empirical validation. Another portion of research focuses on national or local case studies, the conclusions of which cannot always be generalized. There is scarcely any study of these processes for the group of LDCs, which is what this chapter strives to do.[1] It shows that brain drain is more prevalent in LDCs than in other developing countries and is especially strong in islands and some African LDCs. However, the potential contribution to the home country stemming from the strong presence abroad of high-skilled LDC nationals and other members of the diaspora is not automatically realized. This is especially true of knowledge transfer and sharing, the strengthening of trade and investment linkages, or the contribution of returnees to their home country. Achieving this potential depends on a series of institutional, economic and political conditions, which are so far missing in most LDCs. Therefore, policy action by home and host countries, as well as by the international community, is crucial in order to foster or strengthen positive diaspora effects on LDCs.

The potential contribution stemming from diaspora is not automatically realized.

Policy action is crucial in order to foster or strengthen positive diaspora effects on LDCs.

The chapter is organized as follows. Section AB explains how home country economies can be adversely affected by brain drain and analyses its trends globally and in the LDCs. Incorporating more recent research on the issue, Section C analyses how the international movement of skilled persons has the potential to benefit the countries of origin, and examines to what extent LDCs are availing themselves of these opportunities. Section D summarizes and concludes.

B. Brain drain and its adverse implications for home countries

1. ANALYTICAL FRAMEWORK

All international movement of labour entails some degree of knowledge flow across countries.

Labour movements and knowledge flows. All international movement of labour entails some degree of knowledge flow across countries, which takes place in two basic forms. First, embodied knowledge directly accompanies people whenever they move across borders temporarily or permanently, "carrying with them" the knowledge which has been accumulated through education, learning and/or experience. Second, once migrants are settled abroad they can share their knowledge, skills and technology with their home country at a distance (e.g. through information and communication technologties (ICTs)), i.e. without this involving the cross-border movement of natural persons.

International migrants consist of people with all levels of educational background, including those with no formal education and those with some degree of primary, secondary or tertiary education. Differences in knowledge and skills between non-migrants and migrants and among the latter tend to become more accentuated as the migratory experience unfolds. Time spent studying, living and working abroad usually allows migrants to be exposed to different cultural and business environments and to acquire new skills, such as language, craft, technological, academic, professional, managerial, networking and relational capabilities. This human capital accumulation abroad takes place through different mechanisms, including formal education, informal channels (e.g. on-the-job training, learning by doing while working) and/or accumulated experience (Dustmann et al., 2011; Domingues dos Santos and Postel-Vinay, 2003). All emigrants can acquire some type of new skills and knowledge, but this tends to happen more intensively the more skilled emigrants are, through a process of cumulative causation driven by the increasing returns that are typical of knowledge and its accumulation.

Time spent studying, living and working abroad usually allows migrants to acquire new skills.

While all international migrants have some knowledge and skills, a large portion of the research and policy discussions on brain drain and brain circulation focuses on so-called "high-skilled migrants". These are migrants who have some length of tertiary (i.e. university-level) education, ranging from one year of study at this level to post-doctorate graduates.[2] Statistics generally use this definition of high-skilled worker. Accordingly, brain drain has been defined as "the migration of engineers, physicians, scientists, and other very highly skilled professionals with university training" (Docquier and Rapoport, 2008).

All emigrants can acquire some type of new skills and knowledge, but this tends to happen more intensively the more skilled emigrants are.

Two other categories largely overlap with that of high-skilled workers: knowledge workers and talent. Knowledge workers are those persons who possess specialized knowledge and are involved in high value-added and high-productivity jobs that are essential for the global knowledge economy and society. The category of internationally mobile talent is composed of three broad types: 1. directly productive talent (entrepreneurs, executives, managers, and technical engineers); 2. scientific talent (academics, scientists and international students); and 3. health and cultural talent (physicians, nurses, artists, musicians, writers, and media-related people) (Solimano, 2008).

Brain drain is the migration of engineers, physicians, scientists, and other very highly skilled professionals with university training.

The knowledge-based economy and brain drain. International movements of skilled people or talent are a feature of the knowledge-based economy (David and Foray, 2002; Foray, 2006; Hollanders et al., 1999). The latter also has the following defining features:

- It produces increasingly knowledge-intensive goods and services, which in turn require skilled labour inputs for their production. This raises demand for skills (or talent) both in terms of the number of workers and in terms of the skill level of each worker;

- The intangible capital stock (resulting from investment in education, training, research and development, health, etc.) tends to become larger than physical capital (physical infrastructure and equipment, natural resources, etc.);

- Knowledge is increasingly becoming the crucial determinant of countries' long-term growth and international competitiveness.

International movements of skilled people or talent are a feature of the knowledge-based economy.

Given these developments, knowledge is part of UNCTAD's definition of productive capacities and plays an essential role in the development of LDCs (UNCTAD, 2006: 59–84, 2007: 1–10).

The agglomeration economies typical of knowledge-intensive activities lead to the concentration of high-skilled people in a few locations (nationally) or countries (internationally). Talented individuals rarely develop their full potential by working in isolation. A new idea, a new product, a new production process or a new scientific theory requires human interaction and cooperation. An entrepreneur needs access to capital, markets and technology to develop his or her new ideas and visions. A scientist needs a certain number of peers to discuss his or her theories and present research papers. As a result, highly skilled people from both developed and developing countries — including LDCs — who decide to emigrate mainly choose developed countries as their migration destination (see subsection B2a below).

The agglomeration economies of knowledge-intensive activities lead to the concentration of high-skilled people in a few countries.

Recent research[3] on high-skilled labour identifies the following main factors that drive its international mobility:

- More favourable conditions for professional development in host countries. In destination countries, high-skilled emigrants typically earn higher salaries than in their home countries. The pay gap is such that salaries in developed destination countries are sometimes 20 times higher than in LDC countries of origin. Host countries allow higher labour productivity, thanks to a better institutional environment and to the externalities stemming from the agglomeration of knowledge workers. Complementarities between talent, capital and technology reinforce these agglomeration economies. Moreover, destination countries offer better opportunities for professional development in terms of career advancement prospects as well as better living conditions for emigrants and their families, superior infrastructure necessary for work and daily life, and political stability. In most cases, host countries offer more favourable conditions for research and academic interaction for scientists, as well as more secure property rights for entrepreneurs;

The main factors driving international mobility of high-skilled labour are: (a) More favourable conditions for professional development in host countries; (b) Adverse conditions in home countries; (c) Lower relative migration costs for the high-skilled; (d) Selective immigration policies for attracting foreign talent.

- Adverse conditions in home countries (e.g. political strife, civil conflict, insecurity), which act as push factors of international migration;

- Lower relative migration costs for the high-skilled as compared to the low-skilled, given the former's easier access to information on host country labour markets, more favourable migration conditions and their greater access to transportation;

- Selective immigration policies for attracting foreign talent enacted especially by several developed countries.

2. Brain drain trends

The following section briefly analyses global trends and future prospects for international flows of high-skilled labour, in order to put trends concerning brain drain and knowledge circulation in LDCs into perspective.

a) Global trends

Brain drain has been increasing worldwide in absolute figures.

Current flows of high-skilled workers. Brain drain has been increasing worldwide in absolute figures. The number of high-skilled international migrants climbed from 16.4 million in 1990 to 26.2 million in 2000, which implies an annual growth rate of 4.8 per cent. Between 2000 and 2010, the emigration of highly educated persons continued to increase, rising at an estimated annual pace of 4 per cent (based on figures for the United States, the largest destination for brain drain worldwide and home to some 40 per cent of all high-skilled emigrants). Complete data on worldwide bilateral flows of high-skilled labour are available for 1990 and 2000, because at the time of writing this Report, most results of the 2010 round of population censuses (the major primary source for brain drain statistics) had not yet been published.[4] The UNCTAD secretariat has collected more updated indicators and information on high-skilled emigration from LDCs and has also commissioned case studies on some of these countries. Together, these sources of information and data provide solid evidence for analysing major flows, trends and structural features of brain drain.

International immigration is selective, since it is skewed towards highly educated people. Twenty-six per cent of all international migrants are tertiary-educated (according to data for 2000), while only 11.3 per cent of the world labour force have tertiary education. In developing countries, university-level workers account for a much lower five per cent of the labour force.

International immigration is selective, since it is skewed towards highly educated people.

The selectivity of international migration is also reflected by the different emigration rates, i.e. the number of emigrants as a share of the corresponding labour force segment. Worldwide, the emigration rate is 6.6 per cent for all tertiary-educated people, well above the 2.63 per cent emigration rate of low-skilled people. Moreover, the degree of skill-based selectivity of immigration varies sharply according to the development level of the host country, rising with the development level of the destination country of international migrants. In developed countries, 35 per cent of immigrants are tertiary-educated, while in other developing countries (i.e. those developing countries which are not LDCs) this share is one-third of that level: 13 per cent. In LDCs, by contrast, a mere four per cent of immigrants are highly skilled (chart 33). Immigration selectivity has been increasing. Worldwide, the total stock of high-skilled immigrants rose by 60 per cent between 1990 and 2000, while that of low-skilled migrants went up by a modest 16 per cent. This is largely driven by immigration trends in developed countries. There, the selection rate (i.e. the tertiary-educated as a share of all immigrants) rose by six percentage points in the ten years to 2000. This confirms the tendency of human capital to agglomerate in locations where it is already relatively abundant (Docquier, Marfouk et al. 2011), a tendency which is reinforced by selective immigration policies in major destination countries.

The degree of skill-based selectivity of immigration rises with the development level of the destination country.

More than half of international high-skilled migration is South–North. The second most important flow of tertiary-educated people is North–North: migration among developed countries amounts to almost one-third of

More than half of international high-skilled migration is South–North.

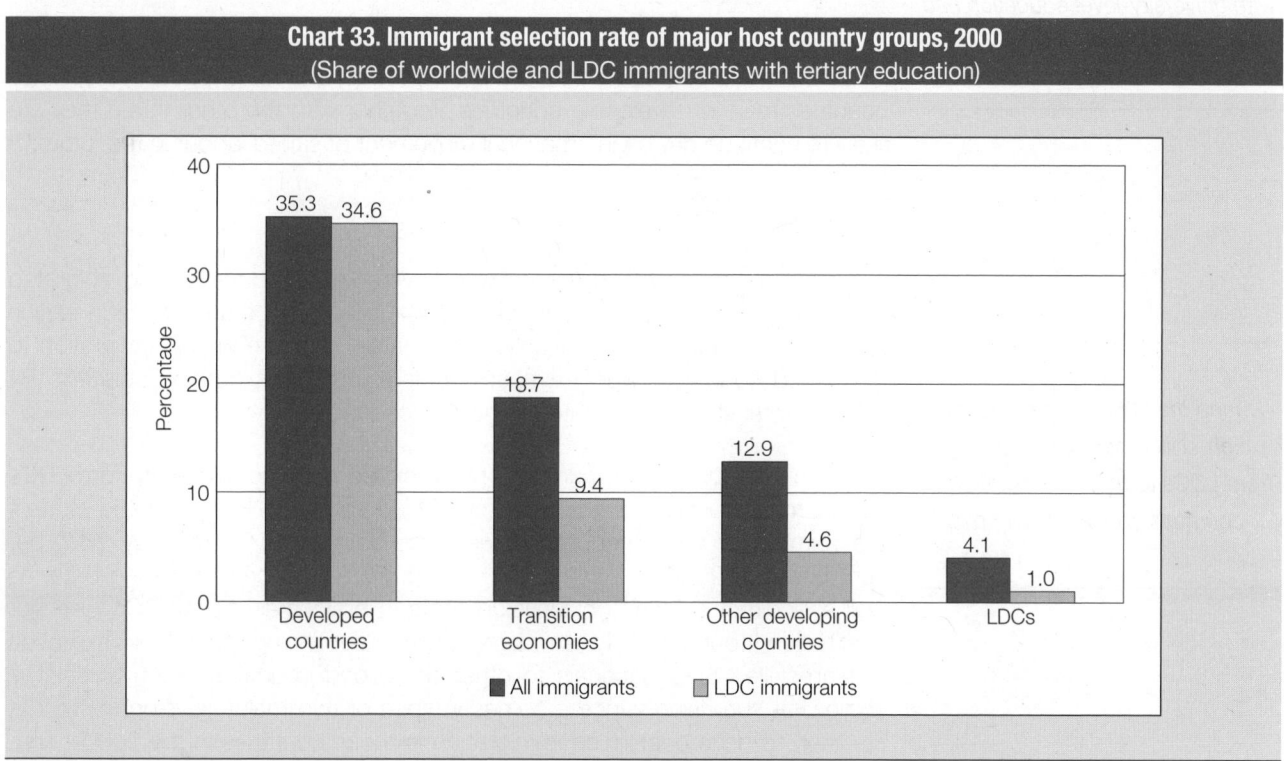

Chart 33. Immigrant selection rate of major host country groups, 2000
(Share of worldwide and LDC immigrants with tertiary education)

Source: UNCTAD secretariat calculations, based on data from Docquier et al. (2011).

international skilled labour flows. Skilled migration flows are highly concentrated in a few destination countries, and developed countries absorb some 80 per cent of all international high-skilled migratory flows. The major country is the United States, which hosts some 40 per cent of all internationally mobile high-skilled people. It is followed by Canada, Australia, United Kingdom, Germany, Russian Federation and France.[5] The professions most affected by brain drain are computer specialists, accountants, managers, medical doctors and nurses and, among higher education levels, scientists and academics.

Skilled migration flows are highly concentrated in a few destination countries, and developed countries absorb some 80 per cent of these flows.

The gender balance of brain drain seems to be closely associated with the level of development of destination countries. In developed countries, high-skilled men and women each account for half of total high-skilled immigration. In the group of other developing countries, two-thirds of all tertiary-educated immigrants are male, while in LDCs this share is 71 per cent. In developing countries of origin, genders differ slightly in their brain drain rates (i.e. the number of tertiary-educated emigrants as a share of the labour force at the same level of education in the home country). They are five per cent for males and six per cent for females. The main reason for this discrepancy is that tertiary education enrolment in home countries is higher for males than for females (Docquier and Rapoport, 2012).

The international mobility of high-skilled persons is likely to continue in the future.

Future outlook. Based on underlying forces pushing current international migratory flows, and barring major disruptions in the international economy, the international mobility of high-skilled persons is likely to continue in the future, largely as a result of the following trends:

- The growing knowledge intensity of the world economy (see section B1);

- The decline in demographic growth and consequent ageing of the world population, as well as the expanding demand for health services which accompanies development;

- The steadily falling costs of transportation and communication;

- Economic interdependence brought about by globalization;

An estimated 1.3 million workers with university-level education had emigrated from LDCs by 2000.

- The lingering income gaps between professionals in developed and in developing countries.

The first two processes above are progressing at a faster pace in developed countries than in developing countries. Together with the other three, they are likely to continue driving international movement of skilled labour in the future.[6]

b) LDC trends

An estimated 1.3 million workers with university-level education had emigrated from LDCs by 2000. While this was 58 per cent more than a decade earlier, bilateral flows developed unevenly. The greatest increase was in emigration to developed countries, which almost doubled during this period (table 13). By now the total stock is estimated to have exceeded two million.

During the 2000s, the number of high-skilled persons migrating from LDCs to the main destination countries continued to grow.

During the 2000s, the number of high-skilled persons migrating from LDCs to the main destination countries continued to grow. In the United States, the number of tertiary-educated residents born in LDCs rose by 78.7 per cent between 2000 and 2010. Table 14 provides the corresponding data, as well as indirect evidence of developments in brain drain from LDCs to major destination countries.[7] These data indicate continuing growth in migration of high-skilled LDC nationals to other developed countries. Such a result is somewhat surprising, since it comes in spite of two major developments that are likely to have depressed immigration in those countries in the 2000s: first, the immigration backlash following the 9/11 attacks; and, second, the world economic and financial crises which started in 2007. These developments seem

Table 13. International high-skilled migration corridors fom LDCs, 2000
(Number of high-skilled migrants and percentage)

Country of origin	Country of destination									
	Developed			Transition economies	Other developing			LDCs		Total
	Asia Pacific	Europe	North America		Africa	America	Asia	Africa	Asia	
Number of migrants										
LDC Africa	14,245	170,814	178,561	55	86,763	380	44,696	29,809	-	525,323
LDC Americas	20	2,127	150,999	0	19	8,138	11	-	-	161,314
LDC Asia	37,179	67,041	192,243	218	2,297	17	295,669	-	2,703	597,367
LDC Pacific	10,450	354	5,762	1	4	1	6	-	-	16,578
LDC Total	61,894	240,336	527,565	274	89,083	8,536	340,382	29,809	2,703	1,300,582
Percentage of destination										
LDC Africa	23.0	71.1	33.8	20.1	97.4	4.5	13.1	100	-	40.4
LDC Americas	-	0.9	28.6	-	-	95.3	-	-	-	12.4
LDC Asia	60.1	27.9	36.4	79.6	2.6	0.2	86.9	-	100	45.9
LDC Pacific	16.9	0.1	1.1	0.4	-	-	-	-	-	1.3
LDC Total	100.0	100.0	100.0	100.0	100.0	100.0	100.0	100	100	100.0
Percentage of origin										
LDC Africa	2.7	32.5	34.0	-	16.5	0.1	8.5	5.7	-	100.0
LDC Americas	-	1.3	93.6	-	-	5.0	-	-	-	100.0
LDC Asia	6.2	11.2	32.2	-	0.4	-	49.5	-	0.5	100.0
LDC Pacific	63.0	2.1	34.8	-	-	-	-	-	0.0	100.0
LDC Total	4.8	18.5	40.6	-	6.8	0.7	26.2	2.3	0.2	100.0

Source: UNCTAD secretariat calculations based on data from Docquier et al. (2011).

Table 14. Indicators of high-skilled immigration from LDCs to selected host countries in the 2000s
(Persons and percentage)

Host country	Indicator	Initial period (A)	Latest period (B)	Persons		Change
				(A)	(B)	(B/A : %)
United States[a,b]	Number of tertiary-educated residents from 15 LDCs (amounting to 91 per cent of total LDC high-skilled residents in 2000)	2000	2010	381,425	681,485	78.7
	Number of non-resident visas for skilled persons granted to nationals from all LDCs	1998-2000	2008-2010	1,289	1,364	5.9
Canada[c]	Permanent residents born in all LDCs	1999-2001	2009-2011	15,950	22,813	43.0
	Arrival of students born in all LDCs	1999-2001	2009-2011	1,514	2,406	58.9
United Kingdom[d]	Nationals from all LDCs given work permit for jobs other than domestic work	2004	2009	676	1,581	133.9
	Nationals from all LDCs granted entry into the UK under PBS Tier 1 (Highly skilled workers) and PBS Tier 2 (Skilled workers) schemes	2009	2010	788	1,077	36.7
France[e]	Number of workers' visas granted to nationals from all LDCs	2004-2005	2007-2008	324	1,214	274.7
	Number of student visas granted to nationals from all LDCs	2004-2005	2007-2008	4,841	4,446	-8.2
Australia[f]	Number of high-skilled nationals from all LDCs arriving for permanent settlement	2000-2001	2010-2011	964	1,121	16.3

Source: UNCTAD secretariat elaboration based on the sources quoted in the notes (see below).
Notes: When periods are indicated, data refer to annual averages. The destination countries above hosted 55 per cent of high-skilled emigration from LDCs in 2000.
   a US Census 2010 (for 2010); American Community Survey 2010 (for 2010) for the number of tertiary-educated residents from 15 LDCs.
   b State Department, for the number of non-resident visas for skilled persons. Includes the following visa types: H1-B, H1-C, L1, O1 and E-2.
   c Statistics Canada.
   d Home Office and National Statistics. PBS: Points Based System for immigration, introduced in 2008.
   e Institut national d'études démographiques.
   f Department of Immigration and Citizenship.

to have been offset by the continuing operation of the push and pull forces driving brain drain mentioned in section B1.

Host countries. Almost two-thirds of LDC high-skilled emigrants live in developed countries, while one-third moved to other developing countries. Skilled migratory flows from LDCs are directed mainly to developed America and Europe, oil-exporting developing countries and neighbouring countries (chart 34). The major destination country of the LDC brain drain is the United States, which hosts one-fourth of all LDC high-skilled emigrants. Other major destination countries are Saudi Arabia, Canada, the United Kingdom, India and France (chart 35). North America hosts almost the entirety of the Haitian brain drain and approximately one-third of high-skilled emigration from the LDCs of Africa, Asia and the Pacific (table 13). The remaining flows from each of these regions differ geographically. For African LDCs, the other major destination is developed Europe (especially the United Kingdom, France and Belgium) and, to a lesser extent, other developing African countries (mainly Côte d'Ivoire, South Africa and Kenya). Asian LDCs are the group for which intraregional South-South flows are the most pronounced: almost half of their high-skilled emigrants live in other Asian developing countries (especially India, Saudi Arabia, Thailand, Iran and the Gulf States). For Pacific LDCs, New Zealand and Australia host almost two-thirds of their high-skilled emigrants.

The selection rate of immigration from LDCs is directly related to the income level of destination countries, as is the case for immigrants from all other countries. In developed countries, the selection rate is highest: 35 per cent of all immigrants born in LDCs are tertiary-educated. In other developing countries, the corresponding share is much lower (five per cent), while in the case of other LDCs it is a scant one per cent. In other words, intra-LDC migration largely consists of low-skilled persons. The total selection rate of LDC immigrants in developed countries is similar to that of immigrants coming from other regions. In developing countries, by contrast, immigration from LDCs is much less selective than migratory flows originating in other country groups (chart 33). This confirms the strong Northern bias of LDC skilled emigration. Available data indicate that LDC emigration selectivity rose in the 2000s. In the United States (the largest host country for LDC high-skilled emigrants), the selection rate for LDC nationals rose from 32.4 per cent in 2000 to 48.3 per cent in 2010 (based on the same sample as table 14).

Home countries. The major source of high-skilled LDC emigrants is Asia, which generates 45.9 per cent of tertiary educated migrants from LDCs. It is followed by African LDCs, which account for 40.4 per cent of the LDC brain drain (table 13). Regional figures, however, mask a very strong concentration of migratory flows in a few countries. The largest LDCs of origin for skilled migrants are Bangladesh and Haiti, both of which have more than 160,000 high-skilled nationals living abroad. These two countries account for 30 per cent of all LDC migration. They are followed by Afghanistan, Yemen, Sudan, Lao People's Democratic Republic, Ethiopia and Cambodia, each of which have more than 50,000 high-skilled people living abroad (chart 36). Taken together, these nine countries account for almost two-thirds of LDC brain drain. Data on the major bilateral high-skilled migration corridors originating in LDCs are shown in table 15.

Brain drain rates. Collectively, the LDCs are by far the most seriously affected by brain drain among the country groups shown in chart 37. They have an average brain drain rate of 18.4 per cent, much higher than other developing countries (10 per cent). Regionally, the worst affected subgroups are LDCs from the Americas (Haiti), Pacific and Africa, which have higher brain drain rates than all other groups of developing countries except the Pacific ODCs. The LDC regional group with the lowest brain drain rate is Asian LDCs (chart 37).

Skilled migratory flows from LDCs are directed mainly to developed America and Europe, oil-exporting developing countries and neighbouring countries.

The selection rate of immigration from LDCs is directly related to the income level of destination countries.

The major source of high-skilled LDC emigrants is Asia (45.9 per cent of the LDC brain drain) followed by African LDCs (40.4 per cent).

The LDCs are by far the group most seriously affected by brain drain.

Chart 34. Main LDC high-skilled emigration corridors

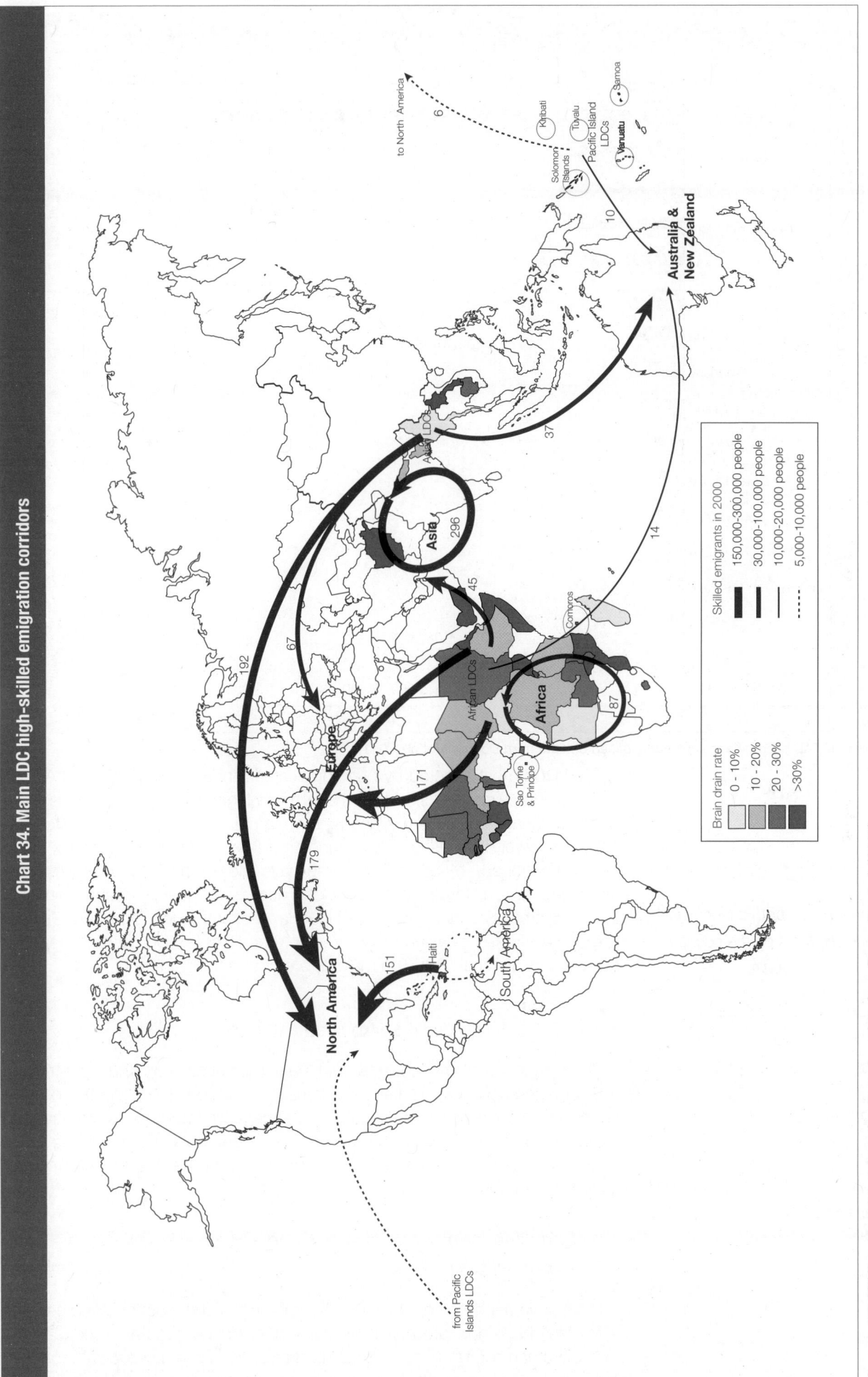

Source: UNCTAD secretariat elaboration based on data from Docquier et al. (2011).

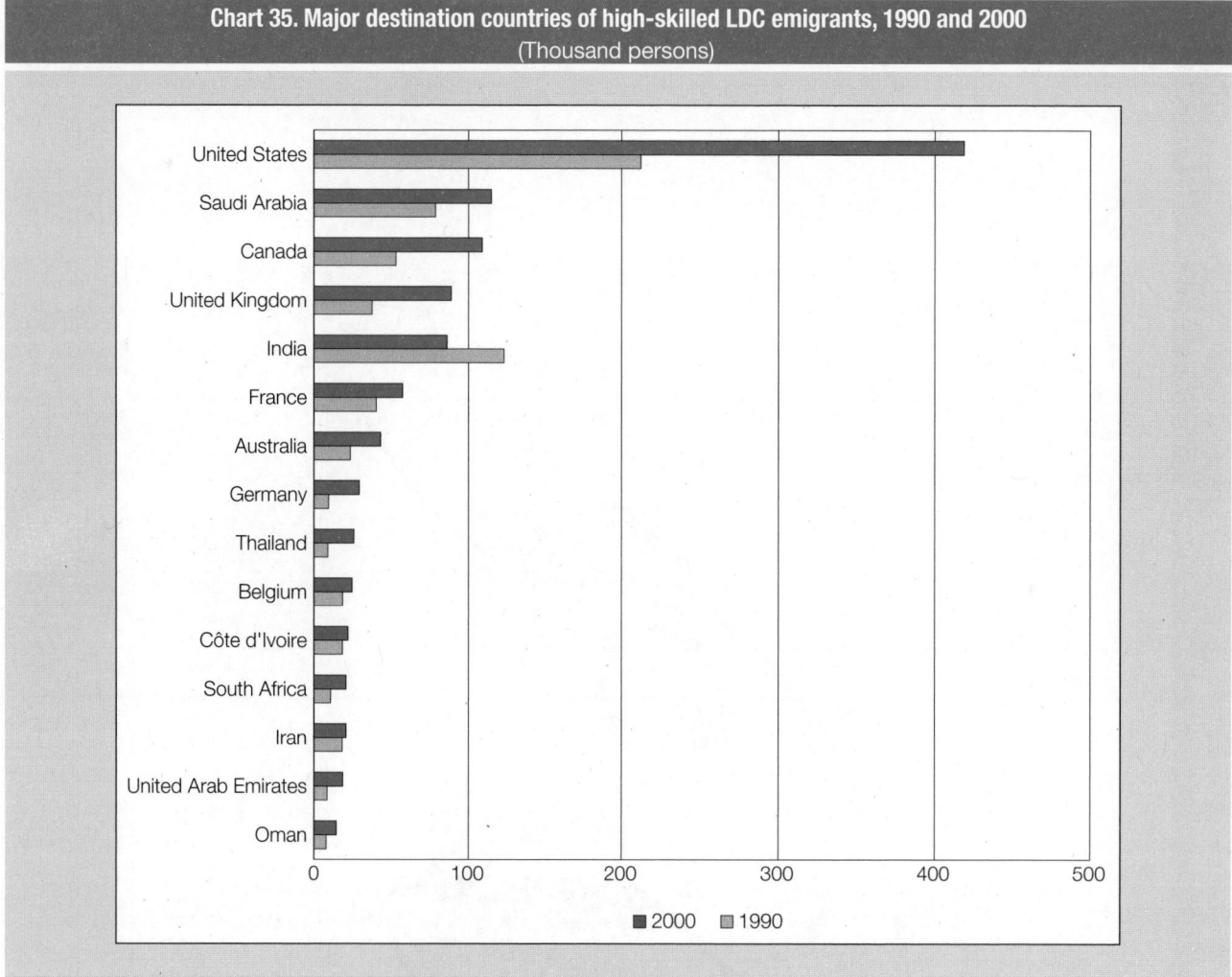

Chart 35. Major destination countries of high-skilled LDC emigrants, 1990 and 2000
(Thousand persons)

■ 2000   ■ 1990

Source: UNCTAD secretariat calculations, based on data from Docquier et al. (2011).

The LDCs most affected by brain drain are islands or relatively small African countries. For example, six LDCs have more high-skilled professionals living abroad than at home: Haiti, Samoa, the Gambia, Tuvalu, Kiribati and Sierra Leone. However, the case of Haiti stands out (box 5). Apart from the six LDCs already mentioned, 11 other LDCs also have more than 30 per cent of their high-skilled labour force living abroad. These are mostly African countries (Liberia, Eritrea, Somalia, Rwanda, Uganda, Mozambique, Togo and Guinea-Bissau), and three are Asian LDCs: Yemen, Lao People's Democratic Republic and Afghanistan (chart 38). The majority are post-conflict States.

3. ADVERSE IMPACTS

Brain drain has both adverse and beneficial effects on the countries of origin of high-skilled emigrants, as summarized in table 16. While the positive aspects are discussed later in section C, the negative implications are analysed below. The adverse impacts of brain drain can be especially damaging when the countries of origin are developing countries and/or they have a small pool of highly qualified human resources.

a) Shrinking human capital stock and slower economic and productivity growth

Brain drain deprives countries of origin of some of the most qualified persons whom they have educated and trained. In the source country, it reduces the stock of human capital, a factor which is already scarce in developing countries, especially in LDCs (box 6). This effect is particularly strong if a large share of

Brain drain has both adverse and beneficial effects on the countries of origin.

Brain drain deprives countries of origin of some of the most qualified persons whom they have educated and trained.

Chart 36. Number of skilled emigrants from LDCs, 1990 and 2000
(Thousand persons)

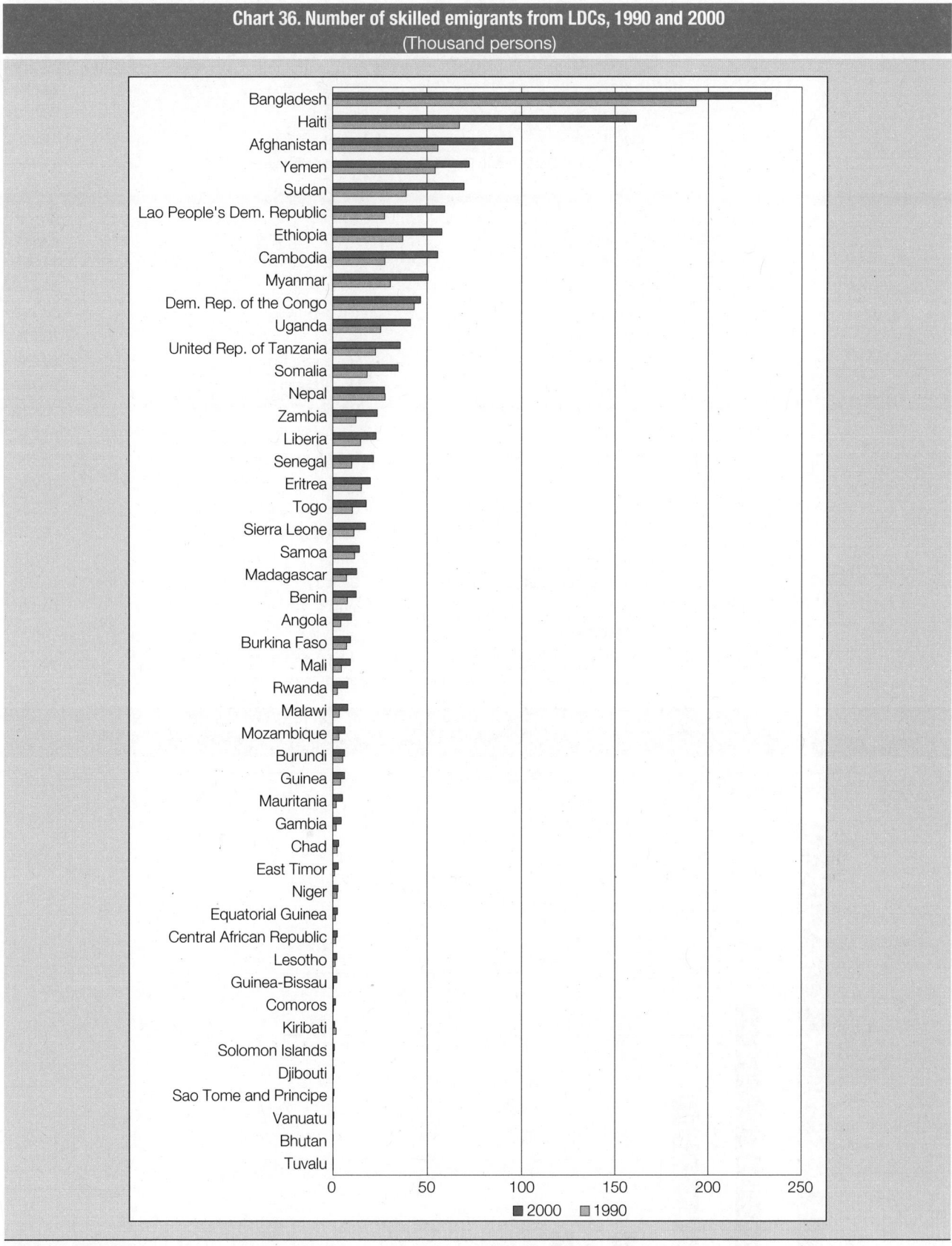

Source: UNCTAD secretariat calculations, based on data from Docquier et al. (2011).

high-skilled people emigrate (Berry and Soligo, 1969; Bhagwati and Hamada, 1974). Given the fundamental role played by human capital in long-term growth and development, brain drain could have the impact of slowing down the origin country's economic growth rate (Miyagiwa, 1991; Haque and Kim, 1995; Wong and Yip, 1999). The adverse impact of shrinking human capital on development is especially acute as the world economy becomes increasingly knowledge-based.

Table 15. Largest bilateral migration corridors for skilled emigrants from LDCs, 2000 (Number of migrants)		
Originating LDC	**Destination country**	**Skilled migrant stock**
Haiti	United States	126,524
Bangladesh	India	70,092
Bangladesh	United States	41,920
Lao People's Democratic Republic	United States	41,440
Bangladesh	Saudi Arabia	41,222
Yemen	Saudi Arabia	39,200
Ethiopia	United States	34,428
Cambodia	United States	32,955
Haiti	Canada	24,475
Sudan	Saudi Arabia	22,399
Afghanistan	Iran	20,715
Afghanistan	United States	19,246
Liberia	United States	18,436
Democratic Republic of the Congo	Belgium	18,428
Myanmar	United States	18,047
Uganda	United Kingdom	17,600
Myanmar	Thailand	15,742
Bangladesh	United Kingdom	15,507
Afghanistan	Germany	14,519
Bangladesh	Oman	12,625
United Republic of Tanzania	Canada	12,220
Nepal	India	11,179
Bangladesh	Canada	11,065
United Republic of Tanzania	United Kingdom	10,535

Source: UNCTAD secretariat calculations based on data from Docquier et al. (2011).

Chart 37. Brain drain rate of country groups, 2000
(Percentage)

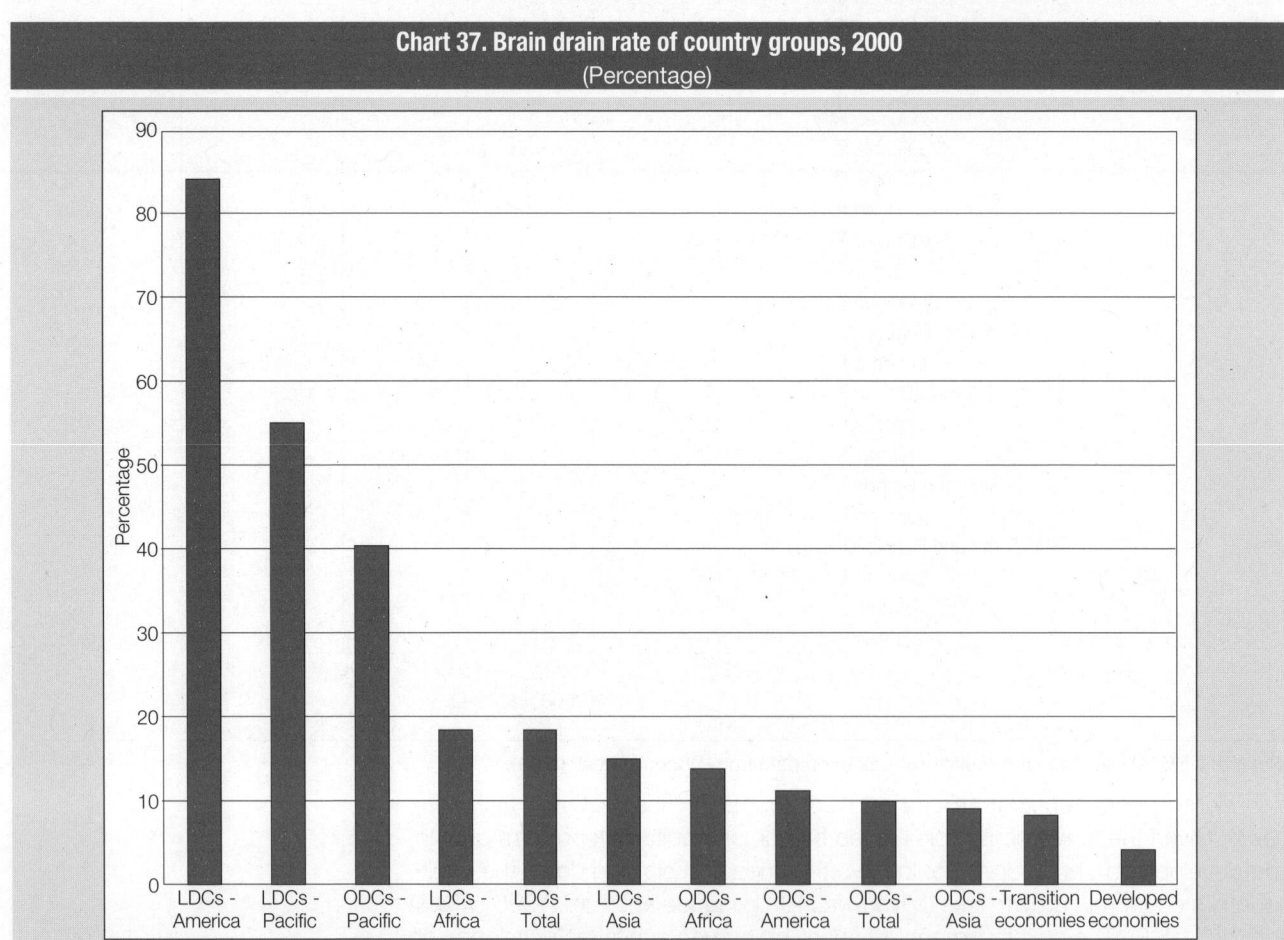

Source: UNCTAD secretariat calculations, based on data from Docquier et al. (2011).
Note: The brain drain rate is the emigrants' share of the correponding age and educational group in the home country.

Box 5. Brain drain and the labour market in Haiti

Most LDCs with very high brain drain rates are countries with a small population. Haiti is an exception. Its population was 8.6 million in 2000 and currently stands at 10.3 million. Yet it has the highest brain drain rate of all LDCs (83.4 per cent). This places Haiti worldwide among the countries most affected by brain drain, since only six other countries have brain drain rates above 80 per cent.

Labour market conditions in the country largely explain the extent of brain drain, according to the national case study prepared for this Report. Although some 200,000 people enter the labour market every year, labour demand does not even represent 10 per cent of this supply. Moreover, almost half of all Haitians over 65 continue to work, due to the lack of a well-functioning retirement pension system. The chances of finding a job are higher for university graduates than for secondary-educated people, but they are still low. Nevertheless, this situation acts as an incentive with regard to higher education, although the additional supply of skills is not met by demand.

A major job website for qualified professionals posted 2,230 positions between 2008 and 2010. Based on the highly conservative assumption that only five per cent of available jobs are advertised, this would bring the total number of jobs to 44,600 for the three-year period, far from matching a labour market supply of 600,000. In view of this labour supply mismatch, especially for skilled labour, there are only two options: resort to informality, which is already the main sector of employment in the country,[1] or emigrate. Orozco (2006) points out that close to 90 per cent of Haiti's skilled emigrants moved abroad due to lack of job opportunities.

Apart from the very difficult conditions of the labour market, other features push skilled Haitians abroad, such as insecurity and the political situation. Conditions were worsened by the earthquake of 2010. It is estimated that after this natural disaster, one-third of the remaining high-skilled persons living in the country decided to emigrate.

[1] Some 57 per cent of employment in Haiti takes place in the informal sector (IHSI, 2010).

Table 16. Possible effects of brain drain on (developing) home countries

Effect types / Processes	Adverse	Beneficial
Knowledge and human capital	• Shrinking human capital base • Less innovation • Sectoral impacts, especially health and education • Brain waste	• Brain gain • Transfer/sharing of skills/technology • Diaspora knowledge networks • Acccumulation of broader/deeper knowledge/skills/experience
Macroeconomic processes	• Slower economic growth • Declining high-skill labour externalities • Lower productivity growth • Less entrepreneurship • (Fiscal) cost of educating high-skilled persons • Foregone taxes paid by high-skilled persons	• Returnee entrepreneurship

Trade / capital flows	• Changing relative resource endowments away from skills	• Remittances
		• Diaspora savings: bonds, deposits, loans, funds, etc.
		• Diaspora effects and business networks:
		  • creation/strengthening of trade flows: merchandise and services (e.g. tourism)
		  • creation/stregthening of foreign direct investment

Institutional processes	• Lower supply of/demand for institutions	• Diaspora assistance in/pressure for institution-building • Returnee supply of/demand for institutions

Source: UNCTAD secretariat.
Note: The table presents the potential effects of brain drain which can generally affect home economies negatively or positively. The actual impact on individual countries depends on their specific conditions and on their level of economic, social and instiutional development.

Brain drain reduces welfare due to the loss of externalities. The high-skilled labour force tends to have a positive externality on the rest of the labour force, since the latter emulates the better qualified workers and thereby achieves higher productivity. Therefore, the positive impact of highly talented persons goes well beyond their small numbers in the population. If many of the most highly skilled workers leave the country, this externality is considerably reduced (Haque, 2005).

Brain drain can have an adverse effect on local science and knowledge systems.

Apart from this general formulation on human capital, brain drain can have an adverse effect on local science and knowledge systems (box 7 provides the example of Ethiopia), impairing the economy's capacity to produce and

Chart 38. Brain drain rate of LDCs, 1990 and 2000
(Percentage)

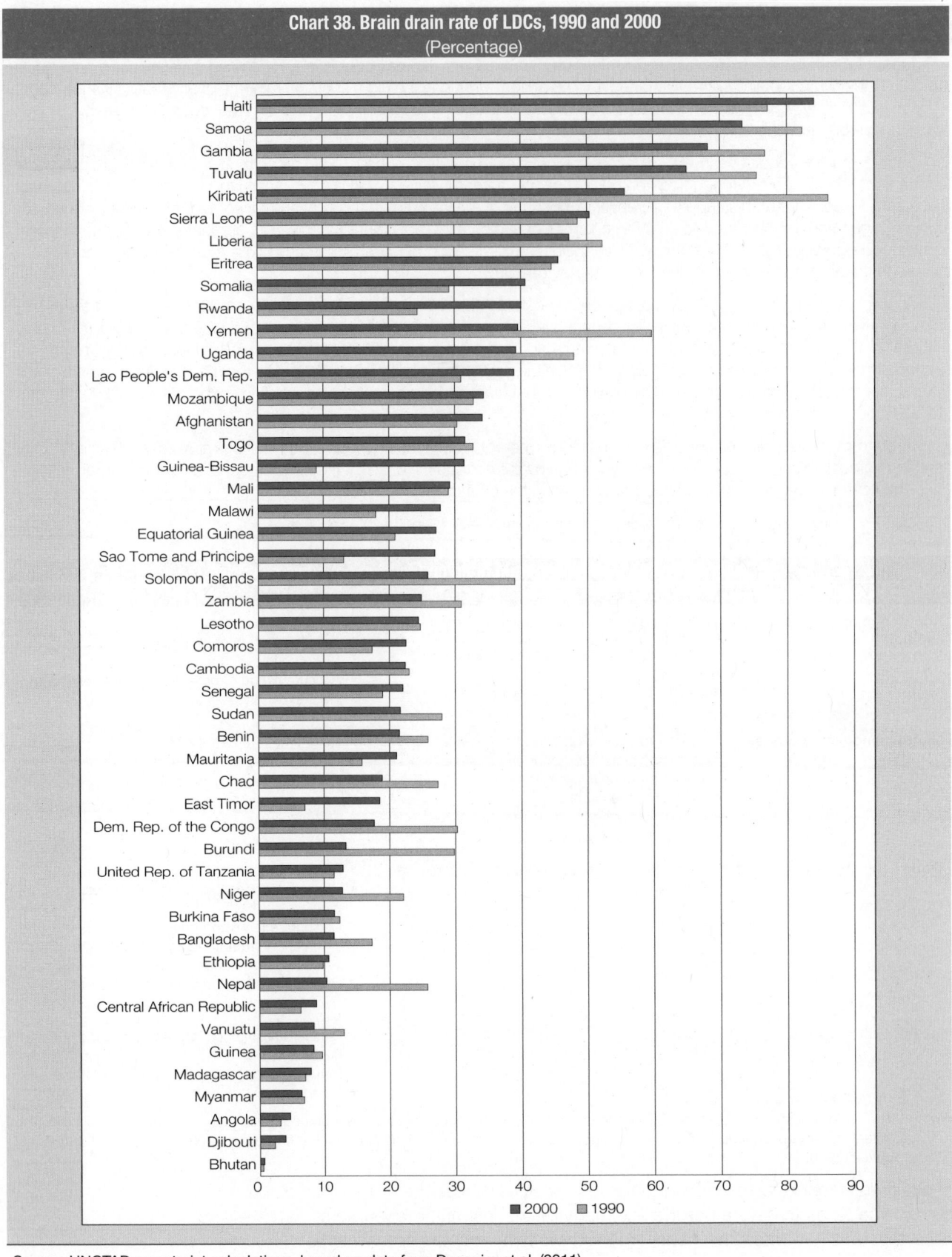

Source: UNCTAD secretariat calculations, based on data from Docquier et al. (2011).

implement innovation. This, in turn, slows down productivity growth (Kapur and McHale, 2005; Agrawal et al., 2011). Schiff and Wang (2009) empirically estimate that higher brain drain rates reduce the technological absorptive capacity of home countries and thereby the degree to which they incorporate technological innovation. As a result, brain drain could lead to lower productivity growth.

Box 6. Human capital endowments and international labour and resource flows

Least developed countries have relatively more low-skilled than high-skilled labour. In the LDCs, the ratio of the former to the latter is 42. This is more than double the level in other developing countries (16) and more than ten times higher than in developed countries, where the ratio is just 4.[1] Prima facie, it could be expected that high-skilled labour has the highest return where it is relatively scarcer, i.e. in developing countries and especially in LDCs. Therefore, highly qualified labour should apparently flow to the latter countries, where human capital is most scarce and knowledge stocks are lowest. In absolute figures, the prediction of the conventional view is verified: low-skilled emigration from LDCs outpaces high-skilled emigration by a ratio of 11. Yet this same ratio shows that LDCs are exporting high-skilled labour more intensively than low-skilled labour, since the low/high-skilled ratio of "labour exports" (i.e. emigration) corresponds to just one-fourth of the ratio of endowments. Another way of measuring the relative "export intensity" at the different skill levels is through the emigration rates for low-skilled and high-skilled labour.[2] In 43 out of the 48 LDCs, the emigration rate of high-skilled labour is higher than that of low-skilled labour, and the opposite is true in only five of these countries.

The above data reveal that the vast majority of LDCs export high-skilled labour more intensively than low-skilled labour. This finding contradicts the expectations mentioned above based on apparent returns to knowledge. The explanation for this apparent paradox seems to lie in the particular nature of human capital embodied in people. Knowledge is subject to increasing returns and to positive agglomeration effects. Agglomeration economies generate centripetal forces, so that human resources tend to agglomerate in locations which already have a considerably stock of qualified persons. Agglomeration leads to higher productivity and earnings in these locations. For instance, Clemens et al. (2008) estimate that on average, Haitians moving to the United States boost their incomes almost sevenfold. Beyond earnings differentials, the significance of agglomeration effects is particularly strong for research and scientific production, which depend on the availability of scientific infrastructure (laboratories, measurement instruments, specific materials, sophisticated machinery, access to databases and libraries, interaction with colleagues, face-to-face discussions and collaboration, etc.).

South–North migration of high-skilled labour amounts to an international transfer of (human) resources from the poorest countries to the richest. Similarly, South–South flows of high-skilled people from LDCs (around one-third of the total) are directed to developing countries with a relatively higher development and income level.

[1] Data are for 2000, the year for which the latest bilateral high-skilled migration matrix is available.

[2] The emigration rate is the number of emigrants divided by the corresponding skill and age group. In the case of high-skilled labour, it is the brain drain rate.

Box 7. The effects of brain drain on higher education and academic research in Ethiopia

The exponential growth of higher education in Ethiopia over the last 15 years (section C1) hides the extent to which the sector is adversely affected by brain drain. The number of students graduating at the bachelor's level rose sharply from 29,800 in 2007 to 75,300 in 2011. At the same time, however, the corresponding figure for higher level education (master's and PhD) rose much more moderately: from 2,700 to 6,200.

As a result, there is a dearth of people with doctorate-level degrees in Ethiopia, and this is especially true where they are most needed, i.e. in higher education. Among the 15,192 teachers and researchers working in the country's 25 universities, only 979 (6.4 per cent) hold a doctoral degree. Moreover, PhD holders are very unevenly distributed, since half of them work at the University of Addis Ababa. The bulk of the country's university teachers and researchers have only a master's degree (43.4 per cent) or a bachelor's degree (42.6 per cent). Ethiopian higher education institutions sorely lack very high-skilled people.

The number of PhD-holding teachers and researchers active in the country's universities is much lower than the members of the Ethiopian diaspora just in the United States and Canada who have that level of education: 1,600, according to conservative estimates. The case study on the Ethiopian academic diaspora prepared for this Report identified 200 Ethiopian professors currently working in foreign universities, of whom 148 are active in the United States. Among these, 72 are full professors. In Ethiopia, by contrast, only 65 persons hold an equivalent position. In other words, there are more Ethiopian full professors working in the United States than in Ethiopia itself, in spite of the strong need of Ethiopian universities for very highly skilled people.

In order to respond to the stringent need for more qualified university teachers and professors, the Ethiopian Government has launched a campaign to recruit 631 teachers and researchers, especially from India. Whether this programme will succeed is not yet clear. Nevertheless, if properly implemented, its implications for the country's limited foreign exchange will be significant.

Brain drain can also comprise entrepreneurs and students (i.e. future professionals). The former's departure deprives the home country of some of the people who create businesses and employment. As for students, most developing countries send some of them abroad for tertiary-level studies, as a means of expanding and improving the human capital stock of the home country. However, this often becomes a route to brain drain. The greater the gap between the conditions in the study country and those in the home country, the higher the probability of graduates staying abroad (Finn, 2010), which shrinks the human capital base of the home country.

b) Sectoral impacts

The impact of reduced availability of qualified professionals could be more acute in some sectors, for instance education and scientific activities (box 7) and health (box 8). These are the main sectors responsible for building and improving countries' human capital endowment. Their malfunction due to brain drain hampers the continuing formation of human capital, which in turn is likely to depress the national long-term growth rate.

The impact of reduced availability of qualified professionals could be more acute in some sectors, for instance education and scientific activities.

c) Fiscal costs and foregone revenues

Expanding a country's human capital base through education has a high cost, which is financed to a large extent by the State.[8] Typically, the persons thus trained work, live and pay taxes in the home country upon completion of education (at whatever level). This allows the State to partly recoup the investment through the taxes (income, property, indirect, etc.) generated by these people. In the case of brain drain, however, this payback does not occur, because emigrants generally live, work and pay taxes abroad (Bhagwati and Hamada 1974; Grubel and Scott 1966; Berry and Soligo 1969; Johnson 1967; Kwok and Leland 1982). Although these effects take place for all sorts of migrants, they are strongest in the case of high-skilled migrants. Their education costs the most for the home country and, since they have the highest earnings, the corresponding foregone fiscal revenues are the highest. Gibson and McKenzie (2010) present the results of survey micro-data for high-skilled emigrants from Tonga, Federated States of Micronesia, Papua New Guinea, Ghana and New Zealand. The developing countries in the sample share several structural characteristics with Pacific and African LDCs. They estimate the net annual fiscal cost per high-skilled emigrant at $6,300–16,900 in Ghana and Papua New Guinea, but a much lower $500–1,000 in Tonga and Micronesia, which have very low tax rates.[9]

If brain drain is significant, it can alter the relative resource endowment of both origin and destination countries.

d) Changing relative resource endowments

If brain drain is significant, it can alter the relative resource endowment of both origin and destination countries. By reducing the human capital stock of countries of origin, it tilts the relative factor endowment of the domestic economy towards other factors (e.g. natural resources), thereby altering the patterns of comparative advantage. At a minimum, it can reinforce the home country's specialization away from skill-intensive sectors or activities.[10] Worldwide, tertiary graduates tend to agglomerate in the United States, the United Kingdom, Australia, Canada and some other developed countries. The pre-existing polarization of the geographical distribution of talent is reinforced by the South–North migration of high-skilled people. These flows amount to a net transfer of resources from the country of origin to the country of destination (box 6).

The degree of brain waste depends to a large extent on home country characteristics.

e) Brain waste

In the context of international labour mobility, brain waste refers to the fact that some immigrants can only find jobs in the host country which are below the skills corresponding to their education level. This happens for instance when medical doctors work as nurses or university graduates work as taxi drivers or waiters. The degree of brain waste depends to a large extent on home country characteristics. In the case of the United States, Mattoo et al. (2008) note that the probability of skilled immigrants finding a job corresponding to their education level rises with the income level of the country of origin and with the level of the latter's expenditure on education. Educated immigrants from Latin America, Eastern Europe and Africa are more likely to take jobs below their education skill level than immigrants from Asia and industrial countries. In

Box 8. Medical brain drain

LDCs form the group of countries with the lowest medical density: 0.12 physician/1000 inhabitants, well below the acceptable threshold recommended by the World Health Organization of 2/1000. The medical density in other developing countries is nine times higher than in LDCs, whereas in developed countries it reaches a multiple of 24. The emigration of doctors from developing countries aggravates these disparities: LDCs also have the highest rate of medical brain drain, i.e. the number of nationally trained physicians who work abroad as a share of those who work at home or abroad. This rate is highest in Haiti (35 per cent) and African LDCs (14 per cent) (box chart 2).[1] Medical brain drain has been growing since the 1990s in both the LDCs and in other developing countries.

In the case study on Ethiopia prepared for this Report, it is estimated that around 1000 Ethiopian medical doctors work in the United States, whereas the number of physicians working in the home country in 2009 was 2,154. Therefore, it can be surmised that out of all Ethiopian doctors, between one-third and one-half work abroad. Bangladesh has a physician density of 0.25/1000 inhabitants and 32 medical schools. Some 2,000 persons graduate annually, of whom some 300 emigrate. Although the share is low, these are generally the best and the brightest. The quality of medical research and intellectual development at the top institutions in the country suffers from this brain drain (Rahman and Khan, 2007).

The main development problems associated with medical brain drain in LDCs are its impacts on the health of the population and the cost of medical education in these countries. Higher brain drain rates are associated with higher infant and child mortality and lower vaccination rates in developing countries, as well as higher adult mortality due to AIDS in the case of sub-Saharan Africa (Bhargava et al., 2011; Bhargava and Docquier, 2008). They also have an indirect negative impact on medical research and innovation in home countries. More broadly, the adverse impact on national health systems has long-term negative consequences on the human capital formation and accumulation of LDCs. Still, brain drain is only one factor in the sub-standard performance of health systems in most LDCs. In various African countries, a number of doctors and nurses are inactive or unemployed, indicating that understaffing of health systems is also due to factors other than brain drain (Skeldon, 2005).

The education of doctors has a very high cost for LDCs, and medical brain drain largely prevents these countries from recouping the educational investment made. It has been estimated that the full cost of educating a medical doctor in sub-Saharan Africa from primary school to university is $66,000, while the corresponding cost of educating a nurse is $43,000. If this investment is lost to the home country, the opportunity cost could be at least $364,000 and $238,000, respectively, for each emigrated professional (Kirigia et al., 2006). These amounts far exceed the remittances that these professionals could send home during their working life.

[1] These rates are low as compared with those for total brain drain quoted in the main text. This is due to methodological differences in computing both sets of rates. The present ones are based on the country of training and on emigration to just 12 developed countries. By contrast, the figures for total brain drain in the main text are based on nationality or country of birth and on all host countries. Clemens and Pettersson (2008) estimate medical brain drain for African countries based on physicians' country of birth and reach rates much higher than the ones quoted in this box. Their median medical brain drain rate for African LDCs is 39 per cent, as opposed to 14 per cent in the database used in the present box. These authors do not provide data for non-African countries.

Box chart 2. Medical brain drain and physician density by country groups, 2004

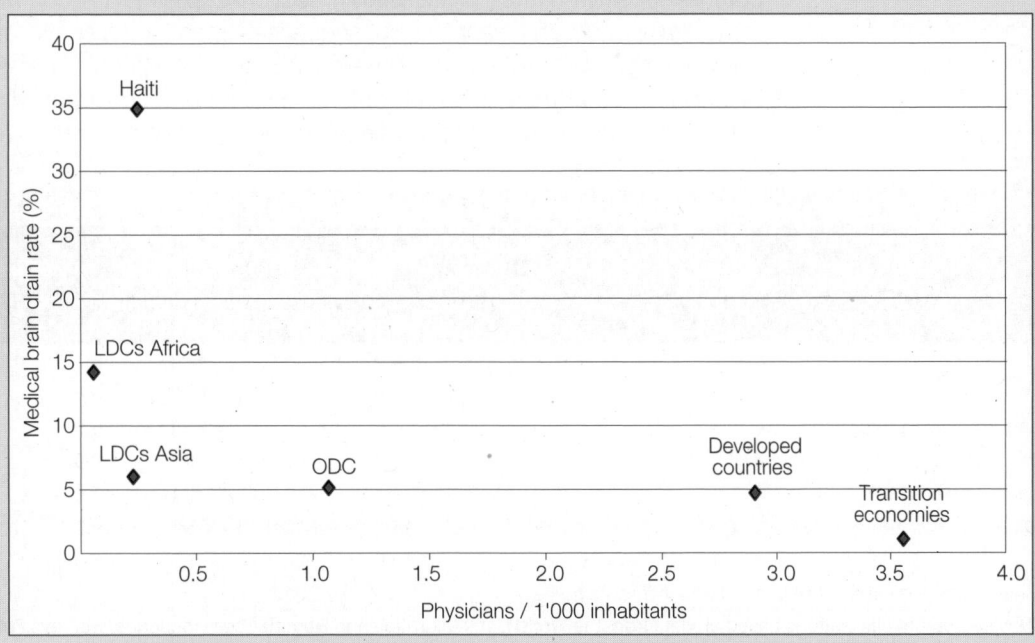

Source: UNCTAD secretariat calculations, based on data from Bhargava et al. (2011).

other words, the lower the economic and institutional development of the home country, the more likely that brain waste takes place.

These findings can be expected to apply to LDCs. The occupational profile of high-skilled emigrants from some of these countries deteriorates with emigration, according to survey data. Comparing the occupations of tertiary-educated migrants from Uganda, Senegal and Burkina Faso before and after migration shows an abrupt fall in the share of managerial posts (by at least 15 percentage points). By contrast, the share of persons performing technical and associated professional occupations rises strongly (by 19 percentage points in the case of Senegal) (table 17). Similarly, in interviews undertaken for this Report with a sample of high-skilled Haitian emigrants living in the United States, Canada, France and Spain, 47 per cent indicated that their present job requires less knowledge than what they had acquired in the home country. Nevertheless, 16 per cent stated that it required the same level and 38 per cent indicated higher skill requirements that those mastered before emigration.

The departure of the most qualified people potentially reduces both the demand and the supply of the institutions required for development.

f) Institution-building

Typically, the most skilled people are those who are best qualified to build and run institutions which are required for the national development process (State and government institutions, policymaking organizations, political debate, etc.).[11] At the same time, the most qualified people are those who are most likely to demand good-quality institutions and press for them. Their departure therefore potentially reduces both the demand and the supply of the institutions required for development and may slow the long-term development of the home country.

4. Implications for LDCs

The net impact of brain drain on home countries depends to a large extent on the intensity of brain drain.

Lack of more comprehensive data makes it difficult to estimate the exact impact of brain drain on home economies, especially LDCs. Existing research has postulated that the net impact of brain drain on home countries depends to a large extent on the intensity of brain drain, though this relationship is not always linear. Some degree of brain drain may be tolerated because of its potential positive effects (discussed in section C below). By contrast, at high brain drain rates, the negative consequences mentioned above are likely to predominate, as they tend to outweigh the positive effects. Therefore, it has been posited that there is some "optimal" level of brain drain, at which the net balance of positive and negative effects on the domestic economies reaches the

Table 17. Occupation of high-skilled international migrants from selected LDCs in home and host countries, 2009						
	Home country					
Occupation	**Uganda**		**Senegal**		**Burkina Faso**	
	Where occupation performed					
	Home[a]	Host[b]	Home[a]	Host[b]	Home[a]	Host[b]
Managers[c]	54.9	3.0	27.7	8.7	48.7	33.7
Professionals	10.9	29.4	18.3	0.6		30.9
Technicians and associate professionals	3.5	10.9	17.4	36.3		
Clerical support workers	1.2	5.7	1.5	8.8		
Service and sales workers		11.7	1.1	1.4		
Other	18.7	12.9	33.3	9.2	-	-
Don't know	10.9	26.5	0.6	35.0	51.3	35.5
Memo item: Share of high-skilled out of international migrants surveyed		31.5		6.6		0.4

Source: UNCTAD secretariat calculations based on data from the World Bank Migration and Remittances Household Surveys 2009 (available at http://microdata.worldbank.org/index.php/catalog/534).
    a Occupation performed in home country before migration.
    b Occupation currently performed in the host country (in 2009, date of the surveys).
    c Includes "Senior management employees" in the case of Burkina Faso.

maximum level. It has been estimated that an "optimal" high-skilled emigration rate lies between five per cent and 10 per cent of the high-skilled workforce, on the basis of a series of empirical studies on the effects of brain drain (Docquier, 2006). By contrast, "high" brain drain rates are considered to be those above the 15–20 per cent range. Beyond this level, the likelihood increases that the negative impacts of brain drain will outweigh its positive consequences.

The actual brain drain rate is "high" in 30 of the 48 LDCs; conversely, it is close to the "optimal" level in only five of these countries. Given the intensity of the phenomenon in these countries, it is likely that economic development in most LDCs has been adversely affected both directly and indirectly. It is, however, not possible to arrive at a precise estimate of the magnitude of its macroeconomic impact in terms of economic or productivity growth rates. Concerning sectoral impacts, by contrast, there is ample evidence of the adverse effect of brain drain on LDCs, especially with regard to health, education and science, technology and innovation (STI). The poor performance of STI in LDCs has adverse second-round impacts across all economic sectors and on LDCs' development of productive capacities (UNCTAD, 2007: 139–160), although brain drain is not the only factor explaining such poor performance.

The actual brain drain rate is "high" in 30 of the 48 LDCs; conversely, it is close to the "optimal" level in only five of these countries.

C. Turning brain drain into benefits for home countries

Since the 1990s, the so-called "new economics of the brain drain" has argued that brain drain can be beneficial to developing countries, through the so-called "beneficial brain drain" or "brain gain".[12] This potential positive effect of labour migration comes alongside other possible beneficial effects of labour migration, which were already recognized by the early literature on migration but have recently received increased attention (table 18). These beneficial effects are presented below and their operation in LDCs is analysed.

There is ample evidence of the adverse effect of brain drain on LDCs, especially with regard to health, education and STI.

1. Brain gain

Beneficial brain drain. The brain gain literature argues that brain drain raises returns to education, providing an incentive for people to obtain additional education in order to increase their chances of emigrating. Out of these educated people, many emigrate (i.e. brain drain). At the same time, some eventually do not settle abroad and thereby help raise the human capital endowment of the home country with respect to what would have been the case if the migration incentive had not been present (i.e. a net brain gain). The evidence on the benefits of migration stressed by the new migration literature is still inconclusive (Solimano, 2010). Schiff (2006) questions the assumptions and conclusions of this literature, arguing that the actual brain gain effect is smaller than what these authors claim and that they fail to take into account several negative externalities caused by brain drain. Still, both he and these authors agree that the net impacts of brain drain on home countries vary with brain intensity and are negative for countries with high brain drain rates.

The net impacts of brain drain on home countries are negative for countries with high brain drain rates.

Tertiary education has been expanding in most LDCs since the 1990s. Between 1999–2000 and 2009–2010, the number of graduates in all tertiary-level programmes in a sample of 16 LDCs more than doubled from 182,000 to 455,000, which corresponds to a 19 per cent annual growth rate.[13] This has been driven by the efforts of the educational sector – mainly public but also private – to respond to previously unmet demand for university-level education in many LDCs.[14] However, it is difficult to attribute this rapid expansion in higher education to the incentive effect of emigration prospects. While part of the repressed demand may have had this motivation, it has probably not been the most important one. In recent decades, the rate of growth of university-level education in LDCs has far outpaced that of high-skilled emigration. Among the sample of Haitian qualified emigrants interviewed for this Report, none indicated the prospect of emigration as a motivation for obtaining tertiary education. In the case of Bangladesh, the case study carried out for this Report indicated that if emigration had been a major motivation for university education, the subjects chosen most frequently would have been different from the actual ones.[15]

While part of the repressed demand for tertiary education may have had the motivation of emigration, it has probably not been the most important one.

Given the difficulties of making direct empirical measures of brain gain, Beine et al. (2008) perform an econometric estimation of the impact of emigration prospects on human capital formation. They find a positive effect for countries at all income levels. However, in order to estimate the net effect after accounting for emigration, they compare the actual human capital stock to what it would have been if high-skilled workers had been allowed to emigrate at the same rate as low-skilled workers. In the case of the LDCs, the negative effect of brain drain on human capital formation predominates (in 20 out of 41 countries) and it is nil in 11 countries, due to the high rates of brain drain in these countries. The effect is positive (i.e. net brain gain) in only 10 LDCs and even there its intensity is low, since the estimated impact is at most an expansion of 0.2 percentage points in the proportion of the high-skilled in the labour force. These findings confirm that the brain gain effect of high-skilled emigration is largely absent from most LDCs.

In LDCs, the negative effect of brain drain on human capital formation predominates (in 20 out of 41 countries) and it is nil in 11 countries.

Broader meaning of brain gain. Besides the technical meaning of brain gain postulated by the "new economics of the brain drain" as mentioned above (i.e. the additional education taken thanks to the migration motivation but which does not actually lead to brain drain), "brain gain" is commonly used in a broader sense. As such, it refers to the expansion of human capital, skills and knowledge which accrue to the home country as an indirect effect of migration, but working through other channels. This includes the use of remittances for education, temporary return of high-skilled diaspora members or definitive return of qualified emigrants.

In home countries, remittances can be used to pay for education, so that recipients of those flows can either finance additional education or avoid taking children out of school (Özden and Schiff 2006; Acosta et al., 2007). In such cases, remittances release the liquidity constraint preventing further education. Evidence on the use of remittances in LDCs (section C2 of chapter 3 of this Report) seems to indicate that the mechanism is at work in some of these countries.

The other channels of "brain gain" in this broader meaning are analysed in sections C3 to C5 below.

In home countries, remittances can be used to pay for education.

2. Financial flows

The most tangible positive impacts of both high- and low-skilled migration are the financial flows to the home country that they generate. These flows are mainly remittances, diaspora bonds and foreign direct investment (FDI). The trends and economic impacts of remittance to LDCs are analysed in detail in chapter 3 of this Report. Therefore, this section focuses on two issues: 1. differences in remitting patterns between emigrants according to their skill profile; and 2. whether remittances offset the costs of brain drain. Diaspora bonds are mentioned in this section, while diaspora FDI is discussed in section C4 below.

a) Brain drain and remittances

It is often difficult to differentiate between remittances flows generated by high-skilled and low-skilled emigrants. However, some recent evidence suggests that high-skilled emigrants have a lower propensity to send remittances but those who do send money transfer larger amounts than the low-skilled emigrants, thanks to their higher earnings abroad (Bollard et al. 2011). The contribution of high-skilled emigrants to total remittances thus depends on their propensity to remit and on their share of total migrant stocks.

High-skilled emigrants have a lower propensity to send remittances but those who do send money transfer larger amounts than the low-skilled emigrants.

Available data for LDCs reveal mixed patterns. High-skilled emigrants have a lower propensity to remit in Senegal, but the opposite is true in Uganda and Burkina Faso. The average amount sent home by high-skilled remitters is predictably a multiple of that of low-skilled emigrants (except for Senegal, where the difference is very small). Consequently, the contribution of high-skilled remitters to the total flow of remittances to the home country is higher than their share of the group of emigrants who do send money home. In Uganda, where almost half of the international remitting emigrants are high-skilled, they account for two-thirds of total remittance flows to the country. In Senegal and Burkina Faso, by contrast, where only a fraction of the remittance-sending emigrants are tertiary-educated, their contribution to total remittances flows is less than 10 per cent (table 18).

High-skilled emigrants have a lower propensity to remit in Senegal, but the opposite is true in Uganda and Burkina Faso.

b) Brain drain costs and remittances

While data on remittances have been calculated and/or estimated and made publicly available, there is no comparable information on the costs and benefits of brain drain. Given the complexity of the multiple impacts of brain drain (table 16) it is very difficult to compute the welfare gains/losses of home and host countries, especially with regard to the associated externalities (both positive and negative) and the value of knowledge flows. Haque (2005), for instance, argues that remittances should not be compared with the externalities generated by human capital.

While data on remittances have been estimated, there is no comparable information on the costs and benefits of brain drain.

Nevertheless, some attempts have been made to appreciate the net results of some of the effects. Easterly and Nyarko (2009) estimate that in Ghana, remittances exceed costs of training tertiary brain-drained citizens (when only the cost of tertiary education is considered). They claim that as long as the remittances of the typical person exceed 30 per cent of GDP per capita of the home country, they exceed the cost of (tertiary) education. LDC mean remittances correspond to four per cent of GDP per capita, exceeding 30 per

Table 18. Emigrant skills and remittance patterns in selected LDCs, 2009			
(Percentage, unless otherwise indicated)			
	Home country		
	Uganda	Senegal	Burkina Faso
Remitting propensity of international migrants (share of migrants who ever sent remittances)			
Low-skilled	27.9	78.8	60.8
High-skilled	51.1	60.6	76.8
Annual amount of money sent per remitter ($)			
Low-skilled	782	1538	98
High-skilled	1882	1545	679
Composition of group of emigrants who ever sent remittances			
Low-skilled	54.2	94.9	99.5
High-skilled	45.8	5.1	0.5
Origin of total remittances sent			
Low-skilled	33.2	94.8	96.9
High-skilled	66.8	5.2	3.1

Source: UNCTAD secretariat calculations, based on data from the World Bank Migration and Remittances Household Surveys 2009 (available at http://microdata.worldbank.org/index.php/catalog/534).

cent in only one case (Lesotho) (table 6, chapter 3).[16] Thus, indications are that remittances do not offset the costs of educating people who leave the country (even if computing solely the costs of higher education). Therefore, it is more likely that these countries lose out on balance when comparing costs of education and remittance recepits.

c) Other financial flows

Indications are that remittances do not offset the costs of educating people who leave the LDCs.

Beyond remittances, diasporas can also be a source of savings, which can be channelled as capital inflows to home countries. Home-based economic agents such as governments mobilize these savings through diaspora bonds and other financial instruments like deposit accounts, transnational loans and diaspora mutual funds (Terrazas, 2010). Among LDCs, Ehtiopia, Nepal and Rwanda have issued diaspora bonds.

3. DIASPORA KNOWLEDGE NETWORKS

a) Diasporas as a knowledge pool

Beyond remittances, diasporas can also be a source of savings, which can be channelled as capital inflows to home countries.

The stock of knowledge and skills of emigrants can potentially contribute to the accumulation of human capital and technological capabilities in the home country, mainly through two mechanisms: first, the operation of diaspora knowledge networks, analysed below; and second, the return to the home country of students[17] and long-term emigrants (whose impacts are discussed in subsection C5).

Diasporas. A diaspora refers to a community of expatriates who are spread or dispersed around the world, outside their homeland. A distinctive feature of diasporas is the sense of national identity and emotional attachment to the homeland. Diasporas are often heterogeneous groups. The degree of cohesion, shared values and motivations may vary depending on the type of diaspora and their histories. Some diasporas have greater political and national motivation and corresponding willingness to contribute to the homeland. Yet this may cut both ways: some diaspora groups that are affected by internal conflicts, exile or persecution may be reluctant to engage if they perceive governments at home as hostile and unfriendly to them. By contrast, other types of diaspora groups, e.g. those formed by internationally mobile professionals and entrepreneurs, can be willing and prepared to cooperate with their homeland in the transfer of knowledge, as well as capital, networks and other attributes if they see the home conditions as propitious and/or a possible source of commercial gain (Solimano, 2010).

A diaspora refers to a community of expatriates who are spread or dispersed around the world, outside their homeland.

Diaspora knowledge networks. Diasporas can thus serve as "brain banks" abroad; when properly organized, they can become a source of knowledge sharing and technology transfer with their home country (Mahroum et al., 2006). Technology appears to diffuse more efficiently through culturally and nationally linked groups. As shown in chapter 5 of this Report, by facilitating international knowledge flows and technology diffusion, diasporas can act as "knowledge brokers" and promote innovation in the home country (Agrawal et al., 2008, 2011). The skills of diaspora members are deemed especially appropriate, thanks to their combination of technical and substantive expertise with their acquaintance with local conditions (language, institutions, culture, etc.). However, the intensity and quality of knowledge flows and transfer between host and home countries depends on how they are organized, the actors involved, the amount of finance mobilized, the commitment of diaspora members, and the institutional and economic development of the home countries. High-skilled emigrants tend to share little knowledge with home countries if these are small or

Diasporas can be willing to cooperate with their homeland in the transfer of knowledge, as well as capital, networks and other attributes.

low-income economies which are not undergoing rapid structural transformation. There, information flows tend to concentrate mostly on emigration itself (i.e. work opportunities abroad, migration mechanisms, etc.) (Gibson and McKenzie, 2010). This is in sharp contrast with the case of home economies which are large or growing rapidly and undergoing structural transformation. Successful examples of diaspora knowledge mobilization (e.g. Israel, Taiwan Province of China, India and China, discussed in chapter 5 of this Report) show that diaspora technological entrepreneurs overseas can play an important role in helping to develop technological firms at home and serve as a two-way link for market knowledge, connections and technological transfer across countries.

High-skilled emigrants tend to share little knowledge with home countries if these are small or low-income economies which are not undergoing rapid structural transformation.

b) Initiatives to harness diaspora knowledge flows to LDCs

The channels used to date to foster the transfer and sharing of diaspora knowledge and skills with LDCs home countries can be grouped into two categories: 1. diaspora-inspired initiatives; and 2. multilateral and bilateral programmes.

Diaspora initiatives. While most LDC diaspora associations, organizations and NGOs have philanthropic objectives, some of them are aimed at assisting home countries in benefiting from the expertise, skills and experience accumulated by diaspora members. This is the case with diaspora associations of medical doctors, scientists, engineers, etc., which strive to transfer and share knowledge and technology with researchers, scientists and entrepreneurs in the country of origin. Most LDC diaspora organizations are based in developed countries. Examples of successful knowledge initiatives and programmes are provided in box 9.

While most LDC diaspora associations have philanthropic objectives, some of them are aimed at assisting home countries in benefiting from the expertise and skills of diaspora members.

Bilateral and multilateral programmes. These include programmes initiated by international organizations (typically acting in collaboration with national governments of both home and host countries) or knowledge components of wider agreements between origin and destination countries initiated to influence bilateral migration and the ensuing flows of expertise and business. The knowledge components of these programmes take the form of either advisory missions or participation in specific projects in the home country. The main beneficiaries in the LDC home countries are universities, government institutions, civil society and the private sector.

At the multilateral level, the United National Development Programme (UNDP) launched the Transfer of Knowledge Through Expatriate Nationals (TOKTEN) in 1977. The International Organization for Migration (IOM) has also been running the Temporary Return of Qualified Nationals (TRQN) and Migration for Development in Africa (MIDA), the latter since 2001. Through MIDA, the following LDCs have created partnerships with destination countries and expatriates: Benin, Burkina Faso, Burundi, the Democratic Republic of the Congo, Ethiopia, Guinea, Mali, Mauritania, Rwanda, Senegal, Sierra Leone and Somalia. Box 10 provides examples of how international programmes operate in LDCs.

Several bilateral programmes have been launched jointly by host and home countries in order to foster cooperation on bilateral migration.

Several bilateral programmes have been launched jointly by host and home countries in order to foster cooperation on bilateral migration. They typically deal with different aspects of international labour flows, including diaspora mobilization though knowledge transfer and direct investment, and assistance to permanent return migration. One example is the Programme d'Appui aux Initiatives de Solidarité pour le Développement (PAISD), jointly undertaken by the Governments of Senegal and France during 2009–2011 in the context of co-development programmes. With total funding of €9 million, its knowledge component financed 52 diaspora experts to transfer knowledge and experience to Senegalese counterparts through short- to medium-term missions. The sectors targeted were health, agriculture and food industry, management, ICTs

Box 9. Examples of successful LDC diaspora initiatives for knowledge sharing and transfer

The national case studies prepared for this Report highlight some examples of how diaspora knowledge, skills and resources can be successfully harnessed and transferred to home countries.

Strengthening PhD education at the University of Addis Ababa. Given the obvious need for more and better training at the doctorate level in Ethiopia, the country's largest university established several PhD programmes. It realized, however, that in order to reach its objectives it could not rely uniquely on its own resources. Accordingly, it decided to mobilize the knowledge of the national diaspora working in foreign academic institutions. To this end, in 2008 it launched a large-scale programme financed by the Ethiopian Government and the Swedish and French official development aid agencies. The main participants abroad have been Ethiopians active in US and European universities, who in several cases convinced their non-Ethiopian colleagues to take part in the project. Their collaboration with the home country has taken the form of participation in research seminars, book donations, links between laboratories in the universities of Addis Ababa and laboratories abroad, and thesis direction by diaspora members. The programme has had a considerable impact on several departments.

Decoding the jute genome in Bangladesh. A Bangladeshi microbiologist and biochemist who studied and worked in the Soviet Union, Germany, United States and Malaysia decoded for the latter country the genome sequencing of its most important plant, rubber. In order to have his country of origin benefit from his knowledge and skills, he later undertook the same type of research for jute. This was done in a joint project with the Global Network of Bangladeshi Biotechnologists (GNOB), the Centre for Chemical Biology, the University of Science (Malaysia) and the University of Hawaii (United States) and a team of Bangladeshi researchers. The discovery facilitates pest control and the manufacturing of better finished industrial products out of jute.

Upgrading the national health sector in Ethiopia. The People to People association was established by Ethiopian diaspora members in the late 1990s with the aim of mobilizing diaspora skills for the benefit of the home country. It operates in several countries in North America and Europe and has been active above all in the health sector. Its activities have included participating in medical training in Ethiopia, advocating for diaspora mobilization with international organizations and donor institutions, mobilizing resources abroad for medical programmes in Ethiopia, setting up a telemedicine system in the home country, restructuring university hospitals, organizing an annual conference on health in Ethiopia, awarding a prize for medical best practice, and maintaining a blog for the exchange of medical best practices and discussions. The association collaborates with other diaspora organizations, NGOs active in Ethiopia and international organizations (e.g. the World Bank), the United States National Institute of Health and universities of host countries.

Mobilizing resources and knowledge transfer to Haiti. In Canada, the Regroupement des organismes canado-haïtiens pour le développement (ROCADH) is an effort to coalesce many philanthropic organizations working for the advancement of Haitian communities back home. ROCADH brings together some 47 home town associations. It has been active in the fields of education and capacity-building (including in agricultural, animal breeding techniques, commodity processing, medical and tourism service skills). ROCADH has been able to channel substantial funding through the Canadian International Development Agency (CIDA). To be eligible for CIDA funds, ROCADH has to contribute one-third of the value of the project.

Medical diaspora network for Bangladesh. Bangladeshi physicians in North America established the Bangladesh Medical Association of North America (BMANA) in 1980. It supports the home country by organizing visits of medical teams to provide training and technology transfer, provision of subsidized/pro bono specialized clinical services, and donation of books, computers and journals to medical colleges and universities in Bangladesh. Its members have been participating in activities of knowledge transfer and training in terms of cutting-edge advances in medical specialities, such as neurology, surgery and infection control.

Water in Ethiopia. A programme of collaboration between an American and an Ethiopian university was put in place in 2009 at the initiative of an Ethiopian working as professor in a United States university, with financing from the United States Agency for International Development (USAID) under the African American Universities Partnership. It was successful in leveraging official financing to obtain financing from the American private sector for project activities. It foresees the establishment of a research centre on water in Ethiopia to conduct academic research and participate in the formulation and planning of the country's policies and programmes for water management.

and biotechnology. In some cases, the projects included financing to upgrade installations and equipment of home country beneficiary institutions (both public and private).[18]

To date, many of the efforts to establish diaspora knowledge networks have not succeeded in creating synergies with other initiatives or ensuring continuity.

c) Effects on LDCs

To date, many of the efforts to establish diaspora knowledge networks and foster knowledge transfer and sharing between diaspora members and home LDC countries have attained their specific and circumscribed goals. However, they have not succeeded in creating synergies with other initiatives or ensuring continuity, both of which are essential for a regular knowledge flow to home countries. As a result, their development impacts have been limited for a number of reasons, such as:

Box 10. International programmes to foster diaspora knowledge transfer to LDCs

Afghanistan. Since the 1980s, the resurgent periods of civil conflict in Afghanistan have spurred brain drain (over one-third of high-skilled workers lived abroad in 2000), low numbers of permanent return migration and the deterioration of the educational system, which failed to modernize. As part of reconstruction efforts of the 2000s, international organizations mobilized high-skilled diaspora members to contribute through transfer of skill and knowledge, and local capacity-building. From 2002 until 2006, 38 volunteers provided assistance to the national capacity-building efforts of the Afghan Interim Administration and the successor government. They were mobilized through the TOKTEN programme of the UNDP. IOM launched a Temporary Return of Qualified Nationals (TRQN) programme together with the Netherlands. It mobilized and financed the temporary return (for three or six months) of members of the Afghan diaspora in the Netherlands in the fields of education, health, engineering, infrastructure and information technology. Despite some initial resistance, diaspora members were able to teach and train locals in new teaching methods, university organization, medical procedures and equipment, building techniques, use of computers and the Internet, software previously not in use in Afghanistan, and work and managerial methods and routines. These innovations had been learned and/or practised by diaspora members in the host country. Participants mentioned as their motivation identification with the home country and their desire to participate in its rebuilding (Siegel and Kuschminder, 2012).

Great Lakes. The MIDA Great Lakes Programme was launched by IOM in 2001 and is expected to continue until 2012. Its main objective was to fill technical skills gaps in the fields of health, education and rural development, by tapping into the knowledge pool of the diasporas of Burundi, Democratic Republic of the Congo and Rwanda in Europe. It started by identifying the technical skills needs of local beneficiary institutions (universities, hospitals, laboratories, professional training centres). To match the demand side, the supply side was organized by mobilizing diaspora experts interested in participating and selecting them. Training and capacity-building activities were undertaken through the return of diaspora members, which could be temporary (ranging from some weeks to several months), virtual (by means of ICTs and e-learning tools) or – exceptionally – permanent. More than 400 short-term expert and capacity-building missions were carried out. The main achievements claimed by the project are training physicians and paramedics; strengthening health institution management and planning; introducing South–North partnerships of health institutions; improving course quality in universities; relaunching courses previously inactive for several years; strengthening libraries and IT infrastructure in education institutions; and building the capacity of ministries and provincial authorities active in rural development. The Programme claims that its actions are aligned with national priorities. It was foreseen that at the end of the project, the functions of diapora mobilization and matching of skills would be transferred to the three national governments and to diaspora associations.[1]

[1] Based on information available at the website of the project (http://mida.belgium.iom.int/).

Dispersion and lack of coordination of resources. The spread and multiplication of actors, initiatives and programmes and the lack of coordination among them result in the dispersion of efforts, energy and resources.[19]

Most LDC diaspora associations and NGOs tend to be ad hoc efforts with very small budgets, and their actions are local and small-scale. Often their members, although willing to engage, are not experts in the field of development, which does not allow them to undertake large-scale development projects that could have a region-wide or country-wide impact on the lives of the beneficiaries. In many cases, emigrants rely on channels such as family members, local chieftains or social and professional networks to carry out their activities, depending on the level of institutional development of the home country. At the same time, they often lack more structured institutional support.[20] The lack of coordination can limit the effectiveness of the initiatives and programmes which are implemented by individual or a small number of organizations and NGOs. This can lead to situations in which "projects carried out by such [diaspora] organisations interfere with mainstream policies carried out by the national government or local organizations" (Zoomers and van Naerssen, 2006: 73).

The multiplication of initiatives and the lack of coordination among them result in the dispersion of resources.

Nevertheless, in some cases, diaspora knowledge-sharing initiatives are undertaken in partnership with home country governments or international organizations. Coordinating the actions and programmes of different actors can leverage existing resources and greatly enhance their development impact (box 9).

Coordinating the actions and programmes of different actors can leverage existing resources and greatly enhance their development impact.

Official international initiatives for diaspora knowledge-sharing and transfer through circular migration or return sometimes encounter problems. First, the financial and human resources involved can be somewhat limited. For instance, the final report of a large project aimed at clarifying the links between migration and development and the impact of official programmes for promoting knowledge transfer concludes that "the numbers are very modest and the success is limited and the number of beneficiaries is not in proportion to the total number of migrants and/or expatriates" (Zoomers and van Naerssen, 2006: 29). Second, such initiatives are frequently inconsistent with national priorities. Knowledge-sharing programmes and activities are often designed without consulting home country governments and are not articulated with broader development strategies or wider national policies and programmes in mind. This thwarts the desired effectiveness of diaspora knowledge initiatives.

Trust. Trust among different groups of the diaspora and stakeholders of knowledge transfer is often lacking, hampering collaboration and coordination between them. In some cases, associations of LDC nationals living abroad prefer not to undertake projects in collaboration with the national government either because of the causes of emigration (civil conflict, political strife, etc.) or due to frustration with bureaucratic delays and uncertainty concerning the use of funds. In other cases, trust is lacking among diaspora associations themselves.

Limited information. Some LDC governments have initiated programmes and action courses to strengthen the engagement of their diasporas with the home country (e.g. Bangladesh, Senegal, Mali, Rwanda, Ethiopia and Haiti). One of the components of these programmes is collecting information on diasporas, including their number, location, professional activities, skills, etc. Information gathering is the first step towards strengthening the engagement of the diaspora in the development of the home country. However, those LDCs which have not initiated an active programme of diaspora engagement are typically not aware of the potential that diasporas represent in terms of skills and knowledge (but also in terms of savings and investment potential). This lack of information prevents them from mobilizing diaspora knowledge effectively.

Differential treatment of nationals. In order to attract diaspora members to work for the home country (temporarily or permanently), national governments and international organizations often mobilize financial resources for and/or provide special treatment to these emigrants (e.g. fiscal breaks, special political rights). Such treatment can generate resentment among national residents working at a comparable grade (e.g. government officials, experts, professors, scientists, researchers), hampering collaboration between national residents and diaspora members.

Cost of technology transfer. The transfer of knowledge, skills and technologies requires efforts by beneficiaries and transferors. It therefore entails costs of local adaptation of procedures, methods and equipment, including the creation of locally appropriate skills and resources. This feature is well known from the literature on transfer of technology (Teece, 1977; von Hippel, 1994). Even if it is easier to learn from fellow countrymen and countrywomen than from foreigners, it still entails costs (Obukhova, 2009). Such costs tend to be overlooked when planning diaspora knowledge transfer programmes and initiatives.

4. Diaspora business networks

a) Potential business impacts of diasporas

Apart from forming diaspora knowledge networks, diasporas can contribute to the development of their home country by facilitating the establishment of business and trade networks between the home and the host country. Diaspora members can help link people and firms in both countries thanks to superior knowledge of, or preferential access to, market opportunities, as well as familiarity with home country markets, language, preferences and business contacts. Emigrants can also help overcome reputational problems their home

---

The number of beneficiaries is not in proportion to the total number of migrants and/or expatriates.

Trust among different groups of the diaspora and stakeholders of knowledge transfer is often lacking.

Even if it is easier to learn from fellow countrymen and countrywomen than from foreigners, it still entails costs.

Diasporas can contribute to the development of their home country by facilitating the establishment of business and trade networks between the home and the host country.

country may have abroad. Diaspora members reduce transaction costs by means of these specific skills and capabilities.

Diasporas can play an important role in fostering business creation and expansion in the home country by participating in external searches for new market opportunities and domestic institutional reform, through their contacts with domestic officials concerning the redesign of relevant institutions and firms. Diasporas have played a major role in the establishment and development of high-tech clusters in India, China, Taiwan Province of China, Israel and Ireland since the 1990s (Saxenian and Sabel, 2008; Saxenian, 2005), as discussed in greater detail in Chapter 5 of this Report.

Business linkages and economic flows between home and host countries can come from either high-skilled or low-skilled emigrants, but they are more likely in the case of high-skilled emigrants, since the latter tend to have wider and higher-level contacts in both home and host countries (Docquier and Lodigiani, 2010).

The presence of a diaspora is therefore often associated with higher bilateral trade flows (Gould, 1994; Mesnard and Ravallion, 2001; Head and Ries, 1998; Rauch and Trindade, 2002; Rauch and Casella, 2003; Combes et al., 2005, Peri and Requena, 2009). The most direct and simple form of a diaspora business network is when the diaspora itself is a prime market for the exports of home country goods, in what has been termed "ethnic trade" or "nostalgia trade". This consists mainly of foodstuffs, but also includes films and music, reading material, utensils and dishes, ornaments, textiles and clothing – goods which, in principle, have more difficulty penetrating international markets than other types of exports (Newland and Taylor, 2010). If home country exporters are successful in exploiting the diaspora market, they can move beyond it to tap other markets. In this case, diasporas serve as a bridge to wider markets.

Beyond merchandise trade, the presence of diasporas also stimulates the export of services, especially international tourism. Diaspora tourism offers domestic agents some advantages over other types of tourism. First, diaspora tourist spending typically reaches domestic goods and services suppliers more directly, as nationals tend to use locally-targeted accommodation, shops and restaurants rather than facilities established for typical international tourists. As a result, this type of spending reduces the well-known phenomenon of tourism leakage (Supradist, 2004). Second, diaspora tourists are more widely spread over the home country territory. Third, their arrivals can be less seasonal than those of other tourists (Newland and Taylor, 2010). Diaspora tourism is therefore likely to have a greater developmental impact than other types of tourism. Moreover, diasporas can serve as a bridge to wider markets by overcoming reputational problems or a lack of information in host countries concerning their home country as a tourist destination, as with the case of nostalgia trade. In most of the countries sampled by Gibson and McKenzie (2010), more than half of high-skilled emigrants advised other people concerning tourism in their home country.

Another, non-exclusive possibility of diaspora business networks is for diaspora members to invest directly in the home economy (Javorcik et al., 2001; Kugler and Rapoport, 2007; Docquier and Lodigiani, 2010). This may take various forms, such as a capital contribution to family business, the acquisition of shares in publicly traded firms, or other forms of direct diaspora investment. Evidence presented by Gibson and McKenzie (2010) shows that this is the exception. Only between five and eight per cent of high-skilled migrants from developing countries invested directly in their home country, and the amounts invested were relatively small (less than $18,000).

Emigrants can help overcome reputational problems their home country may have abroad.

The presence of a diaspora is often associated with higher bilateral trade flows.

The most direct form of a diaspora business network is when the diaspora itself is a prime market for the exports of home country goods.

If home country exporters are successful in exploiting the diaspora market, they can move beyond it to tap other markets.

Diaspora tourism is likely to have a greater developmental impact than other types of tourism.

b) Initiatives to strengthen diaspora business effects

In order to engage diasporas and encourage them to invest part of their savings in LDC home countries, action has been taken at the international, bilateral and national levels. Programmes have targeted both individual and collective investment. LDCs like Burundi, Democratic Republic of the Congo, Ethiopia, Senegal and Rwanda have launched initiatives to attract direct investment of their diasporas by organizing roadshows for investor; publishing investment guides geared to their diasporas; encouraging diaspora investors' associations; initiating dialogues on major constraints for emigrant investment in the home country, including diaspora investment in bilateral cooperation programmes, etc.

At the multilateral level, some Migration for Development in Africa (MIDA) projects carried out by IOM feature a component aimed at strengthening diaspora investment in the home country and mobilizing diaspora business and professional networks in order to strengthen international business activity of home countries. This comes in addition to the MIDA components designed to foster knowledge flows to home countries.

At the bilateral level, several agreements launched in conjunction with European co-development initiatives have incorporated a component to foster diaspora investment in the home country. In some cases, programmes foresee co-financing of development projects by diasporas and donor countries. In 2009, Senegal launched the Plateforme d'appui au Secteur Privé et à la Valorisation de la Diaspora Sénégalaise en Italie (PLASEPRI) together with Italy, and another programme, Programme d'Appui aux Initiatives de Solidarité pour le Développement (PAISD), together with France. These three-year programmes aim to boost SME development and employment generation in regions with high emigration rates.

Among national initiatives, in 2009, Senegal launched the Fonds d'Appui aux Investissements des Sénégalais de l'Extérieur (FAISE), aimed at encouraging diaspora members to invest in their region of origin.

c) Diaspora business effects in LDCs

There is a very high participation of migrants in the United States in the market for home-country goods, according to Orozco (2008). Each migrant spends almost $1000 per year on nostalgia products, and the total may exceed $20 billion annually. Orozco and Burgess (2011) estimate that some 90 per cent of Haitians living in the United States consume nostalgia goods to the tune of $800 per person per year, which amounts to a potential market of some $285 million. For the home country, this represents a major export market allowing the diversification of its exports. While 80 per cent of Haitian exports consist of manufactures, nostalgia goods are mostly agriculture-based. Similarly, Debass and Orozco (2008) estimate that the Ethiopian diaspora in the United States spends $1,077 on nostalgia goods annually. Going beyond diaspora markets, in the United Kingdom, part of the Ethiopian diaspora has established a niche market by marketing home coffee to independent delicatessens, ethically aware food shops, corporate purchasers and faith groups through the Oromo Coffee company (Newland and Taylor, 2010).

Econometric evidence computed by the UNCTAD secretariat indicates that worldwide, the presence of both skilled and unskilled immigrants helps to expand merchandise trade between home and host countries. The former have a trade-creating impact which is double that of the latter. In the case of the LDCs, by contrast, unskilled immigrants have such an impact, but there is little corresponding evidence in the case of skilled immigrants. This indicates that so

---

In order to engage diasporas and encourage them to invest part of their savings in LDC home countries, action has been taken at the international, bilateral and national levels.

There is a very high participation of migrants in the United States in the market for home-country goods.

Diasporas represents a major export market allowing the diversification of home country exports.

far, low-skilled LDC immigrants have been more involved in facilitating bilateral trade in their destination countries than their more educated fellow countrymen and countrywomen.

With regard to tourism, 70 per cent of the 254,000 tourists arriving in Haiti are Haitian-born or of Haitian origin, with the United States, Canada, France and the Dominican Republic as the leading sources (data for 2011). These are the main host countries of the Haitian diaspora. Haitian diaspora tourists spend amounts ranging from $1000-5000 per person on each trip, and it is therefore likely that they account for a larger share of the country's tourism receipts than the number of tourists arriving in the country.

The diapora business network effect of generating bilateral FDI is expected to vary according to the size of the diaspora and of the home country (Docquier and Lodigiani, 2010). FDI by diasporas in LDC home countries (which are mostly small economies) is still limited. According to concerns expressed by potential LDC diaspora investors, the main reported deterrents are lack of support from the home government, a dearth of incentives for investment, and diasporas' demand for guarantees for their investments. Still, some LDC diasporas have started gearing up to invest in their home country. Members of the Haiti diaspora are active in FDI in the areas of mining, tourism, energy and financial services. They seem to be cautious and risk-averse, typically taking minority stakes in projects and companies and shunning larger investment projects. The diasporas of Rwanda and Liberia have launched or planned diaspora funds, which are professionally managed vehicles that allow individual investors to diversify risk by purchasing shares of a basket of investment products – typically including money market funds, sovereign and corporate bonds, and equities (Terrazas, 2010).

In Senegal, PAISD provided technical assistance for 221 investment projects in the country in agriculture, domestic trade, handicraft, services, tourism, ICT, consultancy, etc. Half of them were undertaken by diaspora members who remained in France, while the others were implemented by investors who returned permanently to Senegal to oversee their projects. The total value of the beneficiary investment projects was $4 million, which represents around 0.1% of gross fixed capital formation in 2010. Some $400 million were mobilized to co-finance them. [21] PLASEPRI had a budget of €24 million, consisting mainly of credits to SMEs and microfinance institutions as well as a grant component. Also in Senegal, in 2010 FAISE had a budget of $323,000 to finance 31 diaspora projects, mainly in fisheries, small industry and services (ANSD, 2011).

5. Returnees

a) Potential contribution to the home country

The potential contributions of permanent returnees to the home country are many and often depend on the level of development of the home country and the range of opportunities for the involvement of returnees. Some of the potential contributions are discussed below.

Knowledge. Returnees can deploy their skills and experience accumulated abroad by working in knowledge-intensive activities, e.g. government, consultancies, managerial positions in firms, etc. (Dustmann and Kirchkamp 2002). They can also forge and sustain simultaneous and multi-stranded relationships that link their societies of origin and destination (Glick Schiller et al., 1992). There is ample evidence demonstrating that the knowledge and skills accumulated abroad and brought home by returnees have significantly boosted

So far, low-skilled LDC immigrants have been more involved in facilitating bilateral trade in their destination countries than their more educated fellow countrymen and countrywomen.

Seventy per cent of the tourists arriving in Haiti are Haitian-born or of Haitian origin.

Some LDC diasporas have started gearing up to invest in their home country.

The potential contributions of permanent returnees to the home country are many and often depend on the level of development of the home country.

the technological capability and innovation activities of economies that have successfully undergone structural change, as shown in chapter 5 of this Report.

Entrepreneurship. Returnees can use their entrepreneurial capabilities to establish new businesses,[22] which may be in technologically more advanced sectors. Compared with their fellow countrymen and countrywomen who did not emigrate, returnees are more likely to be entrepreneurs thanks to:

Returnees are more likely to be entrepreneurs than their fellow countrymen and countrywomen who did not emigrate.

- Savings accumulated during emigration;
- Additional skills acquired abroad (McCormick and Wahba, 2001; Wahba and Zenou, 2011);
- Connections to business networks established while living abroad, which can be mobilized for the purposes of foreign trade, marketing, financing, access to technology, etc.

Entrepreneurial activities of returnees can arise from both high-skilled and low-skilled emigration, but are more likely to have an impact in the former case. High-skilled emigrants are more likely to have acquired managerial experience abroad and to have put aside savings necessary to start businesses.

Institutions. Returnees can participate in institution-building in the home country by strengthening both supply of and demand for institutions (Docquier, Ldogiani et al., 2011; Easterly and Nyarko 2009). This is a mirror effect of the loss incurred by the home country due to brain drain (see section B3f above), with the major difference that returnee actions are enriched by their learning and experience abroad.

Returnees can participate in institution-building in the home country by strengthening both supply of and demand for institutions.

However, the various potential positive contributions of permanent returnees to the home country mentioned above are not always realized. This depends on the conditions of return, in particular returnees' motivation, preparedness and time spent abroad (Cassarino, 2004), as well as local conditions. Typically, home economies that are not undergoing structural transformation are less likely to attract returnees who want to participate actively in local development. By contrast, highly dynamic home economies stand a greater chance of luring migrants back. Sustained growth over many years tends to precede permanent return, especially for high-skilled migrants. This has been the experience of Republic of Korea and Taiwan Province of China. It means that permanent return of the high-skilled is more often a consequence than a trigger of economic growth (Docquier, 2006).

Sustained growth over many years tends to precede permanent return, especially for high-skilled migrants.

b) The experience of LDCs

The conditions of LDCs have generally not been very conducive to active contributions by permanent returnees to home country development. The major driver is family reasons, but other motivations seem to vary according to conditions prevailing locally in LDCs. In Haiti, these include above all involuntary return (e.g. deportation, work permit expiry, failure to find a job, etc.). In Senegal, Uganda and Burkina Faso, the fact that emigrants had no intention of staying abroad is the second most important reason quoted for return. By contrast, Bangladeshi returnees interviewed for this Report cited positive motivations besides family reasons, such as the desire to have a greater impact on society and willingness to make own knowledge and experience available to the home country.

The conditions of LDCs have generally not been very conducive to active contributions by permanent returnees to home country development.

Most LDCs have only been able to attract return migration in very low numbers, a factor which has constrained their contribution to home country development. The rate of return (i.e. the number of returnees as a share of the emigrant stock plus returnees) in a selection of LDCs varies from six per cent in Uganda to 10 per cent in Senegal and approximately 15 per cent in Haiti and

Burkina Faso. As a share of the population, they account for less than two per cent in all four cases.[23] It should be borne in mind that in these countries (except for Uganda) the vast majority of returnees are low-skilled, which means that they are less likely to have accumulated resources and new knowledge abroad. As for the time spent abroad, in Haiti, out of returned emigrants 78.4 per cent have lived six years or less abroad. Only 6.7 per cent of all returnees have spent ten years or more abroad, which means that most returnees have had little time to accumulate resources.

On the whole, professional and business development opportunities have not been very common in most LDCs, so they have not been very successful in attracting returnees and benefiting from their professional and entrepreneurial activities. In many cases, LDC returnees have tried to start new businesses, but have been discouraged by lack of support for enterprise development (extension services, financing, etc.) or have found bureaucratic requirements too demanding. This contrasts with the experience of more vibrant economies which offer wider opportunities for returnees in terms of both economic activities and professional prospects, as exemplified by Bangladesh (box 11).

Professional and business development opportunities have not been very common in most LDCs.

Despite these caveats, there is evidence of positive effects for migration and returnees' activities in the home country and for returnees' contribution to economic activities in LDCs. In Senegal, research findings show that returnees

---

Box 11. Contributions of returnees to the Bangladeshi economy and society

The highly skilled knowledge workers who migrated from Bangladesh through State-sponsored scholarships from the 1950s to the 1980s rarely returned or circulated to the home country. Since the 1990s, however, private universities, technical institutions, research bodies and NGOs have provided a launching pad for temporary or permanent return. At present, the country has reached a social and economic stage where the return and circulation of knowledge workers are sustainable (RMMRU-DRC, 2005). Some examples of the contribution of permanent returnees to Bangladesh in different domains are given below.[1]

Education. After studying and working at Harvard University (United States), a scientist returned to Bangladesh, where he is contributing to the development of a leading private university. He has successfully developed collaborative research relationship with different United States and United Kingdom universities, including for an international centre for climate change and development in his institution. After having studied and worked in the United States, a computer scientist returned to Bangladesh to become a professor of computer science and engineering at a public university. He is a public activist and part of the nationwide campaign using contests and science fairs, for example, to encourage young students to concentrate on science and mathematics. He has been a member of the technical committee which prepared the draft national education policy.

Medicine. After working as a senior physician in a leading US hospital, a Bangladeshi doctor returned to his home country to use his expertise in pathology and improve the quality of pathology tests. There are only a few individuals in the country with exposure to leading-edge pathology, which is one of the most technology-intensive branches of medicine. Some Bangladeshi doctors, after finishing their post-graduate studies in Japan, returned to their home country, where they established the Japan Bangladesh Friendship Hospital (JBFH) in 1993 in partnership with Japanese doctors. The Hospital has initiated a grassroots programme entitled "Krishoker Sashtho Seba" (health care for farmers). It has been conducted in the remote areas of Bangladesh in order to provide health-care facilities to farmers since 2006. JBFH also provides health-care facilities to the marginal and underprivileged and organizes workshops on issues such as first aid training and awareness of common diseases.

Telecommunications. A top Bangladeshi manager studied in the United States, where he worked in both the public and private sectors. He returned to his home country, where he contributed to providing access to telephone services and increasing self-employment opportunities for the rural poor through connectivity. In 1993, he started a company with the backing of a Norwegian telecom company and financing from aid agencies and development banks. The company later became a major telephone operator, with 16 million subscribers providing telephone access to more than 100 million people covering 60,000 villages.

Finance. A Bangladeshi returnee from the United States and one from the United Kingdom have successfully contributed to the strong spread of microcredit in Bangladesh, first to the country's subsistence farmers then to urban areas. Rahman (2010) argues that this helped foster entrepreneurship among the rural poor.

Media. Two communications professionals developed international careers as journalists and worked for several public affairs and media bodies in Asia, North America and Europe, including international organizations. They later returned to Bangladesh, where they launched a newspaper in 1991, with the stated aim of strengthening democracy and freedom of expression. The newspaper has become the country's English-language daily with the largest circulation.

1 The individual cases presented in this Box as examples derive from a country study prepared for this Report.

have some characteristics which differentiate them favourably from non-migrants: 1. returnees have higher labour force participation rates and have a stronger tendency to be self-employed; 2. they are more likely to have skilled jobs; 3. they are more present in commercial and handicraft activities; 4. they have higher earnings (Mezger, 2008; Mezger and Flahaux, 2010). Beyond self-selection at the moment of deciding whether to migrate or not, it is likely that the knowledge and experience accumulated abroad contribute to further differentiating returnees from non-migrants.

In Senegal, returnees have some characteristics which differentiate them favourably from non-migrants.

Survey evidence on the investment activity of returnees in LDCs shows that in Burkina Faso, 32.5 per cent of them have invested based on the savings accumulated abroad, whereas in Senegal the corresponding share is 17.3 per cent.[24] In the former country, all individual returnee amounts invested were smaller than $5,000, while in Senegal they ranged as high as $20,000. The total cumulative amount invested by returnees in Senegal corresponds to 2.6 per cent of the country's gross fixed capital formation in 2009, whereas in Burkina Faso, the corresponding share is a higher 6.2 per cent. [25] In both countries, returnees have invested mainly in traditional sectors. In Burkina Faso, the primary sector accounted for 65 per cent of returnee investment projects, whereas in Senegal, 60 per cent of the projects were in trade and services, while the remainder was in the primary sector and real estate. A fraction of returnee investment involved international partners: two per cent or less in both cases. It is likely that a significant share of these business partnerships resulted from contacts held while living abroad, possibly indicating some form of diaspora business network.

In Senegal and Burkina Faso, returnees have invested mainly in traditional sectors.

These case studies do not correspond to the typical examples of transformative returnee entrepreneurship in modern sectors which assists the structural transformation of home country economies, as was the case with a few successful dynamic developing countries mentioned above. Still, they do show that the potential of returnees and their entrepreneurship is far from negligible. The example of the contribution of Bangladeshi returnees (box 7) reveals that, given a conducive domestic environment and policy action, this potential can be developed to a much greater extent.

Given a conducive domestic environment and policy action, the potential of returnees and their entrepreneurship can be developed to a much greater extent.

c) International programmes to assist permanent return

International action has striven to assist return migration by facilitating their permanent resettlement in the home country and providing financial assistance in that respect. This was the case for the Return and Reintegration of Qualified Nationals (RQN) programmes of the International Organization for Migration (IOM) and the Transfer of Knowledge Through Expatriate Nationals (TOKTEN) programme of the United Nations Development Programme (UNDP), mentioned above. However, these programmes have generally failed to meet expectations. They have been very costly, considering the amounts allocated to individual returnees. At the same time, the financing required to effectively help returnees resettle in their home country has been much higher than what is available through the programmes. In several cases, beneficiary nationals returned to the home country temporarily but subsequently emigrated again.[26] Therefore, the emphasis of international programmes has mostly shifted to temporary return, i.e. from return migration to circular migration. TOKTEN was mainly reoriented towards temporary return. IOM has launched the *Temporary* Return of Qualified Nationals (TRQN) and Migration for Development in Africa (MIDA) focusing on temporary return to replace previous programmes aimed at permanent return (see section C3b above).[27] In bilateral initiatives, by contrast, assistance to permanent return remains one of the components, as in the case of the bilateral programmes and agreements on co-development to which European countries are a party.

The emphasis of international programmes has mostly shifted to temporary return, i.e. from return migration to circular migration.

D. Conclusions

According to Gibson and McKenzie (2011: 125), "we are still some way from a comprehensive global answer on the effect of brain drain on sending country growth and development outcomes". This is certainly true of LDCs. Nevertheless, this chapter has presented analysis and information which help us to identify some major features of high-skilled migration and the potential impact of diasporas on LDC home country development.

We are still some way from a comprehensive global answer on the effect of brain drain on sending country growth and development outcomes.

On average, LDCs are more affected by brain drain than any other group of countries. The intensity is especially acute in islands (where more than half of the high-skilled workers often live abroad) and in African LDCs, 21 of which have more than one-fifth of their high-skilled population abroad. The brain drain rate is lower is Asian LDCs, though even there it is still higher than in other developing countries. There is strong variation in the rates of brain drain of LDCs, but it is close to the estimated "optimal" level (5–10 per cent) in only five of these countries. Apart from the likely adverse macroeconomic effects to be expected at these high rates of brain drain, emigration of highly qualified LDC nationals has adverse consequences, especially in the activities of health, education and STI. This brain drain primarily amounts to a South–North transfer of resources.

Available evidence shows that the (positive) developmental impacts of brain drain on LDCs have been limited so far. Concerning their human capital base, since the 1990s, education enrolment in most LDCs has been expanding rapidly at all levels, including the tertiary stage. This expansion is driven mainly by public policies and by the increased supply of educational services. It is very difficult to attribute improving educational attainment (or a significant share of it) to the incentive effect of emigration, although some observers argue that it has been one of the factors pushing demand for higher education.

The (positive) developmental impacts of brain drain on LDCs have been limited so far.

There are indications of embryonic diaspora business network effects in a few LDCs. With respect to financial and capital flows, beyond the remittances analysed in chapter 3 of this Report, a few LDCs have taken initial steps to mobilize the savings of their diaspora through diaspora bonds and FDI. Some fledgling diaspora business network effects are starting to appear in terms of strengthening trade and investment ties between home and host countries. The current impact pertains especially to bilateral trade in services (especially tourism) and goods (e.g. nostalgia trade). LDC diaspora FDI in home countries is still very limited compared to its potential.

Some fledgling diaspora business network effects are starting to appear.

Diaspora knowledge networks are incipient in most LDCs. A number of initiatives and programmes to leverage diaspora knowledge for the benefit of LDC home country development have been launched. They are undertaken by individuals, diaspora associations and NGOs, national home and host country governments and/or international organizations, often in an uncoordinated way. They generally have positive effects, but these are very localized and specific. In most cases, these initiatives do not have a broader impact because the multitude of actions by different stakeholders tends to dilute resources, efforts and energies. They are often isolated programmes, which are not linked to broader development strategies and policies. The few cases of more effective initiatives have typically been a result of coordinated action by different stakeholders — including the home government —, which creates synergies among agents and leverages resources.

The few cases of more effective diaspora mobilization initiatives have typically been a result of coordinated action by different stakeholders, which creates synergies among agents and leverages resources.

Returnees' contribution to investment, innovation and institution-building in LDCs has varied according to local conditions in home countries. Where local conditions are unfavourable to investment and innovation and/or policy has

The contribution of diasporas and other positive effects of brain circulation to the development of LDCs is below its potential.

Initiatives can be taken to strengthen the home country benefits associated with brain drain. This will require policy action by LDC themselves and by the international community.

not been supportive, returnee investment has been limited and has tended to reinforce existing patterns of specialization. By contrast, in some larger LDC economies or those that are growing and undergoing structural transformation, returnees have made significant contributions to economic activity and social innovation.

The contribution of diasporas and other positive effects of brain circulation to the development of LDCs is below its potential. There are two main reasons for this: the development stage of LDCs themselves, and the initiatives put in place. First, prevailing conditions in most LDCs are quite different from those in countries which benefitted greatly from diaspora knowledge and business networks and were able to attract return emigrants. In the latter case, diaporas contributed significantly to home country development, helping many of these countries to become high-income countries.

Second, although most LDCs at present reap limited gains from their diasporas, it is likely that the positive effects of brain circulation will strengthen later during the economic development of these countries. While this is a long-term perspective, initiatives can be taken in the short term to strengthen the home country benefits associated with brain drain. This will require policy action by LDC themselves and by the international community. The next chapter of this Report provides an analysis of policy alternatives and options needed to achieve this objective.

Notes

1 This chapter builds on UNCTAD (2007: 139–160) by updating the statistical information and broadening the scope of analysis and policy recommendations.

2 By contrast, low-skilled migrants are those whose highest educational attainment is at the secondary or primary level or who did not undergo any formal schooling.

3 Bhagwati and Hanson (2009); Docquier and Rapoport (2012); Kapur and McHale (2005); IOM (2008); Solimano (2010); Pritchett (2006).

4 The most widely used database on worldwide brain drain is that of Docquier and Marfouk (2006), which was later revised to provide a gender breakdown (Docquier, Lowell and Marfouk, 2009). It was subsequently expanded in Docquier et al. (2011), which includes non-OECD host countries and therefore captures South–South flows. The first version of this database was kindly made available to the UNCTAD secretariat by its authors.

5 High-skilled people flows are in sharp contrast with those of overall migration, where South–South movements predominate, as seen in chapter 2 of this Report. The latter are strongly influenced by the migration of low-skilled people.

6 Given the preponderance of oil exporters among developing host countries, developments in the price of this commodity are also likely to play a role in determining brain drain trends in the future.

7 The indicators include the number of LDC students, since studying abroad is often the first step towards long-term emigration.

8 Even if education is financed privately, this is an investment in human capital formation made under the expectation that it will bring returns.

9 These costs are net of: 1. the estimated fiscal gains from domestic consumption funded by remittances; and 2. the Government savings from not having to provide services to people who no longer live in the home country.

10 By the same token, host countries become better endowed with skills or human capital, which tends to reinforce their specialization in the corresponding goods and services.

11 On the importance of institutions to economic growth and development, see Szirmai (2012) and Bluhm and Szirmai (2012).

12 Mountford (1997); Stark (2004); Stark et al. (1997, 1998); Vidal (1998); Beine et al. (2001); Docquier and Rapoport (2007, 2012); Kangasniemi et al. (2007); Commander et al. (2004).

13 Angola, Bangladesh, Benin, Burundi, Cambodia, Comoros, Djibouti, Eritrea, Ethiopia, Lao People's Democratic Republic, Lesotho, Madagascar, Malawi, Niger, Uganda and United Republic of Tanzania (UNCTAD secretariat estimates, based on data from the UNESCO Institute for Statistics: http//www.uis.unesco.org, accessed on 22/06/2012).

14 In Ethiopia, for example, in the mid-1990s, university-level institutions hosted only 15,000 students, but received 300,000 applications annually. However, the introduction of new policies by the Government to boost investment in human capital formation resulted in a rapid expansion of the number of universities and students. During the academic year 2006/2007, universities hosted 203,000 students at the bachelor's level and within five years the number of enrolments had more than doubled to 448,000. Similarly, in Senegal, the number of students enrolled in tertiary-level education institutions swelled from 30,000 in 2001 to 86,000 in 2008, as the expansion rate was double that of the preceding decade. By 2012, total enrolment had reached 91,000.

15 Similarly, in Gibson and McKenzie's (2010) survey data for high-skilled emigration from Tonga, Federated States of Micronesia, Papua New Guinea, Ghana and New Zealand, the migration incentive generally pushed respondents to learn a language or take test preparation classes, but not to lengthen schooling itself.

16 Even considering that high-skilled emigrants tend to remit more than low-skilled emigrants (and remittance data refer to all migrants), remittances as a share of GDP per capita exceed 20 per cent in only four LDCs: Lesotho, Haiti, Samoa and Nepal.

17 Rogers (2004) finds that countries with relatively high numbers of students studying science and engineering abroad experience faster subsequent growth.

18 Source: http://www.codev.gouv.sn.

19 The Government of Senegal, for instance, has recorded as many as 741 associations of the Senegalese diaspora (ANSD, 2011).

20 The lack of linkages to national government sometimes stems from limited trust of diaspora organizations in the latter or from missing interest or institutional capacity of the national government to engage with diaspora organizations active in specific projects.

21 This share provides an order of magnitude, since the diaspora investment was made over several years.

22 A survey of Turkish returnees shows that more than half are economically active upon return and most of them engage in entrepreneurial activities (Dustmann and Kirchkamp 2002). In Egypt, returning migrants tend to have higher levels of human capital than non-migrants, and are likely to be more entrepreneurial the longer they have worked abroad (McCormick and Wahba 2001; Wahba 2007).

23 Data for 2009 for Uganda, Senegal and Burkina Faso, and for 2001 in the case of Haiti.

24 Based on the same source as table 17.

25 These shares provide an order of magnitude, since the returnee investment was made over several years.

26 In Ethiopia, out of 30 expatriates who participated in a TOKTEN programme in the home country, only one decided to resettle there permanently (Adredo, 2002).

27 In the MIDA Great Lakes Programme (box 10), just 15 permanent returnees were aided financially, as compared with more than 400 missions, often involving more than one expert.

CHAPTER 5

TOWARDS A POLICY AGENDA FOR THE LDCs: AN INTEGRATED APPROACH TO MIGRATION, REMITTANCES AND MOBILIZATION OF DIASPORA KNOWLEDGE

A. Diasporas and capacity-building

---

1. INTRODUCTION

This Report examines the impact on LDCs of past and current migration that has created diasporas in different parts of the world, and the potential for utilizing these diasporas for development of the home country. It is evident that migration and its varied consequences have become increasingly significant for developing countries in general and LDCs in particular, and these trends are likely to continue in the medium term.

In this Report, various forms of migration have been considered, with a more specific focus on high-skilled migrants. It has been seen that while concerns about brain drain and other costs associated with the migration of skilled personnel are still valid in LDCs, there is also potential for both residents and governments of home countries to utilize the presence of skilled, high-earning diasporas in other parts of the world. It is useful for analytical purposes to distinguish between three sets of resources, capabilities and assets associated with diasporas and their contributions to home countries. They are:

1) Diasporas as sources of capacity-building;

2) Diasporas as sources of knowledge and learning; and

3) Diasporas as sources of development finance

Each of these features could contribute to the development of home countries in different ways, depending on the context, the economic processes at work within the country, and of course the overall policy framework as well as the specific policies applied in different sectors and areas. These aspects of the relationship between cross-border migration and diasporas' links with their countries of origin, along with some specific policies that could be utilized to enhance the relationship in a mutually beneficial way, are outlined in the table 19 and considered in more detail below.

Migration and its varied consequences have become increasingly significant for developing countries in general and LDCs in particular.

2. CREATING THE POLICY FRAMEWORK

a) The need for information

To start with, governments in LDCs need to be aware of the actual extent and pattern of cross-border migration, the location, spread and nature of diaspora activities and the extent and pattern of remittances. On these issues, the current state of knowledge in most LDCs is relatively poor. Therefore, one part of the issue to be addressed is statistical in nature. There is hardly any official apparatus to report on and monitor many of the facets of migration and its results, and what does exist is mainly concerned with remittances. Yet this is to be expected, given that central banks normally monitor and register the flows of remittances coming in through formal channels. Central banks are natural stakeholders in this process since the inflow of remittances alleviates a country's balance of payments constraints. For other aspects of migration, however, there are no natural stakeholders in the government administration, or at best they are dispersed and only loosely connected. Consequently, data on these phenomena are sparse and incomplete, and sometimes do not exist at all. This is especially true of data on the geographic location of diasporas; the costs of remitting; the extent of brain drain; and the current professional and educational status of emigrants.

While concerns about brain drain are still valid in LDCs, there is also potential to utilize the presence of skilled, high-earning diasporas in other parts of the world.

Table 19. Key objectives and possible activities of a diaspora strategy for LDCs		
Key objectives	**Possible activities**	**Rationale**
Making diaspora mobilization and engagement a priority in the development agenda of the home countries	Creating a ministry-level institution to link diaspora issues with national development agenda, identifying goals and policies and coordinating inclusion of all stakeholders	Given the cross-cutting nature of migration, remittances and diaspora engagement, a highest representation in government institutions is necessary
Improving the knowledge of the location, size, and characteristics of the diaspora	Improving data collection, compiling of inventories of diaspora skills and experience, and the like	Policies cannot be based on anecdotal evidence and wrong assumptions
Contacting and engaging diaspora organizations abroad	Organizing high profile events, appointing diaspora members as spoke persons on diaspora issues, partnering with host countries when possible	Engagement of diaspora has to be a continuous process built on trust and thus needs to be nurtured
Defining the role of embassies and consulates with a goal of supporting and mobilizing the diasporas living abroad	Strengthening the role of diplomatic representation in topics that are of special importance to diaspora (legal counseling in host countries, information on options for investment, return, and the like)	Diplomatic representation should promote a quid pro quo relationship with the diaspora members and stand ready to help them in the host country and inform them of options in the home country
Encouraging circular migration, return migration and providing return facilitation services	Recruiting highly skilled diaspora members for temporary return in key government and/or academia positions, providing material and non-material incentives for return migration	Circular migration and temporary return would increase the chances of permanent collaboration of locals with diaspora members; incentives might entice some diaspora members to return for good
Defining and establishing the main mechanisms of diaspora engagement	Depending on the policy goals, activities such as financial assistance, tax incentives, strengthening of cultural and national identity, etc. could be considered	Mechanisms of diaspora engagement would depend on policy goals, the structure of diaspora and the resources the Government has to meet these goals
Extending and upholding citizenship rights	Engaging diaspora will be easier if its members are granted voting rights, dual citizenship, etc.	Having a dual citizenship might strengthen the identification with the home country and could result in stronger engagement
Defining financial vehicles and legal frameworks for attracting specific diaspora resources	Providing incentives for savings, investment, skills, knowledge and technology transfers	Depending on the type of diaspora resources that is targeted, a proper mix of incentives would be needed
Creating a favourable economic environment for attracting diaspora resources	Taking any measures that help to create a favourable economic environment in general	The likelihood of diaspora engagement is higher if the economic environment in the home country is favourable
Facilitating short-term and tourist home visits by the diaspora	Simplifying visa procedures for diaspora members, organizing specific, heritage-tourism programmes, etc.	Diaspora members could provide an impetus for the local tourist industry and also play a key role in converting the country into a new tourist destination
Establishing links of diasporas and diaspora business networks with the private sector of the home country and the national strategy of development	Organizing business events to promote the country's investment opportunities, creating a one-stop shop for investment information, matching local business leaders with diaspora counterparts	Promote links between diaspora and local businesses to make sure that national development goals are supported by the engagement of diaspora resources; use diaspora knowledge networks to enhance national industrial policy
Encouraging philanthropy to support the homeland	Engaging high-profile individuals (artists, sport stars, or wealthy businesspeople) to serve as "goodwill ambassadors" and promote philanthropy in diaspora; when possible, providing matching funds, especially for investment in public goods	Philanthropic activities of diaspora members could substantially improve local conditions, especially in terms of public goods provision

Source: UNCTAD secretariat, based on literature review and Agunias and Newland (2012).

It may be argued that the costs of collecting such information and monitoring the activities of emigrants can be disproportionately large for LDC governments that are cash-strapped and have many other competing uses for their resources. However, with creative policies to engage diasporas and to increase and direct the flow of inward remittances, the benefits to LDCs of such data collection and monitoring are likely to significantly outweigh the costs. The establishment of a migrant remittance observatory for LDCs in Benin is a positive first step,[1] but should be complemented by concrete national measures in other LDCs.

With creative policies to engage diasporas and to increase and direct the flow of inward remittances, the benefits to LDCs of such data collection and monitoring are likely to significantly outweigh the costs.

b) Policy coherence for diaspora engagement

Policies on migration, remittances and diaspora engagement should be formulated as an integral part of national development strategies, not in isolation. This is partly because different forms of migration — internal migration, emigration, immigration, and return migration — are all interlinked, and various macroeconomic and sectoral policies affect each of these. Agricultural and rural development policies influence rural–urban migration patterns. Trade policies affect domestic employment creation (or the lack thereof) and thus influence emigration trends. Monetary and exchange rate policies affect both remittance costs and sending channels. Educational policies influence brain drain processes, and so on. This being so, a piecemeal approach is inappropriate. Not only must migration policies be coherently included in a development strategy, but other policies need to take migration issues into account. This is complicated by the tendency of different ministries and agencies of government to work in a compartmentalized fashion that fails to take other factors and outcomes into consideration.

A further consideration when formulating a development strategy is the presence of multiple stakeholders. When designing policies, it is necessary to bear in mind that there are at least four sets of stakeholders driving the processes related to remittances, diasporas and migration: migrants themselves; migrants' families in the home country; the government in the home country; and the government in the host country. Interests and priorities may vary across groups of stakeholders and even within them (as in the case of migrants from different locations or income groups). For all these reasons, a pragmatic yet holistic and coherent approach to policymaking is required.

Clearly, governments of LDCs cannot control either the pull factors in developed countries or the decisions of their neighbours that sometimes result in flows of refugees or other migrants. In both cases, however, a development strategy should incorporate such considerations. For example, it might be possible to reach bilateral agreements with certain vitally important developed countries to try to regulate migration flows and encourage circular migration. In the case of developing countries, regional cooperation can play a key role, especially since a great deal of international migration from LDCs is from nearby countries.

In effect, an agency, ideally at ministerial level, is required to deal with the cross-cutting nature of these issues; ensure policy coherence and consistency across the board; and coordinate potential actors around a set of identified priorities. Some LDCs have already established ministries that are dedicated exclusively to the issues of migration, remittances and diasporas. For example, the Government of Bangladesh, responding to demands by expatriate Bangladeshis, created a Ministry of Expatriates' Welfare and Overseas Employment (MoEWOE) in 2001, two years before India and the Philippines. Its prime function is the creation, promotion and regulation of employment overseas. One important motive for promoting employment abroad is to ensure a steady flow of remittances. However, the Ministry's functions have been expanding, so it now also deals with the creation of an investment-friendly economic policy package for diaspora members. Some other LDCs, like Haiti and Senegal, have also established ministerial positions for dealing exclusively with diaspora issues, while in others, these issues are dealt with by ministries with hybrid functions. Thus, Ministries of Foreign Affairs often have the additional function of dealing with diaspora issues (for example in Benin, Comoros, Ethiopia), while in other cases this role is played by a Ministry of Regional Integration, as in the cases of Mali, Niger and Somalia. However, most other LDCs do not give these issues adequate institutional importance and deal with them at subministerial level (Agunias and Newland, 2012).

Not only must migration policies be coherently included in a development strategy, but other policies need to take migration issues into account.

In the case of developing countries, regional cooperation can play a key role, especially since a great deal of international migration from LDCs is from nearby countries.

While the specific mix of policies and concrete measures for diaspora engagement will vary for each country, the overall direction should be to provide an enabling environment for development of productive capacities. Like both domestic residents and other foreign residents, diaspora members are more likely to be interested in investing and participating in an economy that has some dynamism, where rules and norms are clearly laid out and followed as much as possible and key institutions can be trusted. The importance of clear, transparent and fair rules and legal infrastructure cannot be overemphasized.

As noted in chapter 4, the issue of trust is crucial. In terms of public policy, one possible way to build trust is to start with small commitments and gradually scale up. If these smaller projects are successful, trust and experience will accumulate on both sides. This approach may be advantageous in cases where previous experiences with mobilization of diaspora resources were unsatisfactory. Further, while it is true that diaspora members are not motivated exclusively by commercial interests, their engagement will fail if they are only expected to contribute and receive nothing in return. For example, the policy approach of the Ethiopian Government recognizes that partnerships should be built with the diaspora in such a way as to benefit both parties and include building capacity, extending rights and extracting obligations (Kuschminder and Siegel, 2011) in mutually beneficial commercial and professional engagement at various levels.

While the specific mix of policies and concrete measures for diaspora engagement will vary for each country, the overall direction should be to provide an enabling environment for development of productive capacities.

3. DIASPORAS AS ENTREPRENEURS

Very little research has been done on how diaspora entrepreneurs contribute to economic development in LDCs. In some middle-income countries, entrepreneurial diasporas have been instrumental in developing the productive capacities of their home countries. For example, migrant entrepreneurs have played an important role in building knowledge-based industries in India, China, Taiwan Province of China, Israel and Ireland in the last two decades or so. One lesson from these experiences is that entrepreneurs abroad can play an important role in helping to develop firms at home and also serve as a two-way link for market knowledge, connections and technology transfer across countries. This has been tried successfully in South America, on a regional basis, through the MERCOSUR Entrepreneurial Portal.

In LDCs, this process may perhaps hold less promise in the short run because of their more limited base of human capital and venture capital to develop high-tech industries at home. Nevertheless, their entrepreneurial diasporas operating in light industry can help develop similar industries at home through contacts, know-how and other valuable inputs and capabilities developed in the host countries. They can also contribute to the upgrading of managerial and innovating capabilities at home.

The issue of trust is crucial. In terms of public policy, one possible way to build trust is to start with small commitments and gradually scale up.

In general, there are at least two conditions that determine migrants' success in establishing thriving firms upon their return. The first is whether they return with more advanced knowledge and skills than before. As discussed in chapter 4, the longer they stay as migrants in foreign countries and the more entrepreneurial experience they accumulate, the more likely this will be. The second condition is the existence of a favourable policy framework in their home country. Return migrants would probably need suitable financial support to start a new firm, even if they have accumulated some savings. At the very least, they would have to be able to get a credit from the financial sector under normal conditions. However, given the reluctance of financial institutions to extend credit to SMEs, a national development bank with special lines of credit for return migrants might be necessary. In addition, return migrants might have accumulated some but perhaps not all of the requisite skills for successful entrepreneurial activity.

In that case, they would need technical assistance to upgrade their managerial, technical, financial, or other skills required for successful management of small and medium-sized enterprises (SMEs). Governments could provide this type of technical assistance and/or education. One option could be to support these entrepreneurs by lowering tariffs on imports of machinery and equipment and raw materials to help them get their businesses off the ground.

Initially, the public policy focus in LDCs would most likely be on small, family firms that create jobs. Later, however, policymakers would have to shift their focus to medium-sized companies that are more likely to boost economic development by moving up the value chain and that have a stronger technology-upgrading potential. The policies then would have to identify strategic sectors for the national economy and provide incentives for entrepreneurial diaspora members to invest in these sectors.

Governments could also provide incentives to migrants to return to the home country once they retire by signing double-taxation avoidance treaties with the main host countries where the majority of their migrants work. Jamaica, for example, has signed double taxation avoidance treaties with all of its major trading partners and also the main destination countries of its migrants (the United Kingdom, the United States, Canada, etc.). The economic rationale is the following: given the income differences, retiring in the home country provides retirees with much greater purchasing power than retiring in the host country. However, if they have to pay taxes on their pensions twice (in both home and host country), this advantage mainly disappears. Thus, double taxation avoidance agreements should, among other things, contain a provision that pensions and other similar remuneration paid in consideration of past employment to a migrant by the host country be taxable only in the country in which a migrant decides to retire. The benefits of higher consumption would then accrue to the home country to the extent that migrants decide to retire there instead of retiring in the host country.

4. DIASPORAS AS TRADE FACILITATORS

A positive empirical correlation has been found between the degree of international trade in source and destination countries and the size of the migrant community in both nations.[2] The dominance of language, culture and knowledge of costumer and supplier markets are all factors that help to develop trade relations among nations, and diaspora communities can be especially well placed to perform this role.

As noted in chapter 4, a distinct niche for LDCs could initially be to seek an advantage in the so-called "nostalgia trade". Orozco (2008) finds that there is a very high participation of migrants in the United States in markets for home-country goods. On average each migrant spends almost $1,000 per year on nostalgia products, and the total volume may top $20 billion annually. A first step for many LDCs could be to try to tap the consumption potential of its own diaspora by exporting goods that are emblematic of the country but are difficult to find in host countries. The potential for policy intervention in nostalgia trade is wide since it is a multistep process that involves producers, home-country distributors, host-country importers, wholesalers and retailers (Newland and Taylor, 2010). Policies in LDCs could be designed to help producers become and stay competitive by upgrading their products and adapting them to changes in final markets, and to enlist diaspora members to help with branding and marketing in the host country. Education and training of producers is crucial if they are to become competitive in foreign markets.

A positive empirical correlation has been found between the degree of international trade in source and destination countries and the size of the migrant community in both nations.

A distinct niche for LDCs could initially be to seek an advantage in the so-called "nostalgia trade". Each migrant in the United States spends almost $1,000 per year on nostalgia products, and the total volume may top $20 billion annually.

Governments should also identify hurdles which local firms encounter in foreign markets and help them overcome them. Typically, local firms are too small to research market conditions abroad. Given the more stringent phytosanitary and other requirements in developed countries, small producers generally cannot meet them without first incurring significant costs for finding the appropriate information and financial resources to invest in technology. Moreover, they lack capabilities to market their products. To capture the lucrative niche markets in developed countries, LDC governments have to make sure that local firms receive support throughout the commercial chain, up to and including the retail phase. Diaspora members could be crucial in providing support for these policies, and could provide strategic guidance throughout the process.

For countries such as South Africa, diaspora-owned companies were partly responsible for the worldwide diffusion and adoption of products such as rooibos tea and South African wine. These companies also imported products from South Africa for sale first to diaspora members, but later to a broader public as well. South African crafts have also benefited from contacts between local producers and the diaspora. Policies to connect diaspora members to local business in the home country could include initiatives such as providing diaspora organizations with information on local producers and their conditions, organizing business events or matching local entrepreneurs with their diaspora counterparts.

Another example, that of the Oromo refugees from Ethiopia in the United Kingdom developing the Oromo Coffee Company (OCC), mentioned in chapter 4, shows that LDC diasporas are succeeding in not only catering to the nostalgic tastes of their countrymen, but also in moving beyond the narrow focus on the consumption potential of diaspora members. In effect, by exporting organic coffee, OCC has succeeded in expanding the appeal of its products to a wider set of consumers. Given that one of the main problems of small producers in penetrating foreign markets is their inability to provide larger quantities of goods, policies in LDCs could encourage producers to organize into clusters. That would allow them to share information and knowledge; upgrade their production processes; improve access to more modern technologies; and penetrate the broader markets of host countries beyond the relatively reduced niches for nostalgia goods.

Finally, the examples of China and India in particular show that diasporas can be instrumental in increasing exports to new markets. In order to do something similar, however, LDCs would first have to substantially strengthen their productive capacities to produce competitive goods and services for exports, and would have to engage much more actively with their own diasporas.

Diaspora members could be a special target group for a strategy of tourist development of the home country as they are more likely to visit the country, even in the absence of a full-fledged tourist infrastructure. Besides utilizing diasporas' motivations to visit countries of origin, governments could also generate other motives related to culture, business, sport, religious, well-being and other activities that also have a strong impact on the development of tourism. These visits could also precipitate interest in so-called "nostalgia" goods, and increase their consumption in the host country.

The following two examples demonstrate how other countries have used specific means of boosting diaspora tourism. One example is the "Homecoming Scotland 2009" project, a series of events with the specific goal of attracting people of Scottish origin to visit their "ancestral homeland". The year 2009 was chosen for a symbolic reason: it was the 250th anniversary of the birth of

To capture the lucrative niche markets in developed countries, LDC governments have to make sure that local firms receive support throughout the commercial chain.

Diaspora members could be a special target group for a strategy of tourist development of the home country as they are more likely to visit the country.

Robert Burns, the national poet of Scotland. The programme consisted of more than 300 events that motivated thousands of people of Scottish ancestry to visit Scotland. The timing of the project could not have been better: the boost to tourism and the economy was a welcome support, as it coincided with the worst global economic crisis since the Great Depression.

The other example shows that sport can connect diaspora members with their home country. The Croatian World Games are an Olympic-style competition in twelve different sports with participation of young Croats from Croatia and from Croatian diaspora communities. The event is organized by the Croatian Olympic Committee and the Croatian World Congress, an umbrella organization of different diaspora communities, and supported by the Government. Besides economic benefits for the home country, its significance is in the outreach to younger members of the Croatian diaspora born abroad who would normally tend to lose their ties with the country of origin of their parents or grandparents. Both examples illustrate a more general point about policies to engage diasporas: it takes some creativity and knowledge to devise policies that will attract diaspora members as tourists.

In 2000, the number of workers with university-level education who emigrated from LDCs reached 1.3 million — an increase of 58 per cent over 1990.

B. Diasporas, knowledge and learning

As indicated in chapter 4, the number of workers with university-level education who emigrated from LDCs reached 1.3 million in 2000 — an increase of 58 per cent over 1990. The latest figures are not yet available, but given recent trends, the total number is estimated to be much higher today. The greatest increase was in emigration to developed countries, in particular the United States, which hosts one-fourth of all LDC high-skilled emigrants. From a home country policy perspective, two points are worth noting: first, brain drain from LDCs is most likely to continue in the foreseeable future, due to strong push and pull forces mentioned in chapter 4 of this Report. This will increase the size of highly skilled professionals in diasporas. Second, in most cases, living and working abroad allows nationals to continue to accumulate and upgrade their knowledge, skills and experience.

Living and working abroad allows nationals to continue to accumulate and upgrade their knowledge, skills and experience.

Home countries can draw on these overseas pools of skills and human resources so that they share knowledge and transfer technology with domestic agents, thereby contributing to national development. As noted above, the burden of devising and implementing development strategies and programmes should not fall solely on diasporas (Skeldon, 2008), although the establishment of diaspora knowledge networks makes the transfer of knowledge to home countries easier. This of course requires the active involvement of home country governments and the formulation of well-targeted policies for diaspora engagement.

LDC governments are starting to realize the potential of their diasporas as sources of knowledge and technology.

LDC governments are starting to realize the potential of their diasporas as sources of knowledge and technology. Home countries have taken the initial steps of devising and implementing policies to mobilize diaspora knowledge for domestic development. In many cases, however, the incipient diaspora policies of LDCs have been designed by government officials without consulting diaspora members. Consequently, the professional priorities, time and financial constraints, willingness of emigrants to engage, and the desired forms of participation have not been taken into account. These design and implementation shortcomings limit policy effectiveness.

Ideally, the planning and design of policies and instruments for diaspora engagement should be made by national home country governments in consultation with diaspora members and their associations. This requires home countries to have a good knowledge of their diasporas and to establish a dialogue with them. Such consultations are also likely to ensure engagement and commitment by diaspora members from the start, as well as coherence between diaspora action and national government priorities and programmes.

Dialogue results in a better acquaintance with diasporas in terms of their geographical location, skills profile, professional activities, areas of expertise and experience. It also allows drawing a clear picture of the way in which a diaspora is willing to engage with the home country for the purpose of knowledge sharing and transfer. The policies, mechanisms and instruments devised and implemented by national policymakers need to be differentiated by diaspora segment (e.g. scientists, professionals, entrepreneurs, low-skilled workers, peasants, artists, etc.) and their forms of engagement. These forms can be "virtual return" (i.e. interaction at a distance), temporary return (through participation in development programmes and projects, training activities, advisory missions, etc.) or definitive return. Each of these forms of diaspora engagement requires different financing mechanisms and institutional support.

The policies, mechanisms and instruments devised and implemented by national policymakers need to be differentiated by diaspora segment (e.g. scientists, professionals, entrepreneurs, low-skilled workers, peasants, artists, etc.) and their forms of engagement.

In many cases, policies and programmes will involve just home country agents and diaspora members and associations. Often, however, it will be advisable to involve more stakeholders in the planning and execution of diaspora knowledge transfer programmes and policies. These include host country governments and other key agents (e.g. businesses, research centres, government institutions and universities), international organizations, and international donors. Such joint action avoids the problems of dispersion and lack of coherence of programmes and actions discussed in chapter 4 of this Report.

Coordinating and leveraging the actions, programmes and resources of different stakeholders will allow LDCs to establish dynamic diaspora knowledge networks (DKNs) and to reap the benefits from the ensuing flows of knowledge and technology transfer to the home country.

Coordinating and leveraging the actions, programmes and resources of different stakeholders will allow LDCs to establish dynamic diaspora knowledge networks (DKNs) and to reap the benefits from the ensuing flows of knowledge and technology transfer to the home country.

1. DIASPORA KNOWLEDGE NETWORKS (DKNs)

DKNs consist of groups of highly skilled expatriate professionals who are interested in maintaining contacts and helping to develop their countries of origin. Thus, DKNs do not refer to all the members of the diaspora, but only to those groups of individuals who are interested in sharing and transferring their knowledge, experience and know-how back home. In order to become agents of change and learning, however, DKNs need to become "search networks",[3] which consist of individuals and institutions who and which link and connect the most effective segments of relevant institutions in order to discover what a country is good at producing (Kuznetsov and Sabel, 2006). As knowledge is neither costless nor easily transferrable, for this to occur, proactive policy is required that incorporates this potentially key function of a diaspora into the government's strategic developmental framework.[4]

DKNs are understood as subsets of international knowledge networks that "govern the transfer of various types of knowledge, such as intellectual property, know-how, software code, or databases, between dependent parties, across the economy" (OECD, 2011b:1).[5] As such, they include a platform for knowledge flows and interaction between diaspora and the local actors in home countries. These flows may incorporate various forms of learning and knowledge creation, such as research and development (R&D), intellectual property, technology licensing, know-how, joint ventures and alliances, technology sharing and best practices. Consequently, DKNs represent a subset of global knowledge

DKNs govern the transfer of various types of knowledge, such as intellectual property, know-how, software code, or databases, between dependent parties, across the economy .

networks, with vast economic potential that remains untapped in most LDCs. For example, as explained in Box 9 of chapter 4 of this Report, the decoding of the jute genome in Bangladesh with the direct involvement of the Bangladeshi diaspora was a very significant innovation, with enormous economic potential and scientific impact. This innovation was produced as a result of knowledge sharing between national and international knowledge providers. It serves as an excellent example of the success of DKNs in LDCs at the current time and the potential of DKNs for building the productive base of LDC economies.

DKNs represent a subset of global knowledge networks, with vast economic potential that remains untapped in most LDCs.

The full economic impact of DKNs is believed to be greatly underestimated, since the methodology for impact assessment remains to be elaborated. For example, how does one measure the impact of research networks on policy development? Obviously, knowledge generation and transfer, and the synergies involved in innovation and productivity increases, have been central to economic growth in developed countries and can be extremely significant in developing countries.

DKNs are generally characterized by the absence of formal governance arrangements, which can have its advantages and disadvantages. They can imply the emergence of non-state actors, thereby potentially generating pressures for democratic structures with greater roles for civil society. Conversely, they can contribute to the further entrenchment of existing inequalities and asymmetries in economies and societies. They should not be perceived as a panacea or a substitute for local efforts to build endogenous productive capabilities; rather, their role is that of an additional actor in the story of growth based on domestic productive capacities.

DKNs should not be perceived as a panacea or a substitute for local efforts to build endogenous productive capabilities; rather, their role is that of an additional actor in the story of growth based on domestic productive capacities.

In this section, it will be argued that there is ample evidence from numerous case studies to show that DKNs have played a critical role in the technological upgrading, industrial development and building of productive capacities of source countries (Meyer and Wattiaux, 2006). However, such transfer of knowledge and learning does not happen automatically but requires an organized and coordinated diaspora network and a home-country national development strategy backed by industrial policy and active government engagement in diaspora affairs. A proactive diaspora policy is essential to ensure that DKNs, which are in essence private voluntary networks, gain the trust and confidence needed to remain engaged and ensure that their activities exert a positive impact.[6] As latecomers to industrial development and given their recent experience with deindustrialization,[7] LDCs need to formulate innovative industrial policies that are compatible with their current conditions and requirements as well as the rapidly evolving global context. Some LDCs have already designed industrial policies with a view to accelerating economic diversification and structural change. This Report will argue that in formulating their industrial policies, LDCs should learn from countries that have benefited most from DKNs by designing their diaspora strategy as an integral part of industrial policy and the broader national development strategy. This has already taken place in Asia, less so in Africa.

A proactive diaspora policy is essential to ensure that DKNs, which are in essence private voluntary networks, gain the trust and confidence needed to remain engaged and ensure that their activities exert a positive impact.

LDCs should learn from countries that have benefited most from DKNs by designing their diaspora strategy as an integral part of industrial policy and the broader national development strategy.

2. Diaspora networks as sources of knowledge and learning

DKNs have been effectively deployed as agents of change in both developed and developing countries. There are successful cases of diaspora networks such as those formed by Indian, Chinese, Korean, Taiwanese, Vietnamese, Turkish and Bangladeshi emigrants, to name but a few. These demonstrate the opportunities associated with the institutionalization of private voluntary networks in promoting horizontal inter-firm networks that enable the transfer of skills and knowledge. The cases of Taiwan Province of China, India, Republic of

Korea and China illustrate, for example, how public policies by developmental states can mitigate the losses of "brain drain". In these countries, government policies were not focused on the return of the members of the diaspora; rather, they highlighted the importance of integration into international networks that would link the professionals overseas with those in the source country (Kapur, 2001). The massive boom of the Indian sector supplying services of information and communication technologies (ICTs) is a good example of how decentralized knowledge transfer arrangements can play a critical role in the emerging model of industrial policy. In this respect, therefore, DKNs represent a new feature in the recent evolution of industrial policy.

There are many reasons for promoting networks, not least of which is knowledge diffusion. It is widely acknowledged that DKNs can lead to knowledge spillovers and greater collective efficiency (Barré et al., 2003; Brinkerhoff, 2006; Chaparro et al., 2004; Kapur and McHale, 2005). One of the key reasons to promote such networks is because they not only help to channel remittances and imply higher savings and income, but also boost collective efficiency. DKNs can supply new technologies and inform government and other residents of the latest technological developments and those appropriate for domestic industrial needs. They can assist in matching the needs of local productive sectors with specific foreign direct investment (FDI) required for upgrading local skills and capacities.

As awareness grows of knowledge's essential role in the development process, hundreds of new DKNs were created throughout the 1990s and 2000s in countries as diverse as Argentina, Mexico, Haiti, Panama, the Philippines, Chile, China, Colombia, India and South Africa. While not all networks have been equally successful, the large Chinese and Indian search networks demonstrate how they can effectively facilitate the transfer of knowledge and technology to the home countries.[8] Moreover, from these experiences, it would appear that horizontal interventions at the network level can enhance market efficiency and lead to higher productivity and upgrading at the firm level (Kaplinsky, 2005). In effect, the significance of the diaspora network to industrial policy is that it makes the shift from hierarchy to search networks an essential component of industrial policy. DKNs help to link up those who want to learn with those that are already learning. Indeed, this shift from hierarchy to horizontal networks has a profound impact on the global supply chains and consequently on new industrial strategies, where "learning to learn" becomes an essential objective of the industrial policy.

What is different about networks from other forms of market coordination? First, within networks, firms relate to each other not through arm's-length market transactions but through long-term, special relationships that are historically determined. Empirical evidence shows that market-based, hierarchical coordination carries much higher costs than network-based coordination, especially when physical proximity is involved, resulting in agglomeration economies. Second, the pooling of skills and resources, even by competing firms, can lead to higher productivity and increased innovation. Third, DKNs can internalize the negative externalities and encourage knowledge sharing within networks.

As noted by Kuznetsov and Sabel (2006), a proliferation of professional associations of diaspora members illustrates this transition to different types of search networks that facilitate trial-and-error experimentation and learning what a country is good at producing. The authors underscore the role of open migration chains and diaspora networks (expatriate networks) in transmitting information about new opportunities and types of skills required in the home and host countries and in advancing the collective interests of diasporas.

The massive boom of the Indian ICT services sector is a good example of how decentralized knowledge transfer arrangements can play a critical role in the emerging model of industrial policy. In this respect, therefore, DKNs represent a new feature in the recent evolution of industrial policy.

DKNs can supply new technologies and inform government and other residents of the latest technological developments and those appropriate for domestic industrial needs. They can assist in matching the needs of local productive sectors with specific FDI required for upgrading local skills and capacities.

DKNs help to link up those who want to learn with those that are already learning.

They also cite the creation of the venture capital industry in Taiwan Province of China and other diaspora-led initiatives to promote productive development in the home country as practical examples of diaspora-induced productive development. According to Kuznetsov and Sabel (2006), "open migration regimes" best accommodate DKNs, as they can also transfer "tacit" knowledge and experience to home countries, largely based on the success cases of the knowledge-intensive sectors, such as Iinformation technology (IT) services and biotech sectors in India, Republic of Korea, Taiwan Province of China, and more recently in China.

The profit motive is an implicit incentive which induces knowledge transfer within networks and encourages information sharing and collaboration not only across firms but within firms and across other entities that make up the production system. While many of these networks are essentially private and voluntary initiatives based on altruism or philanthropy, several well-known DKNs have been institutionalized and become effective agents of change and transmission of knowledge, including through student mentoring, policy advice, technical assistance and other channels of tacit as well as embodied technology transfer. There are several such examples, such as the Chilean "Primera" business innovation organizations and SENSA, the South African Network of Skills Abroad.

3. THE POTENTIAL ROLE OF DKNs IN LDCs' INDUSTRIAL DEVELOPMENT

In recent years, UNCTAD has repeatedly argued that progressive transformation in economic structure is a prerequisite for LDCs to achieve accelerated and sustained economic growth and poverty reduction. The policies and strategies required for structural transformation will involve, inter alia: (a) the development of a new industrial policy based on a strategic approach which reflects the specific needs and conditions of LDCs; (b) a catalytic developmental State to compensate for the incipient and weak private sector in LDCs; (c) measures to encourage private investment in productive activities and public investment in basic infrastructure, including the development of skills and support institutions; and (d) the promotion of domestic technological learning and innovation and improvements in productivity in both the agricultural and manufacturing sectors.

UNCTAD (2011a) argued that there is an urgent need for LDCs to espouse innovative industrial policies instead of imitating industrial policy practices in other countries. The Report articulated why the hierarchical industrial policies adopted in many of the emerging economies (for example, the East Asian model of industrial policy) are not likely to be the most appropriate ones for the LDCs, owing to the dearth of conditions and institutions required for these approaches to function. The internal conditions, which allowed other more successful developing countries to harness market forces for development, simply do not exist in most LDCs. These conditions include close alliances between the State and the private sector, including financial institutions, expansionary macroeconomic policies, and a high degree of strategic integration with the global economy, relatively high levels of education of the population, developmental elites, and a high level of the institutional development of the State itself. Instead, it was argued that the LDCs needed to adopt catalytic development policies that are not primarily aimed at market development but rather diversification of their productive structures at the sectoral and enterprise levels.

In the wake of the recent global financial and economic crisis, which has exerted a negative impact on the economic performance of LDCs, a renewed

"Open migration regimes" best accommodate DKNs, as they can also transfer "tacit" knowledge and experience to home countries.

UNCTAD has repeatedly argued that progressive transformation in economic structure is a prerequisite for LDCs to achieve accelerated and sustained economic growth and poverty reduction.

There is an urgent need for LDCs to espouse innovative industrial policies instead of imitating industrial policy practices in other countries.

LDCs needed to adopt catalytic development policies that are not primarily aimed at market development but rather diversification of their productive structures at the sectoral and enterprise levels.

interest in industrial policy has emerged, as indicated in the final outcome of the UNCTAD XIII Conference. The Doha Mandate stresses that:

> "Industrial policies play an important role in establishing dynamic and sustainable development in many countries. These need to be complemented with other policies in relevant areas if they are to have their full and intended effect. This includes economic diversification, improving international competitiveness and realizing more sustainable and inclusive outcomes."

This Report reinforces the case for a new industrial policy in LDCs, arguing further that such a policy should reflect the role of DKNs because they carry a potentially transformative impact on knowledge accumulation, especially in accelerating technological change and foreign direct investment.[9] At a minimum, DKNs can partly offset the huge knowledge gap created by the shortage of skills and knowledge in LDCs. For example, underdevelopment of local SME sectors, along with development financing gaps, has been identified as a major weakness in the industrial structures of most LDCs. These gaps are viewed as major stumbling blocks to LDCs' efforts to foster technological learning and upgrading and build their productive capacities (UNCTAD, 2007). In principle, DKNs can act as bridging institutions for the LDCs, as they are more familiar with the best practices acquired abroad in more advanced countries while possessing sensitivity and knowledge of their own developmental needs and weaknesses. Moreover, even though physically apart, through the intense use of ICTs, DKNs could assist the State in linking local firms up with foreign ones in order to address specific bottlenecks and shortages. DKNs, if organized, could play a key intermediary role in linking local research capacity and local systems of production diffusion with global knowledge and production systems.

However, the mere existence of DKNs does not necessarily imply a beneficial impact on economic development, as much depends on complementary policy initiatives and practices towards diasporas, which can be seen as sources of financial flows and opportunities for technology transfer and political support. As shown in box 12, there are a number of developing countries, including some LDCs, primarily in Asia, that have already deployed DKNs effectively in their efforts to industrialize and develop. Governments in LDCs would be well advised to take a closer look at certain of these success cases, as some of them provide useful lessons on how to organize and tap into DKNs.

Unfortunately, to date, there is very little empirical information on measurable impacts of DKNs, particularly in African LDCs. This lacuna calls for further research, especially detailed case studies, as the macro indicators do not necessarily tell the whole story, owing to the high degree of informality. Informal channels of transmission and transfer of remittances and knowledge dominate all other channels, making formal analysis very daunting.

This Report recognizes the new opportunities for LDCs arising from collaboration with DKNs (table 20). However, it does so in full awareness that the fundamental patterns of underdevelopment, which have become deeply entrenched in the LDCs' economies, will not change automatically or without strong and active engagement by policymakers themselves. The Report proposes that as LDCs formulate new industrial policies, their governments need to bear in mind that DKNs, if coordinated through networks, can help catalyse and facilitate the process of structural transformation in LDCs. Failure to recognize this fact may mean that DKNs will remain untapped resources and missed opportunities.

This Report reinforces the case for a new industrial policy in LDCs, arguing further that such a policy should reflect the role of DKNs because they carry a potentially transformative impact on knowledge accumulation, especially in accelerating technological change.

DKNs, if organized, could play a key intermediary role in linking local research capacity and local systems of production diffusion with global knowledge and production systems.

The mere existence of DKNs does not necessarily imply a beneficial impact on economic development, as much depends on complementary policy initiatives and practices toward diasporas.

The Report proposes that as LDCs formulate new industrial policies, their governments need to bear in mind that DKNs, if coordinated through networks, can help catalyse and facilitate the process of structural transformation in LDCs. Failure to recognize this fact may mean that DKNs will remain untapped resources and missed opportunities.

Box 12. International best practices

The empirical literature shows that there is a variety of experiences with diaspora engagement strategies, policies and actions. Two very interesting cases are Ireland and Scotland. These are high-income countries with significant diasporas abroad and with diaspora-oriented strategies supported at the highest political level. The size of the Irish diaspora can be very large depending on the definition used.[1] Scotland and Ireland in the 2000s, acknowledging the potential of their diasporas and mindful of the attractiveness of home country conditions, started a process of developing national diaspora strategies led by the First Minister (Scotland) and the presidency (Ireland). The two diaspora strategies are broadly similar but not exactly the same. Ireland has followed a sort of "light touch" diaspora strategy, network-based -- rather than heavy top-down (and bureaucratic). Scotland, in turn, followed a more State-active strategy but without adopting a dirigiste approach of weighty statist intervention. The Irish diaspora strategy is multidimensional in scope and built around economic, social, cultural and affinity networks. Business and economic considerations are certainly important but are not the only overriding concern. The main Irish networks and initiatives comprise the Irish Abroad Unit, established in 2004, which comes under the Department of Foreign Affairs and has a mandate to coordinate the Emigrant Support Programme reoriented to centralizing previous support programmes for the diaspora such as the Emigrant Advice Network, Enterprise Ireland, Culture Ireland, Emigrants News online and Ireland Funds. Most of these efforts were initially geared to the Irish communities residing in the United Kingdom and the United States but later were extended to Irish communities in Australia, Canada, Argentina, South Africa, Zimbabwe, the Netherlands, France and, most recently, China.

Diaspora strategies vary across nations. Unlike Ireland and Scotland, several countries have created a principal and single government institution (a government minister or full government department) that coordinates diaspora strategy around such issues as the legal status and voting rights of diaspora members, the welfare and labour rights of diaspora members in their new locations, remittances and philanthropy, cultural and social links to the diaspora, and the development of business relationships with the diaspora. In this more centralized model of diaspora strategy, we find the case of India (Ministry of Overseas Indian Affairs), Armenia (Ministry of Diaspora) and Jamaica (Diaspora and Consular Affairs Department in the Ministry of Foreign Affairs and Foreign Trade), and Lithuania (Department of National Minorities and Lithuanians Living Abroad).

In Chile, DICOEX — the Directorate for Chileans Abroad, a State agency — was established in 2000.[2] In turn, a business network called Chile Global stands out as an active network geared to attracting successful Chilean entrepreneurs located mainly in advanced economies. A new programme, Start-Up Chile, directed to nationals of any country in the world, was recently set up by the industrial promotion agency CORFO to attract foreign technological and innovative entrepreneurs to do business and create new ventures in Chile, taking advantage of the favourable business climate and overall macro stability. This is an interesting programme that provides grants of $40,000 to prospective foreign entrepreneurs seeking to go to Chile to develop a productive venture. In addition, the inflow of foreign entrepreneurs is facilitated by a system of (one-year) working visas granted in one week's time. In Chile, the network Fundación Chile has played a major role in building not only Chilean but also regional and technological capacities. Fundación Chile has served as a bridging institution for enhancing technological capacities in local firms, combined with foreign knowledge. It illustrates the benefits of institutionalized networks supporting technological development in the whole region.

Some developing countries have established formal channels for counseling their diaspora on a variety of issues: Jamaica has formed the Jamaican Diaspora Advisory Board, while India has created the Prime Minister's Global Advisory Council of Overseas Indians. Two high-skilled, entrepreneurial networks are the Mexican Talent Network and the TiE organization in India. Kuznetsov (2011) makes a distinction between "sophisticated" and "emerging" diasporas facing a variety of country conditions in which countries such as China, Republic of Korea, Taiwan Province of China, Ireland and Scotland belong to a first group of "sophisticated diaspora/favourable country conditions", while Chile, Hungary, Slovenia, Croatia, Malaysia and Thailand belong to a second group of "emerging diaspora/favourable country conditions. LDC efforts to attract diasporas (see below) may be classified as "emerging diasporas". National country conditions, in turn, may vary across countries, although today we can say that progress in terms of having some kind of diaspora policy is greater than in the past.

From this perspective, a variety of diaspora initiatives have been developed in Africa in recent years, showing that African middle-income countries and sub-Saharan African LDCs are also participating in this global trend of engaging national diasporas for development. Examples include the Council of the Moroccan Community Abroad, the Ethiopian Expatriate Affairs of the Ministry of Foreign Affairs and the Diaspora Coordinating Office in the Ministry of Capacity-building, the National Diaspora Council of Kenya, the Senegalese Diaspora Foundation, and the Diaspora Desk in the President's Office in Zambia.[3]

High-income nations such Norway, Finland, Sweden, France (Assemblée des Français de l'étranger) and Switzerland (Organisation des Suisses de l'étranger) have recently established expatriate parliaments. Italy also has a parliamentary representation system for nationals residing abroad.

New Zealand and Australia have been active in trying to build broad global networks of talented and professional people living overseas. They are more broadly designed than simple business networks. KEA, in New Zealand, has 25,000 subscribers in over 174 countries and 14 international chapters in eight countries. It works to connect the estimated 750,000 New Zealand-born people living overseas with home, and specifically seeks to connect to talented New Zealanders in order to share knowledge, contacts and opportunities. Australia's Advance initiative, in turn, is headquartered in New York; it has over 12,000 members in 63 countries and has chapters in 14 countries. Advance activates and engages overseas Australians to use their expertise, contacts, and positions of influence for Australia. It creates industry-specific networks; partners with tourist agencies in promoting tourism to Australia; and facilitates return migration.

One of the best examples of what a government can do through its industrial policy to attract diaspora to build productive capacities and to maximize the developmental impact of a diaspora is to be found in China. The Chinese diaspora, estimated at

Box 12 (contd.)

anywhere between 35 to 50 million people, has exerted a major impact on the growth of the Chinese economy. However, this did not happen automatically but in response to policy measures taken by the Government. Since the late 1980s, the Chinese Government has undertaken major efforts to combine sentiment and incentives to attract investment from the diaspora. The Chinese strategy was a combination of efforts by entrepreneurial local officials and Chinese diaspora investors to promote a pro-investment policy toward the diaspora. Substantial increases of FDI into China (estimated at as much as 80 per cent of the total) largely originate from the Chinese diaspora. Their efforts have helped to make China one of the world's leading manufacturing centres. It is true that the growth was also driven by significant public investment, especially in infrastructure. The particular institutional conditions of China also encourage the phenomenon known as round-tripping whereby domestic resources were transferred to the Chinese diaspora to enter the country again as diaspora investment. While no precise claims can be made, estimates suggest that a significant part of Chinese diaspora investment has been of this type, aided by the fact that the Chinese Government made investment a major focus of its relationship with the diaspora. Such investment was important, not just for the financial resources it provided but probably more so for the technical skills, external contacts, organizational approaches and other "soft" aspects of production with which it was associated.

The Chinese Government has also actively solicited highly skilled professionals to return to China permanently or for a few years, with incentives such as relatively higher pay than local counterparts; better working conditions such as laboratories and research assistants; and provision of research grants. In many technological areas, diaspora members are also actively encouraged to mentor younger skilled people who are still in China, as well as visit and nurture their previous institutions, which has been an important part of the strategy of encouraging innovation and technological upgrading.

As a vital element of its diaspora policy, India granted generous incentives to diaspora investors who actively promoted and supported the Indian software sector in the late 1990s. Indian-born entrepreneurs and those of Indian descent, particularly from the United States, accumulated significant financial capital and acquired human capital and business networks that enabled them to play a salient role in foreign direct investment and technology transfer.

Indian overseas migrants have also contributed through investment, transfer of skills and technology, and through networking. For instance, returnee Indian doctors from the United Kingdom and United States, along with Indian diaspora associations in the medical profession, have helped to set up world-class corporate hospitals and extremely specialized health-care establishments in India. They have also assisting in procuring the latest equipment and technology and in providing specialized skills and expertise accumulated overseas. Professionals in other areas such as software and engineering services have helped provided venture capital for start-up companies in India. They have also supported the development of their sectors by bringing in projects; facilitating the outsourcing of services to Indian companies; providing contacts to overseas clients; and facilitating further inward and outward movement of service providers.

Following the exodus of approximately 90,000 Taiwanese in the second half of the 20th century, the Government of Taiwan Province of China focused its attention on the acquisition of skills, technology transfer and "brain gain" through an emphasis on networking and return migration. It has designed numerous initiatives on order to maximize the development impact of its diaspora. Some of these public policy initiatives include:

- Establishing a database that tracks skilled emigrants and matches job opportunities in Taiwan Province of China;
- Coordinating efforts to convince emigrants to return home by providing them with competitive salaries, improved working conditions and financial subsidies;
- Setting up networks with its Taiwanese counterparts, officials and foreign investors;
- Sponsoring national development conferences and bringing Taiwanese back home to participate in the formation of multinational networks, geared to building Taiwanese business and technological advantages;
- Setting up the Hsinchu Science and Industrial Park and diaspora incubator firms; and strongly encouraging investment in R&D and innovation.

The novelty of the approach was that the Taiwanese Government did not treat its diaspora only as a source of investment, but as a source of human capital and technology transfer which could support the development of endogenous knowledge-based industries. The example of Taiwan Province of China offers many valuable lessons for LDCs, especially in regard to the variety of intellectual property they may be invited to consider. And while traditional infant industry protection is theoretically justified in the presence of Marshallian externalities, and may indeed be welfare-enhancing (Rosenthal and Strange, 2004), policy plurality should nonetheless not be abandoned.

The diaspora played a critical role in the technological development of the Republic of Korea. Kuznetsov (2008), notes that in the late 1990s, when chaebols (large family-owned business conglomerates) like Samsung were unable to obtain critical United States technologies through licensing, the Korean diaspora of the United States intervened and succeeded in obtaining these critical technologies. In this way, the networks proved not only critical in identifying binding constraints but also designed the way to obtain a transfer of the necessary knowledge. It obtained critical technical knowledge abroad and demonstrated how trust and cooperation can outperform competition.

[1] The population of the Irish Republic was 4.4 million in 2009 and over 70 million people worldwide claimed Irish descent; 3.2 million Irish are citizens (passport holders) and 800,000 Irish born citizens lived overseas (Ancien et al., 2009a, 2009b, 2009c). In turn, millions in the world also claim Scottish descent, and nearly 900,000 people born in Scotland live abroad (including the UK).

[2] DICOEX has been complemented by the Inter-ministry Committee for Chileans Abroad and ProChile (export promotion) and ChileGlobal; as well as BIONEXA; PymeGlobal; ChileTodos; and EuroChile.

[3] See Ratha et al. (2011), Annex chapter 4.

Geographical Zone/County	Name of network	Website address
Table 20. Selected examples of DKNs in LDCs and regional groupings		
Africa		
Africa	International Society of African Scientists (ISAS)	http://www.dca.net/isas
Africa	African Community International (The African Center)	http://www.africancommunity.net/
Africa	International African Students Association (IASA)	http://www.iasaonline.org
Africa	African Distance Learning Association	http://www.physics.ncat.edu/~michael/adla/
Africa	Africa In the Netherlands	http://www.africaserver.nl/africadirectory/
Cameroon	Cameroon Society of Engineers (CSE), USA	http://www1.stpt.usf.edu/njoh/cse/cseusa.htm
Ethiopia	Federation Ethiopian Organizations for the Spread of Knowledge (FEOSK)	http://www.physics.ncat.edu/~michael/vses/genet/ees/
Ethiopia	Society of Ethiopians Established in the Diaspora	http://www.ethioseed.org/
Ethiopia	Ethiopian Professionals Association Network (EPAN)	http://www.ethiotrans.com/epan/
Ethiopia	Ethiopian Professors	http://www.angelfire.com/de/Ethiopian Professors/index.html
Ethiopia	Ethiopian Students Association International	http://www.esai.org/
Ethiopia	Ethiopian Distance Learning Association	http://www.physics.ncat.edu/~michael/edla/
Ethiopia	Ethiopian Chemical Society in North America	http://www.ourworld.cs.com/ecsnal/index.htm?f=fs
Ethiopia	Ethiopian North American Health Professionals Association	http://www.enahpa.org/
Ethiopia	Addis Ababa University Alumni Association	http://www.aau.ed.et/alumni/president.php
Ethiopia	Ethiopian Economic Policy Research Institute (EEA/EEPRI)	http://www.eeaecon.org/news.htm
Ethiopia	Ethiopian Scientific Society (ESS)	http://www.his.com/~ess/
Ethiopia	Gesellschaft zur Förderung der Medizin, Ingenieur und Naturwissenschaften in Äthiopien	http://www.emenssg.de/
Ethiopia	Ethiopian Diaspora Association (EDA)	ababum@yahoo.com
Malawi	Malawi Knowledge Network, The Malawi Polytechnic	http://www.maknet.org.mw
Mali	Malinet, the Malian World Network	http://callisto.si.usherb.ca/~malinet/
Mali	Malilink Discussion Forum	http://www.malilink.net/
Sudan	Sudan-American Foundation for Education, Inc.	http://www.sudan.com/safe/
Togo	Communauté Togolaise au Canada (CTC)	http://www.diastode.org/ctc/index.html
Asia		
Asia	Asian American Manufacturers Association (AAAMA)	http://www.aamasv.com/
Asia	Asia-Silicon Valley Connection (ASVC)	http://www.asvc.org/
Asia: Middle East		
Arab States	Islamic Medical Association of North America	http://www.imana.org/
Arab States	National Arab American Medical Association (NAAMA)	http://www.naama.com/
Arab States	Association of Muslim Scientists and Engineers (AMSE)	http://www.amse.net/
Arab States	Union Arabischer Mediziner in Europa e.V. (Arabmed)	http://www.arabmed.de/
Asia: South		
Bangladesh	EB2000:Expatriate Bangladeshi 2000	http://www.eb2000.org/
Bangladesh	TechBangla for transferring to and developing indigenous technology and products in Bangladesh	http://www.techbangla.org/
Bangladesh	Banglasdesh Environment Network	http://www.ben-center.org/
Bangladesh	Bangladesh Medical Association, North America	http://www.bmana.com
Bangladesh	American Association of Bangladeshi Engineers and Architects, NY-NJ-CT, Inc. (AABEA Tristate, Inc.)	
Bangladesh	Bangladeshi-American Foundation, Inc. (BAFI)	http://www.bafi.org/
Bangladesh	Association for Economic and Development Studies on Bangladesh (AEDSB)	http://www.aedsb.org/index.htm
Bangladesh	Alochona	http://www.alochona.org/
Bangladesh	North American Bangladeshi Islamic Community (NABIC)	http://www.nabic.org/
Bangladesh	North American Bangladeshi Statistics Association	mail to: mali@gw.bsu.edu
Bangladesh	Bangladesh Chemical and Biological Society of North America (BCBSNA)	mail to: kamal.das@netl.doe.gov
Nepal	Network of Nepalese Professionals	http://www.netnp,org/index.html
Nepal	Association of Nepalis in America	http://www.anaonline.org/index.php
Nepal	Nepalese Entrepreneurs Group (NEG)	
Nepal	Nepal United States Educational Network	http://www.nusf.homestead.com
Nepal	America Nepal Medical Foundation	http://www.anmf.net/
Nepal	Empower Nepal Foundation	http://www.empowernepal.hypermart.net/
Nepal	Sajha Career Network	http://www.sajha.com/sajha/html/network.cfm
Nepal	Society of Ex-Budhanilkantha Students	http://www.sebsonline.org/
Central America and Carribean		
Haiti	Association of Haitian Physicians Abroad (AMHE)	http://www.amhe.org/

Source: UNCTAD, based on Meyer and Wattiaux (2006).

C. Diasporas as sources of development finance

1. THE ROLE OF REMITTANCES

One of the more obvious effects of external migration for the home country is in terms of increased inflows of remittances. Although remittances are private flows, they can play a positive role in not only easing balance of payments gaps, but also fostering the development of home countries. However, this role is obviously conditional on government policies that enhance their developmental impact. It is important to remember that remittances cannot lead development.

As noted in chapter 3, in many countries, remittances have grown remarkably and amount to a significant proportion of national income and export revenues. These relatively more stable inflows may prevent balance of payments crises; allow trade deficits to be financed; and even generate current account surpluses in many recipient countries. In addition to the microeconomic benefits for the recipient families, the macroeconomic advantages of remittance incomes are beyond question. They provide an important (and often the largest) source of foreign exchange; they can lead to increases in investment and therefore output; they tend to be more stable over economic cycles in both home and host economies; they may offset the losses involved in terms of brain drain and tax revenue; and they are often associated with an increase in the marginal propensity to save (Ratha, 2003).

However, as noted in chapter 3, the mobilization of remittances for productive purposes requires policy and institutional improvements, aimed at reinforcing both the "investment channel" and the impact of remittances on financial deepening. To ensure that this is indeed the case, more active government policies are required which would encourage certain types of expenditure. In general, a significant proportion of remittance income — especially for relatively less well-off families — tends to be used directly for consumption. This is not necessarily bad, since improved consumption patterns are desirable per se given prevailing relatively low standards of living. In some countries, it has been found that this high and relatively stable source of income has become an important source for eliminating hunger and reducing poverty in communities which have experienced substantial short-term migration.

Earlier studies for some LDCs suggest that remittance incomes can work to diversify economic activities even independently of government policies. For example, a survey in Bangladesh (IOM-UNDP, 2002) found that expatriate workers tend to spend 30 per cent of their income on personal consumption abroad, send 45 per cent back and save the rest (around 25 per cent). Of the amount remitted to families back home, 36 per cent was used for consumption, including spending on food, education and health care; 20 per cent was used for investing in land or other property; and 14 per cent was used for improving housing arrangements, including additions/renovations on existing property. It was also found that with a relatively prolonged and constant inward flow of remittances, families tended to move away from wage employment to self-employment and from sole reliance on cultivation to various non-farm activities.

Policies to channel remittances into domestic financial sector have substantially evolved in the last couple of decades. In the past, rules governing remittances were part of the larger goal of tightly controlling the flow of foreign exchange. One of the earliest efforts was a policy adopted by the Government of Lesotho for its migrants working in South Africa. In 1974, it passed the Deferred Pay Act establishing the legal terms and conditions of a compulsory remittance system for mineworkers. A portion of miners' wages (initially between

Although remittances are private flows, they can play a positive role in not only easing balance of payments gaps, but also fostering the development of home countries. However, this role is obviously conditional on government policies that enhance their developmental impact.

In general, a significant proportion of remittance income — especially for relatively less well-off families — tends to be used directly for consumption. This is not necessarily bad, since improved consumption patterns are desirable per se given prevailing relatively low standards of living.

A survey in Bangladesh found that expatriate workers tend to spend 30 per cent of their income on personal consumption abroad, send 45 per cent back and save the rest (around 25 per cent). Of the amount remitted to families back home, 36 per cent was used for consumption, including spending on food, education and health care; 20 per cent was used for investing in land or other property.

60 to 90 per cent) was compulsorily deferred and paid into a special account at the Lesotho National Development Bank. Miners received some interest on their deposits. The funds could only be withdrawn in Lesotho by the miners themselves at the end of a contract. The compulsory deferred pay (CDP) system ensured that the bulk of migrants' earnings returned to Lesotho as remittances. While it had the effect of directing remittances to formal channels, it also represented a restriction on migrants' freedom to remit as they saw fit. The Deferred Pay Act has been amended several times to reflect changes in the composition of migrants from predominantly young, single males to a mixed group, with a growing number of women migrating to South Africa. Currently, miners defer 30 per cent of their gross earnings for 10 months of every 12-month contract (Crush and Dodson, 2010). This alteration of the rules has also been part of a broader drive to liberalize the flow of foreign exchange.

Formal mechanisms of remitting are preferable to informal ones. They can stabilize the balance of payments; enhance the developmental impact of remittances; enable the monitoring of monetary and exchange rate consequences of such flows; improve countries' external creditworthiness; help to prevent fraud and money laundering; and encourage financial deepening of the economy.

Since then, the policy tide has turned away from the strict control of remittances, so LDC governments nowadays rarely impose restrictions on remitting. Now, the overall direction of policy is to try to make formal channels of remitting more attractive than informal channels and to reduce the cost of remitting. As discussed in chapter 3, formal mechanisms of remitting are preferable to informal ones. They can stabilize the balance of payments; enhance the developmental impact of remittances; enable the monitoring of monetary and exchange rate consequences of such flows; improve countries' external creditworthiness; help to prevent fraud and money laundering; and encourage financial deepening of the economy. For individual recipients, they allow for more reliable service as well as access to other financial services. By contrast, informal channels create distortions in a country's exchange rate and reduce the other benefits of remittances.

Policies designed to increase the use of formal channels have to address the factors that make informal networks attractive, such as high costs of remitting; unavailability of services, especially in rural areas; and unreliability. It was noted in chapter 3 that the costs of remitting to LDCs are among the highest in the world, so one of the urgent issues which governments should address is how to bring the cost of remitting down. There are various measures to be taken on both the sending and receiving ends of the process.

The costs of remitting to LDCs are among the highest in the world, so one of the urgent issues which governments should address is how to bring the cost of remitting down.

In many sending countries, a key prerequisite is the regularization of the status of migrants and their eligibility to open bank accounts, which would enable them to utilize the host country's financial services for transferring remittances. A larger volume of remittances would be an incentive for other players from the financial sector in both sending and receiving countries to enter the market, so that competition would drive the cost of remitting down. While policymakers in LDCs cannot influence the financial policies and regulatory frameworks of sending countries, it may be worthwhile to pursue bilateral agreements to regulate this and other issues with some of the major sending countries.

In some cases, the high cost of sending remittances reflects institutional and regulatory barriers in the home country, which can be adjusted to reduce such costs.

In some cases, the high cost of sending remittances reflects institutional and regulatory barriers in the home country, which can be adjusted to reduce such costs. In Ethiopia, for example, in 2004 the National Bank of Ethiopia (NBE) allowed Ethiopians abroad and foreign nationals of Ethiopian origin to open foreign currency accounts in any of the authorized commercial banks in the country. The result was an elimination of the exchange rate risk for diaspora members, and indirectly an increase in the attractiveness of formal channels of remitting. In 2006, the NBE issued a directive regulating the activities and rates charged by international remittance service providers. The aim was to improve service delivery in Ethiopia; increase the cost-effectiveness of remittance transfers; and make the service faster, more accessible and more reliable. Finally, the NBE's exchange rate policy, which has recently been geared towards eliminating the gap between the official exchange rate and the parallel (black market) exchange rate, has also enticed senders to remit through official channels.

Further, the formal remittance channels for most LDCs are currently controlled by a small number of such service providers. The practice of "exclusive agreements", which are mostly to be found in African LDCs, stifles competition by preventing competitors from entering the market. Such concentration is then associated with high fees and a lack of branches next to potential customers. Many poorer migrants and their families are forced to rely to a large extent on less secure informal channels, and many of the rural poor end up being excluded from financial services altogether. Allowing greater competition would reduce the monopolistic rents that current market leaders enjoy (Mundaca, 2009; Orozco, 2007; Sander, 2003).

The formal remittance channels for most LDCs are currently controlled by a small number of such service providers. The practice of "exclusive agreements", which are mostly to be found in African LDCs, stifles competition by preventing competitors from entering the market.

There are several strategies available for increasing such competition. For example, it is possible to tap the wide range of financial institutions specialized in catering for the rural poor, with track records in reducing their financial exclusion. Regulations on money transfers and supervision of financial institutions could be revised to allow microfinance institutions and post offices to increase their participation in the remittance market (Maimbo and Ratha, 2005; Orozco and Fedewa, 2006). This would encourage greater use of formal rather than informal remittance channels; reduce costs of remitting and ensure greater access for the poor, especially in underserved remote and rural areas; increase banking breadth and depth; and allow for better surveillance of transferred amounts. Yet promoting competition raises regulatory issues, primarily the need to ensure the reliability and integrity of the transfer systems and to avoid the system being abused (e.g. for money laundering), which is why only regulated financial service entities are usually permitted to provide remittance services. Policymakers face a challenge in striking the right balance between promoting competition in this market and maintaining supportive regulation.

There are several strategies available for increasing such competition.

A central policy conclusion is, thus, to open up the remittance market, particularly by encouraging the participation of regulated finance institutions targeting the poor. Possible measures could include the following:

- Directly increasing the range of financial actors involved, especially in rural areas, by changing regulations to allow the participation of especially microfinance institutions, savings and loans cooperatives, credit unions, and post offices;

- Promoting partnerships among banks and microfinance institutions;

- Strengthening post office involvement by improving their Internet connectivity, increasing their technical capabilities and cash resources, and promoting a wider selection of savings products;

- Improving telecommunications infrastructure;

- Harmonizing banking and telecommunications regulations to enable banks to participate in mobile remittances;

- Actively promoting competition through specialized remittances trade fairs;

- Discouraging exclusivity agreements between all market participants, in particular, banks and money transfer companies.

Promoting competition raises regulatory issues, primarily the need to ensure the reliability and integrity of the transfer systems and to avoid the system being abused (e.g. for money laundering), which is why only regulated financial service entities are usually permitted to provide remittance services. Policymakers face a challenge in striking the right balance between promoting competition in this market and maintaining supportive regulation.

All of these policies must obviously be part of prudential and careful regulatory regimes that recognize the country's degree of financial development and the need to avoid the instabilities and fragilities that may arise from financial market failures.[10]

The use of new technologies, particularly Internet-based and mobile telephony-driven methods of transmitting funds, can be exploited to a greater extent. Mobile phones as a delivery channel have untapped potential, especially in the more remote areas where banking branches are not present.

These conventional measures could be accompanied by other, more innovative approaches in some LDCs. It may be worth having a public sector institution compete with private sector providers of remittance services. The example of Mexico and the United States is interesting in that respect. As part of the Partnership for Prosperity action plan between Mexico and the United States, the central banks of both countries (Banco de México and the U.S. Federal Reserve) established a payment system in 2003 that offers a reliable, low-cost formal transfer channel, initially as a way of sending government pension payments to recipients in Mexico. In 2004, a "Directo a México" programme was established to make financial transactions between the two countries available to any individual with a bank account in Mexico, creating a cost-effective alternative to other payment channels. Moreover, the beneficiaries are able, from 2010, to cash their payments in post offices in Mexico. The benefits of this programme are transparency for the participants, transactions guaranteed by the highest monetary authorities, reliability, speed and low cost.

In LDCs, something similar could be done by establishing a public corporation or using existing institutions like public, development, or central banks. Such an institution would provide the same service as the private sector but would charge a lower cost for remitting. Since there is less pressure on public corporations to make a profit, the fee could be substantially lower. The corporation would only need to recuperate the operational cost through fees, which could be much lower than the cost currently charged by remittance service providers in most LDCs. Instead of opening up its own branches, the public corporation could team up with the postal service. Working with post offices could help to reach customers in remote areas where there are no branches of private financial institutions, given its geographic spread.

The use of new technologies, particularly Internet-based and mobile telephony-driven methods of transmitting funds, can be exploited to a greater extent. Mobile phones as a delivery channel have untapped potential, especially in the more remote areas where banking branches are not present. Since brick-and-mortar branches are costly, especially when there is no critical mass of clients, central banks should encourage "branchless banking" via the use of modern technologies, which would expand the outreach of financial institutions to hard-to-reach areas and reduce operating costs of financial institutions. The growing application of new technologies and their potential role in Africa in serving as money transfer channels are analysed in detail in chapter 3.

The feasibility of such innovations, especially in places like rural Africa, will be influenced to a large extent by the availability of supportive infrastructure, in particular telecommunications infrastructure, and sociocultural factors like widespread illiteracy in rural areas, which may detract from the use of the new technology.

At present, there is little evidence of significant penetration of the market of remittance service providers (RSPs) by mobile money services in LDCs, and mobile money RSPs still face significant operational, infrastructural and regulatory constraints to market entry. CGAP (2010; 2012) recommends a careful cost-benefit analysis of any technological innovation as well as an assessment of an institution's information systems prior to commitment. The feasibility of such innovations, especially in places like rural Africa, will be influenced to a large extent by the availability of supportive infrastructure, in particular telecommunications infrastructure, and sociocultural factors like widespread illiteracy in rural areas, which may detract from the use of the new technology. This highlights the importance of complementary policies promoting both financial deepening and the development of infrastructure and productive capacities in LDCs.

Despite the constraints, as noted in chapter 3, several global money transfer companies have been promoting the use of mobile phones in rural areas to facilitate access to remittances. According to CGAP (2012), mobile money has achieved the broadest success in sub-Saharan Africa, with 16 per cent of adults having used a mobile phone to pay bills or send or receive money in the last 12 months. Despite the potential, however, this mechanism poses supervisory challenges, and is bound to have an impact on remittance costs and efficiency for the recipients.

Nevertheless, there are important caveats. Since regulators in LDCs are at the forefront of developments in the area of mobile money, they have few countries to turn to for policy options and lessons learned. This compounds the challenge of effectively regulating the activity and protecting consumers without stifling innovation. In addition, the previously distinct regulatory sectors of telecommunications and finance will now have to interact more closely, addressing new issues like security, consumer protection, money laundering, etc. Addressing these issues will be a challenge for regulators, central banks and policymakers in general.

The development of new products within the formal financial sector can be another means of improving service delivery for remittance transfers (Buencamino and Gorbunov, 2002; Shaw, 2007; Omer, 2003). For example, through groups such as Sénégal Conseils, an association in Lyon, Senegalese migrants in France can remit funds to Senegal both in cash and in the form of goods. Those remitters who are unable to cover the entire cost of goods immediately are allowed to pay in instalments over six months, incurring interest charges. Similarly, in Egypt several exchange companies offer door-to-door delivery of money, following the example of Philippine banks that successfully introduced and implemented the service to compete with unofficial market operators (Dieng, 2002; Russell, 1986, 1990; Shaw, 2007).

Since the cost of remitting is the highest within Africa (see chapter 3), there is scope for regional initiatives to bring such costs down, for example through coordination of measures as a result of formal regional integration initiatives or through the good offices of the regional development bank (the African Development Bank- AfDB). This regionally driven process led by the AfDB should be linked to the international goal of reducing remittance costs known as the "5 x 5" initiative discussed in chapter 3.

While policies to increase the ease of remitting money and reduce the costs involved are clearly necessary and desirable, they need to be part of a broader macroeconomic framework that would enhance the developmental role of such remittance transfers. Accordingly, central banks need to monitor the impact of remittances on exchange rates and tailor exchange rate and monetary policies to compensate for possible undesirable consequences, including through open market operations when necessary. More generally, a consistent set of trade, industrial and macroeconomic policies that sustainably foster growth and economic diversification will obviously be crucial in ensuring that remittance flows also contribute to the process of development rather than simply enhancing consumption in recipient families.

On the microeconomic level, governments could enhance the developmental impact of remittances by offering migrants additional incentives. For example, future remittances could be used as collateral to guarantee small business loans in sub-Saharan African countries. The experience of Banco Salvadoreño in El Salvador provides a model, whereby the bank offers remittance recipients the opportunity to borrow up to 80 per cent of their last six months' remittance flows and provides them with debit cards. Another policy could be to allow migrants to open foreign currency accounts in the home country, providing them with insurance against the exchange rate risk. Given exchange rate expectations in the home country, commercial banks could feasibly accept such foreign currency deposits as collateral for loans at preferential terms (lower rates or longer maturities). Once again, it is worth noting that when the domestic context is favourable for development (also because of appropriate public policies in education and health care, macroeconomic stability, supportive industrial policy, investment in infrastructure that removes bottlenecks, and the like), remittances allow households to save or to invest in their future income (education, health care, small businesses and so on) rather than simply in ensuring survival.

The development of new products within the formal financial sector can be another means of improving service delivery for remittance transfers.

Since the cost of remitting is the highest within Africa, there is scope for regional initiatives to bring such costs down, for example through coordination of measures as a result of formal regional integration initiatives.

While policies to increase the ease of remitting money and reduce the costs involved are clearly necessary and desirable, they need to be part of a broader macroeconomic framework that would enhance the developmental role of such remittance transfers.

On the microeconomic level, governments could enhance the developmental impact of remittances by offering migrants additional incentives. Future remittances could be used as collateral to guarantee small business loans.

2. Diaspora savings and investment

Out-migration can be associated with higher levels of savings and investment over time in a country. In addition to the savings transferred by the diaspora, households that receive remittances in the home country can also generate extra savings. The savings potential of diasporas needs an outlet or vehicle to be invested. It is useful to make a distinction between portfolio investment and diaspora direct investment (DDI) (Terrazas, 2010; Newland and Tanaka, 2010). Portfolio investment comprises a variety of financial instruments, such as deposits, bonds and mutual funds. Another, non-exclusive possibility would be for diaspora members to invest directly in the home economy. This could take various forms, such as a capital contribution to family business, acquisition of existing firms, a greenfield investment, or other forms of DDI.

In addition to the savings transferred by the diaspora, households that receive remittances in the home country can also generate extra savings.

In terms of portfolio investment, LDCs typically have higher domestic interest rates because of the increased risk perception in these economies, part of which is usually currency risk. Reducing or eliminating this particular risk could make saving in the financial instruments of LDCs more attractive. For example, if financial institutions in the home country were to offer bank deposits or other financial assets denominated in foreign currency, this could be an attractive option for members of the diaspora. This would combine a return on saving higher than in the case in developed countries with a risk that is lower than in the case of saving instruments in the local currency of a typical LDC. The Central Bank of Turkey, for instance, offers foreign-currency-denominated fixed-term deposit accounts and "Super FX" accounts that are similar to certificates of deposit, to Turkish passport holders living abroad. Interested policymakers should bear in mind the limitations of this strategy; while it transfers the currency risks to the central banks of the countries concerned, it may not actually result in a net increase in foreign exchange inflows, but simply transfer resources from non-interest-bearing remittances to foreign exchange-denominated interest-bearing investments.

LDCs typically have higher domestic interest rates because of the increased risk perception in these economies, part of which is usually currency risk. Reducing or eliminating this particular risk could make saving in the financial instruments of LDCs more attractive.

Issuing diaspora bonds (see also box 13) could provide LDCs with an important source of long-term financing. Diaspora bonds are debt instruments issued by a sovereign country to raise funds by placing them among its diaspora population. Ideally, the conditions for issuing diaspora bonds would be a sizeable and wealthy diaspora; a strong and transparent legal system for contract enforcement; absence of civil strife; earmarking of proceeds for specific projects to help marketability; and although not a prerequisite, the presence of national banks in the destination countries could facilitate the marketing of bonds (Ketkar and Ratha, 2010). The relevant concern is whether the cost of capital acquired through diaspora bonds is lower than the cost of capital raised in international capital markets. For many LDCs, however, this issue is irrelevant because they have little or no access to international capital markets. In such cases, diaspora bonds are attractive options because they can increase the pool of development financing sources. It may be argued that patriotic motives for investing in diaspora bonds make these instruments less procyclical than other external capital flows, and could thereby allow governments to issue them not only in good times but also in bad (e.g. natural disasters or external economic shocks).

Issuing diaspora bonds could provide LDCs with an important source of long-term financing. Diaspora bonds are debt instruments issued by a sovereign country to raise funds by placing them among its diaspora population.

If sub-Saharan countries were to issue diaspora bonds, they could face non-trivial costs of marketing and retailing that could offset the benefits of the lower interest rates paid to bond holders. However, it has been estimated that there is potential for such bonds to raise between $5 to 10 billion annually, which is not a small amount (Ratha et al., 2008). One idea worth exploring could be regional issuance of diaspora bonds by a group of countries supported by a regional development bank. Such an initiative would help make up for the lack of concentration of migrants from individual countries in any single developed country.

The relevant concern is whether the cost of capital acquired through diaspora bonds is lower than the cost of capital raised in international capital markets. For many LDCs, however, this issue is irrelevant because they have little or no access to international capital markets.

Box 13. Diaspora investment

Some countries have been exceptionally successful in attracting diaspora investment. For example, the Chinese diaspora provided 80 per cent of total foreign direct investment (FDI) in China between 1979 and 1995, and the Indian diaspora is estimated to have invested $2.6 billion out of $10 billion of FDI between 1991 and 2001 (see references in Riddle et al., 2011). Both India and China have established special export processing zones and have given diaspora investors priority for establishing operations in these zones. They have created specific incentives for businesses owned and operated by diaspora members, such as tax breaks and access to free or cheap land, to convince them to invest in the home country. Where appropriate, LDC governments could consider such measures for attracting investment from their diaspora members.

Israel has issued diaspora bonds since 1951, keeping the Jewish diaspora community interested in this asset class by offering a menu of options in terms of maturities and interest rates. The Indian Government has used this instrument only occasionally, when having difficulty accessing international capital markets (e.g. after the nuclear tests of 1998). While bond prices have been close to market values of non-Indian bonds, a premium may have been paid given that access to other sources of international finance was limited at the moment of issuance of the diaspora bonds. Institutionally, the Government of Israel established the Development Corporation for Israel to issue diaspora bonds, while India relied on the Government-owned State Bank of India.

Ethiopia is one of the few LDCs that have introduced diaspora bonds to complement domestic resource mobilization for financing major development projects. The Government of Ethiopia is implementing a five-year (2011-2015) Growth and Transformation Plan (GTP). The GTP envisages intensifying the GDP growth rate and maintaining the country's recent record as one of the ten fastest-growing economies in the world. As part of this plan, the Government has embarked on substantial expansion of social services and investment in physical infrastructure, in particular the construction of road and railways and hydropower supply. One of the mega flagship projects launched in April 2011 is the construction of the Ethiopian Renaissance Dam on the Blue Nile. When completed, the dam will generate 5250 MW of electricity to supply Ethiopian consumers as well as consumers in some neighbouring countries. The project is estimated to cost $4.8 billion and the bulk of the financing will be mobilized from Ethiopians — both within the country and among the diaspora. For this purpose, the Government has introduced the Ethiopian Grand Renaissance Dam Bond, which includes specific features aimed at the Ethiopian diaspora.

In addition to these strategies for boosting investment by diasporas, there are new modalities for using remittances to enable greater domestic investment through securitization or collateralization of these flows. Since these have recently been receiving a great deal of attention, it is worth considering the advantages and risks associated with such mechanisms.

Since remittance flows have proved relatively stable over the medium to longer term, it has been argued that these future flow receivables can be used as collateral for securitization or long-term loans. For some LDCs, this could even represent the only possible access to international capital markets, thereby increasing funds available for development, and could become a stepping stone to establishing international creditworthiness. Ratha et al. (2008) have constructed a hierarchy of future flow receivables for potential securitization by developing countries, based on information from credit rating agencies. Remittances are among the top of the list of future flows, with only heavy crude oil receivables considered lower risk. Further, there is now considerable experience with securitizing future flow receivables, following the Mexican experience with oil since 1987. However, the amounts involved still represent a small percentage of total debt.

In addition, there are several areas of concern which LDC governments must consider before engaging in such a process. A typical example of a future flow remittance securitization involves a bank in a recipient country establishing an offshore special purpose vehicle, to which future remittance receivables are pledged. This special vehicle issues bonds, which are then placed in the international capital markets. Correspondent banks and/or remittances transfer companies are instructed to channel remittances to an offshore account managed by a trustee. The trustee makes principal and interest payments to bondholders and remits excess funds to the recipient bank. This bank has thereby funded itself on the international capital markets at presumably lower costs than on the domestic market or if it had attempted to access unsecured credit internationally. These funds can then be used to finance consumption and investment in the recipient country. Sovereign risk for creditors or holders of the asset are minimized since the remittances do not enter the recipient country, and potential instability in remittance flows is to be covered by over-collateralization, at ratios varying from 5:1 to 10:1.

It has been estimated that there is potential for such bonds to raise between $5 to 10 billion annually, which is not a small amount. One idea worth exploring could be regional issuance of diaspora bonds by a group of countries supported by a regional development bank.

There are new modalities for using remittances to enable greater domestic investment through securitization or collateralization of these flows.

Remittances are among the top of the list of future flows, with only heavy crude oil receivables considered lower risk.

It can be seen that this could be an expensive route for LDCs, and is truly justified when there is no possible alternative means of accessing international capital markets. Even to benefit from such a possibility, countries would typically have to have credit ratings of B or above, receive a minimum of $500 million per year in remittances and allow a few banks to handle the majority of the remittance flows. Few LDCs, other than Bangladesh, can meet these stringent criteria, and introducing such instruments in other LDCs would involve fairly extensive financial deregulation without the requisite institutional support for monitoring and supervision. Given these constraints, as well as the global concerns with securitization that have emerged in the wake of the United States subprime crisis and the financial crisis in the eurozone, it is not clear that the benefits of such measures clearly outweigh the costs and potential risks of financial fragility.

Another interesting financial innovation, and one which probably offers more potential than securitization for LDCs, is the use of remittances as collaterals for arranging long-term syndicated loans. Conditions for arranging remittance-backed loans are less stringent than those required for securitization, and may have greater potential for many LDCs.

Another interesting financial innovation, and one which probably offers more potential than securitization for LDCs, is the use of remittances as collaterals for arranging long-term syndicated loans. Conditions for arranging remittance-backed loans are less stringent than those required for securitization, and may have greater potential for many LDCs. Sovereign risk can be mitigated by remittances, and development banks can offer credit enhancement instruments. The African Export-Import Bank has experience in arranging remittance-based future-flow syndicated loans. Indeed, in 2001 it launched its Financial Future-Flow Pre-Financing Programme to expand the use of remittances and other future flows as collateral to leverage external financing at lower costs and longer maturities. It has led various future-remittance-flow collateral-backed loans in Ghana, Nigeria and Ethiopia in recent years (AFREXIMBANK, 2005). The Bank has received awards for such activities, since they have enhanced the access of Africa counterparties to reasonably priced external trade and project financing from the markets using remittances by Africans in diaspora as collateral and the main source of repayment.

The African Export-Import Bank has experience in arranging remittance-based future-flow syndicated loans.

Given that LDCs have only limited access to development finance, these strategies can form part of an approach of building up local institutions and the legal framework for financial deepening as well as establishing an international track record on sovereign risk. This could eventually facilitate greater access to international capital markets for LDCs.

Given that LDCs have only limited access to development finance, these strategies can form part of an approach of building up local institutions and the legal framework for financial deepening as well as establishing an international track record on sovereign risk.

Moreover, similarly to current flow of remittances, from a macroeconomic perspective, the additional funds received either through a process of securitizing remittances or a remittances-backed syndicated loan could imply additional pressure on the exchange rate, and hence on the country's competitiveness. Monetary authorities should always keep this in mind in order to fine-tune policies designed to take this potential effect into account, although (given the likely small magnitudes involved) it is unlikely that such an effect would have significant repercussions. However, the risks of financial pyramiding and entanglement that can come from such financial deepening without adequate regulation and supervision are more serious, and should be duly considered by LDC policymakers.

Other initiatives include the idea of promoting "community remittances" to improve infrastructure and the provision of basic amenities in migrants' local areas of origin. One prominent example is Mexico's Programa Tres por Uno .

Other initiatives include the idea of promoting "community remittances" to improve infrastructure and the provision of basic amenities in migrants' local areas of origin (box 14). One prominent example is Mexico's *Programa Tres por Uno* (box 15), which has sought to coordinate the activities of the diaspora, local communities and governments at national and local level through a system of matching funds for remittances directed to such uses. Despite some drawbacks, *Programa Tres por Uno* offers an interesting model for encouraging and maximizing the developmental impact of collective remittances on migrants' communities of origin. Yet the administrative, fiscal and regulatory requirements are high, and could be challenging for some LDCs.

Box 14. A proposal to combine efforts of diasporas, governments and donor countries

Given that the fiscal requirements of Programa Tres por Uno could be quite high and make it inoperable in a typical LDC context, a proposal to include the international community and LDC governments could be designed to similar effect. The international community could help LDCs develop faster and harness the potential of remittances for development by adopting an international support measure that would provide matching funds through ODA. LDC governments would show their commitment to the provision of public goods by matching the collective remittances in equal proportions. The three-stakeholder programme would thus include the diaspora, the LDC government and the international community with equal contributions.

This would function as follows. The money from collective remittances earmarked for investment in local infrastructure (potable water, sewage, roads, electrification, etc.) or educational and health facilities (schools and hospitals) would be matched by ODA. This would double the impact of remittances on local development conditions, and would provide incentives for hometown associations to finance even more development projects. The LDC government would provide matching funds equal to the amount of collective remittances, but in local currency. Thus, the final result would be to triple the original amount sent through collective remittances.

UNCTAD (2010a) argues that a "matching fund" approach to aid flows could be a useful element of reforms to strengthen government capacities for greater domestic resource mobilization. Such additional matching funds would constitute an incentive to recipient governments to raise more revenues. The current proposal to match collective remittances would by the same token constitute an incentive for governments to strengthen domestic resource mobilization.

An additional ODA fund would be needed for this purpose. It would have to provide disbursements over and above the existing commitments of development partners. Given that activities related to the Millennium Development Goals (MDGs) are scheduled to end in 2015, this proposal could be a way for the international community to continue supporting LDCs in their quest for economic and social development. It would not only provide a means of continuing in some form MDG-related activities of the international community, but would also involve substantial private-sector financing (remittances) of these activities. It would constitute an international public–private partnership for development.

Box 15. Harnessing "community remittances" for local infrastructure development in Mexico

Mexico's "Programa Tres por Uno" is an interesting public policy initiative which attempts to harness and prioritize efforts by the organized diaspora community. The basic idea is that migrants send the so-called "community remittances" to places they came from for investment in local public goods like roads, schools, hospitals, potable water, sewage, electric grid or other public spaces and objects (monuments, churches, community centres, sports facilities, etc.). The Programa has been designed to maximize the impact of migrant organizations' commitment to their communities of origin through a system of matching public funds. It has attracted considerable attention for its attempt to integrate joint investments between migrant organizations and the three levels of government (federal, state and municipality) to finance basic infrastructure (public goods) in the communities of origin of migrants through matching funds to the migrant organizations' contributions. Other governments and/or migrant communities already implementing or considering variants of Tres por Uno include El Salvador, the Philippines, Peru, Colombia and Ecuador.

García Zamora (2007) argues the Programa has evolved from a first phase of "clubs" financing "superfluous" works such as church repairs, soccer fields, parks, etc., to a second phase of organized processes enhancing transnational communal cohesion to include more ambitious projects of basic infrastructure: water, electricity, drainage, streets and roads. In its third phase, the Programa's investments cover social infrastructure: schools, clinics, computing centres, scholarships programmes both in Mexico and the United States, environmental projects, and homes for the elderly. Currently, some of the better organized federations of migrant organizations, such as those from Michoacán and Zacatecas, are attempting to move into productive investments aiming at generating income and employment in their communities.

It should be noted that Tres por Uno has been challenging in terms of administrative capacity even in Mexico, as it requires the coordination of four actors at three different levels of government and a civil organization abroad to bear fruit in jointly financed projects. Regarding the regulatory set-up, García Zamora (2007) suggests the need to avoid overregulation and avoid the exclusion of migrants that are not formally organized in clubs and federations.

Another line of critique of Tres por Uno is its lack of focalization on the poorest communities. The programme is based on self-selection of projects and municipalities by migrants' organizations. This does not correlate with the

Box 15 (contd.)

poorest municipalities, as migration has a non-linear relationship with poverty. Consequently, poorer municipalities would tend to receive less matching funds or none at all.

By nature, Tres por Uno is a meso-level public policy and is not designed to meet macro considerations. Its self-selection bias, in a context of a macro-poverty reduction strategy, should be taken into account to ensure geographical equity in the allocation of public funds. In this sense, a macro programme aimed at geographical equity encompassing meso interventions of matching grants should take into consideration such steps as: (i) earmarking funds for the poorest municipalities; (ii) capping the maximum per capita income for beneficiary municipalities of Tres por Uno; and (iii) making the public matching funds proportional to poverty levels in the municipality.

Given the scale of the needs for infrastructure development in the LDCs, efforts should also be made to increase private sector participation in the provision of infrastructure. Programmes that combine collective remittances and matching funds could accelerate the provision of public goods.

Creating capable and efficient institutions that can provide public goods in sufficient quantity and of highest quality remain one of the paramount developmental objectives of LDCs. In the meantime, however, programmes that combine collective remittances and matching funds could accelerate the provision of public goods. Upgrading much of the existing infrastructure and implementing new infrastructure projects to provide more and better quality services such as potable water, electricity, communications and transport are top development priorities for most LDCs.

It could be argued that encouraging LDC governments to tap into voluntary contributions from their diaspora population for financing public goods involves some degree of transferring government responsibilities to private citizens. In theory, governments tax their citizens to provide for the provision of public goods. The fact remains, however, that many LDC governments are unable to provide adequate public goods, either partially or in extreme cases at all, which means that some basic needs of the population would remain unsatisfied for the foreseeable future. Given the scale of the needs for infrastructure development in the LDCs, UNCTAD (2006) argued that efforts should also be made to increase private sector participation in the provision of infrastructure. Programmes that combine collective remittances and matching funds could accelerate the provision of public goods.

Box 16. WTO General Agreement on Trade in Services (GATS) — Mode 4

The WTO General Agreement on Trade in Services (GATS) is the binding multilateral trade agreement to address, *inter alia*, the movement of persons engaged in the supply of services with temporary stays in the host country (the so-called Mode 4). The definition of Mode 4 is narrower than migration as the latter also includes movement of persons not supplying services. Mode 4, in turn, considers the supply of a service by a service supplier of one Member, through the presence of natural persons of a Member in the territory of any other Member.

The GATS has no standard definition of what qualifies as "temporary" movement, so the proposals go from three months to five years. Although there are several controversies, including the scope of commitments under GATS on Mode 4, it is important that LDC policymakers consider the potential policy implications of GATS Mode 4, as migration is often a critical livelihood strategy for parts of their population. The contribution of Mode 4 to development could potentially be significant, as global labour migrants represent an important channel for transfer of knowledge, skills, ideas, and technology.

The current round of the services trade negotiations under GATS was launched in January 2000. LDCs have made several requests for Mode 4 which have yet to be satisfied. They have identified market access for Mode 4 in the low- and semi-skilled categories as the most important element for the group in the negotiations. LDCs have also suggested widening the scope of Mode 4 and streamlining the process of verification and recognition of competence, skills and qualifications. Thus, provisions of services through Mode 4, broader labour movement covering all skill categories, as well as facilitated recognition of qualification, would be important for LDCs.

However, the degree to which Mode 4 commitments can be improved to incorporate requests made by LDCs depends on LDC trading partners. Given the current situation of negotiations in general and the employment situation in many developed countries in particular, the prospects for adoption of a commitment that would include most of these requests are not very likely.

To bridge this gap, the Eighth WTO Ministerial Conference adopted in December 2011 a decision whereby *"members may provide preferential treatment to services and service suppliers of least-developed countries"* for 15 years.[1] While this has the potential to open up new opportunities for LDC service suppliers, including Mode 4, its implementation depends crucially on the willingness of other Members to provide preferential treatment to LDCs. The challenge which remains is to effectively secure preferential market access opportunities for service providers from all LDCs in a predictable, sustained and general manner.

1 "Preferential treatment to services and service suppliers of Least-developed countries", World Trade Organization, Eighth Ministerial Conference, 15–17 December, 2011, Geneva.

D. Harnessing diaspora knowledge to build productive capacities in LDCs: An international support measure

The challenge. LDCs have an abundant low-skilled labour force but scarce high-skilled professionals. At 1:42, the ratio of high-skilled (i.e. with tertiary level education) to low-skilled workers in LDCs is staggeringly low, compared with 1:16 in other developing countries and 1:4 in developed economies. As a result, the lack of skilled personnel, especially in the fields of science, engineering, medical research, education, health-care services, agriculture, accounting, administration and other related areas, which are critical for building productive capacities and knowledge-based industries, is a major constraint for LDCs. Brain drain through the emigration of highly skilled professionals from LDCs has further intensified this problem. As shown in this Report, LDCs are disproportionately affected by brain drain. The evidence presented in chapter 4 suggests that:

By 2000, more than 1.3 million high-skilled LDC nationals lived and worked abroad. Current estimates put this figure at more than 2 million.

- By 2000, more than 1.3 million high-skilled LDC nationals lived and worked abroad. Current estimates put this figure at more than 2 million;

- Six LDCs have more high-skilled nationals living abroad than at home. Another 24 LDCs have more than one-fifth of their high-skilled workers in the diaspora;

At high levels of brain drain, the adverse effects on LDCs outweigh potential benefits from remittances.

- The brain drain rate in the LDCs is 18.4 per cent, much higher than in other developing countries (10 per cent) and in developed countries (4.1 per cent);

- At these high levels of brain drain, the adverse effects on LDCs outweigh potential benefits from remittances;

- Brain drain is worst in certain sectors such as health, education and activities relating to science, technology and innovation (STI). These are critical skills that make up the backbone of a country's technological and knowledge base. Constraints in these skills and knowledge usually have a negative ripple effect on the rest of the economy;

Brain drain is worst in certain sectors such as health, education and activities relating to science, technology and innovation.

- Brain drain is becoming even more of a concern for LDCs, given that these countries are now facing the dual challenge of promoting structural transformation through industrialization while adopting technologies and production processes that are sustainable and environmentally sound;

- Investing in replenishing the human resources lost to brain drain has a very high opportunity cost for LDCs. Paradoxically, it often results in further brain drain. LDCs are generally resource-poor economies in terms of capital (physical, financial and human), knowledge and technological capabilities, and therefore lack the means to offset loss of human resources by accumulating other types of resources.

Efforts to date. The adverse effects of brain drain on home countries, in particular poor economies that are least endowed with high-skilled professionals, are widely recognized. In the last four decades, several initiatives have been launched, at both multilateral and host country level, aimed at facilitating knowledge transfer and knowledge sharing between the diaspora and home countries. Examples include the Transfer of Knowledge Through Expatriate Nationals (TOKTEN) programme managed by the United Nations Development Programme (UNDP); and Migration for Development in Africa (MIDA) and Temporary Return of Qualified Nationals (TRQN) initiated by the International Organization for Migration (IOM). However, as explained in this Report, these programmes have had a limited impact due to inadequate resources and lack of effective coordination. Many of the bilateral initiatives, for example, the "Co-development" programmes adopted by some European countries, are aimed

In the last four decades, several initiatives have been launched, aimed at facilitating knowledge transfer and knowledge sharing between the diaspora and home countries.

The impact of these programmes on reversing the brain drain processes by transferring knowledge and skills to the home country has been limited.

at diaspora members who are encouraged to return to their home country permanently and/or to invest in their home country. Often, they are provided with financial assistance to enable them to start a business in an area of their choice. The evidence shows that in most cases, the ensuing investment projects are carried out in traditional sectors and/or are small-scale. Moreover, the returnees who are assisted through these initiatives are typically low-skilled. Consequently, although these programmes are useful in facilitating diaspora members who wish to return back home or to invest in their home country, their impact on reversing the brain drain processes by transferring knowledge and skills to the home country has been limited.

Existing multilateral initiatives are aimed at developing countries in general, rather than specifically targeting LDCs. In view of the latter's special status — owing largely to their structurally weak economies — and in line with the principles of international support measures for LDCs, this Report proposes the introduction of a new international support measure aimed at offsetting the adverse impact of brain drain by facilitating investment in diaspora knowledge transfer. The main objectives of the new measure or scheme would be twofold: (a) enabling home countries to benefit from the knowledge and experience accumulated by diasporas, which could be tapped through diaspora knowledge networks; and (b) facilitating diasporas' access to part of the capital needed to start investment projects in knowledge-based productive activities.

The scheme. The proposed scheme — "Investing in Diaspora Knowledge Transfer" (IDKT) — is a financial instrument in support of knowledge and learning targeting the diasporas. It could be operated by regional development banks, more specifically the African Development Bank (AfDB), the Asian Development Bank (ADB) and the Inter-American Development Bank (IDB), working closely with national development banks or a special diaspora support window in the central bank of home countries. The rationale for relying on regional development banks to manage LDC-targeted investment initiatives is analysed in UNCTAD (2011a: 114–117). Some advantages are the facts that regional development banks have a proven track record in screening and monitoring national investment projects; they work closely with home governments and could therefore assist diaspora investors in aligning projects with national development priorities; the established credibility of regional development banks would generate confidence and trust in diasporas; and regional banks are already involved in financing knowledge-based regional investment projects that could benefit from links with diaspora knowledge networks. The involvement of home-based diaspora associations and the specific government department responsible for diaspora engagement in this scheme is critical. The latter could also help monitor whether the proposed investment projects are in line with current national development objectives, and whether or not the proposed diaspora investments through the proposed scheme are compatible with activities that enhance home countries' productive and innovative capacities. Therefore, the scheme is not aimed at all diaspora members but only those with the knowledge, skills and technical know-how needed to broaden the knowledge, innovative and productive base of home countries.

As a result, the scheme would target diaspora members who:

a) Have expertise in a specific field with high knowledge content which is amenable to enterprise development and could contribute to building productive capacities; and

b) Are willing to invest in this field in the home country and share knowledge.

Investments in productive activities in general, and in knowledge and innovation capability-building in particular, often carry risks. The proposed scheme is designed to reduce such risks by giving diaspora members who meet the above conditions access to a certain proportion of the capital (e.g. half) required to initiate the investment. The finance would be made available at

This Report proposes the introduction of a new international support measure aimed at offsetting the adverse impact of brain drain.

The scheme is aimed at diaspora members with the knowledge, skills and technical know-how needed to broaden the knowledge, innovative and productive base of home countries.

preferential interest rates. Therefore, what is being proposed is not a grant system but a sort of diaspora venture-capital initiative to help motivate and lead highly skilled diaspora members to engage in home country development. Diaspora knowledge networks, as well as business associations and academic networks, would serve as important search mechanisms for mobilizing diasporas.

In principle, the scheme would encourage investment in middle-to-high level technology industries (e.g. machinery, information and communication technologies, biotech, precision instruments), and skill-intensive activities (e.g. engineering, consultancy, software). These are the types of knowledge-based activities that are currently less prominent or even totally absent in LDCs. Consequently, the scheme would ensure that the investment projects proposed are innovative in the sense that they should contribute to the creation of activities that are new to the home countries (or underdeveloped there), although they may not be new to the rest of the world.

In order to strengthen the knowledge-sharing aspect of the investment projects initiated through the new scheme and to spread their benefits to domestic agents through linkages, joint ventures with local firms would be encouraged. In this way, the scheme would serve as a catalyst for knowledge diffusion and sharing. For their part, domestic partners would contribute their knowledge of local business conditions and their domestic business networks.

Financing. Multiple sources of financing may be required to raise adequate funds to launch the scheme. As shown in this Report, skilled emigrants from LDCs live mainly in developed countries. The funds needed to launch the scheme could be raised from developed countries and other countries in a position to contribute to such funds, and from international and regional financial institutions. The details of the function of the scheme would require further work and a full-fledged feasibility study, including the scale of financing needed, how these funds would be made available to potential skilled diaspora members, how the potential bankable projects would be assessed, who should screen investment projects and according to which criteria, etc. From the evidence presented in this Report, it is clear that there is a need for a special scheme to motivate skilled LDC diaspora members to help build the knowledge base and innovative capabilities of home countries.

The role of home countries. Home countries should provide a supportive environment favourable to knowledge diffusion and to innovative investment, at different levels. At the macro level, home countries should define clearly the national development priorities, strengthen the State's capacity to formulate and implement policies, and develop essential infrastructure, including adequate energy supply capacity (UNCTAD, 2009: 57–90).

At the meso level, a series of industrial policy instruments could be put in place to favour innovation, technological upgrading and knowledge diffusion in the productive sphere. This may include preferential treatment reflected in incentives or targeted supports, a plethora of fiscal and investment incentives, as well as trade policy tools (tariffs and non-tariff barriers), subsidies, grants or loans, fiscal and investment incentives. Even in the absence of a formally articulated industrial policy, home country governments could adopt some of these instruments. Also at the meso level, different economic agents could be involved in the scheme, such as national chambers of commerce, sectoral business associations and relevant ministries (e.g. industry, technology).

At the micro level, home country governments and agencies could adopt some of the following actions and instruments:

- Identifying potential domestic business partners for investment projects stemming from the diaspora and encouraging both sides to form joint ventures or enter into other forms of partnership;

What is being proposed is a sort of diaspora venture-capital initiative to help motivate and lead highly skilled diaspora members to engage in home country development.

The scheme would encourage investment in middle-to-high level technology industries and skill-intensive activities.

Multiple sources of financing may be required to raise adequate funds to launch the scheme.

Home countries should provide a supportive environment favourable to knowledge diffusion and to innovative investment.

- Developing other elements of the national innovation system (e.g. research centres, laboratories, technical schools) which could potentially establish links with diaspora investment projects;

- Establishing industrial parks with favourable physical, business and knowledge infrastructure and legal frameworks, possibly including include business incubators;

- Promoting conferences which facilitate the interaction between diaspora members and domestic businesses;

- Easing conditions of movement of diaspora members between home and host countries;

- Establishing communication channels between diaspora members (including potential entrepreneurs) and the national government.

Home countries can identify potential domestic business partners and develop other elements of the national innovation system.

E. Conclusions and key policy recommendations

1. OVERALL STRATEGIES WITH REGARD TO DIASPORAS

LDCs with a critical mass of migrants need to strengthen their policy framework in order to better harness the development impact of remittances and engage diasporas as agents of development and structural transformation.

- LDCs with a critical mass of migrants need to strengthen their policy framework in order to better harness the development impact of remittances and engage diasporas as agents of development and structural transformation. In doing so, it is important to note that policies on migration, remittances and diaspora engagement should not be formulated in isolation, but as integral parts of national development strategies.

- The responsibility for formulating and implementing the diaspora policy framework in home countries should lie at the highest level of Government, ideally at ministerial level. Moreover, while the specific mix of policies and concrete measures for diaspora engagement will vary between countries, the overall direction should be to provide an enabling environment for enhancing diasporas' contributions to the development of productive capacities.

- Building "trust" between diasporas and home governments is central for sustaining the engagement and contributions of diasporas. While it is true that diaspora members are not motivated exclusively by commercial interests, their engagement will fail if they are only expected to contribute and receive nothing in return. Policies aimed at diasporas should bear this crucial point in mind.

Building "trust" between diasporas and home governments is central for sustaining the engagement and contributions of diasporas.

2. HARNESSING REMITTANCES TO BUILD PRODUCTIVE CAPACITIES

It is critical that LDCs make formal channels of remitting more attractive.

- It is critical that LDCs make formal channels of remitting more attractive through targeted policies, incentive measures and institutional improvements aimed at reducing the cost of remittances sent through formal remittance service providers. Opening the remittance market to competition would help to lower significantly the cost of remitting. Possible policy initiatives in this area could include the following:

  » Directly increasing the range of financial actors involved in the remittance market, especially in the rural areas, by reforming the regulatory framework in order to enable a wider participation of RSPs, particularly of microfinance institutions, savings and loans cooperatives, credit unions and post offices;

  » Promoting partnerships among banks, microfinance institutions and other financial intermediaries;

  » Strengthening post office involvement by improving their Internet connectivity, increasing their technical capabilities and cash resources, and promoting a wider selection of savings products;

- » Improving telecommunications infrastructure;
- » Harmonizing banking and telecommunications regulations in order to enable banks to participate in mobile remittances;
- » Discouraging exclusivity agreements between all market participants, in particular, banks and money transfer companies.
- » Where necessary, intensifying the market competition by allowing a public sector institution to compete with private sector providers of remittance services.

Governments could enhance the developmental impact of remittances by providing additional incentives to migrants.

- Since, as shown in this Report, the cost of remitting is highest in Africa, the scope of bringing down the rate through regional initiatives, including with the involvement of the African Development Bank (AfDB), should be explored.

- At the microeconomic level, governments could enhance the developmental impact of remittances by providing additional incentives to migrants. For example, migrants may be encouraged to open a foreign currency account in the home country; an option to use foreign-currency deposits as collateral to get loans at preferential terms could be provided; incentives to migrants to return to the home country once they retire could be provided by signing double-taxation avoidance treaties with the main host countries where the majority of its migrants work; the creation of education and housing accounts at home for migrants and their families, and a higher rate of return on these deposits than on ordinary saving accounts would provide an incentive to save more out of remittances and for purposes that would help ensure productive use of remittances. The appropriate mix of measures would have to be decided by the competent authorities.

Home governments should explore the option of using diaspora bonds to mobilize additional external finance for development projects.

- Home governments should explore, where appropriate, the option of using diaspora bonds to mobilize additional external finance for development projects with high prospective social returns (for example, infrastructure development or trade facilitation projects).

- Whilst being wary of the risks of excessive indebtedness, remittances future-flows could be used as collateral for securitization or long-term syndicated loans, thanks to their relative stability compared with other receivables. In addition, the institutional and regulatory strengthening required for the securitization process could represent a stepping stone to establish or improve the international creditworthiness of the recipient country.

LDCs could strengthen the provision of public goods by combining collective remittances and matching funds.

- With the assistance of the international community, LDCs could strengthen the provision of public goods by combining collective remittances and matching funds.

3. HARNESSING DIASPORA KNOWLEDGE TO BUILD PRODUCTIVE CAPACITIES

- Home countries should assess the market potential for the so-called "nostalgic trade". Policies in LDCs could be designed to sustain the competitiveness of producers of nostalgic goods, by upgrading their products and processes and to engage diaspora members to help with branding and marketing in the host country. Education and training of producers is crucial if they are to become competitive in foreign markets.

Strengthen coordination across the array of different stakeholders who engage in activities and programmes targeting the diaspora.

- Improve income, working conditions and career prospects in some key sectors, especially in the national health and education systems, universities and research centres, including with the assistance of donors, so as to reduce the intensity of brain drain.

- Strengthen coordination across the array of different stakeholders who engage in activities and programmes targeting the diaspora: home and host country governments, diaspora associations, NGOs, international organizations, private foundations, etc.

Home country governments could assist diasporas to create diaspora knowledge networks and leverage resources.

The international community could consider establishing an international support measure to harness diaspora knowledge to build productive capacities in LDCs.

- Promote an industrial policy framework that enhances the role of DKNs, and taps their potential to reinforce the processes of learning, technology transfer, and structural transformation in the LDC economies.

- Policy actions and incentive measures that home country governments could implement to engage diasporas and facilitate the transfer of knowledge and technical know-how would include:

  » Monitoring and building reliable database on the diaspora, its skills and professional profile, earnings, aspirations and expectations vis-à-vis the home country in terms of knowledge transfer, investment, business networks, and return (temporary or permanent);

  » Assisting diasporas to create diaspora knowledge networks and leverage resources (e.g. through umbrella organizations, joint activities with other stakeholders) from host countries for productive capacity-building in home countries;

  » Involving the diaspora from the start in planning and designing national development strategies and programmes, so as to ensure the convergence of government and diaspora priorities;

  » Promoting diaspora FDI through road shows, investment promotion strategies targeted at diasporas;

  » Facilitating the assimilation of returnees and diaspora investment though agricultural and industrial extension services, incentives to encourage enterprise development, investment promotion policies and instruments geared specifically to diaspora financing and technical advice.

- The international community could consider establishing an international support measure to harness diaspora knowledge to build productive capacities in LDCs through the proposed IDKT scheme.

Notes

1 The creation of the Migrant Remittances Observatory in Benin is one of the recommendations of the Ministerial Declaration adopted at the Ministerial Conference of the Least Developed Countries on Migrants' Remittances held in Cotonou, 9-10 February 2006.

2 See World Bank (2011a).

3 "Search networks allow us to find and collaborate with those who are already learning what we need to know." (Kuznetov and Sabel, 2006, p. 1)

4 See UNCTAD (2007) and discussion in Haussman and Rodrik (2003).

5 The objectives of DKNs are multifold: (1) to disseminate knowledge; through Self Discovery Networks, (2) to build alternative communication infrastructure for communication via websites, blogs, reports, papers, etc.; and (3) to attract more media attention and consequently higher funding than individual entities can.

6 It is possible that diaspora activities may not always result in positive effects. They are by definition elitist, exclusive and non transparent, often not accountable to anyone and may become subject to internal disputes (Meyer and Wattiaux, 2006). As Kapur (2001) argues, DKNs can also transfer fads and fashions as well as inappropriate technologies to home countries.

7 Since the 2000s, 27 LDCs have experienced some degree of deindustrialization, reflected in the declining share of value added in the manufacturing sector (UNCTAD, 2010a).

8 Indeed, the behaviour and impact of DKNs has been studied and positively evaluated by a number of scholars of industrial policy in recent years (Saxenian, 2006, Kuznetsov and Sabel, 2006; Lamoureaux et al., 2003; Kuznetsov and Torres, 2006; Kuznetsov, 2008; Iskander and Lowe, 2011).

9 Interest in industrial policy in developing countries has re-emerged following the disappointing economic performance prescribed by the Washington Consensus. (Altenburg et al., 2008; Altenburg, 2011; Hausmann and Rodrik, 2003; Rosendahl 2010; Wade 2010).

10 See table 8 in chapter 3 for "regulatory challenges facing international remittance service providers (RSPs) in LDCs".

BIBLIOGRAPHY

Abdih Y, Chami R, Dagher J and Montiel P (2012). Remittances and institutions: Are remittances a curse? *World Development.* 40(4): 657–666.

Acosta P, Calderón C, Fajnzylber P and Lopez H (2008). What is the impact of international remittances on poverty and inequality in Latin America? *World Development.* 36(1): 89–114.

Acosta P, Fajnzylber P and Lopez JH (2007). The impact of remittances on poverty and human capital: Evidence from Latin American household surveys. In: Özden Ç and Schiff M, eds. *International Migration, Economic Development and Policy.* World Bank and Palgrave Macmillan: 59–98. Washington (DC) and London.

Acosta P, Lartey E and Mandelman F (2009). Remittances and the Dutch disease. *Journal of International Economics.* 79(1): 102–116.

Adams R (2011). Evaluating the economic impact of international remittances on developing countries using household surveys: A literature review. *Journal of Development Studies.* 47(6): 809–828.

Adams R and Page J (2005). Do international migration and remittances reduce poverty in developing countries? *World Development.* 33(10): 1645–1669.

Adepoju A, ed. (2009). *International Migration within, to and from Africa in a Globalised World.* Sub-Saharan Publishers. Accra.

Adredo D (2000). Human capital from Africa: An assessment of brain drain from Ethiopia. In: Tapsoba S et al., eds. *Brain Drain and Capacity Building in Africa.* United Nations Economic Commission for Africa, International Development Research Centre and International Organization for Migration: 122–147. Addis Ababa, Ottawa and Geneva.

AFREXIMBANK (2005). Annual Report 2005. African Export-Import Bank. Cairo.

African Union (2006). Draft African common position on migration and development. Report of Experts' Meeting on Migration and Development, Algiers, 3-5 April. Available at: http://www.africa-union.org/root/au/Conferences/Past/2006/April/SA/Apr5/Draft%20AFRICAN%20COMMON%20POSITION%20ON%20MIGRATION%20AND%20DEVELOPMENT%20-final-5%20April2006.pdf.

African Union Commission (2004). Draft Strategic Framework for a Policy on Migration in Africa. Experts Group Meeting on Policy Framework on Migration in Africa; Addis Ababa 29–30 March, Social Affairs Department, African Union Commission.

Aggarwal R, Demirguc-Kunt A and Martinez Peria MS (2006). Do workers' remittances promote financial development? Policy Research Working Paper Series, No. 3957. World Bank. Washinton (DC).

Agrawal A, Kapur D and McHale J (2008). How do spatial and social proximity influence knowledge flows? Evidence from patent data. *Journal of Urban Economics.* 64(2): 258–269.

Agrawal A, Kapur D, McHale J and Oettl A (2011). Brain drain or brain bank? The impact of skilled emigration on poor-country innovation. *Journal of Urban Economics.* 69(1): 43–55.

Agunias DR and Newland K (2012). Developing a Road Map for Engaging Diasporas in Development: A Handbook for Policymakers and Practitioners in Home and Host Countries. International Organization for Migration and Migration Policy Institute. Geneva and Washington (DC).

Altenburg T (2011). Industrial policy in developing countries: Overview and leassons from seven country cases. DIE Discussion Paper 4/2011. Deutsches Institut für Entwicklungspolitik. Bonn.

Altenburg T, Rosendahl C, Stamm A and Drachenfels C (2008). Industrial policy: A key element of the social and ecological market economy. In Küsel C, Maenner U and Meissner R, eds. *The social and ecological market economy: A model for Asian development?* Deutsche Gesellschaft für Technische Zusammenarbeit. Eschborn.

Amuedo-Dorantes C, Georges A and Pozo S (2010). Migration, remittances, and children's schooling in Haiti. *The ANNALS of the American Academy of Political and Social Science.* 630(1): 224–244.

Amuedo-Dorantes C and Pozo S (2004). Workers' remittances and the real exchange rate: A paradox of gifts. *World Development.* 32(8): 1407–1417.

Amuedo-Dorantes C and Pozo S (2010). Accounting for remittance and migration effects on children's schooling. *World Development.* 38(12): 1747–1759.

Ancien D, Boyle M and Kitchin R (2009a). *The Scottish Diaspora and Diaspora Strategy: Insights and Lessons from Ireland.* Scottish Government Social Research. Edinburgh.

Ancien D, Boyle M and Kitchin R (2009b). Exploring diaspora strategies: An international comparison. National Institute for Regional Spatial Analyses. NUI Maynooth. June.

Ancien D, Boyle M and Kitchin R (2009c). Exploring diaspora strategies: Lessons for Ireland. National Institute for Regional Spatial Analyses. NUI Maynooth. June.

ANSD (2011). *Situation économique et sociale du Sénégal en 2010.* Agence Nationale de la Statistique et de la Démographie. Dakar.

Anyanwu JC and Erhijakpor AEO (2010). Do international remittances affect poverty in Africa? *African Development Review.* 22(1): 51–91.

Anzoategui D, Demirguc-Kunt A and Peria MSM (2011). Remittances and financial inclusion: Evidence from El Salvador. Policy Research Working Paper Series, No. 5839. World Bank. Washington (DC).

Barré R, Hernandez V, Meyer J-B and Vinck D (2003). *Diasporas Scientifiques/Scientific Disaporas.* IRD Editions. Paris.

Beine M, Docquier F and Rapoport H (2001). Brain drain and economic growth: Theory and evidence. *Journal of Development Economics.* 64(2): 275–289.

Beine M, Docquier F and Rapoport H (2008). Brain drain and human capital formation in developing countries: Winners and losers. *Economic Journal*. 118(528): 631–652.

Berry RA and Soligo R (1969). Some welfare aspects of international migration. *Journal of Political Economy*. 77(5): 778–94.

Bhagwati J and Hamada K (1974). The brain drain, international integration of markets for professionals and unemployment: A theoretical analysis. *Journal of Development Economics*. 1(1-2): 19–42.

Bhagwati J and Hanson GH, eds. (2009). *Skilled Immigration Today: Prospects, Problems, and Policies*. Oxford University Press. Oxford and New York.

Bhargava A and Docquier F (2008). HIV pandemic, medical brain drain, and economic development in Sub-Saharan Africa. *World Bank Economic Review*. 22(2): 345–366.

Bhargava A, Docquier F and Moullan Y (2011). Modeling the effects of physician emigration on human development. *Economics and Human Biology*. 9(2): 172–183.

Bluhm R and Szirmai A (2012). Institutions and long-run growth performance: An analytical literature review of the institutional determinants of economic growth. UNU-MERIT Working Paper, No. 2012-033. United Nations University - Maastricht Economic and Social Research Institute on Innovation and Technology. Maastricht.

Bollard A, McKenzie D, Morten M and Rapoport H (2011). Remittances and the brain drain revisited: The microdata show that more educated migrants remit more. *World Bank Economic Review*. 25(1): 132–156.

Brinkerhoff J (2006). Diasporas, skills transfer, and remittances: Evolving perceptions and potential. In: Wescott C and Brinkerhoff J, eds. *Converting Migration Drains Into Gains: Harnessing the Resources of Overseas Professionals*. Asian Development Bank. Manila.

Brown RPC (1997). Estimating remittance functions for Pacific Island migrants. *World Development*. 25(4): 613–626.

Brown RPC and Jimenez E (2007). Estimating the net effects of migration and remittances on poverty and inequality: comparison of Fiji and Tonga. WIDER Research Paper, No. 2007/23. United Nations University - World Institute for Development Economic Research. Helsinki.

Buencamino L and Gorbunov S (2002). Informal money transfer systems: opportunities and challenges for development finance. DESA Discussion Paper no.26 (ST/ESA/2002/DP/26). United Nations Department for Econonmic and Social Affairs. New York.

Bugamelli M and Paternò F (2008). Output growth volatility and remittances. Working Papers (Temi di discussione), No. 673. Bank of Italy. Rome.

Bugamelli M and Paternò F (2009). Do workers' remittances reduce the probability of current account reversals? *World Development*. 37(12): 1821–1838.

Cali M (2010). Restricting migration: a bad (development) idea. Policy Brief. Overseas Development Institute (ODI). May. London.

Cassarino J-P (2004). Theorizing return migration: A revisited conceptual approach to return migration. EUI Working Paper, No. RSCAS No. 2004/02. European University Institute. Florence.

Catrinescu N, Leon-Ledesma M, Piracha M and Quillin B (2009). Remittances, institutions, and economic growth. *World Development*. 37(1): 81–92.

CGAP (2010). Financial Access 2010: The State of Financial Inclusion Through the Crisis. Consultative Group to Assist the Poor. Washington (DC).

CGAP (2012). Landscape study on international remittances through mobile money. Consultative Group to Assist the Poor. Washington (DC).

Chami R et al. (2008). *Macroeconomic Consequences of Remittances*. International Monetary Fund. Washington (DC)

Chami R, Fullenkamp C and Jahjah S (2005). Are immigrant remittance flows a source of capital for development? *IMF Staff Papers*. 52(1): 55–81.

Chami R, Hakura D and Montiel P (2010). Do worker remittances reduce output volatility in developing countries? Department of Economics Working Paper, No. 2010-19. Williams College Center for Development Economics. Williamstown (MA).

Chaparro F, Jaramillo H and Quintero V (2004). Aprovechamiento de la Daispora e Insercion de Colombia en Redes Globales de Conocimiento: El Caso de la Red Caldas. World Bank and Universidad del Rosario. Washington (DC) and Bogota.

Chenery HB and Bruno M (1962). Development alternatives in an open economy: The case of Israel. *Economic Journal*. 72(285): 79–103.

Clemens MA, Montenegro CE and Pritchett L (2008). The place premium: Wage differences for identical workers across the US border. Policy Research Working Paper Series, No. 4671. World Bank. Washington (DC).

Clemens MA and Pettersson G (2008). New data on African health professionals abroad. *Human Resources for Health*. 6(1): 1.

Combes P-P, Lafourcade M and Mayer T (2005). The trade-creating effects of business and social networks: Evidence from France. *Journal of International Economics*. 66(1): 1–29.

Commander S, Kangasniemi M and Winters LA (2004). The brain drain: Curse or boon? A survey of the literature. In: Baldwin RE and Winters LA, eds. *Challenges to Globalization: Analyzing the Economics*. National Bureau of Economic Research: 235–278. Cambridge (MA).

Cox-Edwards A and Rodríguez-Oreggia E (2009). Remittances and labor force participation in Mexico: An analysis using propensity score matching. *World Development*. 37(5): 1004–1014.

Crush J, Dodson B Gay J, Green T and Leduka C (2010). *Migration, Remittances and Development in Lesotho*. Southern African Migration Programme. Cape Town.

David PA and Foray D (2002). An introduction to the economy of the knowledge society. *International Social Science Journal.* 54(171): 9–23.

Debass T and Orozco M (2008). Digesting nostalgic trade: A prequel to a value chain approach. USAID Breakfast Seminar Series Presentation. US Agency for International Development. Washington (DC).

Demirgüç-Kunt A, Córdova EL, Pería MSM and Woodruff C (2011). Remittances and banking sector breadth and depth: Evidence from Mexico. *Journal of Development Economics.* 95(2): 229–241.

Dieng SA (2002). Les pratiques financières des migrants Maliens et Sénegalais en France. Epargne sans frontières, Techniques financières et développement. International Workshop on Migration and Poverty in West Africa, University of Sussex. March.

Docquier F (2006). Brain drain and inequality across nations. IZA Discussion Paper, No. 2440. Institute for the Study of Labor (IZA). Bonn. November.

Docquier F and Lodigiani E (2010). Skilled migration and business networks. *Open Economies Review.* 21(4): 565–588.

Docquier F, Lodigiani E, Rapoport H and Schiff M (2011). Emigration and democracy. CReAM Discussion Paper, No. 02/11. Centre for Research and Analysis of Migration. London. January.

Docquier F, Lowell BL and Marfouk A (2009). A gendered assessment of highly skilled emigration. *Population and Development Review.* 35(2): 297–321.

Docquier F and Marfouk A (2006). International migration by education attainment, 1990 - 2000. In: Özden Ç and Schiff M, eds. *International Migration, Remittances and the Brain Drain.* World Bank and Palgrave Macmillan: 151–200. Washington (DC) and London.

Docquier F, Marfouk A, Özden Ç and Parsons CR (2011). Geographic, gender and skill structure of international migration. Report written for the Economic Research Forum. Institut de Recherches Économiques et Sociales de l'Université catholique de Louvain. Louvain-la-Neuve. September.

Docquier F and Rapoport H (2007). Skilled migration: The perspective of developing countries. IZA Discussion Paper, No. 2873. Institute for the Study of Labor (IZA). Bonn.

Docquier F and Rapoport H (2008). Brain drain. In: Durlauf S N and Blume L E, eds. *The New Palgrave Dictionary of Economics.* London.

Docquier F and Rapoport H (2012). Globalization, brain drain and development. *Journal of Economic Literature.* 50(3): 681–730.

Domingues dos Santos M and Postel-Vinay F (2003). Migration as a source of growth: The perspective of a developing country. *Journal of Population Economics.* 16(1): 161–175.

Ducanes G and Abella M (2008). *Overseas Filipino workers and their impact on household employment decisions.* International Labour Office - ILO Regional Office for Asia and the Pacific. Asian Regional Programme on Governance of Labour Migration. Bangkok.

Dustmann C, Fadlon I and Weiss Y (2011). Return migration, human capital accumulation and the brain drain. *Journal of Development Economics.* 95(1): 58–67.

Dustmann C and Kirchkamp O (2002). The optimal migration duration and activity choice after remigration. *Journal of Development Economics.* 67(2): 351–372.

Easterly W and Nyarko Y (2009). Is the brain drain good for Africa? In: Bhagwati J and Hanson G H, eds. *Skilled Immigration Today: Prospects, Problems, and Policies.* Oxford University Press: 316–360. Oxford and New York.

Ehrenreich B and Hochschild AR, eds. (2003). *Global Woman: Nannies, Maids and Sex Workers in the New Economy.* Granta Books. London.

Eichengreen B, Park D and Shin K (2011). When fast growing economies slow down: International evidence and implications for China. NBER Working Paper 16919. National Bureau of Economic Research. Cambridge (MA).

Esim S and Smith M (2004). Gender & Migration in Arab States: The Case of Domestic Workers. International Labour Organisation. ILO, Regional Office for Arab States, Beirut. June.

Faini R (2006). Remittances and the brain drain. IZA Discussion Paper, No. 2155. Institute for the Study of Labor (IZA).

Finn MG (2010). Stay rates of foreign doctorate recipients from U.S. universities, 2007. Oak Ridge Institute for Science and Education. Oak Ridge (TN).

Foray D (2006). *The Economics of Knowledge.* MIT Press. Cambdige (MA).

Freund C and Spatafora N (2005). Remittances: Transaction costs, determinants, and informal flows. Policy Research Working Paper Series, No. 3704. World Bank. Washington (DC).

Garcia Zamora R (2007). Nota Critica. El Programa Tres por Uno de remesas colectivas en México. Lecciones y desafios. *Migraciones Internacionales.* 4(1).

Ghosh J (2009). Migration and gender empowerment: Recent trends and emerging issues. Human Development Research Paper 2009/04. United Nations Development Programme.

Gibson J and McKenzie D (2010). The economic consequences of "brain drain" of the best and brightest: Microeconomic evidence from five countries. Research Policy Working Paper, No. WPS 5394. World Bank. Washington (DC). August.

Gibson J and McKenzie D (2011). Eight questions about brain drain. *Journal of Economic Perspectives.* 25(3): 107–28.

Gibson J, McKenzie D and Rohorua H (2006). How cost-elastic are remittances? Estimates from Tongan migrants in New Zealand. Working Paper in Economics, No. 2/06. University of Waikato. Hamilton. March.

Giuliano P and Ruiz-Arranz M (2009). Remittances, financial development, and growth. *Journal of Development Economics*. 90(1): 144–152.

Glick Schiller N, Basch L and Blanc-Szanton C (1992). *Towards a Transnational Perspective on Migration: Race, Class, Ethnicity and Nationalism Reconsidered.* New York Academy of Sciences. New York.

Glytsos NP (2005). The contribution of remittances to growth: A dynamic approach and empirical analysis. *Journal of Economic Studies*. 32:468–496.

Goldstein S, A. Goldstein A and Gurmu E (2000). Migration, gender and health survey in five regions of Ethiopia: 1998. Population Studies and Training Center, Brown University. Providence.

Gould DM (1994). Immigrant links to the home country: Empirical implications for U.S. bilateral trade flows. *Review of Economics and Statistics*. 76(2): 302–16.

Grabel I (2008). The political economy of remittances: What do we know? What do we need to know? Working Papers, No. 184. Political Economy Research Institute, University of Massachusetts. Amherst (MA).

Grubel HB and Scott AD (1966). The international flow of human capital. *American Economic Review*. 56(1/2): 268–274.

De Haas H (2005). International migration, remittances and development: Myths and facts. *Third World Quarterly*. 26(8): 1269–1284.

Hammar T, Brochmann G and Tamas K, eds. (1997). *International Migration, Immobility and Development: Multidisciplinary Perspectives.* Berg Publishers, Oxford and New York.

Haque NU (2005). Brain drain or human capital flight. Lectures in Development Economics, No. 11. Pakistan Institute of Development Economics. Islamabad.

Haque NU and Kim S-J (1995). "Human capital flight": Impact of migration on income and growth. *IMF Staff Papers*. 42(3): 577–607.

Hausmann R and Rodrik D (2003). Economic discovery as self discovery. *Journal of Development Economics*. 72(2): 603–633.

Head K and Ries J (1998). Immigration and trade creation: Econometric evidence from Canada. *Canadian Journal of Economics*. 31(1): 47–62.

von Hippel E (1994). "Sticky information" and the locus of problem solving: Implications for innovation. *Management Science*. 40(4): 429–439.

Hollanders H, Soete L and ter Weel B (1999). Trends in growth convergence and divergence and changes in technological access and capabilities. MERIT Research Memoranda, No. 018. United Nations University – Maastricht Economic Research Institute on Innovation and Technology. Maastricht.

IFAD (2009). Sending money home to Africa: Remittance markets, enabling environment and prospects. International Fund for Agricultural Development. Rome.

IHSI (2010). Enquête sur l'emploi et l'économie informelle. Premiers résultats de l'enquête emploi, Phase I. Institut Haïtien de Statistique et d'Informatique. Port-au-Prince.

IILS and ILO (2012). *World of Work Report 2012 : Better Jobs for a Better Economy.* International Institute for Labour Studies and International Labour Office. Geneva.

ILO (2011). Growth, Employment and Decent Work in the Least Developed Countries. Report of the International Labour Organization for the Fourth UN Conference on the Least Developed Countries. Turkey.

IMF (2005). *World Economic Outlook April 2005: Globalization and External Imbalances*. International Monetary Fund. Washington (DC).

IMF (2011). *Balance of Payments and International Investment Position Manual.* International Monetary Fund. Washington (DC)

IMF (2012). The IMF and the Fight Against Money Laundering and the Financing of Terrorism. Factsheet. March. Available at: http://www.imf.org/external/np/exr/facts/aml.htm.

IMF and World Bank (2009). A Review of Some Aspects of the Low-Income Country Debt Sustainability Framework. Prepared by the Staffs of the IMF and the World Bank. Available at: http://www.imf.org/external/pp/longres.aspx?id=4358.

IMF and World Bank (2012). Revisiting the Debt Sustainability Framework for Low-Income Countries. Prepared by the Staffs of the IMF and the World Bank. Available at: http://www.imf.org/external/np/pp/eng/2012/011212.pdf.

IOM (2008). *World Migration 2008: Managing Labour Mobility in the Evolving Global Economy*. International Organization for Migration. Geneva.

IOM-UNDP (2002). Contribution of returnees: An analytical survey of post return experience. International Organization for Migration and United Nations Development Programme. Dhaka.

Iskander N and Lowe N (2011). The transformers: Immigration and tacit knowledge development. NYU Wagner Research Paper, No. 2011-01. New York University. New York. January.

Jadotte E (2009). International migration, remittances and labour supply: The case of the Republic of Haiti. WIDER Research Paper, No. 2009/28. United Nations University - World Institute for Development Economic Research.Helsinki.

Javorcik BS, Özden Ç, Spatareanu M and Neagu IC (2011). Migrant networks and foreign direct investment. *Journal of Development Economics*. 94(2): 231–241.

Johnson H (1967). Some economic aspects of the brain drain. *Pakistan Development Review*. 7(3): 379–411.

Jones A (2008). A silent but mighty river: The costs of women's economic migration. Signs: *Journal of Women in Culture and Society*. 33(4): 761–769.

Kabbucho K, Sander C and Mukwana P (2003). Passing the buck in East Africa. Money transfer systems: The practice and potential for products in Kenya. MicroSave Study. May.

Kaplinsky R (2005). *Globalization, Poverty and Inequality: Between a Rock and a Hard Place.* Polity. Cambridge (UK) and Malden (MA).

Kapur D (2001). Diasporas and technology transfer. *Journal of Human Development.* 2(2): 265–286.

Kapur D (2004). Remittances: The new development mantra? G-24 Discussion Paper, No. 29. United Nations Conference on Trade and Development. New York and Geneva.

Kapur D and McHale J (2005). *Give us your Best and Brightest: The Global Hunt for Talent and its Impact on the Developing World.* Center for Global Development. Washington (DC).

Ketkar SL and Ratha D (2010). Diaspora bonds: tapping the diaspora during difficult times. *Journal of International Commerce, Economics and Policy.* 01(02): 251.

Kim N (2007). The impact of remittances on labor supply: The case of Jamaica. Policy Research Working Paper Series, No. 4120. World Bank. Washington (DC).

Kirigia J, Gbary A, Muthuri L, Nyoni J and Seddoh A (2006). The cost of health professionals' brain drain in Kenya. *BMC Health Services Research.* 6(1): 89.

Kugler M and Rapoport H (2007). International labor and capital flows: Complements or substitutes? *Economics Letters.* 94(2): 155–162.

Kuschminder K and Siegel M (2011). Understanding Ethiopian diaspora engagement Policy. UNU-MERIT Working Paper, No. 2011-040. United Nations University - Maastrict Economic and Social Research Institute on Innovation and Technology. Maastrict.

Kuznetsov Y (2008). Why is diaspora potential so elusive? Towards a new generation of Initiatives to leverage countries' talent abroad. World Bank. Washington (DC).

Kuznetsov Y (2011). Why is diaspora potential so elusive? Towards a new generation of initiatives to leverage countries' talent abroad. In: Sharma K, Kashyap A, Montes M F, and Ladd P, eds. *Realizing the Development Potential of Diasporas.* United Nations University Press. Tokyo and New York.

Kuznetsov Y and Sabel CF (2006). Global mobility of talent from a perspective of new industrial policy open migration chains and diaspora networks. WIDER Research Paper, No. 2006/144. United Nations University - World Institute for Development Economic Research. Helsinki.

Kuznetsov Y and Torres F (2006). *Diaspora Networks and the International Migration of Skills: How Countries can Draw on Their Talent Abroad.* World Bank. Washington, (DC).

Kwok V and Leland H (1982). An economic model of the brain drain. *American Economic Review.* 72(1): 91–100.

Lamoreaux NR, Raff D and Temin P (2003). Beyond markets and hierarchies: Toward a new synthesis of American business history. *American Historical Review.* 108(2): 404–433.

Leliveld (1997). The effects of restrictive South African migrant labor policy on the survival of rural households in southern Africa: A case study from rural Swaziland. *World development.* 25(11): 1839–1849.

Lucas REB (2008). *International Migration and Economic Development: Lessons from Low-Income Countries.* Edward Elgar. Cheltenham.

MacMaster J (1993). Strategies to stimulate private sector development in the Pacific Island economies. In: Cole R V and Tambunlertchai S, eds. *The Future of Asia-Pacific Economies: Pacific Islands at the Crossroads?* Australian National University. Asian and Pacific Development Centre and National Centre for Development Studies.

Mahler SJ and Pessar PR (2001). Gendered geographies of power: Analyzing gender across transnational spaces. *Identities.* 7(4): 441–459.

Mahroum S, Eldridge C and Daar AS (2006). Transnational diaspora options: How developing countries could benefit from their emigrant populations. *International Journal on Multicultural Societies.* 8(1): 25–42.

Maimbo SM, Qorchi ME and Wilson JF (2003). Informal funds transfer systems: An analysis of the informal Hawala system. IMF Occasional Paper, No. 222. International Monetary Fund. Washington (DC).

Maimbo SM and Ratha D, eds. (2005). *Remittances: Development Impact and Future Prospects.* World Bank. Washington (DC).

Mattoo A, Neagu IC and Özden Ç (2008). Brain waste? Educated immigrants in the US labor market. *Journal of Development Economics.* 87(2): 255–269.

McCormick B and Wahba J (2001). Overseas work experience, savings and entrepreneurship amongst return migrants to LDCs. *Scottish Journal of Political Economy.* 48(2): 164–78.

McDowell C and de Haan A (1997). Migration and sustainable livelihoods: a critical review of the literature. IDS Working Paper, No. 65. Institute of Development Studies, University of Sussex. Brighton.

Melde S and Ionesco D (2010). Mainstreaming Migration, Development and Remittances in the LDC Post-Brussels Plan of Action. International Organization for Migration. New York.

Mesnard A and Ravallion M (2001). Wealth distribution and self-employment in a developing economy. CEPR Discussion Paper, No. 3026. Centre for European Policy Research. London.

Meyer J-B and Wattiaux J-P (2006). Diaspora knowledge networks: Vanishing doubts and increasing evidence. *Social and Human Sciences.* 8(1): 4–24.

Mezger C (2008). Who comes back? The case of Senegalese returning to Dakar. MAFE Working Paper, No. 4. The Migrations between Africa and Europe Project. Louvain-la-Neuve. December.

Mezger C and Flahaux M-L (2010). Returning to Dakar: The role of migration experience for professional reinsertion. In: Beauchemin C, Kabbanji L, and Schoumaker B, eds. *Entre Parcours de Vie des Migrants et Attentes Politiques, quel Co-Développement en Afrique Subsaharienne?* Documents de travail INED: 61–90. Institut national d'études démographiques. Paris.

Mitchell S (2006). Migration and the remittance euphoria: Development or dependency? The New Economics Foundation. London.

Miyagiwa K (1991). Scale economies in education and the brain drain problem. *International Economic Review*. 32(3): 743–59.

Mohapatra S, Joseph G and Ratha D (2009). Remittances and natural disasters: Ex-post response and contribution to ex-ante preparedness. Policy Research Working Paper Series, No. 4972. World Bank. Washington (DC).

Mohapatra S, Ratha D and Silwal A (2011). Outlook for remittance flows 2012-14: Remittance flows to developing countries exceed $350 billion in 2011. Migration and Development Brief, No. 17. World Bank. December. Washington (DC).

Mountford A (1997). Can a brain drain be good for growth in the source economy? *Journal of Development Economics*. 53(2): 287–303.

Mundaca BG (2009). Remittances, financial market development, and economic growth: The case of Latin America and the Caribbean. *Review of Development Economics*. 13(2): 288–303.

Neagu IC and Schiff M (2009). Remittance stability, cyclicality and stabilizing impact in developing countries. Policy Research Working Paper Series, No. 5077. World Bank. Washington (DC).

Newland K and Taylor C (2010). Heritage tourism and nostalgia trade: A diaspora niche in the development landscape. Diasporas & Development Policy Project. Migration Policy Institute and USAID. Washington (DC). September.

Obukhova E (2009). Does brain circulation promote development? High-skilled migration and organizational performance. MIT Sloan School of Management. Cambridge (MA). February.

OECD (2011a). *Doing better for families*. Organisation for Economic Co-operation and Development. Paris.

OECD (2011b). Summary of the proceedings OECD workshop on knowledge networks and markets. Paris. 15 June. Available at: http://www.oecd.org/sti/innovationinsciencetechnologyandindustry/48850067.pdf.

Omer A (2003). Supporting systems and procedures for the effective regulation and monitoring of Somali remittance companies (Hawala). UNDP.

Orozco M (2006). Understanding the remittance economy in Haiti. Paper commissioned by the World Bank. Inter-American Dialogue. Washington (DC). March.

Orozco M (2007). International money transfers: Issues, and development on IT models. IDB Publications, No. 7333. Inter-American Development Bank. Washington (DC).

Orozco M (2008). Tasting identity: Trends in migrant demands for home country goods. United States Agency for International Development. Washington (DC).

Orozco M (2010). Migration, remittances, and the rural sector in Latin America. IDB Publications, No. 8598. Inter-American Development Bank. Washington (DC).

Orozco M and Burgess E (2011). A commitment amidst shared hardship: Haitian transnational migrants and remittances. *Journal of Black Studies*. 42(2): 225–246.

Orozco M and Fedewa R (2006). Leveraging efforts on remittances and financial intermediation.INTAL Working Paper, No. 1448. Institute for the Integration of Latin America and the Caribbean. Buenos Aires.

Özden Ç and Schiff M (2006). Overview. In: Özden Ç and Schiff M, eds. *International Migration, Remittances and the Brain Drain*. World Bank and Palgrave Macmillan: 1–18. Washington (DC) and London.

Peri G and Requena F (2009). The trade creation effect of immigrants: Testing the theory on the remarkable case of Spain. CreAM Discussion Paper Series, No. 0915. Centre for Research and Analysis of Migration (CReAM), Department of Economics, University College London. London.

Pessar PR and Mahler SJ (2003). Transnational Migration: Bringing Gender In. *International Migration Review*. 37(3): 812–846.

Poirine B (1997). A theory of remittances as an implicit family loan arrangement. *World Development*. 25(4): 589–611.

Pradhan G, Upadhyay M and Upadhyaya K (2008). Remittances and economic growth in developing countries. *European Journal of Development Research*. 20(3): 497–506.

Pritchett L (2006). *Let their people come: Breaking the gridlock on global labor mobility*. Center for Global Development. Washington (DC).

Rahman HZ (2010). Bangladesh: Strategy for accelerating inclusive growth. Dhaka Chamber of Commerce and Industry and Power and Participation Centre. Dhaka.

Rahman O and Khan R (2007). Out migration of health professional from Bangladesh: Constraints, opportunities and prospects of diaspora formation for homeland development. *Asian Population Studies*. 3(2): 135–151.

Rajan RG and Subramanian A (2005). What undermines aid's impact on growth? NBER Working Paper, No. 11657. National Bureau of Economic Research. Cambridge (MA).

Ratha D (2003). Workers' remittances: An important and stable source of external development finance. *Global Development Finance 2003: Striving for Stability in Development Finance*. World Bank. Washington (DC).

Ratha D (2006). *Economic Implications of Remittances and Migration*. World Bank. Washington (DC).

Ratha D, et al. (2011). *Leveraging Migration for Africa: Remittances, Skills, and Investments*. World Bank. Washington (DC).

Ratha D, Mohapatra S and Plaza S (2008). Beyond aid: New sources and innovative mechanisms for financing development in Sub-Saharan Africa. Policy Research Working Paper Series, No. 4609. World Bank. Washington (DC).

Ratha D, Mohapatra S and Scheja E (2011). Impact of migration on economic and social development: A review of evidence and emerging issues. Policy Research Working Paper Series, No. 5558. World Bank. Washington (DC).

Ratha D and Shaw W (2007). *South-South Migration and Remittances.* World Bank. Washington (DC).

Rauch JE and Casella A (2003). Overcoming informational barriers to international resource allocation: Prices and group ties. *Economic Journal.* 113(484): 21–42.

Rauch JE and Trindade V (2002). Ethnic Chinese networks in international trade. *Review of Economics and Statistics.* 84(1): 116–130.

Riddle L, Nielsen TM and Hrivnak GA (2011). Bridging the divide between diaspora investment interest and action. *Emerging Markets Case Studies Collection.* 1(1): 1–13.

RMMRU-DRC (2005). Return Migration of the Highly Skilled: Concepts, Issues and Experiences. Report of an international workshop. Refugee and Migratory Movement Research Unit and Development Research Centre. Brighton.

Rogers M (2004). Absorptive capability and economic growth: How do countries catch-up? *Cambridge Journal of Economics.* 28(4): 577–596.

Rosendahl C (2010). *Industrial policy in Namibia.* Deutsches Institut für Entwicklungspolitik. Bonn.

Rosenthal SS and Strange WC (2004). Evidence on the nature and sources of agglomeration economies. In: Henderson J and Thisse J, eds. *Handbook of Regional and Urban Economics.* Elsevier: 2119–2171. Amsterdam.

Russell SS (1986). Remittances from international migration: A review in perspective. *World Development.* 14(6): 677–696.

Russell SS (1990). *International migration and development in sub-Saharan Africa.* World Bank. Washington (DC).

Sander C (2003). Capturing a market share? Migrant remittance transfers and commercialization of microfinance in Africa. Paper prepared for the Conference on Current Issues in Microfinance Johannesburg, 12-14 August 2003. 12 August. Available at: http://dspace.cigilibrary.org/jspui/bitstream/123456789/11317/1/Capturing%20a%20Market%20Share%20Migrant%20 Remittance%20and%20Transfers%20and%20Commercialization%20of%20Microfinance%20in%20Africa.pdf?1.

Saxenian A (2005). From brain drain to brain circulation: Transnational communities and regional upgrading in India and China. *Studies in Comparative International Development.* 40(2): 35–61.

Saxenian A (2006). *The New Argonauts: Regional Advantage in a Global Economy.* Harvard University Press. Cambridge (MA).

Saxenian A and Sabel CF (2008). Roepke Lecture in Economic Geography Venture Capital in the "Periphery": The New Argonauts, global search, and local institution building. *Economic Geography.* 84(4): 379–394.

Schiff M (2006). Brain gain: Claims about its size and impact on welfare and growth are greatly exaggerated. In: Özden Ç and Schiff M, eds. *International Migration, Remittances and the Brain Drain.* World Bank. Washington (DC).

Schiff M and Wang Y (2009). North-South trade-related technology diffusion, brain drain and productivity growth: Are small states different? Policy Research Working Paper Series, No. 4828. World Bank. Washington (DC).

Shaw W (2007). Migration in Africa: A review of the economic literature on international migration in 10 countries. April. World Bank. Washington (DC).

Siegel M and Kuschminder Katie (2012). Highly skilled temporary return, technological change and innovation: The case of the TRQN project in Afghanistan. UNU-MERIT Working Paper, No. 2012-017. United Nations University - Maastricht Economic and Social Research Institute on Innovation and Technology. Maastricht.

Skeldon R (2005). Globalization, skilled migration and poverty alleviation: Brain drains in context. Migration DRC Working Paper, No. WP-T15. Development Research Centre on Migration, Globalisation and Poverty, University of Sussex. Brighton. November.

Skeldon R (2008). International migration as a tool in development policy: A passing phase? *Population and Development Review.* 34(3): 1–18.

Solimano A (2005). Remittances by Emigrants: Issues and Evidence. In: Atkinson A B, ed. *New Sources of Development Finance.* Oxford University Press.

Solimano A (2010). *International Migration in the Age of Crisis and Globalization: Historical and Recent Experiences.* Cambridge University Press.

Solimano A, ed. (2008). *The International Mobility of Talent: Types, Causes, and Development Impact.* Oxford University Press. Oxford and New York.

Stark O (2004). Rethinking the brain drain. *World Development.* 32(1): 15–22.

Stark O, Helmenstein C and Prskawetz A (1997). A brain gain with a brain drain. *Economics Letters.* 55(2): 227–234.

Stark O, Helmenstein C and Prskawetz A (1998). Human capital depletion, human capital formation, and migration: A blessing or a "curse"? *Economics Letters.* 60(3): 363–367.

Supradist N (2004). Economic leakage in tourism sector. Master's thesis. International Institute for Industrial Environmental Economics, University of Lund. October. Available at: http://lup.lub.lu.se/luur/download?func=downloadFile&recordOId=132 9250&fileOId=1329251.

Szirmai A (2012). Proximate, intermediate and ultimate causality: Theories and experiences of growth and development. UNU-MERIT Working Paper, No. 2012-032. United Nations University - Maastricht Economic and Social Research Institute on Innovation and Technology. Maastricht. January.

Tati G (2008). The immigration Issues in the Post-Apartheid South Africa: Discourses, Policies and Social Repercussions. *Espace populations sociétés*. 2008/3: 423–440.

Teece DJ (1977). Technology transfer by multinational firms: The resource cost of transferring technological know-how. *Economic Journal*. 87(346): 242–261.

Terrazas A (2010). Diaspora investment in developing and emerging country capital markets: Patterns and prospects. Diasporas & Development Policy Project. Migration Policy Institute. Washington (DC). August.

Thakur S (1999). *Migration and Its Impact on the Families Left Behind in Kangra District.* Department of Family Resource Management.

Thirlwall AP (1979). The balance of payments constraint as an explanation of international growth rate differences. *Banca Nazionale del Lavoro Quarterly Review*. 32(128): 45–53.

Thirlwall AP (2011). Balance of payments constrained growth models: History and overview. Studies in Economics, No. 1111. Department of Economics, University of Kent. Canterbury.

Toit BM (1990). People on the move: Rural-urban migration with special reference to the Third World: theoretical and empirical perspectives. *Human Organization*. 49(4): 305–319.

UNCTAD (2006). *The Least Developed Countries Report 2006: Developing Productive Capacities.* United Nations publication. Sales No. E.06.II.D.9. New York and Geneva. November.

UNCTAD (2007). *The Least Developed Countries Report 2007: Knowledge, Technological Learning and Innovation for Development.* United Nations publication. Sales No. E.07.II.D.8. New York and Geneva.

UNCTAD (2009). The Least Developed Countries Report 2009: The State and Development Governance. United Nations publication. Sales No. E.09.II.D.9. New York and Geneva.

UNCTAD (2010a). *The Least Developed Countries Report 2010: Towards a New International Development Architecture for LDCs.* United Nations publication. Sales No. E.10.II.D.5. New York and Geneva.

UNCTAD (2010b). *Information Economy Report 2010.* United Nations publication. Sales No. E.10.II.D.17. New York and Geneva.

UNCTAD (2011a). *The Least Developed Countries Report 2011: the Potential Role of South-South Cooperation for Inclusive and Sustainable Development.* United Nations publication. Sales No. E.11.II.D.5. New York and Geneva.

UNCTAD (2011b). *Trade and Development Report 2011: Post-Crisis Policy Challenges in the World Economy.* United Nations publication. Sales No. E.11.II.D.3. New York and Geneva.

UNCTAD (2012a). *World Investment Report 2012.* United Nations publication. Sales No. E.12.II.D.3. New York and Geneva.

UNCTAD (2012b). The paradox of finance-driven globalization. UNCTAD XIII Policy Brief, No. 1.

UNCTAD (2012c). Mobile Money for Business Development in the East African Community: A Comparative Study of Existing Platforms and Regulations. No. UNCTAD/DTL/STICT/2012/2. UNCTAD.

UNCTAD (2012d). Maximizing the Development Impact of Remittances. United Nations publication. Sales No. UNCTAD/DITC/TNCD/2011/8, New York and Geneva.

UNDESA (2011). World population prospects, the 2010 revision. (updated: 28 June 2011). Available at: http://esa.un.org/wpp/Excel-Data/migration.htm.

UNDESA (2012a). *World Economic Situation and Prospects 2012.* United Nations publication. Sales No. E.12.II.C.2. New York.

UNDESA (2012b). *World Economic and Social Survey 2012.* United Nations publication. New York.

UNDP (2009). *Human Development Report 2009: Overcoming Barriers: Human Mobility and Development.* United Nations Development Programme and Palgrave Macmillan. New York and Basingstoke.

UNECA (2007). The Monterrey Consensus and development in Africa: progress, challenges and way forward. United Nations Economic Commission for Africa. Addis Ababa. August.

Valensisi G and Davis J (2011). Least Developed Countries and the green transition: Towards a renewed political economy agenda. MSM Working Paper Series, No. 2011/27. Maastricht School of Management. Maastricht.

Vertovec S (2007). Circular migration: The way forward in global policy? Working paper, No. 4. International Migration Institute. University of Oxford. Oxford.

Vidal J-P (1998). The effect of emigration on human capital formation. *Journal of Population Economics*. 11(4): 589–600.

Wade R (2010). After the crisis: Industrial policy and the developmental state in low-income countries. Global Policy. London School of Economics and Political Science. London. May.

Wahba J (2007). Returns of overseas work experience: The case of Egypt. In: Özden Ç and Schiff M, eds. *International Migration, Economic Development and Policy.* World Bank and Palgrave Macmillan: 235–258. Washington (DC) and London.

Wahba J and Zenou Y (2011). Out of sight, out of mind: Migration, entrepreneurship and social capital. CReAM Discussion Paper, No. 30/09. Centre for Research and Analysis of Migration. London. September.

Widgren J and Martin P (2002). Managing migration: The role of economic instruments. *International Migration*. 40(5): 213–229.

Wimaladharma J, Pearce D and Stanton D (2004). Remittances: The new development finance? *Small Enterprise Development*. 15(1): 12–19.

Wise T and Murphy S (2012). Resolving the Food Crisis: Assessing Global Policy Reforms Since 2007. Global Development and Environment Institute at Tufts University.

Wong K and Yip CK (1999). Education, economic growth, and brain drain. *Journal of Economic Dynamics and Control*. 23(5-6): 699–726.

Woodruff CM and Zenteno R (2007). Remittances and microenterprises in Mexico. *Journal of Development Economics*. 82(2): 509–528.

World Bank (2005). *Agriculture Investment Sourcebook: Agriculture and Rural Development.* World Bank. Washington (DC).

World Bank (2006a). *Global Economic Prospects 2006: Economic implications of remittances and migration.* World Bank. Washington (DC).

World Bank (2006b). *Diaspora Networks and the International Migration of Skills: How Countries Can Draw on Their Talent Abroad.* World Bank. Washington (DC).

World Bank (2008a). *Remittances and Development Lessons from Latin America.* World Bank. Washington (DC).

World Bank (2008b). *World Development Report 2009: Reshaping Economic Geography.* World Bank. Washington (DC).

World Bank (2011a). *Migration, Remittances, and Development in Africa.* World Bank. Washington (DC).

World Bank (2011b). *Migration and Remittances Factbook 2011.* World Bank. Washington (DC).

World Bank (2011c). *Payment Systems Worldwide a Snapshot Outcomes of the Global Payment Systems Survey 2010.* World Bank. Washington (DC).

Ziesemer THW (2009). Worker remittances and growth: The physical and human capital channels. *Journal of Economics and Statistics*. 229(6): 743–773.

Ziesemer THW (2012). Worker remittances, migration, accumulation and growth in poor developing countries: Survey and analysis of direct and indirect effects. *Economic Modelling*. 29(2): 103–118.

Zoomers A and van Naerssen T (2006). International migration and national development in sub-Saharan Africa. Viewpoints and policy initiatives in the countries of origin. Migration and Development Working Papers, No. 14. Radboud University. Nijmegen.